Author
Rabbi Naftali Silberberg

Course Development
Rabbi Mordechai Dinerman
Mrs. Rochel Holzkenner
Rabbi Eli Raksin
Rabbi Yanky Raskin
Mrs. Chava Shapiro
Rabbi Shmuel Super

Editorial Board
Rabbi Yisroel Mangel
Rabbi Sholom Raichik
Rabbi Avrohom Sternberg

Design and Layout
Mendel Schtroks

Printed in the United States of America
© Published and Copyrighted 2015 by
The Rohr Jewish Learning Institute
822 Eastern Parkway, Brooklyn, NY 11213

(888) YOUR-JLI/718-221-6900
www.myJLI.com

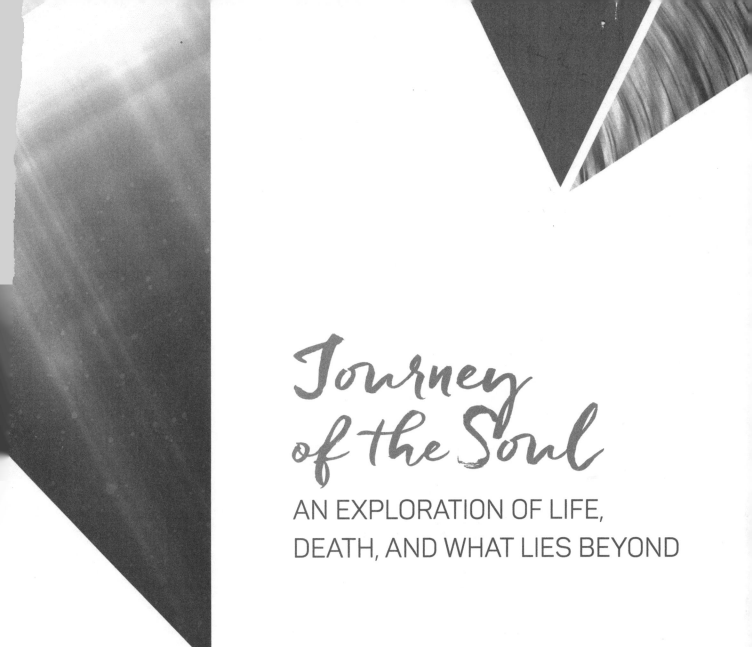

Journey of the Soul

AN EXPLORATION OF LIFE, DEATH, AND WHAT LIES BEYOND

JLI

JEWISH LEARNING INSTITUTE

The **Rohr Jewish Learning Institute**
gratefully acknowledges
the pioneering support of

George and Pamela Rohr

SINCE ITS INCEPTION,
the **Rohr JLI** has been
a beneficiary of the vision, generosity,
care, and concern
of the **Rohr family**

In the merit of
the tens of thousands of hours of Torah study
by **JLI** students worldwide,
may they be blessed with health,
Yiddishe nachas from all their loved ones,
and extraordinary success
in all their endeavors ೞ

Dedicated to

Dr. Michael Maling

President and Director of the

 **Crain-Maling Foundation**

With deep appreciation for his leadership
and partnershipin bringing Torah study
to all corners of the world.

May he and his family enjoy health, happiness,
nachas, success, and abundance in all their endeavors,
as they go from strength to strength in their service
of G-d and the Jewish people.

ENDORSEMENTS

It seems clear to me that this will be a very valuable course that will help people come to grips with their mortality, a topic that is too often avoided. By addressing this critical aspect of being human head on, people can lead more thoughtful, focused, and enriched lives, and this course looks to be an excellent path toward doing so.

Jeff Greenberg, PhD
Professor of Psychology, University of Arizona
Co-author, *In the Wake of 9/11:*
The Psychology of Terror
Co-author, *The Worm at the Core:*
On the Role of Death in Life

Awareness of death provides us with a valuable opportunity to identify and address our fears about our own death—which can help to demystify and lessen those fears—and to discuss our concerns with the people around us, who can make a difference to our experience of death. A course such as this has never been more important, at a time when we risk losing sight of the value of death as an opportunity to explore who we are and to connect on a profound level with those we love.

Bianca Nogrady
Journalist
Author, *The End: The Human Experience of Death*

I believe *Journey of the Soul* is comprehensive in its approach and promises to offer a deeper exploration of what awaits us when our earthly mission is complete.

Pamela D. Blair, PhD
Psychotherapist, Shelburne, VT
Co-author, *I Wasn't Ready to Say Goodbye*

This course strikes me as a very fine juxtaposition of ancient theological wisdom with contemporary empirical science. My sense is that this would be an interesting and rewarding educational and personal experience.

Sheldon Solomon, PhD
Professor of Social Psychology, Skidmore College
Co-author, *In the Wake of 9/11:*
The Psychology of Terror
Co-author, *The Worm at the Core:*
On the Role of Death in Life

The Rohr Jewish Learning Institute's newest course, *Journey of the Soul*, examines death—and Jewish life—with an uplifting blend of Torah-based scholarship and contemporary psychological perspectives. Inspirational and thought-provoking text materials provide insight into understanding life's purpose. Highly recommended, especially for members of the Helping Professions.

Casey Skvorc, PhD, JD
Medical Psychologist
National Institutes of Health

It is one of life's great ironies that mortality is one of the few things we share with every other person, and yet when we are dealing with it ourselves, it's the loneliest feeling in the world. This course helps detoxify death by placing it in a spiritual context.

Combining ancient wisdom with modern psychological concepts, it encourages a thoughtful exploration of what can be a very scary but important subject. After all, it is the specter of death that compels us to find a sense of meaning and purpose in our lives.

Mindy Greenstein, PhD
Clinical Psychologist and Psycho-oncologist,
Author, *The House on Crash Corner (and Other Unavoidable Calamities)* and *Lighter as We Go: Virtues, Character Strengths, and Aging*

ACCREDITATION
FOR MENTAL HEALTH
AND MEDICAL PRACTITIONERS

ACCREDITATION STATEMENT

*This activity has been planned and implemented through a joint sponsorship of **The Rohr Jewish Learning Institute (JLI)** and the **Washington School of Psychiatry (WSP)**. The Washington School of Psychiatry is approved by the **American Psychological Association (APA)** to sponsor continuing education for psychologists. Participants may earn up to **seven and a half (7.5) CE credits** from the APA: four and a half (4.5) credits for participation in lessons one, two, and five of the live course, and up to three (3) additional credits for self-study of the corresponding Additional Readings.*

*The School is accredited by MedChi, The Maryland State Medical Society, to provide continuing medical education for physicians. The school designates sessions one, two, and five for 1.5 **AMA PRA Category I Credit(s)™** each and an additional three (3) credits for self-study of the corresponding Additional Readings for a total of up to **seven and a half (7.5) credits**. Physicians should claim only the credit commensurate with the extent of their participation in the activity.*

*The School is approved by the **California Board of Behavioral Sciences** as provider #5691 of continuing education to Social Workers, Licensed Marriage and Family Therapists and Certified Counselors in California. Participants may earn up to **seven and a half (7.5) CE credits**: four and a half (4.5) for participation in lessons one, two, and five of the live course and up to three (3) additional credits for self-study of the corresponding Additional Readings.*

*The School is approved by the **Social Work Board of the State of Maryland** as a provider of continuing education for social workers. The Maryland Social Work Board is an accredited member of the **Association of Social Work Boards**. Participants may earn up to **seven and a half (7.5) CE credits**: four and a half (4.5) for participation in lessons one, two, and five of the live course and up to three (3) additional credits for self-study of the corresponding Additional Readings.*

DISCLOSURE OF COMMERCIAL SUPPORT AND THE UNLABELED USE OF A COMMERCIAL PRODUCT: No member of the planning committee and no member of the faculty for this event have a financial interest or other relationship with any commercial product.

TO CLAIM CREDIT *for attending the accredited lessons of the course (4.5 credits), professionals should submit their name, profession, e-mail, and mailing address to their instructor, or online at **www.MyJLI.com/ continuingeducation**. To obtain credit for self-study of the Additional Readings (3 credits), professionals should take the brief online quiz at the above Web address.*

TABLE OF CONTENTS

Lesson One

Higher Life
A Jewish Perspective on Life and Beyond

Do you find the notion of death disquieting? Terrifying? Some social psychologists posit that the human fear of death and the innate desire to avoid this ultimate fate is at the root of some of our most complex feelings and the impetus behind many of our lifelong endeavors. To be comfortable with death, however, we must understand what it really is. And any discussion about death needs to begin with a discussion about the nature of life.

JLI

Jewish Learning Institute

Thanatophobia

QUESTIONS FOR DISCUSSION

1. How do you feel about death?
2. What is frightening about mortality?
3. Is the fear of death healthy or paralyzing?

Text 1

Nathan A. Heflick, PhD, "How We Cope with Death: A theory of terror management," www.psychologytoday.com, June 10, 2012

Nathan A. Heflick, PhD

Psychologist. Heflick obtained his PhD in social psychology from the University of South Florida in 2012. He is currently a senior lecturer in psychology at the University of Lincoln in the United Kingdom.

Terror Management Theory (building mostly from the ideas of Ernest Becker) starts with the idea that humans, unlike other animals, face something that is potentially terrifying: the awareness of our own mortality coupled with the desire to live. To paraphrase TMT co-creator Sheldon Solomon, the awareness that you are destined to wither away to nothingness, and in turn are no more significant than a lizard or a potato, is not particularly uplifting. So how do humans cope with this awareness?

From a TMT approach, humans cope with mortality by denying their own mortality, and avoiding thinking about it. They repress the terror, basically.

Soul Survivor

The Immortal You

Text 2

Rabbi Chaim Vital, *Sha'arei Kedushah* 1:1 📖

נוֹדַע אֶל בַּעֲלֵי מַדָּע, כִּי גוּף הָאָדָם אֵינֶנּוּ הָאָדָם עַצְמוֹ מִצַּד הַגּוּף, כִּי זֶה נִקְרָא
בְּשַׂר הָאָדָם . . . נִמְצָא הָאָדָם הוּא הַפְּנִימִיּוּת, אֲבָל הַגּוּף הוּא עִנְיָן לְבוּשׁ אֶחָד
תִּתְלַבֵּשׁ בּוֹ נֶפֶשׁ הַשִּׂכְלִית אֲשֶׁר הִיא הָאָדָם עַצְמוֹ בְּעוֹדוֹ בָּעוֹלָם הַזֶּה.

It is known to the wise that the human body is not the human being; it is merely the body of the human being. . . . When we speak of the human being, we are referring to his inner dimension. The body is merely a garment in which the intellectual soul is attired during its sojourn in this world.

Rabbi Chaim Vital
ca. 1542–1620

Lurianic Kabbalist. Rabbi Vital was born in Israel, lived in Safed and Jerusalem, and later in Damascus. He was authorized by his teacher, Rabbi Yitschak Luria, the Arizal, to record his teachings. Acting on this mandate, Vital began arranging his master's teachings in written form, and his many works constitute the foundation of the Lurianic school of Jewish mysticism. His most famous work is *Ets Chaim*.

thanatophobia \than-ət-ə-ˈfō-bē-ə\ *n* :
fear of death

Text 3a

Genesis 2:7

וַיִּיצֶר ה' אֱלֹקִים אֶת הָאָדָם עָפָר מִן הָאֲדָמָה וַיִּפַּח בְּאַפָּיו נִשְׁמַת חַיִּים. וַיְהִי הָאָדָם לְנֶפֶשׁ חַיָּה.

God formed man of soil from the earth and breathed into his nostrils the *neshamah* (soul) of life. And man became a living being.

Text 3b

Genesis 1:24

וַיֹּאמֶר אֱלֹקִים תּוֹצֵא הָאָרֶץ נֶפֶשׁ חַיָּה לְמִינָהּ בְּהֵמָה וָרֶמֶשׂ וְחַיְתוֹ אֶרֶץ לְמִינָהּ וַיְהִי כֵן.

God said, "Let the earth bring forth living beings of differing species: cattle, creeping things, and beasts of the earth according to their species." And it was so.

What is the primary difference between the manner in which the human being was created and the manner in which animal life was created?

Text 3c

Rabbi Chezekiah ben Mano'ach, *Chizkuni*, Genesis 2:7

וַיִּפַּח בְּאַפָּיו נִשְׁמַת חַיִּים: בִּנְפִיחָתוֹ שֶׁל הַקָּדוֹשׁ בָּרוּךְ הוּא שֶׁהִיא רוּחַ הַקּוֹדֶשׁ, מַה שֶׁלֹּא נָפַח בְּשׁוּם אַף בְּרִיָּה . . . נְשָׁמָה שֶׁהִיא חַיָּה לְעוֹלָם וְאֵינָהּ מֵתָה בְּמוֹת הַגּוּף.

God did what He had not done with any other creature: He blew [into Adam] with His holy breath a *neshamah* that is immortal and does not perish when the body does.

Rabbi Chezkiah ben Mano'ach
(Chizkuni)
ca. 1250–1310

French rabbi and exegete. His commentary on the Torah, *Chizkuni*, is based principally on the work of Rashi, and according to the author's testimony, also draws upon nearly 20 earlier sources which he collected during his travels. He focuses on elucidating the straightforward meaning of the text of the Torah.

The Antechamber and the Palace

Text 4

Midrash Tanchuma, Pekudei 3 📖

מִיַּד רוֹמֵז הַקָּדוֹשׁ בָּרוּךְ הוּא לַמַּלְאָךְ הַמְמוּנֶּה עַל הָרוּחוֹת וְאוֹמֵר לוֹ, "הָבֵא לִי רוּחַ
פְּלוֹנִי שֶׁהִיא בְּגַן עֵדֶן, שֶׁשְּׁמוֹ פְּלוֹנִי וְתֹאֲרוֹ כָּךְ וְכָךְ". לְפִי שֶׁכָּל הָרוּחוֹת שֶׁעֲתִידִין
לְהִבָּרְאוֹת כּוּלָּן הֵן נִבְרָאוֹת מִיּוֹם שֶׁבָּרָא הָעוֹלָם עַד שֶׁיִּכְלֶה כָּל הָעוֹלָם . . .

מִיַּד הוֹלֵךְ הַמַּלְאָךְ וּמֵבִיא אֶת הָרוּחַ לִפְנֵי הַקָּדוֹשׁ בָּרוּךְ הוּא, וּכְשֶׁהִיא בָּאָה
מִיַּד כּוֹרַעַת וּמִשְׁתַּחֲוָה לִפְנֵי הַמֶּלֶךְ מַלְכֵי הַמְּלָכִים הַקָּדוֹשׁ בָּרוּךְ הוּא. אוֹתָהּ
שָׁעָה אוֹמֵר הַקָּדוֹשׁ בָּרוּךְ הוּא לָרוּחַ, "הִכָּנְסִי בְּטִיפָּה זוֹ שֶׁבְּיַד פְּלוֹנִי".

פָּתַח הָרוּחַ פִּיו וְאוֹמֵר לְפָנָיו, "רִבּוֹנוֹ שֶׁל עוֹלָם! דַּי לִי הָעוֹלָם
שֶׁהָיִיתִי דָר מִיּוֹם שֶׁבְּרָאתַנִי, לָמָּה רְצוֹנְךָ לְהַכְנִיסֵנִי בְּטִיפָּה זוֹ
סְרוּחָה, שֶׁאֲנִי קְדוֹשָׁה וּטְהוֹרָה וַאֲנִי גְּזוּרָה מִגְּזֵרַת כְּבוֹדֶךָ?"

Midrash Tanchuma

A midrashic work bearing the name of Rabbi Tanchuma, a 4th century Talmudic sage quoted often in this work. Midrash is the designation of a particular genre of rabbinic literature usually forming a running commentary on specific books of the Bible. *Midrash Tanchuma* provides textual exegeses, expounds upon the biblical narrative, and develops and illustrates moral principles. *Tanchuma* is unique in that many of its sections commence with a halachic discussion, which subsequently leads into non-halachic teachings.

Forty days before the conception of a child, God summons the angel in charge of the souls and tells him, "Bring before Me a certain soul who is now in paradise. Its name is such-and-such and its appearance is such-and-such." This is because all the souls that are born in this world were created on the day the world was created and last until the end of time. . . .

The angel goes and brings the soul before God. The soul bows down and prostrates itself before the supreme King of kings. "I want you to enter the seminal drop that is currently in the hands of [the angel in charge of pregnancy]," God instructs the soul.

The soul opens its mouth and says, "Master of the universe! I am quite satisfied with the world I inhabited since the day You created me. I am holy and pure, hewn from Your Throne of Glory—why do You wish to cause me to enter this putrid drop?"

Text 5

Mishnah, Avot 4:16–17 📖

הָעוֹלָם הַזֶּה דּוֹמֶה לַפְּרוֹזְדוֹר בִּפְנֵי הָעוֹלָם הַבָּא. הַתְקֵן
עַצְמְךָ בַּפְּרוֹזְדוֹר, כְּדֵי שֶׁתִּכָּנֵס לַטְּרַקְלִין . . .

וְיָפָה שָׁעָה אַחַת שֶׁל קוֹרַת רוּחַ בָּעוֹלָם הַבָּא, מִכָּל חַיֵּי הָעוֹלָם הַזֶּה.

This world is like an antechamber before the World to Come. Prepare yourself in the antechamber, so that you may enter the palace. . . .

A single moment of bliss in the World to Come is greater than all of this world.

Mishnah

The first authoritative work of Jewish law that was codified in writing. The Mishnah contains the oral traditions that were passed down from teacher to student; it supplements, clarifies, and systematizes the commandments of the Torah. Due to the continual persecution of the Jewish people, it became increasingly difficult to guarantee that these traditions would not be forgotten. Rabbi Yehudah Hanasi therefore redacted the Mishnah at the end of the 2nd century. It serves as the foundation for the Talmud.

On the Other Hand . . .

Culture of Life

Text 6

Rabbi Shlomo Yitschaki
(Rashi)
1040–1105

Most noted biblical and Talmudic commentator. Born in Troyes, France, Rashi studied in the famed *yeshivot* of Mainz and Worms. His commentaries on the Pentateuch and the Talmud, which focus on the straightforward meaning of the text, appear in virtually every edition of the Talmud and Bible.

Rashi, Yoma 82b

חֲבִיבָה נַפְשָׁן שֶׁל יִשְׂרָאֵל לִפְנֵי הַמָּקוֹם יוֹתֵר מִן הַמִּצְווֹת;

אָמַר הַקָּדוֹשׁ בָּרוּךְ הוּא, "תְּבַטֵּל הַמִּצְוָה וְיִחְיֶה זֶה".

More precious before God than the *mitzvot* are the lives of Israel. God says, "Let the commandment remain unfulfilled, so that this person may live."

QUESTION FOR DISCUSSION

How do we reconcile the value Judaism places on *bodily* life with its belief in the immortality of the *soul*?

The Universe's Ground Zero

Text 7

Talmud, Shabbat 88a

שֶׁהִתְנָה הַקָּדוֹשׁ בָּרוּךְ הוּא עִם מַעֲשֵׂה בְרֵאשִׁית, וְאָמַר לָהֶם: "אִם יִשְׂרָאֵל מְקַבְּלִים הַתּוֹרָה, אַתֶּם מִתְקַיְּימִין; וְאִם לָאו, אֲנִי מַחֲזִיר אֶתְכֶם לְתוֹהוּ וָבוֹהוּ".

God created the universe on one condition: "If the Jews receive the Torah," He stipulated, "you will continue to exist. If, however, they do not accept the Torah, I will return you to nothingness."

Babylonian Talmud

A literary work of monumental proportions that draws upon the legal, spiritual, intellectual, ethical, and historical traditions of Judaism. The 37 tractates of the Babylonian Talmud contain the teachings of the Jewish sages from the period after the destruction of the 2nd Temple through the 5th century CE. It has served as the primary vehicle for the transmission of the Oral Law and the education of Jews over the centuries; it is the entry point for all subsequent legal, ethical, and theological Jewish scholarship.

Text 8

Talmud, Ketubot 103b

כְּשֶׁחָלָה רַבִּי, נִכְנַס רַבִּי חִיָּיא אֶצְלוֹ וּמְצָאוֹ שֶׁהוּא בּוֹכֶה. אָמַר לוֹ, "רַבִּי, מִפְּנֵי מָה אַתָּה בּוֹכֶה? וְהָתַנְיָא, 'מֵת מִתּוֹךְ הַשְּׂחוֹק סִימָן יָפֶה לוֹ, מִתּוֹךְ הַבְּכִי סִימָן רַע לוֹ'" . . . אָמַר לֵיהּ, "אֲנָא אַתּוֹרָה וּמִצְוֹת קָא בָּכִינָא".

When Rebbi [Judah the Prince] fell ill [and was lying on his deathbed], Rabbi Chiya entered and found him weeping. "Master," said Rabbi Chiya, "Why are you weeping? Was it not taught: '[If a man] dies smiling, it is a good sign for him; if he is weeping, it is a bad sign for him . . .'?"

Rebbi replied, "I weep because of the Torah and the commandments [that I will no longer be able to study and observe]."

Conflicted Feelings

Text 9

Mishnah, Avot 4:22 📖

שֶׁעַל כָּרְחֲךָ אַתָּה נוֹצָר, וְעַל כָּרְחֲךָ אַתָּה נוֹלָד, וְעַל כָּרְחֲךָ אַתָּה חַי, וְעַל כָּרְחֲךָ אַתָּה מֵת.

Against your will you are formed, against your will you are born, against your will you live, and against your will you die.

Text 10

Midrash Tanchuma, Pekudei 3 📖

מִיַּד אוֹמֵר הַקָּדוֹשׁ בָּרוּךְ הוּא לַנְּשָׁמָה, "עוֹלָם שֶׁאֲנִי מַכְנִיסֵךְ בּוֹ יָפֶה יְהֵא לְךָ מִמַּה שֶׁהָיִיתְ דָּר בּוֹ, וּבְשָׁעָה שֶׁיְּצַרְתִּיךְ לֹא יְצַרְתִּיךְ אֶלָּא לְטִיפָּה זוֹ". מִיַּד מַכְנִיסוֹ הַקָּדוֹשׁ בָּרוּךְ הוּא לְשָׁם בַּעַל כָּרְחוֹ.

God responds to the soul: "The world to which I am sending you is better for you than the one in which you have dwelt until now. When I created you, I did so for this drop." At that moment, God inserts it against its will.

Text 11

Mishnah, Avot 4:17 📖

יָפָה שָׁעָה אַחַת בִּתְשׁוּבָה וּמַעֲשִׂים טוֹבִים בָּעוֹלָם הַזֶּה, מִכָּל חַיֵּי הָעוֹלָם הַבָּא, וְיָפָה שָׁעָה אַחַת שֶׁל קוֹרַת רוּחַ בָּעוֹלָם הַבָּא, מִכָּל חַיֵּי הָעוֹלָם הַזֶּה.

A single moment of repentance and good deeds in this world is greater than all of the World to Come. And a single moment of bliss in the World to Come is greater than all of this world.

Thanatophobia Resolution

Silencing the Revolver

Text 12a

Ecclesiastes 3:1–2 📖

לַכֹּל זְמָן וְעֵת לְכָל חֵפֶץ תַּחַת הַשָּׁמָיִם.

עֵת לָלֶדֶת וְעֵת לָמוּת.

Everything has an appointed season, and there is a time for every matter under the heaven.

A time to be born and a time to die.

Text 12b

Midrash, *Kohelet Rabah* 3:4

"עֵת לָלֶדֶת", מֵעֵת לָלֶדֶת הִיא "עֵת לָמוּת". מִשָּׁעָה
שֶׁאָדָם נוֹלַד הוּא נִגְזַר עָלָיו כַּמָּה שָׁנִים יִחְיֶה.

Kohelet Rabah

A Midrashic text on the Book of Ecclesiastes. Midrash is the designation of a particular genre of rabbinic literature. The term "Midrash" is derived from the root d-r-sh, which means "to search," "to examine," and "to investigate." This particular Midrash provides textual exegeses and develops and illustrates moral principles. It was first published in Pesaro, Italy, in 1519, together with four other Midrashic works on the other four biblical *megilot*.

"A time to be born and a time to die": From the time of birth, there already is a time to die. From the moment of birth, it is already destined how many years a person will live.

Text 13

Rabbi Bachya ibn Pakuda, *Chovot Halevavot, Sha'ar Yichud Hama'aseh*, ch. 2

שֶׁיַּאֲמִין, כִּי הַתּוֹעֶלֶת וְהַנֵּזֶק אֵינָם בְּיָד (בַּעֲצַת) נִבְרָא
וְלֹא בִּיכָלְתּוֹ מִבִּלְתִּי רְשׁוּת הַבּוֹרֵא.

Rabbi Bachya ibn Pakuda
11th century

Moral philosopher and author. Ibn Pakuda lived in Muslim Spain, but little else is known about his life. *Chovot Halevavot (Duties of the Heart)*, his major work, was intended to be a guide for attaining spiritual perfection. Originally written in Judeo-Arabic and published in 1080, it was later translated into Hebrew and published in 1161 by Judah ibn Tibbon, a scion of the famous family of translators. Ibn Pakuda had a strong influence on Jewish pietistic literature.

We must believe that no created being can benefit or harm us without the permission of the Creator.

Life Beyond Death

Text 14

Talmud, Berachot 18a 📖

אֵלּוּ צַדִּיקִים, שֶׁבְּמִיתָתָן נִקְרְאוּ חַיִּים.

Tsadikim (righteous people) are considered alive even after their demise.

QUESTION FOR DISCUSSION

What is the Talmud's definition of "life" in the above statement?

Text 15

Rabbi Shne'ur Zalman of Liadi, *Tanya*, *Igeret Hakodesh*, epistle 27 📜

שֶׁחַיֵּי הַצַּדִּיק אֵינָם חַיִּים בְּשָׂרִיִּים כִּי אִם חַיִּים רוּחָנִיִּים, שֶׁהֵם אֱמוּנָה וְיִרְאָה וְאַהֲבָה.

כִּי בָּאֱמוּנָה כְּתִיב, "וְצַדִּיק בֶּאֱמוּנָתוֹ יִחְיֶה" (חֲבַקּוּק ב, ד);

וּבְיִרְאָה כְּתִיב, "וְיִרְאַת ה' לְחַיִּים" (מִשְׁלֵי יט, כג);

וּבְאַהֲבָה כְּתִיב, "רוֹדֵף צְדָקָה וָחֶסֶד יִמְצָא חַיִּים" (מִשְׁלֵי כא, כא), וְחֶסֶד הוּא אַהֲבָה.

Rabbi Shne'ur Zalman of Liadi (Alter Rebbe)
1745–1812

Chasidic rebbe, halachic authority, and founder of the Chabad movement. The Alter Rebbe was born in Liozna, Belarus, and was among the principal students of the Magid of Mezeritch. His numerous works include the *Tanya*, an early classic containing the fundamentals of Chabad Chasidism, and *Shulchan Aruch HaRav*, an expanded and reworked code of Jewish law.

The life of the *tsadik* is not physical but spiritual, and it consists of faith, reverence, and love.

[There is scriptural support for equating these three qualities with life:]

Of faith it is written (Habakkuk 2:4): "The *tsadik* lives by his faith."

Of reverence it is written (Proverbs 19:23): "Reverence of God produces life."

Of love it is written (ibid. 21:21): "He who pursues charity and kindness will find life"; and kindness is [rooted in] love.

Text 16

Rabbi Shalom Dovber Schneersohn, *Sefer Hama'amarim* 5670, p. 19 📖

"רְאֵה נָתַתִּי לְפָנֶיךָ אֶת הַחַיִּים וְאֶת הַטּוֹב וְאֶת כו'".

דְּפֵירוּשׁ "חַיִּים" וּ"מָוֶת" אֵין הַכַּוָּונָה בְּחַיִּים בָּעֵת שֶׁהַנִּבְרָא חַי, וּמָוֶת הוּא לְאַחַר פֵּירוּד הַחַיּוּת כו', דְּמִי זֶה פֶּתִי לֹא יִבְחַר בַּחַיִּים כו'?

רַק הַכַּוָּונָה שֶׁבְּכָל דָּבָר נִבְרָא, בָּעֵת שֶׁהוּא בְּחַיּוּתוֹ וְקִיּוּמוֹ, יֵשׁ בּוֹ חַיִּים וּמָוֶת. וְהוּא, שֶׁגַּשְׁמִיּוּת הַדָּבָר וְחוּמְרִיּוּתוֹ הוּא מָוֶת בְּעֶצֶם, דְּהַיְינוּ שֶׁהוּא כָּלֶה וְנִפְסָד, וְכַאֲשֶׁר רוֹאֶה הָאָדָם הֶפְסֵד כָּל דָּבָר גַּשְׁמִי, וְכַאֲשֶׁר מַרְגִּישׁ גַּם בְּעַצְמוֹ כִּלְיוֹן הַכֹּחוֹת הַגּוּפָנִיִּים שֶׁלּוֹ שֶׁכָּלִים וְנִפְסָדִים מִזְּמַן לִזְּמַן כו', וְהָרוּחָנִיּוּת וְהַכֹּחַ הָאֱלֹקִי הוּא הַחַיִּים שֶׁאֵין בָּזֶה כִּלְיוֹן וְהֶפְסֵד חַס וְשָׁלוֹם, כִּי אִם הוּא בִּבְחִינַת קִיּוּם נִצְחִי כו'.

> ❝**B**ehold, I have set before you today life and goodness and [death and evil. . . . And you shall choose life]!" (Deuteronomy 30:15, 19)

The word "life" in this verse does not mean physical life, nor does "death" refer to the time when the soul departs the body. For which simpleton needs to be instructed to choose to live?

Every creation, even when alive and fully existent, contains both life and death. The physicality of the object is intrinsically lifeless; it is in a constant state of decline and deterioration. We see this decline in every physical object as well as in ourselves, as our physical capabilities and powers weaken with time.

The spiritual and divine within everything, on the other hand, is alive and eternal, and not subject to destruction or deterioration, God forbid.

Rabbi Shalom Dovber Schneersohn
(Rashab)
1860– 1920

Chasidic rebbe. Rabbi Shalom Dovber became the 5th leader of the Chabad movement upon the passing of his father, Rabbi Shmuel of Lubavitch. He established the Lubavitch network of *yeshivot* called Tomchei Temimim. He authored many volumes of Chasidic discourses and is renowned for his lucid and thorough explanations of Kabbalistic concepts.

LEARNING EXERCISE

1. Write down the point from today's lesson that resonated with you most on a personal level.

_____

_____

_____

_____

_____

2. Identify a change that you can make in your life to live in a manner that is more "alive" and consistent with your immortal soul.

_____

_____

_____

_____

_____

Key Points

1. The awareness of our mortality and the resulting natural fear of death influence many elements of our psyche, behavior, and life choices. Thus, our perspective on death influences many areas of our lives.

2. The *neshamah* (human soul), the true essence of the human being, is eternal; it precedes the body and continues to exist after the body is gone. While still in heaven, it has no desire to descend into a body, and when the time of death arrives, it resumes its native spiritual state.

3. According to Jewish law, preserving life takes precedence over nearly every mitzvah. This is because the *raison d'être* of the *neshamah* is its achievements in *this* world.

4. One hour in this world is more *important* than all of the next. One hour in the next world is more *pleasurable* than all of this one. This perspective allows us to appreciate and value life—without fear of death.

5. Every person is given a certain number of years. Death cannot be prematurely imposed by illness, accident, or even another's evil deeds or negligence. So, we need not fear dying before our time.

6. Our bodily needs and endeavors die with the body; our soulful aspirations and actions live on eternally. We can live a life of "death," by making choices that are not in synch with our souls, and we can be alive even after our death, when we live and identify with eternal values.

This lesson explored the Jewish perspective on life and death.

Continue your learning experience ONLINE

Visit www.myJLI.com/journey1

for insightful and inspiring videos, articles, and readings on this topic.

Appendix A

Rabbi David ibn Zimra, *Metsudat David*, mitzvah 70 📖

Rabbi David ibn Zimra
(Radvaz)
1479–1573

Noted halachist. Radvaz was born in Spain and immigrated to Safed, Israel upon the expulsion of the Jews from Spain in 1492. In 1513, he moved to Egypt and served as rabbi, judge, and head of the yeshivah in Cairo. He also ran many successful business ventures and was independently wealthy. In 1553, he returned to Safed where he would later be buried. He authored what would later become a classic commentary to Maimonides' code of law, and wrote many halachic responsa, of which more than ten thousand are still extant.

וְטַעַם הַשְׂרִיטָה עַל הַמֵּת לְפִי הַפְּשַׁט, כִּי הָעוֹשֶׂה מַעֲשֶׂה בָּזֶה מוֹרֶה שָׁאֵין לַמֵּת הַשְׁאָרַת הַנֶּפֶשׁ. וְעוֹד, כִּי אֵין רָאוּי לְבַעַל הַשֵּׂכֶל וְהַתּוֹרָה לְהִצְטַעֵר עַל מַעֲשֵׂה הָאֵ-ל וּמִשְׁפָּטָיו יוֹתֵר מִדַּאי. וְכֵן אָמְרוּ רַזַ"ל, שָׁאֵין לְהִתְאַבֵּל יוֹתֵר מִדַּאי, וְזֶה דֶּרֶךְ הַגּוֹיִם שָׁאֵינָם מַאֲמִינִים בְּהַשְׁאָרַת הַנֶּפֶשׁ.

וְרָאִיתִי הַיִּשְׁמְעֵאלִים מַרְחִיקִים דָּבָר זֶה הַרְבֵּה, וַאֲפִילוּ הַקְּרִיעָה עַל הַמֵּת אוֹסְרִים.

וְהַמִּדָּה וְהַדֶּרֶךְ הַמְּמוּצָע לְעוֹלָם הוּא טוֹב כַּאֲשֶׁר כָּתַבְנוּ. וּלְפִיכָךְ רָאוּי לְהִתְאַבֵּל אֲבֵילוּת מְמוּצָע.

On the simplest level, the Torah prohibits self-mutilation [in reaction to the death of a loved one] because one who does so demonstrates a lack of belief in the soul's immortality. Moreover, it is not proper for an intelligent person who has studied Torah to be exceedingly pained over God's ways and decisions. Therefore, our sages advised against excessive mourning, for this is the convention of the nations who do not believe in the eternal nature of the soul.

I have observed that the Ishmaelites greatly abhor [displays of mourning]; they even prohibit rending one's garments.

The middle path is always proper. Therefore, it is proper to mourn—but not excessively.

Appendix B

Maimonides, *Mishneh Torah*, Laws of the Fundamentals of the Torah 5:1

כְּשֶׁיַּעֲמוֹד גּוֹי וְיֶאֱנוֹס אֶת יִשְׂרָאֵל לַעֲבוֹר עַל אַחַת מִכָּל מִצְוֹת הָאֲמוּרוֹת
בַּתּוֹרָה אוֹ יַהַרְגֶנּוּ, יַעֲבוֹר וְאַל יֵהָרֵג, שֶׁנֶּאֱמַר בְּמִצְוֹת (וַיִּקְרָא יח, ה), "אֲשֶׁר
יַעֲשֶׂה אוֹתָם הָאָדָם וָחַי בָּהֶם". "וָחַי" בָּהֶם, וְלֹא שֶׁיָּמוּת בָּהֶם.

If a Gentile attempts to force a Jew to violate one of the Torah's commandments at the pain of death, the Jew should violate the commandment rather than be killed, because it is stated concerning the *mitzvot*: "A person shall do them and live by them" (Leviticus 18:5). One should *live by them* and not die because of them.

Rabbi Moshe ben Maimon
(Maimonides, Rambam)
1135–1204

Halachist, philosopher, author, and physician. Maimonides was born in Cordoba, Spain. After the conquest of Cordoba by the Almohads, he fled Spain and eventually settled in Cairo, Egypt. There, he became the leader of the Jewish community and served as court physician to the vizier of Egypt. He is most noted for authoring the *Mishneh Torah*, an encyclopedic arrangement of Jewish law, and for his philosophical work, *Guide for the Perplexed*. His rulings on Jewish law are integral to the formation of halachic consensus.

Appendix C

בְּרֹאשׁ הַשָּׁנָה יִכָּתֵבוּן וּבְיוֹם צוֹם כִּפּוּר יֵחָתֵמוּן:

כַּמָּה יַעַבְרוּן וְכַמָּה יִבָּרֵאוּן,

מִי יִחְיֶה וּמִי יָמוּת,

מִי בְקִצּוֹ וּמִי לֹא בְקִצּוֹ,

מִי בַמַּיִם וּמִי בָאֵשׁ,

מִי בַחֶרֶב וּמִי בַחַיָּה,

מִי בָרָעָב וּמִי בַצָּמָא,

מִי בָרַעַשׁ וּמִי בַמַּגֵּפָה,

מִי בַחֲנִיקָה וּמִי בַסְּקִילָה.

מִי יָנוּחַ וּמִי יָנוּעַ, מִי יִשָּׁקֵט וּמִי יְטָרֵף, מִי יִשָּׁלֵו וּמִי
יִתְיַסָּר, מִי יֵעָנִי וּמִי יֵעָשֵׁר, מִי יִשָּׁפֵל וּמִי יָרוּם.

O n Rosh Hashanah they are inscribed, and on the day of the fast of Yom Kippur they are sealed:

How many shall pass away and how many shall be born;

who shall live and who shall die;

who shall live out his allotted time and who shall depart before his time;

who [shall perish] by water and who by fire;

who by the sword and who by the wild beast;

who by hunger and who by thirst;

who by earthquake and who by pestilence;

who by strangulation and who by stoning.

Who shall be at rest and who shall wander; who shall be tranquil and who shall be harassed; who shall enjoy well-being and who shall suffer tribulation; who shall be poor and who shall be rich; who shall be humbled and who shall be exalted.

Appendix D

Midrash Hagadol, Genesis 47:29 📖

"וַיִּקְרְבוּ יְמֵי יִשְׂרָאֵל" (בְּרֵאשִׁית מז, כט). רַבִּי שִׁמְעוֹן בֶּן לָקִישׁ אוֹמֵר: יְמוֹתֵיהֶן שֶׁל צַדִּיקִים מֵתִין וְהֵן אֵינָן מֵתִין. מַאי טַעֲמָא? "וַיִּקְרַב יִשְׂרָאֵל לָמוּת" אֵין כְּתִיב, אֶלָּא "וַיִּקְרְבוּ יְמֵי יִשְׂרָאֵל לָמוּת". וְכֵן בְּדָוִד: "וַיִּקְרְבוּ יְמֵי דָוִד לָמוּת" (מְלָאכִים א, ב, א). וְכֵן בְּמֹשֶׁה: "הֵן קָרְבוּ יָמֶיךָ לָמוּת" (דְּבָרִים לא, יד).

> "The days of Israel neared death" (Genesis 47:29). Said Rabbi Shimon ben Lakish: The days of the righteous die, but they themselves do not die. This is indicated by this verse, which does not say that "Israel neared death," but that Israel's days neared death. A similar statement is made regarding David, "The days of David neared death" (I Kings 2:1), and also regarding Moses, "[God told Moses,] behold your days are nearing to die" (Deuteronomy 31:14).

Midrash Hagadol

A midrashic work on the five books of the Pentateuch. Midrash is the designation of a particular genre of rabbinic literature usually forming a running commentary on specific books of the Bible. *Midrash Hagadol* quotes widely from Talmud and other earlier midrashic works, serving as a valuable resource to reconstruct lost sections of Midrash. A traveler, Yaakov Sapir, first discovered the anonymous Midrash in Yemen in the middle of the 19th century. Some ascribe it to Rabbi Avraham, son of Maimonides.

Appendix E

The Rebbe, Rabbi Menachem M. Schneerson, *Torat Menachem* 5715 1:67–68

Rabbi Menachem Mendel Schneerson
1902–1994

The towering Jewish leader of the 20th century, known as "the Lubavitcher Rebbe," or simply as "the Rebbe." Born in southern Ukraine, the Rebbe escaped Nazi-occupied Europe, arriving in the U.S. in June 1941. The Rebbe inspired and guided the revival of traditional Judaism after the European devastation, impacting virtually every Jewish community the world over. The Rebbe often emphasized that the performance of just one additional good deed could usher in the era of Mashiach. The Rebbe's scholarly talks and writings have been printed in more than 200 volumes.

כְּתִיב (בְּרֵאשִׁית לג, יז), "וּלְמִקְנֵהוּ עָשָׂה סֻכֹּת". "מִקְנֵהוּ" – הֵם דְּבָרִים הַנִּקְנִים ("אײַנגֶעקוֹיפְטֶע זאַכְן"), דְּהַיְינוּ, כָּל הַדְּבָרִים הַגַּשְׁמִיִּם שֶׁהַנְּשָׁמָה מִצַּד עַצְמָהּ אֵין לָהּ שׁוּם שַׁיָּיכוּת אֲלֵיהֶם, אֶלָּא שֶׁ"נִּקְנוּ" וְנִיתוֹסְפוּ אֵצֶל הַנְּשָׁמָה ("אַ צוּגֶעקוּמֶענֶע זאַךְ") עַל יְדֵי יְרִידָתָהּ בַּגּוּף. וְעַל זֶה נֶאֱמַר "וּלְמִקְנֵהוּ עָשָׂה סֻכֹּת" – שֶׁכָּל הָעִנְיָנִים הַגַּשְׁמִיִּים צְרִיכִים לִהְיוֹת בְּאוֹפָן דְּ"סֻכּוֹת", בְּדֶרֶךְ עֲרַאי בִּלְבַד, וּכְמַאֲמַר רַזַ"ל "הָעוֹלָם הַזֶּה דּוֹמֶה לַפְּרוֹזְדוֹר בִּפְנֵי הָעוֹלָם הַבָּא, הַתְקֵן עַצְמְךָ בִּפְרוֹזְדוֹר כְּדֵי שֶׁתִּכָּנֵס לַטְּרַקְלִין", דְּהַיְינוּ שֶׁכָּל עוֹלָם הַזֶּה אֵינוֹ אֶלָּא כִּ"פְרוֹזְדוֹר".

וּמַה שֶּׁכָּתוּב "כְּדֵי שֶׁתִּכָּנֵס לַטְּרַקְלִין" – אֵין הַכַּוָּונָה לְאַחֲרֵי מֵאָה וְעֶשְׂרִים שָׁנָה דַּוְקָא, אֶלָּא עַל דֶּרֶךְ מַאֲמַר רַזַ"ל "עוֹלָמְךָ תִּרְאֶה בְּחַיֶּיךָ", דְּהַיְינוּ שֶׁכַּאֲשֶׁר הָאָדָם נִמְצָא כָּאן לְמַטָּה צְרִיכִים הַדְּבָרִים הַגַּשְׁמִיִּים לִהְיוֹת אֶצְלוֹ בְּאוֹפָן שֶׁל "אֲרַעי".

"Jacob constructed temporary huts for his cattle" (Genesis 33:17). The Hebrew word for cattle, *miknehu*, also translates as "acquisitions," and refers to all things to which the soul has no innate connection but are considered "acquired tastes," acquired after the soul enters a body. The verse teaches us that we must make "temporary huts" for all these acquisitions, i.e., we must relegate all these physical accouterments to the realm of the temporary. This is in accordance with the teaching of our sages, "This world is like an antechamber before the World to Come. Prepare yourself in the antechamber, so that you may enter the palace."

It should be noted, however, that the words "so that you may enter the palace" do not necessarily refer to "after 120 years." Rather, as our sages tell us, it is possible for one to experience the hereafter while still alive. This is accomplished when a person deems all his physical acquisitions as "temporary" [and not of primary importance].

ADDITIONAL READINGS

DEATH: A JEWISH/PSYCHOLOGICAL PERSPECTIVE THROUGH LOGOTHERAPY

BY RABBI REUVEN BULKA, PhD

Reflections on Past and Future

The two words characteristic of the most prevalent human moods are *hope* and *despair*. Hope, an optimistic frame of mind, is generally associated with the future; *despair* by contradistinction is a sense of future*lessness*, either because of the feeling of emptiness that no future can rectify, or because of the inevitableness of death.

Existentialism, focusing on the here-and-now of woes and predicaments, has popularized numerous pessimistic terms, such as dread, sickness unto death, nausea, anxiety, crisis, etc. Although identified with existentialism, logotherapy, the analytical method developed by Viktor E. Frankl, is unique in its optimistic approach to life. Logotherapy is future-oriented. It emphasizes hope and meaning rather than despair. It accentuates the positive of future promise and not past failure.

Judaism, too, is future-oriented. It knows that while humans are finite and imperfect, and therefore liable to err and sin, we are also capable of self-perfection to a certain degree. Judaism does not explain sinfulness as a "spur of the moment reaction," "haphazard occurrence," or an act caused by "temporary insanity." Indeed, the Talmud asserts that *"a person does not sin unless a spirit of folly (shetut) enters into him,"*[1] but this is not intended to condone misbehavior or punishment. Rather this talmudic statement is expressive of Judaism's optimism. If one sins, it is because some foreign ingredient—a spirit of folly—has taken possession of him. As Judaism sees it, if transgressors want to mend their ways, they need only divest themselves of "the spirit of folly" and return to their selfhood.

One of the Hebrew terms for sin is *averah,* derived from a root meaning "to pass" and linked to "the past." It is not overindulgence in homiletics to equate the Jewish concept of wrongdoing with the past; that is, sin, after being committed, is a thing of the past which need not determine the future. Judaism rejects the notion that sin constitutes an eternal burden of guilt, that one's future is doomed because of the past. Repentance *(teshuvah)* can erase the past if implemented by good deeds in the future. This conviction is expressed as follows:

> If you see a scholar who has committed an offense by night, do not cavil at him by day, for perhaps he has done penance. 'Perhaps,' say you?—Nay, rather, he has certainly done penance.[2]

Even if we have witnessed wrongdoing, we should assume that the wrong has been righted and that, as a result, the past has been deprived of power. We can always mend our ways:

> Even if one has been completely wicked all his life but repents at the end, he is not reproached for his wickedness.[3]

I have heard many, almost hostile, reactions to this Talmudic passage. It is not right, it is argued, that a rascal should get away with last minute repentance.

---

[1] Talmud, *Sotah* 3a.

[2] Talmud, *Berakoth* 19a.
[3] Talmud, *Kiddushin* 40b.

But the Sages referred to *sincere* repentance. The Sages refused to concede that the human situation is ever hopeless. Retrievement is always possible. There is no hopeless situation.

II

Viktor Frankl sets the same optimistic tone in logotherapy. He stresses that the endeavor to find meaning in life is the primary human motivation. Frankl insists there is always meaning in life—to the very end. He does not acknowledge the inevitableness of the consequences of inherited dispositions or environmental coercion. He emphasizes the human ability to exercise free choice despite circumstances, and asserts that we can surmount any and every situation. As proof he cites the many, including himself, who retained hope and trust in meaning in the Nazi death camps.

Logotherapy focuses on the future, both in the clinical and meta-clinical situations. In Frankl's words:

> But man cannot really exist without a fixed point in the future. Under normal conditions his entire present is shaped around that future point, directed toward it like iron filings toward the pole of a magnet.[4]

In the Nazi concentration camp, Frankl tried to alleviate the despair of fellow-sufferers by finding some task in the future that called upon their inner resources. He challenged those who despaired to struggle and survive in order to fulfill that future task. Frankl never lost faith and hope, and he instilled that faith and hope in some of his fellow prisoners. Logotherapy asserts that man can bear suffering if he can see beyond it, however remotely, into the future. This insight is based on Frankl's own experience.

But there are situations when finding a meaning seems futile. But even then, Frankl writes, "A human being, by the attitude he chooses, is capable of finding and fulfilling meaning in even a hopeless situation."

The faith in the unconditional meaningfulness of life enables one to elicit a positive response in all situations. Thus, a nurse suffering from a terminal illness was told that her attitude to pain would go a long way in helping the many patients in her care. This gave her a meaning in suffering.

Facing death is the main challenge to the meaning-orientation of logotherapy. It is the sorrow and agony of the person who is facing his end, as well as of those who suffer a tragic loss. In trying to meet this challenge, logotherapy is compatible, if not consistent, with Jewish thought.

> Actually, the only transitory aspects of life are the potentialities; as soon as we have succeeded in actualizing a potentiality, we have transmuted it into an actuality and, thus, salvaged and rescued it into the past. Once an actuality, it is one forever. Everything in the past is saved from being transitory. Therein it is irrevocably stored rather than irrecoverably lost. Having been is still a form of being, perhaps even its most secure form.[5]

Frankl therefore concludes:

> This leads to the paradox that man's past is his true future. The dying man has no future, only a past. But the dead 'is' his past. He has no life, he is his life. That it is his past life does not matter; we know that the past is the safest form of existence—it cannot be taken away.[6]

There is a parallel to this approach in a Midrashic exegesis of *and the day of death (is better) than the day of one's birth*.

> To what can this be compared? To two ships laden with merchandise sailing the ocean, one coming in and the other going out, and the people praised the one coming in. Some people stood there and wondered: 'Why are you praising this one and not the other?' They replied to them: 'We are praising

---

[4] Viktor E. Frankl, *The Doctor and the Soul: From Psychotherapy to Logotherapy* (New York: Bantam Books, 1967), p. 80.

[5] Frankl, *Psychotherapy and Existentialism: Selected Papers on Logotherapy* (New York: Simon and Schuster, 1968), pp. 30–31.

[6] Frankl, "Time and Responsibility," *Existential Psychiatry,* Vol. 1 (1966), pp. 365–366.

the ship that came in, because we know that she went out in peace and has returned in peace. As to the one now going out, we do not know what her fate will be.' Thus when a man is born we do not know what the nature of his deeds will be, but when he departs this world, we already know of what nature his deeds are.[7]

Here, as in Frankl's thought, there is a balanced attitude to the future. While both Judaism and logotherapy concern themselves with the manifold possibilities of the future, they do not become obsessed with it. After all, is not every future moment destined to become part of the past? Past accomplishments are always better than future possibilities. On this logotherapy and Judaism are agreed.

III

Logotherapy extends its affirmative attitude also to aging. Our culture's glorification of youth has induced fear of aging and envy of the young. Frankl writes:

> Even in advanced years one should not envy a young person. Why should one? For the possibilities a young person has or for his future? No, I should say that, instead of possibilities in the future, the older person has realities in the past—work done, love loved, and suffering suffered.[8]

Logotherapy insists, as Judaism does, that even in the twilight of life man should not stop working and being active. The inability to do one's best in later years need not deter a person from trying. Here, too, the delicate balance between future promise and past accomplishment must be maintained. In his positive attitude to the past, Frankl also points to solace for the individual who has experienced a tragic loss.

> Imagine what consolation the logotherapeutic attitude to the past would bring to a war widow who has only experienced, say, two weeks of marital bliss. She would feel that this experience can never be taken from her. It will remain her inviolable treasure, preserved and delivered into her

past. Her life can never become meaningless even if she might remain childless.[9]

Indeed, memory is transient. Frankl properly asks who will keep the memory alive after the widow dies. He thinks that an appropriate response is the following:

> To this one may answer, it is irrelevant whether anyone remembers or not; just as it is irrelevant whether we look at something, or think about something, that still exists and is with us. For it exists regardless of whether we look at it or think about it. While it is true that we can't take anything with us when we die, the totality of our life, which we have lived to completion and death, remains outside the grave, and outside the grave it remains. And it remains not although, but because, it has slipped into the past and has been preserved there.[10]

The concept of a deed *remaining in the world* raises questions about the meaning of existence proper. Frankl comments:

> Now it is my contention that man really could not move a limb unless deep down to the foundations of existence, and out of the depths of being, he is imbued by a basic trust in the ultimate meaning. Without it he would have to stop breathing.[11]

> This ultimate meaning necessarily exceeds and surpasses the finite intellectual capacities of man; in logotherapy, we speak in this context of a supra-meaning.[12]

Frankl takes the daring step of suggesting that this world may not be the ultimate reality.

> For all that man may occupy an exceptional position, for all that he may be unusually receptive

---

[7] *Tanhuma*, Vayakhel 1; *Ecclesiastes Rabbah* 7:1.
[8] Frankl, *Psychotherapy and Existentialism*, p. 31.

[9] *Ibid.*, p. 32.
[10] Frankl, "Time and Responsibility," *op. cit.*, p. 363.
[11] Frankl, *The Will to Meaning: Foundations and Applications of Logotherapy* (New York: World Publishing Co., 1969), pp. 150–151.
[12] Frankl, *Man's Search for Meaning: An Introduction to Logotherapy* (New York: Washington Square Press, 1963), p. 187.

to the world, and that the world itself may be his environment—still, who can say that beyond this world a superworld does not exist? Just as the animal can scarcely reach out of his environment to understand the superior world of man, so perhaps man can scarcely ever grasp the superworld, though he can reach out toward it in religion—or perhaps encounter it in revelation.[13]

Frankl's concept of a "supra-world" is, I suggest, a synonym for *olam haba*—the world-to-come.

Logotherapy has a perspective of time totally differing from the time concepts of philosophy and psychology. The future is potential fulfillment and, moreover, it is extended beyond existence as we know it. Frankl has an elastic approach to time, which extends the future into the past as well as into a supra-world. The broad ramifications of logotherapy's meaning-orientation encompass all of life from past reality to all future possibilities.

Death in Life—Talmudic and Logotherapeutic Affirmations

In spite of all the sophistication of a highly technologized 20th century, man has essentially still not come to grips with the psychologically traumatic and emotionally enervating experience of death. To be sure, one finds the odd intellectual or the odd man-in-the-street who is philosophical about death, who is ready, so to say, to live with death. In the main, however, the average man still fears death, the process of dying, and the experiencing of death. Perhaps it should be this way. Perhaps it is ridiculous for philosophers and psychologists to attempt pseudo-explanations which explain, even explain away, death. Perhaps it is the height of obscenity to reduce what is assuredly an awesome reality into an acceptable experience. Then, too, it is possibly self-contradictory for man to, at one and the same time, glorify life and accept death. After all, if life is so valuable, and human existence so beautiful, death should be avoided. And, even though death cannot be avoided in fact, it can be avoided in mind. Taking into consideration man's preoccupation with life, it is to be expected that

thoughts of death should be suppressed. The thought of death having been suppressed, man becomes psychologically unequipped to face death when death confronts him.

If what we have said is true, then the secularized 20th century technology as a creeping philosophy does not enhance, rather it exacerbates the problem. Man's cold and calculated sophistication, designed to mediate between man and nature in a this-worldly setting, almost totally ignores what may be called "the ultimate problems of man's being." The concerns of a dubious tomorrow are muted in the obsessive preoccupation with today. And, as long as death and what follows death are relegated to the "tomorrow," the "today" world will find it increasingly difficult to properly understand death.

What is needed to deal with the problem on a meta-clinical level is an acceptable philosophy of life which fuses together the today and tomorrow, a philosophy which goes beyond the "as if" of a Camus but is more livable than the *sein-zum-tode* of a Heidegger. If the today and tomorrow can be shown to be intermingled and intertwined, then perhaps the philosophical problems of death can be tackled. The hope is that the psychological aspect would follow.

II

In attempting to formulate a philosophy of life and death to deal with the aforementioned problems, the present paper will present two traditions, one religious, the other secular, relating to the role of death in life. The religious tradition is that found in the Talmudic and Midrashic literature of Judaism. The secular tradition is the logotherapy of Viktor E. Frankl.

Even a cursory glance at the legislative structure of Judaism indicates an appreciation for life. With few exceptions, man is, in Judaism, at all times excused from the performance of a commandment when this endangers his life.[14] Danger to life suspends the code of Jewish existence. According to some,[15] this does not even allow man the possibility of being a theo-

---

[13] Frankl, *The Doctor and the Soul*, pp. 25–26.

[14] Talmud, *Yoma* 85b.

[15] Maimonides, *The Foundations of Torah* 5:4.

logical hero. He must suspend religious observance for the higher reality, life itself. At the same time, the attitude to death in Judaism is a surprisingly positive one. Midrashic comment on the verse "and God saw everything that He had made, and behold, it was very good" (Genesis 1:31) suggests that "very good" can be equated with death.[16] In a similar vein, it is said of the psalmist David that "He looked upon the day of death and broke into song."[17] At once, we are thus confronted with an affirmative attitude to life and a positive outlook to death. In simple terms, the two ideas can be reconciled with the mediating principle that man would not be faced with an imperative to act and accomplish if his life were endless. That his existence may be terminated suddenly is a reality which forces, or should force, man to utilize his allotted moments as meaningfully as possible.

It seems, though, that awareness of death in the abstract is not deemed enough to act as imperative. Thus, to prevent transgression, the Talmud proposes that man be mindful, among other things, of where he is eventually going, to a place of dust, worms, and maggots.[18] Of the righteous it is said that they "set their death in the forefront of their thoughts."[19] And a famous sage, to bring home the importance of awareness of death, suggested to his disciples that they repent one day before their death. Immediately he was confronted with the expected question, does then man know on what day he will die? To which the sage responded, "Then all the more reason that he repent today, lest he die tomorrow, and thus his entire life is spent in repentance."[20] Repentance here is presented in the existential sense, as the constant process of investigating the past to improve the future. In any event, we have here an ancient thought system which correlates the fact of death with meaningful life. Admittedly, there is a danger in proposing an extreme such as constantly being mindful of death, which can easily give birth to neurotic behavior. It would be more realistic to take this extreme as a counter to the extreme of neglect, with man in his own unique situation striking a delicate balance. The balance might rest in the awareness of death when establishing the "game-plan" for life, and in investing one's life energies in carrying out the plan.

The paradoxical nature of man's relation to death is best expressed in a dialogue between Alexander of Macedon and the elders of the south city.

> He said to them: What shall a man do to live? They replied: He should mortify himself. What shall a man do to kill himself? They replied: He should keep himself alive.[21]

A Midrashic counterpart of the same is the following: "Death is near to you and far from you, as well as far from you and near you."[22] The more man is interested merely in keeping himself alive the more he cuts himself off from meaningful living. In the pursuit of years he wastes the days. The more man realizes he is mortal, destined to die, the more he will try to accomplish, thus perhaps even gaining immortality. Basic to the Talmudic approach is the inherent notion that death, properly understood, can be a vital life force. Needless to say, the element of fear can easily enter into the religious sphere, as when man is urged to behave in life because of the consequences he might face afterwards. Such a confrontation with life and death out of fear, which might yield positive results on a quantitative level, nevertheless falls short on the qualitative level. To propose transcending death in an atmosphere of fear is to circumvent the trauma of death with an even greater disease, the life lived in fear. An affirmation of the role of death in life on an existential level would thus seem to be most appropriate. For this, we turn to the existential philosophy underlying the logotherapeutic system of Viktor E. Frankl.

III

Logotherapy is the school of psychotherapy fathered by Frankl and focusing on the importance of meaning in life. Logotherapy proposes the existence of unconditional meaningfulness and posits the no-

---

[16] *Genesis Rabbah* 9:5.
[17] Talmud, *Berakoth* 10a.
[18] Talmud, *Aboth* 3:1.
[19] *Ecclesiastes Rabbah* 7:9.
[20] Talmud, *Shabbath* 152a.

[21] Talmud, *Tamid* 32a.
[22] *Ecclesiastes Rabbah* 8:17.

tion that man's primary motivational force is to find meaning in life.[23] Logotherapy, unlike other existential systems, is basically an optimistic, future-oriented system, focusing on man's freedom and the multitude of possibilities for man to find meaning. Logotherapy carefully avoids injecting such ideas as fear, trembling, sickness-unto-death, nausea, anxiety, etc., into the human situation. Instead, ideas such as hope, meaning, joy, ecstasy, and values form its basic lexicon. Nevertheless, logotherapy does not recoil from facing squarely the issues of suffering and death.

The process of death, according to Frankl, is not a severed fragment of the human biography. Death is part of life. "Without suffering and death human life cannot be complete."[24] In projecting the notion of "unconditional meaningfulness," man is called upon to elicit meaning up to and including the moment of death. For "human life, under any circumstances, never ceases to have meaning, and this infinite meaning of life includes suffering and dying, privation and death."[25] The thesis of logotherapy is that man is to live, and die, meaningfully.

So much for the moment of death. What bearing does the inescapability of death have on life itself?

Frankl believes the fact of death is crucial to life; "only in the face of death is it meaningful to act."[26] Contrary to the thought that death indicates the futility and meaninglessness of life, Frankl asserts that if man's life tenure were really infinite in duration, he could continually, and legitimately, postpone every action forever. It would not really matter whether a deed was performed now, or ten years from now. "But in the face of death as absolute finis to our future and boundary to our possibilities, we are under the imperative of utilizing our lifetimes to the utmost, not letting the singular opportunities—whose 'finite' sum constitutes the whole of life—pass by un-

used."[27] In a word, man exists in time and time exists in man. In the becoming process, the man-time combination is utilized. The death of man in time signifies the passing of a life. The death of time in man signifies the passing of a moment. Ultimate death is only a more radical form of expiration, more radical than the death in installments involved in the wasting of time.

On the other hand, proper utilization of time signifies a positive irreversibility, for that which has been accomplished remains as a reality forever. Transitoriness applies only to the potentialities, which, once actualized, are, so to say, "rescued . . . into the past."[28] Death poses a constant imperative to man, an imperative which says that each moment, as life itself, is irrepeatable, and must be utilized. Death makes life meaningful. The challenge of life is how to use each moment, which values are to be actualized, and which doomed to nonexistence.[29] In logotherapy this is taken to indicate the importance of the past, that "man's past is his true future."[30] The past deeds are "safely stored," immune from any erasure. And, for the dying man who has no future, the past, which is really his life, is the eloquent testimonial to his existence. Death ends the becoming process. In death man "is" what he was in life.[31]

Ironically, Frankl, to counter the negativism usually linked to the fact of death, actually introduces the ubiquity of death even in life, in the passing of time, as a counter to nihilism.

The fact that not only life, but also the moment can be lost, and are in fact irreversible, leads to the logotherapeutic notion of man's responsibleness in life. For, if what has been done can forever be undone, and vice versa, then virtue and vice would disappear in uncertainty, praise and blame would be impossible and education unmanageable. Human beings would

23 Viktor E. Frankl, *Man's Search for Meaning: An Introduction to Logotherapy* (New York: Washington Square Press, 1963), p. 154.

24 *Ibid.,* p. 106.

25 *Ibid.,* pp. 131–132.

26 Frankl, *Psychotherapy and Existentialism: Selected Papers on Logotherapy* (New York: Simon and Schuster, 1968), p. 30.

27 Frankl, *The Doctor and the Soul: From Psychotherapy to Logotherapy* (New York: Bantam Books, 1967), p. 52.

28 Frankl, *Psychotherapy and Existentialism*, p. 30.

29 Frankl, *Man's Search for Meaning*, p. 191.

30 Frankl, "Time and Responsibility," *Existential Psychiatry*, Vol. 1 (1966), p. 365.

31 *Ibid.*

be free from the responsibilities which underlie their humanness. Responsibleness is a responsiveness to the challenges posed by life, challenges which call for undelayed response. If the existence of man in time is "temporality" and the existence of time in man is "singularity," the following statement capsules these ideas: "The meaning of human existence is based upon its irreversible quality. An individual's responsibility in life must therefore be understood in terms of temporality and singularity."[32]

Irretrievability of a past moment, singularity, and of a past life, temporality, constitute the basis of human existence, and are the impetus for man's responsibleness to life. Frankl thus sees death as an ongoing life process, not in the pessimistic sense, but in the positive sense. Just as total death, the death of man in time, challenges man's life in its totality, so fragmentary death, the death of time in man, challenges man in each moment. The sum of these moments constitutes the existence of man.

IV

It is instructive at this point to note the striking similarities between the Talmudic and logotherapeutic attitudes to death. Although they are separate systems, the one religious, the other secular, nevertheless both take an affirmative attitude to death. The affirmative attitudes are no doubt born of differing assumptions. At work in the Talmud is the fundamental faith that God would not have put in the world a purely negative reality or fact of life. This is not to glorify or seek death, rather to indicate that death enhances the human situation. In logotherapy one senses an optimism with life which is, at once, a philosophical and psychological proposition. As death is unavoidable, it is psychologically silly and philosophically untenable to deny its importance. And, to avoid the dangers of negativism, which can only impede the human situation, it is vital to say yes to life in its totality. Even if life appears senseless, and death more than meaningless, it is vital for man to make life and death as meaningful as possible, to make life philosophically justifiable and psychologically livable. In both these systems, there is an inherent affirmation of the natural order, and an implicit faith in all life contingencies.

In a sense, one may argue that logotherapy presents nothing new, taking into account the fact that its ideas already appear centuries ago in the Talmud. Then, too, the affirmative attitude to death is already found in the writings of so many existential thinkers. Perhaps the uniqueness of the logotherapeutic approach is that it is so affirming while being a secular system, and is affirming with a positive and realistic bent.

For the man-in-the-street, theological or logical propositions are not likely to evoke any excitement. Theology and philosophy have a habit of finding the ear of few people. If Hegel is correct in saying history is what man does with death, then the 20th century poses a unique challenge. Some see in the proliferating abundance of life-saving techniques and their use on the dying person a denial of the individual's right to his own death.[33] It is almost as if science is doing its utmost to see if it can beat the death force, if it can conquer nature. And, ironically, the same medical prowess which tries to conquer death is the judge of when medicine can no longer help, when the situation is hopeless to the point that euthanasia is indicated. In these attitudes one senses a trend to deny nature, to let medicine prolong, and, if need be, to terminate. The affirmative view of logotherapy is consistent when it asks if "we are ever entitled to deprive an incurably ill patient of the chance to 'die his death,' the chance to fill his existence with meaning down to its last moment."[34] For, "the way he dies, insofar as it is really his death, is an integral part of his life, it rounds that life out to a meaningful totality."[35]

Perhaps what we should be arguing for is a return to nature, to an awareness and appreciation of the natural, unavoidable aspects of human existence. Feifel hints at this when he argues that "the concept of death must be integrated into the self to subdue estrangement from the fundamental nature of our

---

[32] Frankl, *The Doctor and the Soul*, p. 52.

[33] Elisabeth Kübler-Ross, *On Death and Dying* (New York: Macmillan, 1970), pp. 8–9.

[34] Frankl, *The Doctor and the Soul*, p. 37.

[35] *Ibid.*

being."[36] Frankl alludes to it when he asserts that "this acceptance of finiteness is the precondition to mental health and human progress, while the inability to accept it is characteristic of the neurotic personality."[37]

In the striving for an orderly, structured world, a world of rules and clear-cut patterns which arc undoubtedly necessary for technology to benefit the masses, the matter of death has suffered the fate that is to be expected when eschewing the inevitable.

The ultimate answers relative to the problem are not logical but paradoxical. From the Talmudic dialogue previously cited to the effect that to live one must mortify himself and to die one should indulge in life, to the Heideggerian idea that one can conquer death by actually willing it, to the logotherapeutic notion that to the extent which man understands his finiteness he also overcomes it,[38] it is evident that man magnifies the problems of death by avoidance, and counters these problems by accepting and affirming the role of death in life. In espousing an affirmative attitude to the natural order, it might be possible not only to effectively overcome the trauma associated with death, but also to re-enter into meaningful dialogue with life, and to project human concerns into the forefront of man's endeavors.

Work, Love, Suffering, Death: A Jewish/Psychological Perspective through Logotherapy. Ch. 8–9 [Northvale, New Jersey: Jason Aronson, 1998], pp. 105–119.
Reprinted with permission of publisher.

---

[36] Herman Feifel, "The Problem of Death." In Hendrik M. Ruitenbeek (Ed.), *Death: Interpretations* (New York: Dell Publishing Co., 1969), p. 129.

[37] Frankl, *Psychotherapy and Existentialism*, p. 47.

[38] *Ibid.*, p. 36.

ESSENCE AND EXPRESSION

BY RABBI YANKI TAUBER

Rabbi Yaakov would say: This world is compared to an antechamber before the world to come. Prepare yourself in the antechamber, so that you may enter the banquet hall.

He would also say: A single moment of repentance and good deeds in this world is greater than all of the world to come. And a single moment of bliss in the world to come is greater than all of this world.

—Ethics of the Fathers, 4:16–17

The Talmud relates that Rabbi Yaakov once witnessed the tragic death of a young man who, at that very moment, was engaged in fulfilling the very two *mitzvot* for which the Torah promises "long life."

"Honor your father and your mother," reads the fifth of Ten Commandments, "that your days be lengthened, and that good befall you."[1] The other *mitzvah* for which the Torah specifically promises reward is *shiluach hakan* ("dispatching the nest"): "If you happen upon a bird's nest… and the mother bird is sitting upon the young or upon the eggs, do not take the mother bird along with the young. Send away the mother bird, and you may then take the young for yourself, that good may befall you and that your days be lengthened."[2]

And yet, here was a man who was fulfilling both these commandments simultaneously. At his father's request, he had climbed a ladder to chase away a mother bird from her nest and collect the chicks. But no sooner had he done so that he slipped from the ladder and fell to his death.

"Where are this person's 'long days'?" asked Rabbi Yaakov. "Where is the 'good' he was promised? But,

when the Torah says 'that your days be lengthened,' it is referring to a world that is wholly long; when the Torah says 'that good befall you,' it is referring to a world that is wholly good."[3]

"Rabbi Yaakov," concludes the Talmud, "is of the opinion that there is no reward for *mitzvot* in this world"—a view expressed in the *Ethics* by Rabbi Tarfon ("Know, that the reward of the righteous is in the World to Come"[4]) and reiterated by Maimonides in his codification of Torah law, the *Mishneh Torah.*[5]

Another talmudic sage, Rabbi Joshua ben Levi, quotes the verse "You shall keep the *mitzvah,* the decrees, and the laws, which I command you today to do them"[6]—"today to do them," Rabbi Joshua reads in the verse's meaning, "and not to do them tomorrow; today to do them, and tomorrow to receive their reward."[7]

In other words, the "present world" and "the world to come" represent two entirely different modes of existence, which, for some reason, must each be confined to a world all its own. Our present existence is the environment for the deed and achievement, but lacks the possibility to enjoy the fruits of our labor. On the other hand, the "world to come" is a world of ultimate reward, bliss, and perfection, but one that precludes any further achievement on the part of man. The Talmud goes so far as to quote the verse, "There will come years of which you will say: I have no desire in them,"[8] and declare: "This refers to the days of the Messianic Era, in which there is neither merit nor obligation."[9]

---

[3] Talmud, Kiddushin 39b.

[4] *Ethics of the Fathers*, 2:16.

[5] Mishneh Torah, Laws of Repentance 9:1.

[6] Deuteronomy 7:11.

[7] Talmud, *Eruvin* 22a.

[8] Ecclesiastes 12:1.

[9] Talmud, *Shabbat* 151b.

---

[1] Deuteronomy 5:16.

[2] Deuteronomy 22:6–7.

Why this dichotomy? On the most basic level, this is a function of G-d's granting freedom of choice to man, without which our deeds would be devoid of moral significance. A world in which the benefits of obeying the Almighty's commandments are self-evident would obviously lack the challenge and the sacrifice which makes their observance worthy of reward. So in this world G-d created an environment in which neither He nor the divine nature of His commandments are openly manifest. A world in which surface appearances shroud and distort the divine truth—a world in which people engaged in life-lengthening *mitzvot* fall off ladders—challenging us to choose between good and evil, between faithfulness to our mission in life and its corruption. Only such a world can serve as the arena for meaningful accomplishment.

The Physics of Will

However, our material world's concealment of the divine truth is much more than an orchestrated moral challenge. On a deeper level, this concealment is significant to the nature of the *mitzvot* themselves.

The *mitzvot* are primarily physical deeds performed with physical objects: animal hides are fashioned into *tefillin* and wrapped around one's head and arm; flour and water become the instrument of a *mitzvah* in the form of the *matzah* eaten on Passover; a ram's horn is sounded on Rosh Hashanah; a citron and palm frond are taken on Sukkot. For the physical world is ultimately the most appropriate environment for the function of the *mitzvah* to be realized.

"*Mitzvot* relate to the very essence of G-d"[10] is a mainstay of chassidic teaching. But the very notion of something relating to another thing's essence is a philosophical oxymoron. The "essence" of something is the thing itself, as opposed to the manner in which it affects and is perceived by that which is outside of it. Hence the axiom: "The essence of a thing does not express itself or extend itself"[11] In other words, if you see it, it is not the thing itself that you see, only the manner in which it reflects light and imprints an image on your retina; if you understand it, then it is not

the thing itself that you comprehend, only a concept that your mind has pieced together by studying its effect on other things, and so on.

Nevertheless, G-d desired to project His essence into the created reality. This is the function of the *mitzvot:* through observing His commandments and fulfilling His will, we "bring" the very essence of G-d into our lives. And this is why He chose the physical object as the medium of the *mitzvah's* implementation.

Spiritual entities (e.g., ideas, feelings, etc.) intrinsically point to a source, a cause, a greater reality which they express and serve. Unlike the physical, whose deeper significance is buried deep beneath the surface of its corporeality, the spiritual readily serves as the express ion of a higher truth. The spiritual is thus the natural medium for the various *expressions* of the divine reality that G-d chose to convey to us.

But when it comes to the projection of G- d's *essence,* the very "virtues" of the spiritual disqualify it: its capacity to convey, to reveal, to manifest, runs contrary to the introvertive nature of "essence." Here, the physical object, the most non-transcendental element of G-d's creation, is the most ideal vehicle for G-d's essence—capturing *mitzvot*.

A physical object merely *is:* "l am," it proclaims, "and my being is wholly defined by its own existence." As such, the physical object constitutes the greatest concealment of the divine truth.[12] Precisely for this reason, it is G-d's medium of choice for man's implementation of His will.

---

[10] *Torat Shalom* pg. 190, see also *Tanya*, part IV, section 20.
[11] *Guide for the Perplexed*, quoted in *Ki Shemesh U'magen* 5692.

[12] Ultimately, however, this "I am, period" quality of the physical reflects on the wholly self-contained quintessence of its Creator. So while the most immediate function of the physical is to obscure the divine truth, a deeper contemplation of its qualities will yield insight into the very beingness of G-d, something that no spiritual expression of Him can convey. (It is told that following the Rosh Hashanah prayers one year, Rabbi Schneur Zalman of Liadi asked his son, Rabbi DovBer: "What did you think of during your prayers?" Rabbi DovBer replied that he had contemplated the meaning of the passage, "and every stature shall bow before You"—how the most lofty supernal worlds and spiritual creations negate themselves before the infinite majesty of G-d. "And you, father," Rabbi DovBer then asked, "with what thought did you pray?" Replied Rabbi Schneur Zalman: "I contemplated the table at which I stood.")

In other words, the object of the *mitzvah* is not a "manifestation" of the Divine. Were it to reflect Him in any way, were it to reveal anything of the "nature" of His reality, it would, by definition, fail to capture His essence. But capture His essence it docs, simply because He willed it to. G-d, of course, could have willed anything (including a manifest expression of His reality) to convey His essence, but He chose a medium that is most appropriate according to logical laws he established in creating our reality - a reality in which "essence" and "expression" are antithetical to each other. He therefore chose the material world, with its virtual blackout on any revealed expression of G-dliness, to serve as the "tool" with which we perform the *mitzvot* and thereby relate to His essence.

Better for Whom

"The reward of a *mitzvah* is a *mitzvah*,"[13] say our sages. For all pleasures and satisfactions (indeed, the very concepts of pleasure and satisfaction) were created by G-d. So what greater delight can there be than to experience the divine essence, the source of all pleasure? Were it possible for a human being to perceive what transpires each time he fulfills G-d's will in his daily life, he would experience the very essence of bliss.

But the very nature of what is accomplished by the performance of a *mitzvah* precludes the possibility of such "reward": as explained above, the concealment of the divine reality which categorizes our material-bound existence is what makes it the appropriate medium for the drawing down of G-d's essence. Reward can only come in a future world, a world that reveals rather than obscures its Creator. And yet, the world to come, precisely because of its manifest G-dliness, can serve only as the environment for the reward of the *mitzvah* but not for its implementation.

Thus, Rabbi Yaakov states in our *mishnah*: "A single moment of repentance and good deeds in this world is greater than all of the world to come. And a single moment of bliss in the world to come is greater than all of the present world."

Regarding the Almighty's purpose in creation—the drawing down of His essence into the physical creation[14]—a single positive act on the part of man is more meaningful than all the bliss experienced in the world to come. Yet the performer of the *mitzvah* remains in the dark. Although he may be aware of the value of what he is doing, he is unable to perceive it and experience it. On the experiential level, a single moment of bliss in the world to come is greater than all the joys of our present world.

The Banquet Hall

In light of this, one may ask: why bother with the reward at all? If G-d's purpose in creation is realized in our present-day lives, of what significance is our personal satisfaction?

One possible answer is that the need for a world to come is a function of G-d's commitment to justice and fairness. In the words of our sages, "G-d does not deprive any creature of its due."[15] If a man is instrumental in satisfying G-d's desire in creation, he deserves the satisfaction of enjoying the fruits of his labor.[16]

But this certainly does not describe the ultimate significance of the world to come. Rabbi Yaakov prefaces his above-quoted saying by comparing our world to an antechamber leading lo the banquet hall, which is the world to come. Clearly, then, the World to Come is not a footnote to our world, but its purpose and goal, a theme that is reiterated by many sayings by our sages.

How, then, do we reconcile this with the concept that "the essence of a thing does not express itself or extend itself"? And that it is, therefore, our present world, *because* of its spiritual darkness and inexpressiveness that facilitates the drawing down of G-d's essence and thereby realizes His purpose in creation?

---

13 *Ethics of the Fathers* 4:2.

14 See *Wood Submerged in Stone*, pgs. 92–94; *Debating Truths*, pgs. 275–284.

15 *Midrash Mechilta*, Exodus 20:30.

16 See *The Resurrection of the Dead* on pg. 212.

Truly Him and Truly Here

In applying terms such as "essence" and "expression" to the Almighty, we must bear in mind that it is He who created logic and its laws. Obviously, He is not governed or limited by any rational "axioms."

Nevertheless, He wishes to relate to our world as it is. So He chooses to make His relationship with us consistent with the basic "truths" that define our reality.

Indeed, since the purpose of creation is that the divine essence be drawn down into the physical reality, the objective is to do so on its (the physical reality's) terms, not by overriding them. So if the logical laws that govern our reality dictate that "expression" is incompatible with "essence," our bringing G-dliness into the world is to be achieved "blindly," without any perceptible manifestations of the divine essence.

On the other hand, however, if G-d's essence is truly to enter our reality, He must enter it as He is, without hindrance or inhibition. If *His* reality tolerates no limits or definitions, "revelation" must be no less conducive to His essence than "concealment."

In other words, for Him to be here implies two (seemingly contradictory) truths: if He is to be truly *here,* then His presence must be consistent with our reality; yet if it is truly *He* who is here, He must be here on His terms.

This is why the created existence has two distinct components: the present world and the world to come—the process and its culmination. The process of drawing down the divine essence into the created reality is carried out under an obscuring veil of corporeality, in keeping with the created rule that "the essence of a thing does not express itself or extend itself." At the same time, the product and end result of this process is a world in which G-d is uninhibitedly present, in which also the *expressions* of His reality fully convey the quintessence of His being.[17]

Beyond the Letter of the Law [Brooklyn, NY: Vaad Hanochos Hatmimim, 1995], pp. 201–209.
Reprinted with permission of the publisher.

[17] Based on an address by the Rebbe, Tammuz 12, 5719 (July 18, 1959).

ETHICS FROM SINAI

BY RABBI IRVING M. BUNIM

He used to say: Better, finer is one hour [spent] in repentance and good deeds in this world than all of life in the world-to-come; and better, finer is one hour of spiritual pleasure in the world-to-come than all of life in this world.

R. Jacob goes on with his contemplation of the known world here on earth and the spiritual world-to-come, to consider how they compare and how they interrelate. This *mishnah* is thus a direct continuation of the previous one.

If this world is merely a foyer or waiting-room, a place to prepare and make ready, and the Hereafter is the great banquet hall, we might well assume that life on earth is of far lesser importance, not to be regarded or valued too highly. If R. Jacob has created any such impression through his first teaching, he corrects it now. True enough, for sheer spiritual bliss and thoroughgoing reward, the world-to-come is incomparably superior. But this world of ours has one overriding importance of its own: Only here is man able to will and act, to achieve, to repent and change for the better; in short, to develop and grow in spiritual maturity. "Whatever your hand finds to do by your strength," says Solomon the wise, "do it; for there is no work or thought, knowledge or wisdom in the nether-world, to which you are going."[1]

It is told that in his last moments, as he knew death to be approaching shortly, the Gaon of Vilna began to weep. His disciples, gathered by his bedside, could not understand. "O Master," they asked, "you have spent a lifetime preparing for the Hereafter. Now that you are about to enter it, why do you weep?" In reply he pointed to the *tzitzith,* the fringes at the four corners of a special white garment *(arba canfoth)* that he constantly wore. "This garment," he said, "I bought for such a little bit of money. Yet by wearing it each day, I was able to fulfill such precious *mitzvoth.* In the world-to-come, even so simple a deed will not be possible. I weep, for I will be deprived of any further chance for *mitzvoth.*"

The Hereafter provides indescribable bliss, but it is a passive realm. There is no further chance for initiative, for conscious arousal to strive and achieve. The Midrash tells that ultimately, when the wicked stand in judgment before the Holy, Blessed One, they will plead, "Permit us, and we will repent." And the Holy One will reply, "You utter fools, the world in which you lived is like a Friday, and this realm is like a Sabbath. If a man does not prepare [food] on Friday, what will he eat on the Sabbath? Shall he then make his preparations on the Sabbath and thus desecrate it? Only one who has made his preparations beforehand can now eat. And do you not know that the world in which you lived is like the shore, while this realm is like the sea? If a man does not prepare for his meals while on shore, what will he eat at sea? Do you not know that this realm is like a wilderness, while the world from which you came is like a settlement? If a man does not prepare [food to take along] from the settlement, what will he eat in the wilderness? Again, the world in which you lived is like a sunny season, while this realm is like the rainy season. If a man does not plow in the sunny months, what will he eat when the rains descend?"[2]

The world-to-come is the realm of incomparable bliss, but this world of ours is the domain of incomparable achievement. Whatever ethereal joy the Hereafter may bring a person, there is one deep satisfaction it cannot give: the satisfaction of overcoming difficulties and making solid achievements. To see oneself grow spiritually, in faith, in religious observance, in Torah study, in deeds of kindness—this brings its own basic joy and contentment. In the Hereafter we can be wafted along on a cloud; in this world we can ourselves scale heights, knowing that our attainments will bring lasting compensation in the after-life.

[1] Ecclesiastes 9:10.

[2] Midrash Mishle, vi; Rabbah, Eccl. i 15; Yalkut Shim'oni II, Mishle § 938.

On one point our Sages are firm and clear: that "there is no reward for a *mitzvah* in this world."[3] Scripture states, "Then you shall keep the commandment and the statutes and the ordinances which I command you this day to do them."[4] And the Talmud tersely comments, "*This day* [you are] *to do them,* but not this day [are you] to receive reward";[5] "you are to do them this day, but receive their reward tomorrow."[6] Again and again is this theme expressed: "The entire recompense of the righteous is held in readiness for them for the world-to-come.[7] The Holy, Blessed One has postponed the reward that the performers of *mitzvoth* receive, so that they should fulfill them in faith and trust."[8] In *Pirke Avoth* itself we learned, "Know that the reward of the righteous is granted them in the world-to-come."[9]

Yet this is in startling contradiction to the countless passages in our Written Torah that distinctly promise a reward of material goods and material well-being for observing the *mitzvoth.* In the *Sh'ma* that the devout Jew recites morning and evening, we read, "If you will carefully heed My commandments which I command you this day, to love the Lord your God and to serve Him with all your heart and all your soul, then will I give the rain for your land in its [proper] season, the autumn rains and the spring rains, that you may gather in your grain, your wine and your oil. And I will make grass grow in your fields for your cattle, and you shall eat and be satisfied."[10] Interpret as we will, neither Heaven nor the Hereafter is mentioned directly here. In its literal meaning, the verse promises the Almighty's recompense in man's everyday life on earth.

First we might note the point that the *Rambam* makes. He concludes that where Scripture promises material rewards, it predicts them not as full and true compensation, but merely as means toward

further goals and ends. If the Torah and its precepts are faithfully observed, there will be the kind of material rewards that will promote Torah living further. The rewards will tend to create economic, political, and social conditions in which it will be easier, more convenient to do *mitzvoth* and flourish in religious growth. The *intrinsic,* essential reward for *mitzvoth,* however, remains spiritual bliss in the world-to-come.[11] As the Talmud states specifically about certain *mitzvoth,* "a man enjoys the 'fruits' in this world [in modern terminology, we might say the dividends] while the principle remains for him [to enjoy] in the Hereafter."[12]

Why does the "principle," the core of true reward, remain for the world-to-come? Why is there "no reward for a *mitzvah* in this world"? As we have mentioned elsewhere, there is not enough true pleasure or treasure in this whole wide world for the reward that a *mitzvah* deserves. It is as though a person earns a check, a bank draft for his Divine merit, but there is no bank here on earth with funds enough to honor it. The reward for *mitzvoth* is so great and sublime that it can be given only in the "currency" or "wealth" of the world-to-come.

What is it like, then—we may ask in curiosity—to receive such recompense in the Hereafter? Try as we will, we cannot imagine or comprehend this kind of experience. Just as earthly goods cannot provide this blissful reward, human words and thoughts cannot describe it. When we sleep and perhaps dream, we are totally unaware of the passage of time; when we are awake and conscious, it is impossible for us to *break out* of the dimensions of time and space and become unaware of them. Then how can we perceive anything clear about eternity, a realm in which the laws of time and space do not exist? The *Rambam* gives analogies: A person blind [from birth] can have no concept whatever of color; the deaf can have not the slightest understanding of sound; live fish can never experience fire for they exist in water. Even so can we, living our normal lives here on earth, know nothing of the sublime joy of the Hereafter through

3 T.B. Kiddushin 39b, Hullin 142a.
4 Deuteronomy 7: II.
5 T.B. Abodah Zarah 3a.
6 T.B. Erubin 22a.
7 Midrash Rabbah ii 3.
8 T.J . Pe'ah i 1.
9 Avoth ii 21.
10 Deuteronomy 11: 13-15.

11 Rambam, *Commentary to the Mishnah,* Sanhedrin x, introduction.
12 T.B. Shabbath 127a.

the cognition of direct experience.[13] The best we can do is to use simile and metaphor, describing the joys of the Hereafter as "pleasure" or "bliss," concepts that are familiar within our range of experience, although such terms are certainly inaccurate and misleading. Perhaps for this reason our *mishnah* uses the term *korath ruah* to denote the happiness in eternity, rather than the more usual *oneg:* The word *korath* seems to be associated with the root *kar,* "cold"; thus it would suggest a cooling or soothing calmness of spirit, in direct contrast to the excitation of the senses associated with intense pleasure here on earth.

In a similar vein, *Mahzor Vitry* explains: Anger and grief (or deep mourning) are passions designated as "heat"; hence pleasure, satisfaction of spirit is called *korath,* "cooling"; the mind is soothed and calmed by great happiness and joy.

A Talmudic passage comes to mind: "There was a habitual saying always on the lips of Rav: Unlike this world is the world-to-come. In the world-to-come there is neither eating nor drinking, neither conjugal intercourse nor business activity, nor envy, hatred, or heated rivalry. Rather do the righteous sit crowned in glory, enjoying the lustre of the *sh'chinah,* the Divine Presence."[14] Without the needs and appetites that the earthbound human being shares with the animal; without the drive to compete, excel, outdo others; without the destructive emotions of envy and hate— the Hereafter indeed offers a glimpse of unparalleled, unimaginable serenity and soothing tranquility, a vista of a new dimension of bliss.

Better, finer is one hour of repentance and good deeds…

Once more we can note that the language of our Sages is not random or haphazard. R. Jacob specifies one hour, one brief span of time: for our tradition teaches that some may achieve immortality, a share of life in the Hereafter, in one hour, while others may have to toil a lifetime.[15] One heroic deed for God or man, one

impassioned response to a crisis, one act of sincerity and sacrifice that brings blessed consequences, may effect a revolution within; to transform a person's entire character and faith. For ever after his vision may be lifted from this world, from hopes and ambitions centered on material gains, to value morality and spiritual growth. When he wins the key to immortal life, that can well be a man's finest hour.

But let us bear in mind that the reverse is also true. Our Rabbinic tradition records that it was R. Judah haNasi who stated that some may win life in the Hereafter in a brief hour, while others toil for years. And he wept as he said this. In one source we read that he added, "some can toil all their living days and lose their entire reward in one brief hour."[16] This indeed is cause for weeping. How tragic for a person to lose so swiftly, through one heinous act, what he may have toiled a lifetime to achieve.

A further nuance lies in these words of R. Jacob: "Better is one hour of repentance and good deeds *miccol* (than all) life in the world-to-come." The prefix *mi* also has the sense of "deriving from, stemming from."[17] Hence R. Jacob's teaching could connote that an hour of turning to religion and good deeds in this world is superior, when it derives from a realization, an awareness of the reality of life in the Hereafter. The way a man chooses to spend a free hour should reflect an entire way of thought about the value and purpose of his being in the world. It will be truly a fine hour if he makes it a stepping-stone on a clear-cut path through life, determined by an awareness of the Hereafter.

The Midrash gives an apt parable: An old man sat at a fork in the road, where two pathways spread out before him. One began smooth and fine, but eventually became a mass of thorns, cedars, and reeds. The other was at first nothing but reeds, cedars, and thorns, but eventually it became a smooth path. And so he would warn the passers-by how each pathway ulti-

---

[13] Rambam, *Commentary to the Mishnah,* Sanhedrin x, introduction.
[14] T.B. Berakoth 17a.
[15] T.B. Abodah Zarah 10b, 17a, 18a.

[16] Midrash Eleh Ezc'rah, on R. Hanina b. T'radyon (Beth haMidrash II p. 68).
[17] R. Abraham Azulai similarly interprets the prefix here as "because of": An hour of repentance, etc. is fine *because of* all the life in the Hereafter that it will earn.

mately was. Now surely (the Midrash concludes) the passers-by should be grateful to him, that he warned them for their own good, so that they could avoid exhausting [waste of time and energy]. So should mankind be grateful to Solomon, for he sits at the gateways of wisdom and warns ... "I have seen everything that is done under the sun, and behold, all is vanity and a striving after wind"[18]—everything except repentance and good deeds.[19]

At every free hour that we can spend in leisure, two roads open before us: one, the way of earthly pleasure, immediate gratification, certainly seems smooth and easy; the other is the path of virtue, to serve Heaven and benefit people, and it may seem beset by difficulties like twisted brambles and thorns; to travel such a road may mean much discomfort and sacrifice. But the wise Solomon sums up the value of earthly goals and gains, like the mathematician who writes a long equation on the blackboard, full of complex terms, and then writes at the end: equals zero. Hence R. Jacob advises: It is fine to devote a free hour to religious return and good deeds, knowing that this thorny way leads to the most blessed path of all.

At any rate, here we have evidence, if evidence is needed, that our Sages did not blindly follow popular concepts or ways of thinking. Through the ages the hedonist approach has never lacked a large enthusiastic following. In the words of Scripture, their cry is, "Let us eat and drink, for tomorrow we die."[20] The quatrains of Omar Khayyam echo and re-echo the yearning for the pleasures of wine and love as long as life allows. And in our own day a popular song dinned into our ears the wise counsel: "Enjoy yourself; it's later than you think." Life on this earth, says the hedonist, should be devoted to pleasure (even if it kills you).

As for religious worship and good deeds, the popular idea would be that this is a matter for angels, winged creatures who fly about heaven. If someone wants to explain that he is not really a good person, he says, "I'm no angel." If someone is being coaxed to do something good or kind, he may be urged, "Be an angel." At best, religious devotion and selfless compassionate kindness are expected of someone who lives an "other-worldly" life as a mystic or saint, without mingling in the ordinary activities of ordinary people, feet on the ground.

R. Jacob teaches the very opposite: The place for pleasure is in the Hereafter. Enjoyments on this earth do not begin to compare to the bliss of eternity. And the place for religiosity and deeds of kindness is here on earth. In the Hereafter no one can take the initiative to do *mitzvoth*. You can only obey and reflect the Divine will. The finest way to spend an hour on this earth is to "be an angel," and fulfill His commandments. The best way to spend an hour in the world-to-come is to enjoy yourself, although there it is never later than you think.

Ethics from Sinai [Feldheim Publishers: New York, 1966], pp. 151–156.
Reprinted with permission of the publisher.

---

[18] Ecclesiastes 1: 14.
[19] Midrash Rabbah to *ibid.*
[20] Isaiah 22: 13.

ON IMMORTALITY AND THE SOUL

BY RABBI ARYEH KAPLAN

Meet the Real You

LOOK AT YOUR HAND. What do you see? A part of your body, an appendage made of bone and sinew covered with flesh and skin. It is filled with nerves, blood vessels and lymph ducts which run through it and connect it to your body, making it part of you.

You can open and close your hand. It obeys every command that your mind sends to it. It is yours—a part *of* you. But what are you? Who is the real you? What happens when you tell your hand to open and close? How does your mind will it to obey its commands?

Now point a finger at yourself. If you are an average person, you will point a finger at your chest. You think *of* yourself as your body. But is your body the real you?

Not too long ago, a person could consider his own body an integral part of himself. You were your body and your body was you. But this is no longer the case. Scientific progress has changed the entire concept of human personality and identity.

Heart transplants are now an almost commonplace occurrence. They do not even make the news any more. A man can live with another person's heart beating in his breast. If we would ask such a man to point to himself, would he point at his heart? Is this transplanted heart really part of him? Is the heart that beats within your breast the real you? Or is it something else entirely?

Researchers are predicting that within the next decade or two, brain transplants may be possible. This would force us to completely reevaluate the concept of human personality.

Imagine what it would be like to undergo a brain transplant. A man might be suffering from an incurable disease in his body, but still have a healthy brain. The donor, on the other hand, would have suffered irreparable brain damage, but otherwise have a perfectly sound body. The brain is removed from the sick body and placed in the healthy one.

Who is the new man? We have an old brain with all its memories, personality traits and behavior patterns. But it has a brand new body. The old body might have been old and sick, while the new one may be young and full of energy.

Let us ask this man to point to himself. Will he point to his body? Is the real you your body or your brain?

(Actually, an analogous question is raised in the Talmud. As is well known, in the case of an unsolved murder, a special sacrifice, the *Eglah Arufah,* was brought by the city nearest the corpse.[1] The Mishnah raises two questions. What if the head is found in one place and the body in another?[2] And, if the body is equidistant from the two cities, from what portion of the body do we measure?[3] In both cases, Rabbi Eliezer states that we measure from the body, while Rabbi Akiba states that we measure from the head. The *Halachah* follows Rabbi Akiba.[4])

A brain transplant raises enough questions. How about a memory transfer? The science of cybernetics has discovered many similarities between computers and the human brain. Computer technology allows one to program a memory transfer, taking all the information contained in one computer and transferring it to another. All that passes from one computer to the other is information.

What if this were done with the human brain? This may lie in the realm of science fiction, but even if it will never be possible in practice, it is certainly possible in theory.

---

[1] Deuteronomy 21:1-9.
[2] *Sotah* 9:3 (45b).
[3] Ibid. 9:4.
[4] *Yad Chazakah, Rotzeach* 9:9.

Let us try to envision such a memory transfer. Assume we have a person with an incurable disease where neither his body nor his brain can be salvaged. We clone a new body for this individual, brain and all. The possibilities of doing this have already been discussed at length in scientific literature. This new body has a blank new brain, capable of functioning, but without any memories or thought patterns. As a final step, we accomplish a memory transfer, bringing all the information from the sick person into the brain of the new body.

We now have a fascinating situation. If all of a man's memories, thought patterns and personality traits are transferred to a new body and brain, this person literally exists in his new body. But nothing physical has been transferred. No physical part of him has been placed in the new body. All that has been placed in this new body is information that previously existed in the old brain. Yet this information contains the sum total of this person's personality.

But if this is true, then it offers us tremendous new insight into our original question: Who is the real you?

The real you is not your body or brain, but the information contained in your brain—your memories, personality traits and thought patterns.

[The philosophical Kabbalists write that the spiritual world is a realm whose substance is information. It is an arena where information can interact without being attached to or dependent on matter. Thus, an angel, for example, can interact with another angel, even though they have no connection with anything material. Angels can also interact with material objects. Such a spiritual world would also be able to interact with the information comprising the human persona.]

What happens then when a person dies? We know that the body ceases to function. The brain becomes inert and the physical man is dead. But what happens to the real you—the human personality? What happens to all this information—the memories, thought patterns and personality traits? When a book is burned its contents are no longer available. When

a computer is smashed, the information within it is also destroyed. Does the same thing happen when a man dies? Are the mind and personality irretrievably lost?

We know that God is omniscient. He knows all and does not forget. God knows every thought and memory that exists within our brains. There IS no bit of information that escapes His knowledge.

What, then, happens when a man dies? God does not forget, and therefore all of this information continues to exist, at least in God's memory.

[An allusion to this is also found in the Kabbalah Gan Eden (paradise) is said to exist in the *sephirah* of *Binah* (Divine understanding).[5] This may well be related to the concept of memory. Souls, on the other hand, are conceived in the *sephirah* of *Daas* (knowledge).[6] One may say that while we live, we exist in God's knowledge *(Daas),* while after death we exist in His memory *(Binah).*]

We may think of something existing only in memory as being static and effectively dead. But God's memory is not a static thing. The sum total of a human personality may indeed exist in God's memory, but it can still maintain its self-identity and volition, and remain in an active state: This sum total of the human personality existing in God's memory IS what lives on even after a man dies.

[This may well be why the Kabbalists speak of this as *Binah* (understanding), rather than memory. For understanding is a dynamic process, where information contained in one's memory interacts in an active manner. The soul is not in a passive state of memory but in a dynamic state of *Binah.*]

The concept of immortality and of the soul may well be outside the realm of human comprehension. "No eye has seen it other than God." However, our limited understanding of both God and man can pro-

---

[5] *Shaarei Orah 8; Pardes Rimonim 8:9, 23:3.*
[6] *Etz Chaim, Shaar MaN U'MaD 4, Shaar HaKlipos 2.*

vide us with some degree of perception into our ultimate future.

[In a Kabbalistic sense, we are here speaking about the lowest level of the soul, the *Nefesh HaBehamis* or "animal soul."[7] This most probably can be identified with the information contained in the human brain. However, this interacts with the higher parts of the soul, *Nefesh, Ruach* and *Neshamah.*]

To speak of a concept such as God's memory is indeed very difficult. It involves a deep discussion of the entire transcendental sphere. We therefore give it names that have meaning to us, such as *Gan Eden,* Paradise, the World to Come, the World of Souls,[8] or the bond of eternal life. However, the Bible speaks of immortality as a return to God Himself (Ecclesiastes 12: 7): "The dust returns to the dust as it was, but the spirit returns *to God* Who gave it."

Naked before God

We have seen that our knowledge of the mind and our traditions regarding God can give us some handle on the question of immortality. But what is immortality like? What is it like to be a disembodied soul? How does it feel to be in the World of Souls?

We know that the human brain, marvelous organ that it is, is still very inefficient as a thinking device. Henri Bergson has suggested that one of the main functions of the brain and nervous system is to eliminate activity and awareness, rather than produce it.

Aldous Huxley[9] quotes Prof. C. D. Broad's comments on this. He says that every person is capable of remembering everything that has ever happened to him. He is able to perceive everything that surrounds him. However, if all this information poured into his mind at once, it would overwhelm him. So the function of the brain and nervous system is to protect us and prevent us from being overwhelmed and confused by the vast amount of information that impinges upon our sense organs. They shut out most

of what we perceive and remember. All that would confound us is eliminated and only the small, special selection that is useful is allowed to remain.

Huxley explains that our mind has powers of perception and concentration that we cannot even begin to imagine. But our main business is to survive at all costs. To make survival possible, all of our mind's capabilities must be funneled through the reducing valve of the brain.

Some researchers are studying this effect. They believe that this reducing-valve effect may be very similar to the jamming equipment used to block out offensive radio broadcasts. The brain constantly produces a kind of static, cutting down our perception and reducing our mental activity.

This static can actually be seen. When you close your eyes, you see all sorts of random pictures flashing through your mind. It is impossible to concentrate on any one of them for more than an instant, and each image is obscured by a host of others superimposed over it. This static can even be seen when your eyes are opened. However, one usually ignores these images, since they are so faint compared to our visual perception. However, they still reduce one's perception, both of the world around him and of himself.

Much of what we know about this static is a result of research done with drugs that eliminate it. According to a number of authorities, this is precisely how the psychedelic drugs work.

Now imagine the mental activity of a disembodied soul, standing naked before God. The reducing valve is gone entirely. The mind is open and transparent. Things can be perceived in a way that is impossible to a mind held back by a body and a nervous system. The visions and understanding are the most delightful bliss imaginable (as per: "the righteous, sitting with their crowns on their heads, delighting in the shine of the *Shechinah*").[10] This is what Job meant when he said (19:26), "And when after my skin is destroyed, then without my flesh shall I see God."

---

[7] Cf. *Zohar* 2:94b.

[8] See *Derech HaShem* 1:3:11.

[9] Aldous Huxley, *The Doors of Perception* (Harper, Row, N.Y. 1970) p. 22f.

[10] *Berachos* 17a.

But then, an individual will also see himself in a new light. Every thought and memory will be lucid, and he will see himself for the first time without the static and jamming that shuts out most thoughts.

Even in our mortal physical state, looking at oneself can sometimes be pleasing and at other times very painful. Certain acts leave us proud and pleased with ourselves. Others cause excruciating pains, especially when we are caught.

Imagine standing naked before God, with your memory wide open, completely transparent without any jamming mechanism or reducing valve to diminish its force. You will remember everything you ever did and see it in a new light. You will see it in the light of the unshaded spirit, or, if you will, in God's own light that shines from one end of creation to the other. The memory of every good deed and *mitzvah* will be the sublimest of pleasures, as our tradition speaks of *Olam Haba.*

But your memory will also be open to all the things of which you are ashamed. They cannot be rationalized away or dismissed. You will be facing yourself, fully aware of the consequences of all your deeds. We all know the terrible shame and humiliation experienced when one is caught in the act of doing something wrong. Imagine being caught by one's own memory with no place to escape. This, indeed, may be what Daniel is alluding to when he says (Daniel 12:2), "And many of them that sleep in the dust shall awake, some to everlasting life, and some to reproach and everlasting shame."

A number of our great teachers[11] write that the fire of *Gehinnom* is actually the burning shame one experiences because of his sins. Again, this may be alluded to in the words of the Prophet (Isaiah 66:24), "And they shall go forth and look upon the carcasses of the men that have rebelled against Me; for their worm shall not die, nor shall their fire be quenched, and they shall be ashamed before all flesh." We find that evil leads to shame, as it is written (Jeremiah 7: 19–20), "'Are they angering Me?' says God. 'Are they not

provoking themselves, to their own shame? ... Behold My anger... shall burn, and shall not be quenched.'" The main concept of reward is that it be without shame, as we find (Joel 2:26), "And you shall eat and be satisfied ... and My people shall never be ashamed."

The Talmud provides us with even stronger evidence that shame burns like fire. It states, "Rabbi Chanina says; this teaches us that each one (in the World of Souls) is burned by the canopy of his companion. Woe, for that shame! Woe, for that humiliation."[12] We find (that shame is a major form of punishment) in the Midrash on the verse (Psalms 6:11), "All your enemies shall be ashamed and very confounded:" Rabbi Joshua ben Levi says, "God only curses the wicked with shame."[13] This is also alluded to in the Talmudic statement, "It is better for Amram to suffer shame in this world, and not in the World to Come."[14] Similarly "Blessed is God who gave him shame in this world and not the next."[15] When the Zohar speaks of the future reward, it says, "Happy is he who comes here without shame."[16]

Of course, these concepts of fire and shame, as used by our Sages, may also contain deeper mysteries and meanings. But taken literally, one says that a major ingredient of fire may be shame.[17] How else could one characterize the agony of unconcealed shame upon a soul?

We are taught that the judgment of the wicked lasts twelve months.[18] Even the naked soul can gradually learn to live with this shame and forget it, and the pain eventually subsides. It may be more than coincidence that twelve months is also the length of time required for something to be forgotten in Talmudic law. Thus, one mourns a parent for twelve months,[19] and says a special blessing upon seeing a close friend after this

---

11 *Ikkarim* 4:33, *Nishmas Chaim* 1:13.

12 *Baba Basra* 75a.

13 *Midrash Tehillim* a.l.

14 *Kidushin* 81a.

15 *Yevamos* 105b.

16 *Zohar* 1:4a.

17 *Toras HaAdam, Shaar HaGamul* (Jerusalem, 5715) p. 78a.

18 *Eduyos* 2:10.

19 *Moed Katan* 22b.

period of time.[20] (Of course, there IS an exception to this rule. There are some people whose entire life is shameful and meaningless. They are the nonbelievers and worst of sinners reckoned in the Talmud.[21] These individuals have nothing else but their shame and have no escape from everlasting torment.)

But even temporary torment is beyond our imagination. The Ramban (Nachmanides) writes that all the suffering of Job would not compare to an instant in *Gehinnom*.[22] Rabbi Nachman of Breslov says the same of a man who suffered for years from the most indescribable torments: it is still better than a single burn in *Gehinnom*.[23] Mental torture cannot be compared to the mere physical.

Here again, when we speak of *Gan Eden* and *Gehinnom*, we find that we are not discussing mystical concepts, but ideas that are well within the realm of scientific psychology, such as shame. We can now proceed a step further.

What the Dead Think of Us

There is another dimension of immortality discussed in the Talmud. It asks: Do the dead know what is happening in the world of the living?[24]

After an involved discussion, the Talmud concludes that they do have this awareness.[25] The Kabbalistic philosophers explain that the soul achieves a degree of unity with God, the source of all knowledge, and therefore also partakes of His omniscience.

When a man dies, he enters a new world of awareness. He exists as a disembodied soul and yet is aware of what is happening in the physical world. Gradually, he learns to focus on any physical event he wishes. At first this is a frightening experience. You know that you are dead. You can see your body lying there, with your friends and relatives standing around crying over you.

We are taught that immediately after death, the soul is in a great state of confusion.[26] What is the main source of its attention? What draws its focus more than anything else?

We are taught that it is the body. Most people identify themselves with bodies, as we have discussed earlier. It is difficult for a soul to break this thought habit, and therefore, for the first few days, the soul is literally obsessed with its previous body. This is alluded to in the verse (Job 14:22), "And his soul mourns for him."[27]

This is especially true before the body is buried.[28] The soul wonders what will happen to the body. It finds it to be both fascinating and frightening to watch its own body's funeral arrangements and preparation for burial.

Of course, this is one of the reasons why Judaism teaches us that we must have the utmost respect for human remains. We can imagine how painful it is for a soul to see its recent body cast around like an animal carcass. The Torah therefore forbids this.

This is also related to the question of autopsies. We can imagine how a soul would feel when seeing its body lying on the autopsy table, being dissected and examined. The disembodied soul spends much of its time learning how to focus. It is now seeing without physical eyes, using some process which we do not even have the vocabulary to describe. The Kabbalists call this frightening process *Kaf HaKela*—it is like being thrown with a sling from one end of the world to another.[29] It is alluded to in the verse (I Samuel 25:29), "The soul of my master shall be bound up in the bundle of life with the Lord, your God, and souls of your enemies shall He sling out, as from the hol-

---

[20] *Berachos* 58b.

[21] *Rosh HaShanah* 17a.

[22] *Ramban*, Introduction to Job.

[23] *Sichos HaRan* 235.

[24] *Berachos* 18b.

[25] See *Tosafos, Shabbos* 153a "*VeNishmaso*," *Sotah* 34b "*Avoi*," *Maaver Yabok* 2:25, *Nishmas Chaim* 2:22.

[26] *Taz, Yoreh Deah* 339:3. Cf. *Avodah Zarah* 20b, *Pirkei DeRabbi Eliezer.*

[27] *Shabbos* 152a, *Midrash Ne'elam, Zohar* 1:222b.

[28] *Shabbos* 152b, *Sefer Mitzvos Gadol, Esin DeRabanan* 2 (Vinitzia, 5307) p. 246a.

[29] *Shabbos*, ibid., *Maharsha ad lac., Zohar* 1:2 17b, 3:3185b, 222b.

low of a sling." The soul perceives things flashing into focus from all over, and is in a state of total confusion and disorientation.

One of the few things that the soul has little difficulty focusing on is its own body. It is a familiar pattern and some tie seems to remain. To some extent, it is a refuge from its disorientation.

Of course the body begins to decompose soon after it is buried. The effect of watching this must be both frightening and painful. The Talmud teaches us, "Worms are as painful to the dead as needles in the flesh of the living, as it is written (Job 14:2 2), 'His flesh grieves for him.'"[30] Most commentaries write that this refers to the psychological anguish of the soul in seeing its earthly habitation in a state of decay.[31] The Kabbalists call this *Chibut HaKever,*[32] the punishment of the grave. We are taught that what happens to the body in the grave can be an even worse experience than *Gehinnom.*[33]

This varies among individuals. The more one is obsessed with one's body and the material world in general during one's lifetime, the more one will be obsessed with it after death. For the man to whom the material was everything, this deterioration of the body is most painful. In the other extreme, the person who was immersed in the spiritual may not care *very* much about the fate of his body at all. He finds himself *very* much at home in the spiritual realm and might quickly forget about his body entirely. This is what we are taught. *Tzaddikim* are not bothered by *Chibut HaKever* at all, since they never consider their worldly body overly important.[34]

In general, adjustment to the spiritual world depends greatly on one's preparation in this world. Our traditions teach us that the main separation is through Torah.

Many of us think of death as a most frightening experience. *Tzadikim,* on the other hand, have looked forward to it. Shortly before his death, Rabbi Nachman of Breslov said, "I *very* much want to divest myself of this garment that is my body."[35] If we truly believe and trust in merciful God, then death has no terror for us.

The Aryeh Kaplan Reader [Mesorah Publications: New York, 1983], pp. 175–183.
Reprinted with permission of the publisher.

---

30 *Berachos* 18b, *Shabbos* 152a.

31 *Emunos VeDeyos* 6:7, *Tshuvos Rashba* 369, *Sefer Chasidim* 1163, *Tosefos Yom Tov* 2:7, *Tshuvos Sh'vus Yaakov* 2:97, Zvi Hirsh Chayos on *Shabbos* 13b. Cf. *Tanchuma, Vayikra* 8.

32 *Emunos VeDeyos,* ibid, *Nishmas Chaim* 2:24, *Maaver Yabok* 2:7.

33 *Midrash Chibut HaKever* in *Reshis Chochmah, Shaar HaYirah* 12, #3.

34 *Emunos VeDeyos,* ibid. Cf. *Midrash Ne'elam, Zohar* 1:123a.

35 *Sichos HaRan* 179.

Lesson Two

Proper Perspective
How Death Informs Life

Imagine a world without death, where practical
consequences such as overpopulation were of no
concern. How would you live differently? Judaism
teaches that death, namely the awareness of
our mortality, improves quality of life. In this
lesson, we will discover how this is so.

JLI

JEWISH LEARNING INSTITUTE

Peculiar Prayers

Text 1

Talmud, Bava Metsi'a 87a

Babylonian Talmud

A literary work of monumental proportions that draws upon the legal, spiritual, intellectual, ethical, and historical traditions of Judaism. The 37 tractates of the Babylonian Talmud contain the teachings of the Jewish sages from the period after the destruction of the 2nd Temple through the 5th century CE. It has served as the primary vehicle for the transmission of the Oral Law and the education of Jews over the centuries; it is the entry point for all subsequent legal, ethical, and theological Jewish scholarship.

עַד אַבְרָהָם לֹא הָיָה זִקְנָה. מַאן דַהֲוָה בָּעֵי לְמִשְׁתָּעֵי בַּהֲדֵי אַבְרָהָם מִשְׁתָּעֵי בַּהֲדֵי יִצְחָק, בַּהֲדֵי יִצְחָק מִשְׁתָּעֵי בַּהֲדֵי אַבְרָהָם. אָתָא אַבְרָהָם בָּעָא רַחֲמֵי וַהֲוָה זִקְנָה, שֶׁנֶּאֱמַר (בְּרֵאשִׁית כד, א), "וְאַבְרָהָם זָקֵן בָּא בַּיָּמִים".

Until Abraham there were no [physical signs of] old age. Consequently, one who wished to speak to Abraham might mistakenly speak to Isaac [who was of identical appearance], and one who wished to speak to Isaac might mistakenly speak to Abraham. Thereupon Abraham prayed, and [physical signs of] old age came into existence, as it is written (Genesis 24:1), "And Abraham was aged, well on in years."

Our world exist of Materialistic but we As Jews Need To Concentrate on un Materialistic Things

Aging Never Started until the Time of Abraham

Text 2

David Crary, "Boomers Will Be Spending Billions to Counter Aging," *USA Today* (from AP), August 22, 2011

Baby boomers heading into what used to be called retirement age are providing a 70 million-member strong market for legions of companies, entrepreneurs and cosmetic surgeons eager to capitalize on their "forever young" mindset, whether it's through wrinkle creams, face-lifts or workout regimens.

It adds up to potential bonanza. The market research firm Global Industry Analysts projects that a boomer-fueled consumer base, "seeking to keep the dreaded signs of aging at bay," will push the U.S. market for anti-aging products from about $80 billion now to more than $114 billion by 2015.

The boomers, who grew up in a culture glamorizing youth, face an array of choices as to whether and how to be a part of that market. . . .

Dr. Peter Schmid, who runs a cosmetic surgery practice in Longmont, Colorado, says his field is flourishing because of evolving attitudes among appearance-conscious boomers. A recent Associated Press-LifeGoesStrong.com poll found that 1 in 5 boomers either have had or would consider cosmetic surgery.

Text 3

Talmud, op. cit. 📖

עַד יַעֲקֹב לֹא הֲוָה חוּלְשָׁא. אָתָא יַעֲקֹב בָּעָא רַחֲמֵי וַהֲוָה חוּלְשָׁא,
שֶׁנֶּאֱמַר (בְּרֵאשִׁית מח, א), "וַיֹּאמֶר לְיוֹסֵף, הִנֵּה אָבִיךָ חוֹלֶה".

Until the times of Jacob, [death was not preceded] by illness. Jacob came along and prayed [for this to change]. Thus it is said (Genesis 48:1), "And it was told to Joseph, 'Behold, your father is ill.'"

QUESTIONS FOR DISCUSSION

1. Why did Abraham want to look old? Is there an advantage to looking old?

2. Why do people today wish to avoid and slow the aging process?

3. If your opinion were asked, would you vote to confirm Abraham's request? Explain your reasoning.

4. Why did Jacob ask for illness before death?

5. If your opinion were asked, would you vote to confirm Jacob's request? Explain your reasoning.

Contemplating Our Mortality

The Benefits

LEARNING EXERCISE 1

What are some benefits, if any, of contemplating our mortality?

1. _____

_____

_____

2. _____

_____

_____

3. _____

_____

_____

Prioritizing and Maintaining Focus

Text 4

Mishnah, Avot 3:1 📖

Mishnah

The first authoritative work of Jewish law that was codified in writing. The Mishnah contains the oral traditions that were passed down from teacher to student; it supplements, clarifies, and systematizes the commandments of the Torah. Due to the continual persecution of the Jewish people, it became increasingly difficult to guarantee that these traditions would not be forgotten. Rabbi Yehudah Hanasi therefore redacted the Mishnah at the end of the 2nd century. It serves as the foundation for the Talmud.

עֲקַבְיָא בֶּן מַהֲלַלְאֵל אוֹמֵר: הִסְתַּכֵּל בִּשְׁלֹשָׁה דְבָרִים וְאֵין אַתָּה בָא לִידֵי עֲבֵירָה.

דַּע מֵאַיִן בָּאתָ, וּלְאָן אַתָּה הוֹלֵךְ, וְלִפְנֵי מִי אַתָּה עָתִיד לִתֵּן דִּין וְחֶשְׁבּוֹן.

מֵאַיִן בָּאתָ? מִטִּפָּה סְרוּחָה.

וּלְאָן אַתָּה הוֹלֵךְ? לִמְקוֹם עָפָר רִמָּה וְתוֹלֵעָה.

וְלִפְנֵי מִי אַתָּה עָתִיד לִתֵּן דִּין וְחֶשְׁבּוֹן? לִפְנֵי מֶלֶךְ מַלְכֵי הַמְּלָכִים הַקָּדוֹשׁ בָּרוּךְ הוּא.

Akavi'a the son of Mahalalel would say: "Reflect upon three things, and you will not near transgression. Know from where you came, to where you are going, and before Whom you are destined to give a judgment and accounting.

"From where you came: a putrid drop.

"To where you are going: a place of dust, maggots, and worms.

"Before Whom you are destined to give a judgment and accounting: the supreme King of kings, the Holy One, blessed be He."

Text 5a

Psalms 4:5 📖

רִגְזוּ וְאַל תֶּחֱטָאוּ,

אִמְרוּ בִלְבַבְכֶם,

עַל מִשְׁכַּבְכֶם,

וְדֹמּוּ סֶלָה.

Study Torah and embrace it To block out Material world + evil

Be agitated and sin not;

say in your hearts,

on your beds,

and be forever silent.

Aggadic elucidation of Text 5a:

Text 5b

Talmud, Berachot 5a 📖

לְעוֹלָם יַרְגִּיז אָדָם יֵצֶר טוֹב עַל יֵצֶר הָרַע שֶׁנֶּאֱמַר, "רִגְזוּ וְאַל תֶּחֱטָאוּ".

אִם נִצְּחוֹ מוּטָב, וְאִם לָאו יַעֲסוֹק בַּתּוֹרָה, שֶׁנֶּאֱמַר, "אִמְרוּ בִלְבַבְכֶם".

אִם נִצְּחוֹ מוּטָב, וְאִם לָאו יִקְרָא קְרִיאַת שְׁמַע, שֶׁנֶּאֱמַר, "עַל מִשְׁכַּבְכֶם".

אִם נִצְּחוֹ מוּטָב, וְאִם לָאו יִזְכּוֹר לוֹ יוֹם הַמִּיתָה, שֶׁנֶּאֱמַר, "וְדֹמּוּ סֶלָה".

We should always agitate our good inclination against our evil inclination, as it is stated, "Be agitated and sin not."

If [this suffices to] vanquish the evil inclination, that is good. If not, we should occupy ourselves with Torah study, as it is stated, "say [words of Torah until they enter] your hearts."

If [this suffices to] vanquish it, good. If not, we should recite the *Shema*, as it is stated, "on your beds."

If [this suffices to] vanquish it, good. If not, we should remind ourselves of the day of death, as it is stated, "and be forever silent."

Humility

Text 6

Zohar 1:202a 📖

Zohar

The seminal work of Kabbalah, Jewish mysticism. The Zohar is a mystical commentary on the Torah, written in Aramaic and Hebrew. According to Arizal, the Zohar contains the teachings of Rabbi Shimon bar Yocha'i who lived in the Land of Israel during the 2nd century. The Zohar has become one of the indispensable texts of traditional Judaism, alongside and nearly equal in stature to the Mishnah and Talmud.

וְתָנָן, לְעוֹלָם יַרְגִּיז אָדָם יֵצֶר טוֹב עַל יֵצֶר הָרַע, וְיִשְׁתַּדֵּל אֲבַתְרֵיהּ . . .
אִי אָזִיל מוּטָב, וְאִי לָאו יִדְכַּר לֵיהּ יוֹמָא דְמוֹתָא בְּגִין לְתַבְרָא לֵיהּ.

הָכָא אִית לְאִסְתַּכְּלָא, דְּהָא דָא הוּא יֵצֶר הָרַע וְדָא הוּא מַלְאַךְ הַמָּוֶת, וְכִי מַלְאַךְ
הַמָּוֶת מִתְּבַּר מִקַּמֵּי יוֹמָא דְמוֹתָא? וְהָא אִיהוּ קְטוֹלָא דִּבְנֵי נָשָׁא הֲוֵי וְאִשְׁתַּמַּע
דְּחֶדְוָה הוּא דִּילֵיהּ, וּבְגִין כָּךְ אַסְטֵי לוֹן לִבְנֵי נָשָׁא תָּדִיר בְּגִין לְאַמַּשְׁכָא לוֹן לְדָא!

אֶלָּא וַדַּאי מָה דְּאִתְּמַר דְּיִדְכּוֹר לֵיהּ בַּר נָשׁ הַהוּא יוֹמָא דְמוֹתָא, וַדַּאי הָכִי הוּא,
בְּגִין דְּמִתְּבַּר לְבָּא דְּבַר נָשׁ, דְּהָא יֵצֶר הָרַע לֹא שַׁרְיָא אֶלָּא בְּאֲתַר דְּאִשְׁתְּכַח חֶדְוָה
דְּחַמְרָא וְגַסּוּתָא דְרוּחָא, וְכַד אַשְׁכַּח רוּחָא תְּבִירָא, כְּדֵין אִתְפְּרַשׁ מִנֵּיהּ וְלֹא שַׁרְיָא
בַּהֲדֵיהּ, וּבְגִין כָּךְ בָּעֵי לְאַדְכָּרָא לֵיהּ יוֹמָא דְמוֹתָא, וְיִתְּבַּר גּוּפֵיהּ וְאִיהוּ אָזִיל לֵיהּ.

We have been taught that we should always agitate our good inclination against our evil inclination. If the temptation departs, well and good, but if not . . . we should subdue the evil inclination by reminding it of the day of death.

This statement requires consideration. We know that the evil inclination and the angel of death are one and the same. How is it possible, then, that the angel of death, the slayer of man, should be subdued and broken by the thought of the day of death? After all, death is its joy and its very objective in leading humans to stray!

The purpose of bringing to mind the day of death is to humble a person's heart, for the evil inclination dwells only in a place where the [false] happiness [induced by] intoxication and pride are rampant. Where it finds a humble spirit, it departs. This is why recalling the day of death is effective: it breaks the ego and causes the evil inclination to leave.

Living in the Now
Your Money or Your Time!

QUESTION FOR DISCUSSION

What is more valuable—time or money? Explain your choice.

Text 7

Rabbi Shimon Hadarshan of Frankfurt
1200s

Exegete and preacher. Not much is known about Rabbi Shimon; there are references to him as "chief of the preachers of Frankfurt," and he and his family may have fled the massacres of 1241. He is very likely the author of the Yalkut Shimoni, the best known and most comprehensive midrashic anthology.

Jewish proverb, cited in Rabbi Shimon Hadarshan of Frankfurt, *Sefer Hachayim*

אָדָם דּוֹאֵג עַל אִבּוּד דָּמָיו וְאֵינוֹ דוֹאֵג עַל אִבּוּד יָמָיו.

דָּמָיו אֵינָם עוֹזְרִים, יָמָיו אֵינָם חוֹזְרִים.

People worry about the loss of a dime, but not about the loss of their time.

Happiness their money will not earn, and their days will never return.

Love Hashim with All your Life even if it means having To give it

Text 8

Tana Devei Eliyahu Rabah, ch. 16 📖

אִלְמָלֵא מַלְאַךְ הַמָּוֶת, מָה אֲנַחְנוּ עוֹשִׂין לְאָבִינוּ שֶׁבַּשָּׁמַיִם?

צֵא וּלְמַד מֵעֲשָׂרָה דוֹרוֹת הָרִאשׁוֹנִים שֶׁהַקָּדוֹשׁ בָּרוּךְ הוּא הִשְׁפִּיעַ לָהֶן טוֹבָה מֵעֵין עוֹלָם הַבָּא, וְהֵם עָמְדוּ לְהַחֲרִיב אֶת כָּל הָעוֹלָם.

f not for [the fear of] the Angel of Death, what wrongs would we commit unto our Father in heaven?

Let us learn from the first ten generations of humanity, upon whom God showered an abundance of good [including abnormally long lifespans]. They lived a paradise-like existence, yet [because of their blessings and their longevity], they were on the brink of destroying the world.

Tana Devei Eliyahu

A midrashic work, sometimes referred to as *Seder Eliyahu*. Midrash is the designation of a particular genre of rabbinic literature usually forming a running commentary on specific books of the Bible. This work deals with the divine precepts, their rationales, and the importance of knowledge of Torah, prayer, and repentance. The work is divided into two sections: *Seder Eliyahu Rabah* and *Seder Eliyahu Zuta*.

Text 9

Talmud, Shabbat 153a 📖

תְּנַן הָתָם (אָבוֹת ב, י): רַבִּי אֱלִיעֶזֶר אוֹמֵר, "שׁוּב יוֹם אֶחָד לִפְנֵי מִיתָתְךָ".

שָׁאֲלוּ תַלְמִידָיו אֶת רַבִּי אֱלִיעֶזֶר: "וְכִי אָדָם יוֹדֵעַ אֵיזֶהוּ יוֹם יָמוּת?"

אָמַר לָהֶן, "וְכָל שֶׁכֵּן! יָשׁוּב הַיּוֹם שֶׁמָּא יָמוּת לְמָחָר, וְנִמְצָא כָּל יָמָיו בִּתְשׁוּבָה". וְאַף שְׁלֹמֹה אָמַר בְּחָכְמָתוֹ, "בְּכָל עֵת יִהְיוּ בְגָדֶיךָ לְבָנִים וְשֶׁמֶן עַל רֹאשְׁךָ אַל יֶחְסָר" (קֹהֶלֶת ט, ח).

אָמַר רַבָּן יוֹחָנָן בֶּן זַכַּאי: מָשָׁל לְמֶלֶךְ שֶׁזִּמֵּן אֶת עֲבָדָיו לִסְעוּדָה וְלֹא קָבַע לָהֶם זְמַן. פִּיקְחִין שֶׁבָּהֶן קִישְּׁטוּ אֶת עַצְמָן וְיָשְׁבוּ עַל פֶּתַח בֵּית הַמֶּלֶךְ, אָמְרוּ, "כְּלוּם חָסֵר לְבֵית הַמֶּלֶךְ?" טִיפְּשִׁין שֶׁבָּהֶן הָלְכוּ לִמְלַאכְתָּן, אָמְרוּ, "כְּלוּם יֵשׁ סְעוּדָה בְּלֹא טוֹרַח?"

בְּפִתְאוֹם בִּקֵּשׁ הַמֶּלֶךְ אֶת עֲבָדָיו. פִּקְחִין שֶׁבָּהֶן נִכְנְסוּ לְפָנָיו כְּשֶׁהֵן מְקֻשָּׁטִין, וְהַטִּיפְּשִׁים נִכְנְסוּ לְפָנָיו כְּשֶׁהֵן מְלוּכְלָכִין. שָׂמַח הַמֶּלֶךְ לִקְרַאת פִּקְחִים וְכָעַס לִקְרַאת טִיפְּשִׁים, אָמַר, "הַלָּלוּ שֶׁקִּישְׁטוּ אֶת עַצְמָן לַסְּעוּדָה יֵשְׁבוּ וְיֹאכְלוּ וְיִשְׁתּוּ, הַלָּלוּ שֶׁלֹּא קִישְׁטוּ עַצְמָן לַסְּעוּדָה יַעַמְדוּ וְיִרְאוּ".

Rabbi Eliezer said, "Repent one day before your death" (Mishnah, Avot 2:10).

His disciples asked, "Does one know on what day one will die?"

"All the more reason that one should repent today, lest one die tomorrow," he replied. "And thus, one's whole life is spent in repentance." As Solomon said in his wisdom, "Let your garments always be white; and let your head never lack ointment" (Ecclesiastes 9:8).

Rabban Yochanan ben Zakai said: This may be compared to a king who invited his subjects to a banquet but did not designate its time. The wise subjects adorned themselves and waited at the door of the palace. For they reasoned, "Is the royal palace ever lacking?" The fools went about their work, saying, "Can there be a banquet without extensive preparations?"

Suddenly, the king summoned his subjects [to the banquet]. The wise entered adorned; the fools entered soiled. The king rejoiced at the wise but was angry with the fools. "Those who adorned themselves for the banquet, let them sit, eat, and drink," he ordered. "Those who did not adorn themselves for the banquet, let them stand and watch."

Relationship Mending

Text 10

Mishnah, Yoma 8:9 📖

דָּרַשׁ רַבִּי אֶלְעָזָר בֶּן עֲזַרְיָה:

"מִכֹּל חַטֹּאתֵיכֶם לִפְנֵי ה' תִּטְהָרוּ" (וַיִּקְרָא טז, ל):

עֲבֵירוֹת שֶׁבֵּין אָדָם לַמָּקוֹם יוֹם הַכִּפּוּרִים מְכַפֵּר, עֲבֵירוֹת שֶׁבֵּין אָדָם
לַחֲבֵירוֹ, אֵין יוֹם הַכִּפּוּרִים מְכַפֵּר עַד שֶׁיְּרַצֶּה אֶת חֲבֵרוֹ.

Rabbi Elazar ben Azari'ah expounded the following verse:

["For on this day . . .] of all your transgressions before God you will become pure" (Leviticus 16:30).

Yom Kippur atones for transgressions between a person and God; Yom Kippur does not atone for transgressions between one person and another until the offender placates the victim.

The Disadvantages

QUESTION FOR DISCUSSION

Do any of the texts we've studied today point to the idea that contemplating one's mortality might have drawbacks?

Text 11

Rabbi Ya'akov Reischer
–1733

Austrian rabbi. Rabbi Reischer was born in Prague and served in the rabbinate there and in other Jewish communities through eastern and central Europe. He moved to Metz in 1719, officiating there until his death. He authored multiple works, including *Chok Ya'akov*, a commentary to the laws of Passover; halachic responsa, titled *Shevut Ya'akov;* and *Iyun Ya'akov,* a commentary to *Ein Ya'akov.*

Rabbi Yaakov Reischer, *Iyun Ya'akov*, Berachot 5a

וְאֵין לְהַקְשׁוֹת דְּלָמָה לִי כּוּלֵי הַאי, הֲוָה לֵיה לְמֵימַר מִיָּד "יִזְכּוֹר יוֹם הַמִּיתָה"?

יֵשׁ לוֹמַר, כִּי לִפְעָמִים אֵין הָעַצְבוּת טוֹב, כְּדִכְתִיב "וְשִׁבַּחְתִּי [אֲנִי] אֶת הַשִּׂמְחָה" (קֹהֶלֶת ח, טו), זֶהוּ שִׂמְחָה שֶׁל מִצְוָה (שַׁבָּת לב), וְ"אֵין הַשְּׁכִינָה שׁוֹרָה אֶלָּא מִתּוֹךְ שִׂמְחָה", כִּדְאַמְרִינָן לְקַמָּן דַּף ל"א ע"א וּבְשַׁבָּת דַּף ל'.

לְהָכִי קָאָמַר תְּחִילָּה שֶׁיַּעֲסוֹק בַּתּוֹרָה אוֹ יִקְרָא קְרִיאַת שְׁמַע, וְאִם בְּכָל זֶה לֹא יוֹעִיל, אֲזַי יִזְכּוֹר יוֹם הַמִּיתָה.

You may ask: why does the Talmud need to list all the suggestions? It ought to have started and sufficed with its counsel to recall the day of death.

I will respond: [excessively contemplating the day of death can lead to dejection, and] dejection is not always beneficial. Solomon said, "I extol the importance of joy" (Ecclesiastes 8:15), which the Talmud (Shabbat 30b) understands as a reference to the joy one takes in the observance of a mitzvah. The Talmud also says (ibid., and Berachot 31a) that the divine presence resides only when a person is in a state of joy.

Therefore the Talmud first advises to study Torah and recite the *Shema*. If, however, that does not suffice, one should contemplate the day of death.

Living Each Day
Choice of Furlough

Text 12a

Rabbi David ibn Zimra, *Responsa* 4:13 📖

שְׁאֵלָה: רְאוּבֵן הָיָה חָבוּשׁ בְּבֵית הָאֲסוּרִים וְלֹא הָיָה יָכֹל לָצֵאת לְהִתְפַּלֵּל בַּעֲשָׂרָה וְלַעֲשׂוֹת הַמִּצְוֹת, וְהִתְחַנֵּן לִפְנֵי הַשַּׂר אוֹ הַהֶגְמוֹן וְלֹא אָבָה שְׁמוֹעַ לְהַנִּיחוֹ זוּלָתִי יוֹם אֶחָד בַּשָּׁנָה, אֵיזֶה יוֹם שֶׁיַּחְפֹּץ. יוֹרֵה הַמּוֹרֶה, אֵיזֶה יוֹם מִכָּל יְמוֹת הַשָּׁנָה יִבְחַר רְאוּבֵן הַנִּזְכָּר לָלֶכֶת לְבֵית הַכְּנֶסֶת?

Question:

Reuben is incarcerated and thus precluded from praying in a synagogue and performing various *mitzvot*. Despite his entreaties to the sovereign, permission was only granted for him to leave prison one day a year—whichever day he chooses. May our teacher instruct us, which day shall Reuben choose to go to the synagogue?

Rabbi David ibn Zimra (Radvaz)
1479–1573

Noted halachist. Radvaz was born in Spain and immigrated to Safed, Israel upon the expulsion of the Jews from Spain in 1492. In 1513, he moved to Egypt and served as rabbi, judge, and head of the yeshivah in Cairo. He also ran many successful business ventures and was independently wealthy. In 1553, he returned to Safed where he would later be buried. He authored what would later become a classic commentary to Maimonides' code of law, and wrote many halachic responsa, of which more than ten thousand are still extant.

What would you answer? What is the most important day on the Jewish calendar?

Text 12b

Rabbi David ibn Zimra, ibid. 📖

תְּשׁוּבָה: . . . קַיְּימָא לָן דְּ"אֵין מַעֲבִירִין עַל הַמִּצְוֹת", וְאֵין חוֹלֵק בָּזֶה כְּלָל. הִלְכָּךְ הַמִּצְוָה הָרִאשׁוֹנָה שֶׁתָּבֹא לְיָדוֹ שֶׁאִי אֶפְשָׁר לַעֲשׂוֹתָה וְהוּא חָבוּשׁ בְּבֵית הָאֲסוּרִים קוֹדֶמֶת, וְאֵין מַשְׁגִּיחִין אִם הַמִּצְוָה שֶׁפָּגַע בּוֹ תְּחִלָּה הִיא קַלָּה אוֹ חֲמוּרָה, "שֶׁאִי אַתָּה יוֹדֵעַ מַתַּן שְׂכָרָן שֶׁל מִצְוֹת" (אָבוֹת ב, א). וְזֶה פָּשׁוּט מְאֹד אֶצְלִי.

Response:

[…] "We don't pass on a mitzvah opportunity" is an established and unanimously held halachic precept. Therefore, precedence should be given to the very first occasion when there's an opportunity to do a mitzvah that cannot be done in prison. It is irrelevant whether it is a weighty mitzvah or a light one, "for we do not know the reward of the *mitzvot*" (Mishnah, Avot 2:1). To me, this ruling is patently obvious.

On Tap for Today

Text 13

Rabbi Yisrael Ba'al Shem Tov, *Tsava'at HaRivash*, ch. 1 📖

וְשֶׁלֹּא יָנִיחַ שׁוּם יוֹם מֵעֲשִׂיַּת מִצְוָה.

Do not allow a single day to pass without performing a mitzvah.

Rabbi Yisrael Ba'al Shem Tov (Besht)
1698–1760

Founder of the Chasidic movement. Born in Slutsk, Belarus, the Ba'al Shem Tov was orphaned as a child. He served as a teacher's assistant and clay digger before founding the Chasidic movement and revolutionizing the Jewish world with his emphasis on prayer, joy, and love for every Jew, regardless of his or her level of Torah knowledge.

The Golden Years

Text 14

Talmud, Yevamot 62b 📖

רַבִּי יְהוֹשֻׁעַ אוֹמֵר: נָשָׂא אָדָם אִשָּׁה בְּיַלְדוּתוֹ, יִשָּׂא אִשָּׁה בְּזִקְנוּתוֹ. הָיוּ לוֹ בָּנִים בְּיַלְדוּתוֹ, יִהְיוּ לוֹ בָּנִים בְּזִקְנוּתוֹ. שֶׁנֶּאֱמַר (קֹהֶלֶת יא, ו), "בַּבֹּקֶר זְרַע אֶת זַרְעֶךָ וְלָעֶרֶב אַל תַּנַּח יָדֶךָ כִּי אֵינְךָ יוֹדֵעַ אֵי זֶה יִכְשָׁר הֲזֶה אוֹ זֶה, וְאִם שְׁנֵיהֶם כְּאֶחָד טוֹבִים".

רַבִּי עֲקִיבָא אוֹמֵר: לָמַד תּוֹרָה בְּיַלְדוּתוֹ, יִלְמוֹד תּוֹרָה בְּזִקְנוּתוֹ. הָיוּ לוֹ תַּלְמִידִים בְּיַלְדוּתוֹ, יִהְיוּ לוֹ תַּלְמִידִים בְּזִקְנוּתוֹ. שֶׁנֶּאֱמַר, "בַּבֹּקֶר זְרַע אֶת זַרְעֶךָ וְגוֹ'".

Rabbi Yehoshua says: If a man married in his youth, he should marry again in his old age. If he had children in his youth, he should also have children in his old age. For it is said, "Sow your seed in the morning and do not withhold your hand in the evening. For you know not which shall prosper, whether this or that, or whether they shall both alike be good" (Ecclesiastes 11:6).

Rabbi Akiva says: If a person studied Torah in his youth, he should also study it in his old age. If he had disciples in his youth, he should also have disciples in his old age. For it is said, "Sow your seed in the morning, etc."

Text 15

"Retirement 'Can Drastically Damage Health,'" *The Telegraph*, May 16, 2013

Retirement can cause a drastic decline in health, according to a new study.

Research by the Institute of Economic Affairs found that both mental and physical health can suffer [after retirement]. . . . The study—Work Longer, Live Healthier: The Relationship Between Economic Activity, Health And Government Policy—shows there is a small boost in health immediately after retirement but that, over the longer term, there is a significant deterioration.

It suggests retirement increases the likelihood of suffering from clinical depression by 40 per cent and the chance of having at least one diagnosed physical condition by about 60 per cent.

The probability of taking medication for such a condition rises by about 60 per cent as well, according to the findings. People who are retired are 40 per cent less likely than others to describe themselves as being in very good or excellent health.

Text 16

Talmud, Megilah 31b

אִם יֹאמְרוּ לְךָ זְקֵנִים "סְתוֹר", וִילָדִים "בְּנֵה", סְתוֹר וְאַל תִּבְנֶה.

מִפְּנֵי שֶׁסְּתִירַת זְקֵנִים בִּנְיָן, וּבִנְיַן נְעָרִים סְתִירָה.

I f the elders advise you to destruct and the youth to construct—heed the counsel of the elders.

Because the destruction of elders is constructive and the construction of youth is destructive.

Provisions

Text 17

Rabbi Yechiel Michel Tukachinsky, *Gesher Hachayim*, 1:41

כָּל בֶּן אָדָם הַיּוֹדֵעַ שֶׁיֵּשׁ מַטָּרָה לְחַיָּיו וּלְחַיֵּי בָּנָיו – כְּשֶׁכּוֹתֵב אֵיזוֹ צַוָּואָה אַל יִשְׁכַּח מִלְצַוּוֹת לְבָנָיו עַל תַּכְלִית הַחַיִּים. כְּנֶאֱמַר בְּאָבִינוּ הָרִאשׁוֹן, "כִּי יְדַעְתִּיו לְמַעַן אֲשֶׁר יְצַוֶּה אֶת בָּנָיו וְאֶת בֵּיתוֹ אַחֲרָיו וְשָׁמְרוּ אֶת דֶּרֶךְ ה'" (בְּרֵאשִׁית יח, יט).

וְכָל אֶחָד וְאֶחָד יְצַוֶּה כִּלְשׁוֹנוֹ וּכְסִגְנוֹנוֹ הוּא, וּלְפִי מַעֲמָד בָּנָיו, לִשְׁמוֹר אֶת דֶּרֶךְ ה', בֵּין בְּנוֹגֵעַ לְבֵין אָדָם לַמָּקוֹם וּבֵין בְּנוֹגֵעַ לְבֵין אָדָם לַחֲבֵרוֹ.

I f we understand that there is purpose to our lives and the lives of our children, when we write a will, we will not forget to instruct our children about fulfilling their purpose in life. As God said regarding Abraham, our first father, "I love him because he instructs his children after him to follow the path of God" (Genesis 18:19).

Rabbi Yechiel Michel Tukachinsky
1874–1955

Halachist. Rabbi Tukachinsky was born in Lithuania. In 1882, his family settled in Israel. He studied in the Ets Chaim Yeshivah, where he eventually became the dean. He published many books and articles on halachic issues, including *Hayomom Bikadur Ha'aretz*, an effort to locate the halachic dateline. His most famous work is *Gesher Hachayim*, a classic treatise on the laws of burial and mourning that examines life as a bridge between past and future.

Every person should instruct—using his or her own words and style and tailored to the children's level and needs—to follow the path of God, to have a proper relationship with the Creator and their fellow human beings.

Text 18

Maimonides, Laws of Temperaments 4:1

הוֹאִיל וֶהֱיוֹת הַגּוּף בָּרִיא וְשָׁלֵם מִדַּרְכֵי [עֲבוֹדַת] הַשֵּׁם הוּא, שֶׁהֲרֵי אִי אֶפְשָׁר שֶׁיָּבִין אוֹ יֵדַע דָּבָר מִידִיעַת הַבּוֹרֵא וְהוּא חוֹלֶה, לְפִיכָךְ צָרִיךְ לְהַרְחִיק אָדָם עַצְמוֹ מִדְּבָרִים הַמְאַבְּדִין אֶת הַגּוּף וּלְהַנְהִיג עַצְמוֹ בִּדְבָרִים הַמַּבְרִין וְהַמַּחְלִימִים.

Maintaining a healthy and sound body is an aspect of our service of God—for one cannot understand or have any knowledge of the Creator when ill. Therefore, one must avoid that which harms the body and accustom oneself to that which is healthful and strengthens the body.

Rabbi Moshe ben Maimon
(Maimonides, Rambam)
1135–1204

Halachist, philosopher, author, and physician. Maimonides was born in Cordoba, Spain. After the conquest of Cordoba by the Almohads, he fled Spain and eventually settled in Cairo, Egypt. There, he became the leader of the Jewish community and served as court physician to the vizier of Egypt. He is most noted for authoring the *Mishneh Torah*, an encyclopedic arrangement of Jewish law, and for his philosophical work, *Guide for the Perplexed*. His rulings on Jewish law are integral to the formation of halachic consensus.

LEARNING EXERCISE 2

(a) Write down the point from today's lesson that resonated with you most.

_____

_____

_____

(b) Identify an important goal in your life that you have postponed pursuing. What step will you take to do so?

_____

_____

_____

(c) Identify a relationship in your life that needs mending. What step will you take to remedy it?

_____

_____

_____

Key Points

This lesson explored how our view of death informs our life.

Continue your learning experience ONLINE

Visit www.myJLI.com/journey2

for insightful and inspiring videos, articles, and readings on this topic.

1. It can be beneficial to occasionally contemplate death. The first step is mitigating our fear of death, so that we can confront our mortality with peace of mind.

2. When we consider our ultimate destination, we stay focused on what's most important in life. We also become humble, for we are reminded of our vulnerability. This humility prevents us from making ego-driven destructive choices.

3. When we avoid thinking about death, we live as if we are immortal and, as a result, fail to properly value the present moment. Contemplating the transience of life inspires us to seize every opportunity to better ourselves and our relationships.

4. The present moment must be cherished not only because life is short, but because it contains Godly potential waiting to be actualized through the performance of a mitzvah.

5. Retirement is not a Jewish concept. Productivity must extend throughout one's life. As our bodily powers diminish, our purpose shifts to giving back by mentoring and sharing our wisdom and experience with others.

6. Notwithstanding the benefits of contemplating death, it should not become an obsession or a cause for depression.

7. When we are at peace with our mortality, we can calmly prepare for our transition to the next world. The ability to prepare for death is a blessing. At the same time, we must place great emphasis on preserving our life and health.

Appendix A

Rabbi Yosef Yitzchak Schneersohn, *Sefer Hama'amarim* 5710, p. 118 📖

דְּיֶשְׁנָם כַּמָּה דְבָרִים בָּאָדָם שֶׁהוּא נוֹהֵג וְעוֹשֶׂה כֵּן וַויילֶע אַזוֹי טוּט
וועלְט, וְהַדְּבָרִים הָאֵלֶּה הֵם כְּמוֹ חוֹק שֶׁבִּלְתִּי מְזִיזִים אוֹתוֹ מִמְּקוֹמוֹ לְפִי
דְכֵן הוּא הַנְהָגַת הָעוֹלָם, וּכְמוֹ בְּכַמָּה עִנְיְנֵי נִימוּס וְהַדּוֹמֶה כוּ' . . .

וּכְמוֹ עַל דֶּרֶךְ מָשָׁל זְמַנֵּי הָאֲכִילָה וּזְמַנֵּי הַשֵּׁינָה, הִנֵּה מִצַּד הֶרְגֵּשׁ הָעוֹלָם הֵם
קְבוּעִים בְּעִתִּים וּזְמַנִּים, וְגַם כְּשֶׁצָּרִיךְ לְהִתְעַסֵּק בְּמִקָּח וּמִמְכָּר וּמַשָּׂא וּמַתָּן, הִנֵּה
זְמַנִּים הָאֵלּוּ עַל פִּי הָרוֹב בִּלְתִּי נִיזָזִים וּבִלְתִּי נִידָחִים כְּלָל וְעִיקָר, וּזְמַנֵּי הַקְּבִיעוֹת
שֶׁל תּוֹרָה וּתְפִלָּה הֵם נִדְחִים וְאֵין לָהֶם קֶבַע, וְיֵשׁ שֶׁהֵם נִדְחִים חַס וְשָׁלוֹם לְגַמְרֵי.

הִנֵּה הָאָדָם אֲשֶׁר נוֹתֵן אֵיזֶה חֶשְׁבּוֹן לְנַפְשׁוֹ, הַאִם יֵשׁ אֵיזֶה חָכְמָה בְּהַנְהָגָה
כָּזוֹ? דְּמִי הוּא הַיּוֹדֵע עִתּוֹ וּזְמַנּוֹ? וּכְדְאִיתָא בְּמִדְרָשׁ רַבָּה (דְּבָרִים רַבָּה
ט, ג) "אֵין אָדָם שַׁלִּיט לוֹמַר הַמְתִּינוּ לִי עַד שֶׁאֶעֱשֶׂה חֶשְׁבּוֹנוֹתַי וְעַד
שֶׁאֲצַוֶּה לְבֵיתִי כוּ'". וְאֵיךְ יִתֵּן כָּל נַפְשׁוֹ עַל דָּבָר שֶׁאֵין בּוֹ מַמָּשׁ כְּלָל, וְעַל
הָעִיקָר מָה שֶׁהָיְתָה הַכַּוָּונָה בִּירִידַת נִשְׁמָתוֹ לְמַטָּה הוּא שׁוֹכֵחַ לְגַמְרֵי.

There are many conventions we keep only because that's what everybody does, yet we take them very seriously, as if these principles are carved in stone. For example, certain rules of etiquette and protocol....

An example would be mealtimes and sleeping hours. The world has an attitude that these things cannot budge. Even when there's important business to take care of, these things stay fixed in place. The times people set aside for Torah study and prayer, on the other hand, are easily brushed aside and rarely stay fixed. Sometimes they are, G-d forbid, discarded altogether.

Think for a minute: Is there any wisdom to this? Who can know when his time will come? Or, as the Midrash (*Devarim Rabah* 9:3) puts it: "No one is able to tell the Angel of Death, 'Wait for me to settle my accounts and instruct

Rabbi Yosef Yitschak Schneersohn
(Rayats, Frierdiker Rebbe, Previous Rebbe)
1880–1950

Chasidic rebbe, prolific writer, and Jewish activist. Rabbi Yosef Yitschak, the 6th leader of the Chabad movement, actively promoted Jewish religious practice in Soviet Russia and was arrested for these activities. After his release from prison and exile, he settled in Warsaw, Poland, from where he fled Nazi occupation, and arrived in New York in 1940. Settling in Brooklyn, Rabbi Schneersohn worked to revitalize American Jewish life. His son-in law, Rabbi Menachem Mendel Schneerson, succeeded him as the leader of the Chabad movement.

my household . . .'" So how could you completely devote yourself to something utterly meaningless, while forgetting all about the main thing—the mission for which you came to this world in the first place?

Appendix B

Rabbi Yonah Gerona, Avot 3:1

"וּלְאָן אַתָּה הוֹלֵךְ? לִמְקוֹם עָפָר רִמָּה וְתוֹלֵעָה". וְכִי תַחְשׁוֹב בְּלִבְּךָ לְאָן אַתָּה הוֹלֵךְ, לֹא תַחְפּוֹץ בְּכָל הַתַּעֲנוּגִים, כִּי לְרִמָּה אַתָּה טוֹרֵחַ. גַּם כָּל עוֹשֶׁר וְכָבוֹד תִּבְזֶה בְּעֵינֶיךָ וְכָל טוֹבָה תַּבְהִיל כִּי הַכֹּל הֶבֶל וּרְעוּת רוּחַ. וְעַל עִנְיָן זֶה עָשָׂה שְׁלֹמֹה הַמֶּלֶךְ סֵפֶר קֹהֶלֶת וְהִתְחִיל, "הֲבֵל הֲבָלִים", לְהַבְהִיל כָּל טוֹבָה וְכָל יָקָר.

וְאַחַר שֶׁהֶהֱבִּיל אֶת הַכֹּל אָמַר (קֹהֶלֶת יב, יג), "סוֹף דָּבָר הַכֹּל נִשְׁמָע, אֶת הָאֱלֹקִים יְרָא וְאֶת מִצְוֹתָיו שְׁמוֹר כִּי זֶה כָּל הָאָדָם".

Rabbi Yonah of Gerona
d. 1263

Spanish rabbi and Talmudist. Rabbeinu Yonah from Gerona, Catalonia, was a cousin of Nachmanides. He is renowned for his outspoken critique of Maimonides' works, and for later recanting his opposition and vowing to travel to Maimonides' grave in Israel to beg his forgiveness. He left France, but was detained in Toledo, Spain, where he stayed and became one of the greatest Talmudists of his time. He is best known for his moralistic works on repentance and asceticism.

Where you are going: to a place of dust, maggots, and worms. When you consider where you are destined to go, you will no longer crave worldly pleasures, for all the effort you exert in their accrual is for the worms. You will also consider all wealth and honor to be inconsequential, for all is but vanity and nothingness. This idea led King Solomon to compose the Book of Ecclesiastes, which opens with the words, "[All is] utterly meaningless" and whose intent is to establish in our hearts the insignificance of all that seems good and precious.

Only after Solomon establishes the meaninglessness of all, he declares, "The end of the matter, all having been heard, fear God and observe His commandments, for this is the entire man" (Ecclesiastes 12:13).

Appendix C

Susie Steiner, "Top Five Regrets of the Dying," *The Guardian*, February 1, 2012

A palliative nurse who has counselled the dying in their last days has revealed the most common regrets we have at the end of our lives. And among the top, from men in particular, is 'I wish I hadn't worked so hard'.

Bronnie Ware is an Australian nurse who spent several years working in palliative care, caring for patients in the last 12 weeks of their lives. She recorded their dying epiphanies in a blog called *Inspiration and Chai*, which gathered so much attention that she put her observations into a book called *The Top Five Regrets of the Dying*.

Ware writes of the phenomenal clarity of vision that people gain at the end of their lives, and how we might learn from their wisdom. "When questioned about any regrets they had or anything they would do differently," she says, "common themes surfaced again and again."

The top five regrets of the dying, as witnessed by Ware:

1. "I wish I'd had the courage to live a life true to myself, not the life others expected of me."

2. "I wish I hadn't worked so hard."

3. "I wish I'd had the courage to express my feelings."

4. "I wish I had stayed in touch with my friends."

5. "I wish that I had let myself be happier."

Appendix D

The Rebbe, Rabbi Menachem Mendel Schneerson,
Sefer Hama'amarim Melukat 1:295 📖

Rabbi Menachem Mendel Schneerson
1902–1994

The towering Jewish leader of the 20th century, known as "the Lubavitcher Rebbe," or simply as "the Rebbe." Born in southern Ukraine, the Rebbe escaped Nazi-occupied Europe, arriving in the U.S. in June 1941. The Rebbe inspired and guided the revival of traditional Judaism after the European devastation, impacting virtually every Jewish community the world over. The Rebbe often emphasized that the performance of just one additional good deed could usher in the era of Mashiach. The Rebbe's scholarly talks and writings have been printed in more than 200 volumes.

יָדוּעַ שֶׁהַתַּכְלִית דְּתוֹרָה וּמִצְוֹות הוּא לִפְעוֹל בֵּירוּר וְזִיכּוּךְ בָּעוֹלָם הַזֶּה הַגַּשְׁמִי
. . . וְזֶהוּ שֶׁצָּרִיךְ לִהְיוֹת "יוֹמִין שְׁלֵימִין" דַּוְקָא, שֶׁבְּכָל יוֹם וָיוֹם צָרִיךְ לִהְיוֹת
קִיּוּם מִצְוָה, כִּי מִכֵּיוָן שֶׁגֶּדֶר הָעוֹלָם הוּא מָקוֹם וּזְמַן, הֲרֵי מוּבָן שֶׁהַתּוֹרָה
וּמִצְוֹות (שֶׁתַּכְלִיתָם הוּא לְתַקֵּן אֶת הָעוֹלָם) צְרִיכִים לְתַקֵּן גַּם אֶת הַזְּמַן. וְלָכֵן
מוּכְרָח שֶׁבְּכָל יוֹם תִּהְיֶה עֲשִׂיַּת מִצְוָה (הֲגַם שֶׁגַּם כְּשֶׁחָסֵר לוֹ יוֹמָא חָדָא
יָכוֹל הוּא לַעֲשׂוֹת אֶת הַלְּבוּשׁ עַל יְדֵי שֶׁיְּקַיֵּים מָחָר ב' מִצְוֹות), כִּי בִּכְדֵי לְתַקֵּן
אֶת הַיָּמִים (הַזְּמַן) גּוּפָא צָרִיךְ לִהְיוֹת כָּל יוֹמָא וְיוֹמָא עָבִיד עֲבִידְתֵּי.

I t is known that the purpose of Torah and *mitzvot* is to effect the refinement and sanctification of this physical world.... This explains why every one of our days must be a "complete day" [with mitzvah observance]. Because the parameters of the world are space and time, it is understood that Torah and *mitzvot*, whose purpose it is to rectify the world, must also rectify the dimension of time. This is why every day must incorporate the observance of a mitzvah, although even if a soul is lacking the spiritual protection provided by a mitzvah today, it can gain that protection by doing two *mitzvot* tomorrow. For in order to rectify the days (time) themselves, every day's service must be done in its proper time.

Appendix E

Avot DeRabbi Natan 11:1

רַבִּי יְהוּדָה בֶּן בְּתֵירָא אוֹמֵר: מִי שֶׁאֵין לוֹ מְלָאכָה לַעֲשׂוֹת, מַה יַּעֲשֶׂה? אִם יֵשׁ
לוֹ חָצֵר חֲרֵבָה אוֹ שָׂדֶה חֲרֵבָה, יֵלֵךְ וְיִתְעַסֵּק בָּהּ, שֶׁנֶּאֱמַר (שְׁמוֹת כ, ח), "שֵׁשֶׁת
יָמִים תַּעֲבוֹד וְעָשִׂיתָ כָל מְלַאכְתֶּךָ". וּמַה תַּלְמוּד לוֹמַר "וְעָשִׂיתָ כָל מְלַאכְתֶּךָ"?
לְהָבִיא אֶת מִי שֶׁיֵּשׁ לוֹ חֲצֵרוֹת אוֹ שָׂדוֹת חֲרֵבוֹת, יֵלֵךְ וְיִתְעַסֵּק בָּהֶן.

Rabbi Yehudah ben Beteira says: "If a person has no work, what should he do? If he has a desolate yard or a desolate field, he should go and work it, as it says, 'Six days you shall work and perform all your labor' (Exodus 20:8). What does '*all* your work' teach us? Even a desolate yard or field."

Avot DeRabbi Natan

A commentary on, and an elaboration of, the mishnaic tractate Avot, bearing the name of Rabbi Natan, one of the sages of the Mishnah. The work exists in two very different versions, one of which appears in many editions of the Talmud.

Appendix F

Halachic will

The Rabbinical Council of America

Halachic Health Care Proxy

Proxy and Directive With Respect To
Health Care and Post-Mortem Decisions

Introduction

This Halachic Health Care Proxy, revised in August of 2009, is designed to help ensure that all medical and post-death decisions made by others on your behalf will be made in accordance with Jewish law and custom (*Halacha*). **This document is of great importance in light of in-roads made by medical service providers to insert themselves into the decision making process of patients and their families regarding end-of-life issues**. The text of this Halachic Health Care Proxy has been approved by attorneys. While we do not expect that any future change in federal or state laws would materially affect the validity of this document, you should show it to your own attorney to confirm its effectiveness in your state and for your specific needs.

Acknowledgment

The Rabbinical Council of America wishes to acknowledge the pioneering work of Agudath Israel of America, whose Health Care Proxy was invaluable in the formulation of this document.

Further Guidelines

The RCA has also prepared a separate document titled **"Halachic Guidelines to Assist Patients and their Families in Making "End-of-Life" Medical Decisions"** which should be reviewed prior to filling out this form. Like this document, it is available for download at www.rabbis.org (and in printed form can be found at the back of this document.)

Halachic Health Care Proxy Registration

The Union of Orthodox Jewish Congregations of America, through an agreement with the New York Legal Assistance Group (NYLAG), has arranged registration of your Halachic Health Care Proxy free of charge with the U.S. Living Will Registry. The Registry will maintain a copy on a secure website that can be accessed instantly by healthcare providers around the country 24 hours a day through its automated service. We encourage registration, because, in many instances, a patient has to be rushed to the hospital and the family may not be able to locate or access the health care proxy.

To register, go to www.nytlc.org and look for the U.S. Living Will Registry Registration Form. Download and complete this form. The registration form, together with your Halachic Health Care Proxy may be returned by: e-mail, mail, or fax.

Registrants will receive confirmation of their registration and labels to affix to their insurance card & driver's license, stating that their advance directive is registered, and a wallet card listing their Registration #. The registrant is contacted annually by mail to confirm that the advance directive has not been changed or revoked, and to update personal and emergency contact information. This annual update is included in this life-time registration; there is never a charge to the registrant for annual updates or for continued registration.

For more detailed information on the registry, see www.oucommunity.org

---

The Rabbinical Council of America

305 Seventh Avenue, New York, NY 10001

www.rabbis.org

Instructions

(a) Print your name on the first line of the form.

(b) In Section 1, print the name, address, and telephone numbers of the person you wish to designate as your agent to make medical decisions on your behalf if you ever become incapable of making them on your own. Be sure to include all numbers (including cell phone and pager) where your agent can be reached in the event of an emergency. If the contact information for your agent changes, you should provide that updated information to everyone whom you have provided with a copy of your Health Care Proxy.

You should also insert the name, address, and telephone numbers of an alternate agent, to make such decisions if your main agent is unable, unwilling, or unavailable to make such decisions.

Before appointing anyone to serve as your agent, or alternate agent, ascertain that person's willingness to serve in such capacity. For your convenience, an addendum at the end of this document provides talking points to facilitate discussion between you and your proxy. In addition, if you have made arrangements with a burial society (*Chevra Kadisha*) for the handling and disposition of your body after death, you may wish to advise your agents of such arrangements.

Note: the law allows virtually any competent adult (an adult is a person 18 years of age or older, or anyone who has married) to serve as a health care agent. Thus, you may appoint as your agent (or alternate agent) your spouse, adult child, parent or other adult relative.

You may also appoint a non-relative to serve as your agent (or alternate agent), provided that individual has not already been appointed by 10 other persons to serve as a health care agent, or, is a non-physician employee of a health care facility in which you are a patient or resident.

(c) In Section 3, please print the name(s), addresses, and telephone numbers of the Orthodox rabbi and the alternate Orthodox rabbi whose guidance you want your agent to follow, should any questions arise as to the requirements of *halacha*.

You are free to insert the name of any Orthodox Rabbi(s) you choose. However, you are encouraged to discuss the matter with the rabbi to ascertain his specialization in end-of-life halachic issues and willingness to serve in such capacity.

(d) In Section 8, sign and print your name, address, phone numbers, and the date. If you are not physically able to sign and date the form, the law allows another person to do so on your behalf, as long as he or she does so at your direction, in your presence, and in the presence of two adult witnesses.

(e) In the Declaration of Witnesses section, two witnesses should sign their names and insert their addresses beneath your signature. These two witnesses must be competent adults. Neither of them should be the person you have appointed as your health care agent (or alternate agent). They may, however, be your relatives.

If you reside in a mental health facility, at least one witness must be an individual who is not affiliated with the facility. In addition, if the mental health facility is also a hospital, at least one witness must be a qualified psychiatrist.

(f) It is recommended that you keep the original of this form among your valuable papers in a location that is readily accessible in the event of an emergency; and that you distribute copies to the health care agent (and alternate agent) you have designated in section 1, to the rabbi(s) you have designated in section 3, as well as to your doctors, your lawyer, and anyone else who is likely to be contacted in times of emergency.

(g) If, at any time, you wish to revoke this Proxy and Directive, you may do so by executing a new one; or by notifying your agent or health care provider, in writing, of your intent to revoke it. To avoid possible confusion, it would be wise to try to obtain all originals and copies of the old Proxy and Directive and destroy them.

If you do not revoke the Proxy and Directive, the Law provides that it remains in effect indefinitely. Obviously, if any of the persons whose names you have inserted in the Proxy and Directive dies or becomes otherwise incapable of serving in the role you have assigned, you should execute a new Proxy and Directive.

(h) It is recommended that you also complete the Emergency Instructions Card contained at the end of this form, and carry it with you in your wallet or purse.

(i) If, upon consultation with your rabbi, you would like to add to this standardized Proxy and Directive any additional expression of your wishes with respect to medical and/or post-mortem decisions, you may do so by attaching a "rider" to the standardized form. If you choose to do so, or if you have any other questions concerning this form, please consult an attorney.

These instructions are not part of the Halachic Health Care Proxy and need not be kept attached to the executed document.

Proxy and Directive With Respect To
Health Care Decisions and Post-Mortem Decisions

I, _____, hereby declare as follows:

1. Appointment of Agent: In recognition of the fact that there may come a time when I will become unable to make my own health care decisions because of illness, injury or other circumstances, I hereby appoint

Agent

    Name _____

    Address _____

    Telephone/Email:
        Office _____   **Home** _____

        Cell _____   **E-mail:** _____

as my health care agent to make any and all health care decisions for me, consistent with my wishes as set forth in this directive. If the person named above is unable, unwilling or unavailable to act as my agent, I hereby appoint

Alternate Agent

    Name _____

    Address _____

    Telephone/Email:
        Office _____   **Home** _____

        Cell _____   **E-mail:** _____

to serve in such capacity.

This appointment shall take effect in the event I become unable, because of illness, injury or other circumstances, to make my own health care decisions.

2. Jewish Law to Govern Health Care Decisions: I am Jewish. It is my desire, and I hereby direct, that all health care decisions made for me (whether made by my agent, a guardian appointed for me, or any other person) be made pursuant to Jewish law and custom as determined in accordance with Orthodox interpretation and tradition. Without limiting in any way the generality of the foregoing, it is my wish that Jewish Law and custom should dictate the course of my health care with respect to such matters as the performance of cardio-pulmonary resuscitation if I suffer cardiac or respiratory arrest; the performance of life-sustaining surgical procedures and the initiation or maintenance of any particular course of life-sustaining medical treatment or other form of life-support maintenance, including the provision of nutrition and hydration; and the criteria by which death shall be determined, including the method by which such criteria shall be medically ascertained or confirmed.

3. Ascertaining the Requirements of Jewish Law: In determining the requirements of Jewish law and custom in connection with this declaration, I direct my agent to consult with the following Orthodox Rabbi and I ask my agent to comply with his halachic decisions:

Rabbi

    Name _____

    Address _____

Telephone/Email:

Office_____ Home _____

Cell _____ E-mail: _____

If such Orthodox Rabbi is unable, unwilling or unavailable to provide such consultation and guidance, I direct my agent to consult with the following Orthodox Rabbi and I ask my agent to comply with his halachic decisions:

Alternate Rabbi

Name_____

Address _____

Telephone/Email:

Office_____ Home _____

Cell _____ E-mail: _____

4. Direction to Health Care Providers: Any health care provider shall rely upon and carry out the decisions of my agent, and may assume that such decisions reflect my wishes and were arrived at in accordance with the procedures set forth in this directive, unless such health care provider shall have good cause to believe that my agent has not acted in good faith in accordance with my wishes as expressed in this directive.

If the persons designated in section 1 above as my agent and alternate agent are unable, unwilling or unavailable to serve in such capacity, it is my desire, and I hereby direct, that any health care provider or other person who will be making health care decisions on my behalf follow the procedures outlined in section 3 above in determining the requirements of Jewish law and custom.

Pending contact with the agent and/or Orthodox Rabbi described above, it is my desire, and I hereby direct, that all health care providers undertake all essential emergency and/or life sustaining measures on my behalf.

5. Access to Medical Records and Information; HIPAA: My agent(s) and Rabbi(s) are hereby authorized under the Health Insurance Portability and Accountability Act of 1996 ("HIPAA") access to any and all protected information, and accordingly all of my protected health information (as such term is defined under HIPAA) and other medical records shall be made available to my agent and rabbi upon request in the same manner as such information and records would be released and disclosed to me, and my agent and rabbi shall have and may exercise all of the rights I would have regarding the use and disclosure of such information and records, as required under HIPAA.

6. Post-Mortem Decisions: It is also my desire, and I hereby direct, that after my death, all decisions concerning the handling and disposition of my body be made pursuant to Jewish law and custom as determined in accordance with

Orthodox interpretation and tradition. For example, Jewish law generally requires expeditious burial and imposes special requirements with regard to the preparation of the body for burial. It is my wish that Jewish law and custom be followed with respect to these matters.

Further, subject to certain limited exceptions, Jewish law generally prohibits the performance of any autopsy or dissection. It is my wish that Jewish law and custom be followed with respect to such procedures, and with respect to all other post-mortem matters including the removal and usage of any of my body organs or tissue for transplantation or any other purposes. I direct that any health care provider in attendance at my death notify the agent and/or Orthodox Rabbi described above immediately upon my death, in addition to any other person whose consent by law must be solicited and obtained, prior to the use of any part of my body as an anatomical gift, so that appropriate decisions and arrangements can be made in accordance with my wishes. Pending such notification, and unless there is specific authorization by the Orthodox Rabbi consulted in accordance with the procedures outlined in section 3 above, it is my desire, and I hereby direct, that no post-mortem procedure be performed on my body.

7. Incontrovertible Evidence of My Wishes: If, for any reason, this document is deemed not legally effective as a health care proxy, or if the persons designated in section 1 above as my agent and alternate agent are unable, unwilling or unavailable to serve in such capacity, I declare to my family, my doctor and anyone else whom it may concern that the wishes I have expressed herein with regard to compliance with Jewish law and custom should be treated as incontrovertible evidence of my intent and desire with respect to all health care measures and post-mortem procedures; and that it is my wish that the procedure outlined in section 3 above should be followed in determining the requirements of Jewish law and custom.

8. Duration and Revocation: It is my understanding and intention that unless I revoke this proxy and directive, it will remain in effect indefinitely. My signature on this document shall be deemed to constitute a revocation of any prior health care proxy, directive or other similar document I may have executed prior to today's date.

My Signature _____
(If you are not physically able to sign, please ask another person to sign your name on your behalf.)

My Name (printed) _____ **Date** _____

Address _____

_____

Telephone/Email:
Office_____   **Home** _____

Cell _____   **E-mail:** _____

Declaration of Witnesses

I, on this _____ day of _____, 20___, declare that the person who signed (or asked another to sign) this document is personally known to me and appears to be of sound mind and acting willingly and free from duress.

He/She signed (or asked another to sign for him/her) this document in my presence (and that person signed in my presence). I am not the person appointed as agent by this document

Signature of Witness 1 _____

Name (printed) _____

Address _____

_____

Telephone/Email:
Office_____   **Home** _____

Cell _____   **E-mail:** _____

Signature of Witness 2 _____

Name (printed) _____

Address _____

_____

Telephone/Email:
Office_____   **Home** _____

Cell _____   **E-mail:** _____

Appendices

Expression of Intent
See Instructions paragraph (i)

The issues surrounding end-of-life medical decisions are critical and most complex. We, therefore, strongly recommend that you discuss your wishes and concerns openly with your Health Care proxy (as well as the alternate) and your designated Rabbi. In order to give them guidance, in the event that you are unable to make your own decisions, we ask you to review the following scenarios and discuss with them whether you wish to be treated aggressively with all appropriate life-support interventions, or palliative/comfort care, which may include pain medications, symptom relief, antibiotics and feeding tubes.

- *If I become terminally ill, I want to be treated.....*

- *If I am in a coma or have little conscious understanding, with no hope of recovery, then I want to be treated.....*
- *If I have brain damage or a brain disease that makes me unable to recognize people or speak and there is no hope that my condition will improve, I wish to be treated.....*

Medical technology is constantly advancing, so that new treatment options may become available in the future. Additionally, your advance directives at this time of your life may not necessarily apply if or when conditions change. We, therefore, urge you to periodically update this HCP, Health Care Proxy form, along with your DBA, Durable Power-of-Attorney, and Will.

Emergency Instructions Card
See Instructions paragraph (h)

Health Care Proxy **Emergency Instructions**	
I _____ have executed a "Halachic Health Care Proxy" (HCP) with respect to medical and post-mortem decisions, dated _____. Pursuant to the Halachic HCP, the persons listed on the reverse of this card are to serve as my agent and alternate agent, respectively, in making health care decisions for me if I become unable to do so. I desire that all such health care decisions, as well as all decisions relating to the handling and disposition of my body after I die, should be made pursuant to Jewish law and custom as determined in accordance with Orthodox interpretation and tradition. If there is any question regarding Jewish law and custom, my agent (or any other person making decisions for me) should consult with and follow the guidance of the rabbi or alternate rabbi identified on the reverse of this card. Pending contact with my agent I desire that health care providers should undertake all essential emergency measures on my behalf; and I desire that no autopsy, organ removal, or other post-mortem procedure be performed on my body without authorization from my agent.	**Agent:**_____ Phone: Office:_____ Home: _____ Cell: _____ E-Mail:_____ **Alternate Agent:** _____ Phone: Office: _____ Home: _____ Cell: _____ Email: _____ **Rabbi:** _____ Phone: Office_____ Home:_____ Cell:_____ E-mail_____ **Alternate Rabbi** _____ Phone: Office:_____ Home:_____ Cell_____ E-Mail _____

ADDITIONAL READINGS

INITIATING PALLIATIVE CARE CONVERSATIONS: LESSONS FROM JEWISH BIOETHICS

BY RABBI MICHAEL SCHULTZ, BCC, AND GIL BAR-SELA, MD

What are the ethical responsibilities of the medical staff (doctors, nurses, social workers, and chaplains) regarding the preservation of meaningful life for their patients who are approaching the end of life (EOL)? In particular, what is the staff's ethical responsibility to initiate a conversation with their patient regarding palliative care? By subjecting traditional Jewish teachings to an ethical analysis and then exploring the underlying universal principles, we will suggest a general ethical duty to inform patients of the different care options, especially in a manner that preserves hope. The principle that we can derive from Jewish bioethics teaches that the medical staff has a responsibility to help our patients live in a way that is consistent with how they understand their task or responsibility in life. For some patients, the best way to preserve a meaningful life in which they can fulfill their sense of purpose in the time that remains is to focus on palliation. For this reason, although palliative and supportive care are provided from the time of diagnosis, it is critical we make sure our patients realize that they have the opportunity to make a decision between either pursuing additional active treatments or choosing to focus primarily on palliative therapies to maximize quality of life. The Jewish tradition and our experience in spiritual care suggest the importance of helping patients preserve hope while, simultaneously, honestly acknowledging their situation. Staff members can play a vital role in helping patients make the most of this new period of their lives.

The period following several unsuccessful attempts at curing a life-threatening illness such as cancer, in which the patient is still relatively high-functioning, can be a very difficult time for patients, their fami-lies, and also for the medical staff (doctors, nurses, social workers, and chaplains). What should happen next—should the patient undergo another active treatment in the hopes of either a cure or of significantly extending their life, or should the patient consider palliative care only to maximize their quality of life (QOL)? Patients and their families are often focused on active therapies whose goal is cure or significantly extending life; and physicians are often willing to collude in that hope. Palliative care itself includes "aggressive" treatments such as radiation or chemotherapy as well as purely supportive care, and patients and doctors alike often favor aggressive palliative therapies without giving serious consideration to other palliative approaches which would likely be better for the patient and their QOL.[1] Our focus here is on palliative treatments that have the primary goal and expected outcome of maximizing QOL. If the staff members do not think that any useful non-palliative treatments remain, how can we best help patients at this critical time?

In such a case, one key question relates to a particular element of truth-telling—do staff members have a duty to tell patients that they do not think cure-oriented treatments are worth pursuing? Historically, doctors often took a paternalistic approach to truth-telling, i.e., withholding information in line with their sense of what was best for patients; however, that attitude has changed over the past 50 years in the United States.[2] At the same time, while the gen-

---

[1] De Haes H, Koedoot N. Patient centered decision making in palliative cancer treatment: a world of paradoxes. Patient Educ. Couns. 2003;50(1):43-49.

[2] Surbone A. Telling the truth to patients with cancer: what is the truth? Lancet Oncol. 2006;7(11):944-950.

eral, ethical, and legal landscape now demands that doctors engage in these kinds of open conversations with patients, many do not for a variety of reasons.[3]

There is increasing awareness that there cannot be a monolithic analysis of the ethics of truth-telling. Culture, society, and ethnicity, among other factors, including each individual's web of relationships, play a major role in influencing whether the patient wants to be told the truth,[2] and whether the doctor is inclined or willing to tell that truth.[4] For this reason, it is important for the doctor to understand the patient's individual circumstances.[2] In addition, in order to fully understand their own decision-making process in these situations, doctors need to consider the influence of their personal backgrounds and the ethical systems from which they operate. These factors weigh heavily in situations such as end of life (EOL) truth-telling or being asked by patients to "do everything" possible.[4,5,6]

Various philosophical or ethical systems have been used to analyze these situations, from both the patient and staff perspectives, by asking what that system's approach would be to address these particular issues.[7,8,9,10,11,12,13] However, are these approaches help-ful for people who do not follow those precise philosophical or ethical systems? Is it possible to draw out the general principles that underlie these approaches, such that any member of any medical staff could develop their own approach to these kinds of situations? That is the methodology employed by several bioethicists discussing this issue[14,15] and the methodology we will employ.

In addition to questions of truth-telling, the medical staff needs to consider some of the other needs they could help address during this transitional period of a patient's life. One study found that these patients need staff members to acknowledge their fears and find a way to balance hope and honesty.[16] Other studies describe the importance of asking about and relating to the patients' spiritual needs at this time to develop an appropriate plan of care.[17]

The medical situation

Case 1. *"I don't want to die before I'm dead." With these words, Yoav (the patient's name has been changed), a 31-year old cancer patient with a wife, a 3-year-old son, and a one-month-old baby, encapsulated his situation. "I want to be able to live the rest of my life, and I'm afraid that I'm already dead."*

Yoav understood that he was not expected to live more than 6 months (retroperitoneal leiomyosarcoma, being treated with adriamycin/ifosfamide), and he wanted to do whatever could be done to help preserve his QOL as much as possible, so that he could enjoy time with his young children, perhaps take a vacation, and finally move into the house that he and his wife had bought just before he became ill. However, he was afraid that the time remaining would contain nothing but unmitigated, overwhelming suffering that would prevent him from really living out the time he had left.

3 Buckman R. Doctors can improve on way they deliver bad news, MD maintains. Interview by Evelyne Michaels. CMAJ. 1992; 146(4):564-566.

4 Mystakidou K, Parpa E, Tsilila E, et al. Cancer information disclosure in different cultural contexts. Support Care Cancer. 2004; 12(3):147-154.

5 Mystakidou K, Liossi C, Vlachos L, et al. Disclosure of diagnostic information to cancer patients in Greece. Palliat Med. 1996;10(3): 195-200.

6 Braun UK, Ford ME, Beyth RJ, et al. The physician's professional role in end-of-life decision-making: voices of racially and ethnically diverse physicians. Patient Educ Couns. 2010;(1):3-9.

7 Steinberg A. Ethical issues involved in the care of dying patients: a problem-oriented approach. Isr J Med Sci. 1987;23(4):305-311.

8 Steinberg A. The terminally ill—secular and Jewish ethical aspects. Isr J Med Sci. 1994;30(1):130-135.

9 Genizi J. The terminally ill patient's right to refuse medical treatment according to Jewish law (in Hebrew). Harefuah. 2000;138(2): 160-164.

10 Hodkinson K. How should a nurse approach truth-telling? A virtue ethics perspective. Nurs Philos. 2008;9(4):248-256.

11 Jotkowitz A, Zivotofsky AZ. "Love your neighbor like yourself": a Jewish ethical approach to the use of pain medication with potentially dangerous side effects. J Palliat Med. 2010;13(1):67-71.

12 Kinzbrunner BM. Jewish medical ethics and end-of-life care. J Palliat Med. 2004;7(4):558-573.

13 Bleich JD. Treatment of the terminally ill. In: Hurwitz PF, Picard J, Steinberg A, eds. Jewish Ethics and the Care of End-of-Life Patients. Jersey city, NJ: Ktav Publishing House, Inc; 2006:57-73.

14 Brody B. Taking Issue: Pluralism and Casuistry in Bioethics. Washington, DC: Georgetown University Press; 2003.

15 Freedman B. Duty and Healing: Foundations of a Jewish Bioethic. New York, NY: Routledge, 1999.

16 Stajduhar KI, Thorne SE, McGuinness L, et al. Patient perceptions of helpful communication in the context of advanced cancer. J Clin Nurs. 2010;19(3-4):2039-2047.

17 Sulmasy DP. Spiritual issues in the care of dying patients: ". . . it's okay between me and god". JAMA. 2006;296(11):385-1392.

Yoav's fear is our question: How can we—patients, family members, and medical staff—work together to preserve life and stave off death? Yoav was not talking about life and death in the clinical sense, but he was talking about life and death in the experiential sense; i.e., preserving a meaningful life and preventing what we could call "death-in-life".

The medical staff generally has a duty to try and preserve life in the clinical sense, but what are the ethical responsibilities of everyone involved? From the doctors to the patients themselves, what are the ethical responsibilities regarding preserving meaningful life for someone who is approaching death? The answer to that question will have major ramifications for our issues of patient doctor communication and truth-telling.

Case 2. *Miriam (the patient's name has been changed), a 38-year old mother of four, including a toddler, came to our department after the surgeons discovered that her pancreatic adenocarcinoma was inoperable. After 2 weeks during which Miriam and her husband feared she would die imminently, I met with them as her condition was stabilizing and they were beginning to think about moving forward. A switch had been turned in her life, she said, and she was accepting and looking for the way in which her medical condition could turn out to be a blessing. At the same time, their focus was on a cure, while the doctor's ideal focus of care would have been purely palliative.*

Our analysis is focused on terminal patients who are not expected to live more than a year for whom there is no curative treatment, only palliative care. It is quite normal for patients to decide to undergo further active treatments in the hopes of a cure or significantly extending life, despite the fact that they have been warned about the likely side effects and the fact that the medical staff does not think any substantial benefit from the treatment will occur. In fact, the medical staff thinks this patient is extremely likely to suffer more than benefit from the treatment. Why, then, do so many of our patients end up undergoing these treatments? Why do they not choose to focus on palliative care, to maintain the best possible QOL for the time that remains? For some patients, it is very

important to feel that they are actively doing something, to feel that they are fighting their illness and not giving up.[18] Other patients may prefer not to acknowledge the medical situation. Too often, though, the decision to continue with another non-palliative treatment is actually a non-decision, where patients do not realize they have different options in front of them.[19] After a patient completes one unsuccessful treatment, they ask what treatment to do next. Unfortunately, many doctors follow the patient's lead. The possibility of no further treatment and focusing on palliating symptoms to enhance one's QOL is not necessarily brought up for discussion, and so it might not be considered. An in-depth conversation about the patient's goals for the time to come is not always facilitated.

Is this *status quo* ideal acceptable, or in need of change? To look for guidance, we will analyze this situation through the lens of Jewish bioethics.

Jewish bioethics
The basis for Jewish bioethics is the body of *halakhic* material (legal rulings in specific cases) and *aggadic* writings (ethical statements or potentially didactic stories) in the Jewish tradition. Brody[14] outlines a challenge in bringing Jewish bioethics to bear on discussions relevant to a wider audience. When faced with a particular medical-ethical dilemma, a rabbinic decisor looks through the legal material to provide the questioner with binding guidance on how to behave in that situation. However, the use of Jewish bioethics to mandate specific behaviors in specific situations only makes sense when writing for an audience of Jews who feel bound by Jewish law. In order to engage with the general Western world of ethics, the Jewish ethicist must use *halakhic* material as a source for ideas about medical ethics which can be defended independently of their origins".[13(pp265-267)] In other words, our interest is in the concepts and principles that can be derived from the Jewish source

---

[18] Grunfeld EA, Maher EJ, Browne S, et al. Advanced breast cancer patients' perceptions of decision making for palliative chemotherapy. J Clin Oncol. 2006;24(7):1090-1098.

[19] Tattersall MH, Gattellari M, Voigt K, et al. When the treatment goal is not cure: are patients informed adequately? Support Care Cancer. 2002;10(4):314-321.

material and then applied by anyone to their own practice, not in determining a legal ruling for Jews bound by the *halakhic* system. We are not writing to suggest how to treat religious Jews; we are offering a general ethical argument based on principles derived from sources in the Jewish tradition. It is important to note that Judaism is not univocal, and we can only offer one voice among many.

An ethic of duty

There are important differences between Western and Jewish ethics. Most significantly, we begin by noting this fundamental difference: "the distinction between an ethics whose foundational language is duty, as is true of the Jewish approach, and contrasting that with our common Western ethical approach, whose basis is rights," as stated by the late Benjamin Freedman, Professor of Bioethics at McGill University.[15(p12)] In Judaism, one has a duty at all moments in life—whether to society, to family and friends, or to God. Duties, rather than rights, are the central consideration. These duties devolve upon individuals and the collective, even against their will. In the Bible, they begin with Adam and Eve's duty upon creation "to work the land and protect it" (Genesis 2:15). The collective duties expand with the acceptance of the Ten Commandments and the Torah at Mount Sinai, following the Exodus from Egypt.

Making joint use of Western and Jewish approaches can be productive. "Secular bioethics . . . has a great deal to say about procedural questions—*who* will decide—but relatively less about substantive questions—*how* to decide;" yet how and what to decide is the almost exclusive focus of Jewish bioethics. In this way, the 2 fields could be highly complementary.[15 (p17)]

If we narrow our focus from ethics to bioethics, we can consider what our duties are in relation to the Jewish system regarding questions of health. Judaism teaches that there is an obligation to seek healing. The obligation to seek healing finds its source in one of several possible texts in the Jewish tradition: "Just take care for yourself, and take great care of your soul" (Deuteronomy 4:9); "Yet your blood of your soul shall I require of you" (Genesis 9:5); and "Do not stand idly by the blood of your neighbor"

together with the presumption that "a person is his own relative," meaning one must treat oneself at least as well as one treats one's neighbor.[13,15[pp142-145]] In Judaism, our bodies are not our own, rather they are objects to be held in trust and used well on behalf of their true owner. (For a discussion of the various Jewish positions on whether God is the sole owner of our bodies or if people can also be considered owners, see Genizi.[9]) God gave us the use of our body, but only on the condition that we care for it and seek medical treatment when necessary so that we can use it to fulfill our other duties, however they may be formulated. Here are 2 traditional Jewish formulations:

- Rabbi Moshe Chaim Luzzatto writes that "this, too, is a commandment upon us, to protect our bodies in a fitting manner to enable us to serve our Creator through it".[20]

- Maimonides writes that "It is impossible to reach completeness of the soul . . . so long as he has pain or strong hunger or thirst or overheating or fierce cold." Therefore, one must strive to treat pain.[21]

The principle is that however one formulates their ultimate duties in life, we have an obligation to enable the fulfillment of that ultimate duty by seeking healing and never intentionally damaging one's own body.

The principle that one's body is held in trust rather than owned seems to be directly opposed to the value of autonomy which is prominent in Western ethics. Nevertheless, one can accept the application of Western ethics in society without fully agreeing with them internally. A great many cultures, or at least individuals, seem actually to also believe in a sense of self-regarding duty. Many cultures believe in the duty to care for one's health for any of a number of possible reasons; ie, "obligations to those who rely upon you or care about your well-being; a belief that one's body is to some degree held in trust or stewardship, whether this be on behalf of God, some ideal that you hold, or some special mission that is

---

[20] Luzzatto MC. [The way of God]. Hebrew. Part I:4:7, Italy: 1730s.
[21] Maimonides. Guide for the perplexed. 3:27, Egypt: 1180s.

yours to accomplish; a duty to your community or tribe, or any entity larger than yourself."[15(p140)] Once broadened in this way, the principles derived from the Jewish approach can be relevant to anyone who feels a sense of responsibility to act to preserve one's health for the sake of another or for the sake of being able to accomplish some larger obligatory purpose.

Finally, Judaism expands the circle of duty to seek healing by taking one further step. Not only does each individual have a duty to preserve their own health in order to be able to perform one's other duties in life, but each individual also has a duty to help preserve the health of others. All people have some sense of duty to help preserve the health of others (in certain situations even against their will), so that they can then fulfill their duties in life; including laymen who can help either their parents and family[22] or anyone else ("do not stand idly by when your neighbor's blood is at stake"; Leviticus 19:16) and doctors with respect to their patients ("and you shall return it [his health] to him"; Deuteronomy 22:4).

Different people and different cultures have an entirely different sense of what their duties are in life. The principle that we derive from Jewish ethics teaches that we have a duty to help enable others to fulfill their duty of living in a way that is consistent with how they each understand their task or responsibility in life.

Applied ethics

In a situation where, from the medical staff's perspective, the only remaining beneficial treatments are palliative, Western ethics might not be helpful, since ethically the doctor has the right to bring up all forms of palliative care or the right to wait for the patient to ask about it. (We are not addressing the varying legal requirements to have such a conversation. Recent Israeli law, for one, does mandate that the doctor initiate such a conversation.) But with an approach based on duty, the picture becomes clearer. Let us begin by considering the situation from the patient's point of view. Leading Jewish thinkers, in discussing the process of deciding between curative and palliative plans of treatment in cases like ours, argue that the decision should be left to the patient.[23,24(2:74)] (See Bleich's dissenting argument[13] and Brody's rebuttal.[14[p223]]) This may seem obvious to today's doctors working on the basis of patient autonomy but, in an ethic of duty, this is very surprising. We expect there to be a clear duty, one way or the other. Why is the decision left to the patient?

To answer this question we must carefully define Judaism's duty of living. The Jewish ethic of the duty of living is not precisely to "extend life as much as possible in order to fulfill their duties in life." If that were the case, we would expect the doctors to decide, not the patient. This definition runs the risk of confusing the means with the ends at the EOL. The purpose of the duty of healing or extending life is a means to enable one to fulfill one's duty in life, but it is not the primary duty itself. At the EOL, extending life is not always the best way to fulfill one's duty. We would like to suggest that Judaism teaches that we each have a responsibility "to maximize one's ability to fulfill one's duties in life". Maximizing one's ability to live life well can differ from extending life. Sometimes, treatments focused on extending life with no hope of curing or mitigating the illness make it harder to fulfill these life duties because of the difficult side effects. For example, if the focus is on doing good deeds, then one may be able to do more good deeds by taking the palliative route and not having to devote most of one's energy to getting through the pain. In this approach, the decision is left to the patient because he and he alone will know what is best and what will enable him to fulfill his duties.

Rabbi M. Feinstein draws a helpful analogy in addressing whether a patient with a fatal illness should undergo a risky procedure that carries a chance of long-term survival but also a chance of immediate death, or forgo the procedure and definitely live but only for a short time. His approach can serve as our paradigm: "Behold, in monetary matters some peo-

---

[22] Berlin NTY. Responsa Meshiv Davar. 2:50, Volozhin, Belarus: late 19th century.

[23] Auerbach SZ. Responsa Minchat Shlomo. I:91.24, Jerusalem, Israel: 1986.

[24] Feinstein M. Responsa Igrot Moshe, Choshen Mishpat. Vol. 2, #73-4, New York, Noble Book Press, 1985.

ple spend what little money they have on the chance of a big windfall, even though in the event that it fails they'll lose what little they had. And some people don't want to spend what little they have when there's a chance of losing it all."[25] It is good for people to get to continue living their lives in the way that is true to how they had lived their lives until then, with the values and duties which guided them through life. In Freedman's words, "It is rational for dying patients to live their last days as though they are living, rather than dying, in a manner fully consistent with how they have lived their lives up until this point."[15(p280)] For some patients, it makes the most sense to do the treatment, even against the doctor's recommendations, because they see their duty in life as being a fighter or a risk-taker, and undergoing a risky procedure or treatment seems right to them. But for other patients, if they understood the full picture, their consistent understanding of their duty in life might tell them to focus on leaving a message for their loved ones, or healing family rifts, or providing a long-term arrangement for their philanthropic concerns. The patients' job is to decide what to do now, based on their over-arching understanding of how to fulfill their duty in life.

Let us return to our original question—what is the staff's duty in such cases? Our duty is to make sure that the patient, and his/her family, knows that there is a decision to be made, and that focusing on palliation is a possibility. By palliation, we mean focusing on maximizing one's QOL. For some people, the way to maximize their ability to fulfill their duties in life would be not to continue with more active treatments but to focus on palliation. If we do not ensure that they know that the possibility of palliation exists, we might fail to give them the opportunity to make the decision that is best for them.

Thus, our presentation of Jewish ethics argues in favor of the importance of truth-telling as it relates to the presentation of treatment options, because that enables patients to make an informed decision in determining how best to fulfill their duties.

The duties of the medical staff

In order for a patient to best fulfill their duty when they are approaching the EOL, we know that some will choose not to undergo further active treatments. Our first responsibility is to be sensitive to the patient and provide information about this potential choice in a caring and non-threatening way, guided by the patient's willingness to listen. (An exception to this conclusion would be if one had a specific reason to believe that having such a conversation would harm the patient or otherwise make it harder for them to use their remaining time well.) Additionally, sharing this treatment option does not necessitate providing all the details of the medical situation, if the patient does not wish to hear them. Grunfeld et al and Alesi et al outline some of the best practices for having these honest and compassionate conversations.[18,26] The ability to choose is itself of therapeutic value to a patient who might be suffering from feelings of powerlessness. It is quite common for a patient to have the doctor decide,[1] and can be considered an active decision that may reflect the patient's approach to life. Perhaps the worries and regrets related to having to make further decisions would negatively impact the patient's ability to fulfill their other duties. The medical staff needs to make sure the QOL option is presented as a real option and is given serious weight in the conversation rather than just briefly mentioned, as often happens.[1]

In these situations, as in all the care that we provide, it is important to get to know the patient as a whole person. The more we know his values, his needs, and what is most important to him, the better we can work with him to find the care plan best suited to the life he is trying to lead. In addition, it can help care providers become more comfortable with providing care even when they feel it is not indicated—"the providers may have missed a reason why there is compensating value in the life of the patient and may become comfortable with providing the care if they understand these compensating values".[14(p17)] At all times, palliative approaches to minimizing pain and

[25] Feinstein M. Responsa Igrot Moshe, Yoreh Deah. Vol. 3, #36, New York, Noble Book Press, 1982.

[26] Alesi E, Bobb B, Smith TJ. Guiding patients facing decisions about "futile" chemotherapy. J Support Oncol. 2011;9(5):184-187.

suffering should be applied, whether they accompany active treatments or stand alone.

Thinking back to Yoav (Case 1), one could imagine that a primary focus on palliative care with a minimum of side effects would be beneficial for him as a means of best fulfilling his sense of duty for the time that remained. However, we cannot be certain of that fact in a vacuum. Once the options are clearly presented to the patient and his concerns are heard and acknowledged, he can then make the decision that is right for him. And in fact, although he initially opted for a more aggressive treatment course, the basis for his decision was the hope that overall it would result in a better quality of life with his family. In the end, unfortunately, the combination of illness progression and treatment side effects led Yoav to abruptly cease all treatment. Although we would certainly have preferred to have had the opportunity to provide palliative care rather than no care, we hope that his decision to cease treatment was an empowering and dignifying one that enabled him to be true to himself.

For Miriam (Case 2), there was an initial treatment decision to be made. Should she begin receiving more intensive chemotherapy—a 3-drug combination of oxaliplatin, irinotecan and 5-FU (folfirinox)—with a greater chance of extending life, but also the likelihood of much worse side effects? Or should she receive gemcitabine, a standard chemotherapy in advanced pancreatic carcinoma, also an appropriate palliative treatment in her case, a treatment that her body could much more likely withstand? Her doctor explained both options and shared her opinion that the folfirinox combination would be too much for Miriam, leaving her in great suffering. Miriam and Shaya decided on what felt to them like a compromise approach of gemcitabine together with a biological treatment (erlotinib). They had the need to preserve hope for a cure, but were also intentionally entering on a new path of personal and spiritual growth that would have been impossible when dealing with overwhelming side effects. As she started the treatment, Miriam pursued an internal process of partnering with God and freeing herself from the need to feel in control, as had been predominant her whole life.

Practical challenges

It can be difficult to have these conversations. For a patient to consider not pushing on with every last curative treatment available, because that might not be the best way to use the time that remains, he needs to acknowledge the possibility that he has transitioned from the period of unending life to the period of life that is coming to an end. He needs to acknowledge that there might not be a cure, which is very difficult to do. However, being able to acknowledge that fact is infinitely valuable. The knowledge that we will die and that our time here is limited is one of the most important motivations in helping us to live our lives to the fullest, something we should strive to remember throughout our whole lives.[27]

It may also be difficult to acknowledge death's approach, especially for family members, for fear of appearing religiously unfaithful.[17, 27] In addition, questions of faith are often inextricably linked with questions of guilt and duty—is it really alright for me to start preparing for the possibility that my loved one is in the final stages of life?

Overwhelming levels of fear or anger can make it hard for a patient to maximize his ability to live life well, which can be hard to overcome on one's own. Patients report wanting staff to help out by acknowledging their fears.[16] We should sit down and take the time to encourage patients to articulate their fears, which, once stated in words, often are not quite as scary as they had seemed. When we enable our patients to let out the full wrath of their anger, we can help weaken the hold of these emotions on their lives. These emotions are entirely natural, and often need a listening ear for the patient to be able to process them so that they are able to put these emotions into perspective and they no longer dominate the patient's life.

The staff might be concerned that by initiating conversations about palliative care, a patient's sense of hope will be taken away. Hope is a very positive outlook for our patients.[3] Preserving hope is also a

27 Schultz M, Baddarni K, Bar-Sela G. Reflections on palliative care from the Jewish and Islamic tradition. Evid Based Complement Alternat Med. 2012;2012:693092.

crucial factor in patients deciding to undergo more aggressive palliative treatments like chemotherapy.[18] However, in our experience, we have seen that it is possible to preserve hope for a miracle while also acting in accordance with the strong likelihood that our patient is in a new period, the period of dying. We cannot dismiss the possibility of a miracle; there are too many stories of people who survived for years against all the doctors' expectations. The key is to reach a balance of hope and reality, so that one can use the time remaining as best as possible. Patients themselves identify balancing hope and honesty as one of the most important things they need from the medical-care team.[16] In the words of Rabbi Maurice Lamm, Judaism is "death-defying," not "death-denying." One must do the utmost to preserve life, but not deny that death lies at the end of the road. In his words, "We struggle to preserve life and, failing that, we struggle to preserve humanity, so long as we live".[28] (pp135–139)

Case 2. Miriam and her husband did an amazing job of achieving that balance. While preserving their hope that her treatment would lead to her tumor shrinking, they set about maximizing the 3 months they had while Miriam was feeling relatively good to do the things they now found most valuable. She spent a lot of time with her children, took a painting course, and practiced new techniques for mindfulness. Her husband joined a men's prayer group and found great release in freeing his unceasing inner prayer voice. In Miriam's words, "If I have the strength for something, then I don't want to miss the opportunity." She knew that her opportunities were likely to be limited, and she made the most of that relatively healthier period in fulfilling her sense of duty to personal spiritual growth and to family.

When tests showed that the tumor was still growing, Miriam and Shaya were badly shaken but were committed to finding the way forward. After two more treatments, Miriam's condition began to deteriorate, and she suffered from liver dysfunction and ascites. When I visited, she was mourning her losses. "If only I could just have a normal life." When I reflected back to

her the ways that I saw that she was still growing, she was strengthened spiritually. Perhaps she had begun to fear that the opportunities for really living were ending and was comforted to be reminded that, as one door closed, others had opened. The next day she shared with me her new approach. She would no longer be a big planner. She wanted to live in the moment, and she knew how to enjoy the moment despite the suffering.

The next time they saw Miriam's doctor, she explained to them that the only remaining treatment had not shown success in cases like hers and would likely make things worse for Miriam's dignity and QOL. It was a very difficult conversation for Miriam and her husband, but they decided to enter a home-hospice framework. They have enjoyed unending support from friends and family and continue to make the most of their time together.

The end of life

As with any period of life, there are innumerable meaningful ways to live one's life. The EOL is no time to stop living. Jewish tradition suggests a number of goals for the EOL, many of which may be shared by other traditions. Ultimately, it is up to the patient to make the most of the time that remains, but staff (and family, of course) can also help facilitate making the most of this time. The first step is simply recognizing that, although one's physical limitations might be greater and the distractions of pain and perhaps ongoing treatment are present, good things are still possible, as was the case for Miriam. Some personal goals can still be achieved, life can still be celebrated, and hope for a positive future for one's loved ones and for one's own soul can still be thought of as sources of comfort. One's relationship with the divine can still be strengthened. Judaism emphasizes that more good deeds can always be done, and that it is a wonderful time for spiritual growth. Relationships can still be healed, and the pure act of forgiveness, even without reconciliation, can be deeply powerful. Some people choose to follow the lead of Jacob in the Bible, leaving ethical wills, providing children, grandchildren, and future generations with guidance on how to live their lives, thereby providing a means for this person's values to live on. This can be a time for love and for giving. As the family draws closer to

---

[28] Lamm M. Implementing empathy at the end of life. In: Hurwitz PF, Picard J, Steinberg A, eds. Jewish Ethics and the Care of Endof- Life Patients. Jersey city, NJ: Ktav Publishing House, Inc; 2006: 131-148.

care for their beloved at the end of his life, the degree of love between them can reach new heights and permanently transform the family's relationships.[28]

Conclusion

The Babylonian Talmud (Tractate Sotah 46b) tells the story of the city of Luz whose residents lived eternally, until the day came, separately for each resident, when the person felt that the time had come for him to leave the city walls and pass away. What was the secret of their longevity? As Rabbi Yitzchak of Karlin explains, "one who is on the path of life need not fear the angel of death".[29] May we all be blessed with staying on the path of living our lives, even and especially at the EOL, so that we will live, and not die, our whole lives.

Acknowledgment

We gratefully acknowledge the ongoing support of the UJA/Federation of New York.

Journal of Supportive Oncology, Vol. 11, No. 1 (March 2013), pp. 1–7.

---

[29] Minkovski Y. Keren Orah on Babylonian Talmud, Tractate Sotah 46b, 19th century.

ARE WE DISPOSABLE?

BY JAY LITVIN

Not long ago, I was in a meeting with someone whose husband had passed away less than a year before. In the midst of the meeting someone cracked a joke and the woman of whom I'm speaking laughed. I was startled. "How can you laugh?" I thought. "Your spouse passed away less than a year ago!" And then an alarming thought occurred to me: "Are we all disposable and that easily replaceable? Can our loved ones laugh so quickly after we're gone?"

Right now and before writing another word, I want to clear up any misconceptions: Within seconds of thinking this I knew that that's not what I really think. My wife suggested that perhaps my own condition had something to do with my response. Being in remission from lymphoma does not mean that I believe 100% of the time that I'm out of the woods. Mainly, I'm very optimistic. But I'm not Mr. Bitachon every second of every day. And, whenever I hear of someone who passes away from some version of what I have (or, please G-d, had), it re-opens unpleasant thoughts and fears. Unfortunately, hearing about such people is all too common these days.

"It was laughter with a broken heart that will never mend in full," my wife assured me.

Are we disposable? Sounds ridiculous doesn't it? And of course we are not. But death is not the only place I find evidence to my fear that our lives are too quickly forgotten and replaced not only by laughter, but by others.

Look at divorce. People marry. People divorce. Their spouse remarries. And there is someone else who comes to take his or her place. In some cases, he or she comes to parent the children. Now you see him, now you don't. There seems to be this space—husband, father, whatever—that can be filled by a variety of candidates. Perhaps not in the same way, but still... filled. What is the message to our children? He was your Daddy. But *he* can be your Daddy, too.

I'm taking a risk here. I know that what I'm writing is an exaggeration, and certainly not the most rational or wisest train of thought. I'm inviting you on a journey with my darker side. My fearful side. The side that emerges when my worst nightmares and thoughts overpower my higher and better self. Can I trust you to come along without too much judgment? Will you hang in there with me a little while longer as I flesh this out?

If Daddies are replaceable, is the same true of the children? In a disposable, replaceable world, do we need ponder too long why kids sometimes wonder if their lives are worth anything? Why we sometimes wonder the same?

But, when we lose someone in our life there is a dilemma. On the one hand we are to mourn. On the other, we are to carry on with our lives. And, in today's modern world, it seems that the faster and fuller we do this, the healthier we are. Rarely, today, do we see a widow or widower whose loss is worn constantly on his sleeve. Whose grief becomes an indelible look in the eyes and tension on the face. And even though someone may have once been the "love of my life," in today's world it seems that after loss we are encouraged to pick ourselves up and begin a new life. But if one creates a new life can't one also then have a new "love of my life"? New life; new love. Disposable life; replaceable love.

I'm traveling further downward. Spinning really. Can you feel it? I've done this before, but it's different having you with me. And not even knowing who you are: faceless, unknown confidants!

Have I come to the point where I trust you all so much? Or is it just the chemo and past months of battle that have left me not even caring what you think?

Perhaps if I thought about my own parents more. Perhaps if they occupied more of my thoughts and speech? Perhaps if I didn't feel that my own life had continued on so easily after they both passed away? Were they disposable? Of course not. Were they replaceable? Impossible. And yet...

No, I don't want anyone to suffer after loss. Not anyone in my family. Not anyone in yours. I want for there to be laughter again. Full lives. Happiness. Joy. Song. A warm, lively Shabbos table filled with children and grandchildren, great-grandchildren. Even the ones I might never meet.

But, oh, how I don't want ever to be forgotten. For life to be as if I never was. Can you understand that? Do you ever feel that? Someone told me recently that they never think about one day not being here, yet for me, not one day passes without that thought.

They say "Jacob lived through the good deeds of his children." But that was Jacob. And look at who his children were. But what about me?

Have you never thought these thoughts? Never felt the fear? Never been caught in the spiral of your own darker self with no escape in view? Never wished you could ascend towards the point of light you know is there, somewhere... but where?

I'm lucky enough to have a person in my life who motivates me to reach a little higher, and helps me get there some of the time. His name is Rav (Rabbi) Gluckowsky. He's the guy in my community who is my teacher and guide. He's someone I learn from not just in a class, but from the way he lives his life.

(A lot of people call him by his first name, but I prefer to always call him "Rav Gluckowsky," even though we're pretty good friends and I'm older by a long shot. Perhaps it's because we're friends that I call him "Rav." I enjoy giving things to my friends. And, in this case, I enjoy giving respect to someone I like very much. The respect and honor I afford him in no way lessens the familiarity and comfort I feel when I'm with him. He is my Rav and we are friends.)

I never met Rav Gluckowsky's father. And yet he accompanies Rav Gluckowsky almost everywhere he goes and certainly in most every meeting I have with him. There is not a talk Rav Gluckowsky gives in which he doesn't quote his father. The other day we were speaking of our sons' singing in the choir and he mentioned what a great voice his father had. Last week I went to a birthday *farbrengen* and Rav Gluckowsky was asked to tell a story. "Let me tell you a story about the previous Rebbe that my father used to tell..." He not only told the story in his father's name, his father was imbedded throughout the story.

His father's picture hangs prominently in his living room. We are invited to his home several times a year to share in some event commemorating his father. And one has the feeling that Rav Gluckowsky's entire life is dedicated to his father, that he is busily and consciously being the son his father would have wanted him to be.

In shul, we all know that many of the tunes he sings during *davening* come from his father. And in our community, we all know we are the beneficiaries of the wonderful man Rav Gluckowsky's father must have been. We, too, are better off because Rav Gluckowsky's father once blessed the earth.

Would Sukkot be Sukkot without the stories of the sukkahs that Rav Gluckowsky built together with his father and brothers? How many times have we heard the one about the last minute car ride with the police chasing behind just minutes before candle lighting time? Would our boys school be the same if it was not filled with the educational adages from Rav Gluckwsky's father, an educator who taught first through eighth grades in Toronto for forty years?

And would we not all love to say to our children as Rav Gluckowsky recently said to his: How proud I would be if you grew up to be a teacher like Zaidy, a man who, through his teaching, improved the lives of so many, many people.

Funny, but when I finally saw a video of Rav Gluckowsky's father, he looked like an ordinary guy. A school teacher. Someone a lot like you and I. But someone who had risen to near mythic stature through the love, respect and devotion of his son.

Listening to Rav Gluckowsky, I, this ordinary father, could imagine one day being lifted to such heights by my own children. And such fantasies fill me with warmth and courage. They ease my fears. They impel me forward to live a life full of actions that will give my children something to talk about one day to their children and to their communities.

If Rav Gluckowsky's father is not disposable, neither am I. Neither are you. We are as irreplaceable as the love we give. Our indelible mark is invisibly carved on the hearts of our children and loved ones. Our mark is contained not only in their laughter, but in the laughter they impart to others. Laughter, as my wife says, that comes from a broken heart. But a heart filled with love breaks and then grows stronger through mending. Its strength comes from its softness, a softness made softer by the love we left behind, perhaps softer, even, through the loss our children feel after we've left.

The woman who laughed came into my office the other day. She stopped by to tell me about the event held in her community the night before to commemorate the first anniversary of her husband's passing. She described the event for a long time and then went on to tell me about the highlight of the evening.

"My daughter read a letter she had written to her Abba," she began. "In the letter she described all the family events of the past year. She described them in detail so that my husband, her father, would be able to take nachas from her piano recital, from her brother's first bike ride, from the first day mommy was able to go back to work after months of feeling too sad to even leave the house..."

As the woman spoke her eyes welled with tears. They never spilled over. It was as if her heart had simply filled with so much love it had to relieve itself through her eyes.

She stood in my doorway for a long time reciting all the events that her daughter had recounted in her letter to her father. She even told me how her daughter had described to her father what she knew her father's reactions would be. "You would have laughed so hard, Abba..." "You would have told us your famous story about the time you..." "Oh, Abba, how you would have enjoyed the music..."

I never grew tired of listening to this woman tell about this evening of remembrance. Long past the time when I should have returned to my work, I listened attentively about her children and their love for their father and for his memory.

And when she finally finished and continued down the hall, I could have continued listening even longer.

But instead I sat down and wrote this article. Perhaps one day my children will read it. Or, better yet, perhaps they'll read to their children one day.

May I live to be 120.

Chabad.org Editor's note: Jay sent us this article two-and-a-half years ago, at a time when—as he writes in its opening paragraphs—he was very optimistic about his prognosis. But shortly thereafter, while we were still working on the article, a blood test result brought the news that his illness had turned once more aggressive. Indeed, such ups-and-downs often occurred during his valiant four-year battle with the disease.

Because of the unfortunate turn of events, Jay felt that the subject of this article was too "close to home" to publish. Now, after the worst has occurred, Jay's family decided that the time has come to share it with our readers. —Rabbi Yanki Tauber

Reprinted with permission from Chabad.org.

JEWISH ETHICAL WILLS: 12TH & 14TH CENTURIES

Many Jews were in the habit of writing wills, in Hebrew, in which they imparted instruction of an ethical and religious nature to their children and to their descendants. Such ethical testaments were not uncommon among Moslems and Christians at this time.

Many of these Jewish ethical wills, such as A Father's Admonition, *which follows, are valuable for the insight they give us into the cultural and social life of the individual Jew of some particular land at some specific period. Others, such as the* Testament of Eleazar of Mayence [Mainz], *are valuable in that they reflect the moral and ethical views of a pious Jew. The texts here are excerpts.*

The Admonition of Judah ibn Tibbon *(1120 about 1190) is thus particularly important because it throws light on the intellectual interests of a cultured Spanish Jew. Judah ibn Tibbon was born in Granada; he migrated to Lunel, in enlightened southern France, probably because of the religious bigotry of the fanatical Moslem Almohades. He was the "father of translators" from Arabic into Hebrew. His son, Samuel ibn Tibbon (about 1150about 1230), for whom this lofty though rather querulous Admonition was written, succeeded in becoming an even greater translator than his father. Samuel's most valuable piece of work is the translation from Arabic into Hebrew of Maimonides'* Guide for the Perplexed.

The Testament of Eleazar of Mayence, *parts of which follow as the second selection, is the work of the simple and frank German Jew, Eleazar ben Samuel HaLevi of Mayence [Mainz], who died in his native city on the first day of the Jewish New Year of 1357.*

1. A Father's Admonition
The Ethical Will of Judah ibn Tibbon,
France, about 1160–1180
My son, list to my precepts, neglect none of my injunctions. Set my admonition before your eyes; thus shall you prosper and prolong your days in pleasantness! ....

You know, my son, how I swaddled you and brought you up, how I led you in the paths of wisdom and virtue. I fed and clothed you; I spent myself in educating and protecting you. I sacrificed my sleep to make you wise beyond your fellows and to raise you to the highest degree of science and morals. These twelve years I have denied myself the usual pleasures and relaxations of men for your sake, and I still toil for your inheritance. [After the death of his wife the father devoted his time to Samuel, his son.]

I have honored you by providing an extensive library for your use, and have thus relieved you of the necessity to borrow books. Most students must bustle about to seek books, often without finding them. But you, thanks be to God, lend and borrow not. Many books, indeed, you own two or three copies. I have besides made for you books on all sciences, hoping that your hand might find them all as a nest. [The father probably compiled reference books for the use of the son.]

Seeing that your Creator had graced you with a wise and understanding heart, I journeyed to the ends of the earth and fetched for you a teacher in secular sciences. I minded neither the expense nor the danger of the ways. Untold evil might have befallen me and you on those travels, had not the Lord been with us!

But you, my son! did deceive my hopes. You did not choose to employ your abilities, hiding yourself from all your books, not caring to know them or even their titles. Had you seen your own books in the hand of others, you would not have recognized them; had you needed one of them, you would not have known whether it was with you or not, without asking me; you did not even consult the catalogue of your library....

Therefore, my son! Stay not your hand when I have left you, but devote yourself to the study of the Torah and to the science of medicine. But chiefly occupy yourself with the Torah, for you have a wise and understanding heart, and all that is needful on your part is ambition and application. I know that you wilt repent of the past, as many have repented before you of their youthful indolence. . .

Let your countenance shine upon the sons of men; tend their sick and may your advice cure them. Though you take fees from the rich, heal the poor gratuitously; the Lord will requite you. Thereby shall you find favor and good understanding in the sight of God and man. Thus wilt you win the respect of high and low among Jews and nonJews, and your good name will go forth far and wide. You wilt rejoice your friends and make your foes envious. For remember what is written in the *Choice of Pearls* [53:617, of Ibn Gabirol]: "How shall one take vengeance on an enemy? By increasing one's own good qualities."....

My son! Examine regularly, once a week, your drugs and medicinal herbs, and do not employ an ingredient whose properties are unknown to your. I have often impressed this on you in vain....

My son! I command you to honor your wife to your utmost capacity. She is intelligent and modest, a daughter of a distinguished and educated family. She is a good housewife and mother, and no spendthrift. Her tastes are simple, whether in food or dress. Remember her assiduous tendance of you in your illness, though she had been brought up in elegance and luxury. Remember how she afterwards reared your son without man or woman to help her. Were she a hired nurse, she would have earned your esteem and forbearance; how much the more, since she is the wife of your bosom, the daughter of the great, art you bound to treat her with consideration and respect. To act otherwise is the way of the contemptible. The Arab philosopher [probably AlGhazali, 1058–1112] says of women: "None but the honorable honors them, none but the despicable despises them."...

If you would acquire my love, honor her with all your might; do not exercise too severe an authority over her; our Sages [Gittin 6b] have expressly warned men against this. If you give orders or reprove, let your words be gentle. Enough is it if your displeasure is visible in your look; let it not be vented in actual rage. Let your expenditure be well ordered. It is remarked in the *Choice of Pearls* [1: 3] "Expenditure properly managed makes half an income." And there is an olden proverb: "Go to bed without supper and rise without debt." Defile not the honor of your countenance by borrowing; may the Creator save your from that habit! ....

Examine your Hebrew books at every New Moon, the Arabic volumes once in two months, and the bound codices once every quarter. [Arabic and Latin were the languages of science in Spain, the Provence, and southern Italy.] Arrange your library in fair orders so as to avoid wearying yourself in searching for the book you need. Always know the case and the chest where the book should be. A good plan would be to set in each compartment a written list of the books therein contained. If, then, you art looking for a book, you can see from the list the exact shelf it occupies without disarranging all the books in the search for one. Examine those leaves in the volumes and bundles, and preserve them. These fragments contain very important matters which I collected and copied out. Do not destroy any writing or letter of all that I have left. And cast your eye frequently over the catalogue so as to remember what books are in your library.

Never intermit your regular readings with your teacher; study in the college of your master on certain evenings before sitting down to read with the young. Whatever you have learned from me or from your teachers, impart it again regularly to worthy pupils, so that you may retain it, for by teaching it to others you wilt know it by heart, and their questions will compel you to precision, and remove any doubts from your own mind.

Never refuse to lend books to anyone who has not the means to purchase books for himself, but only act thus to those who can be trusted to return the volumes. [Before the invention of printing each book was written by hand and was therefore expensive.]

You know what our sages said in the Talmud, on the text: "Wealth and riches are in his house; and his merit endures forever." [Ketubot 50a applies this verse, Psalm 112: 3, to one who lends his copies of the Bible.] But, [Proverbs 3:27] "Withhold not good from him to whom it is due," [you owe it to your books to protect them] and take particular care of your books. Cover the bookcases with rugs of fine quality, and preserve them from damp and mice, and from all manner of injury, for your books are your good treasure. If you lend a volume, make a memorandum before it leaves your house, and when it is returned, draw your pen over the entry. Every Passover and Tabernacles [that is, every six months] call in all books out on loan.

I enjoin on you, my son, to read this, my testament, once daily, at morn or at eve. Apply your heart to the fulfillment of its behests, and to the performance of all therein written. Then wilt you make your ways prosperous, then shall you have good success.

2. The Testament of Eleazar of Mayence
Germany, about 1357

These are the things which my sons and daughters shall do at my request. They shall go to the house of prayer morning and evening, and shall pay special regard to the *tefillah* [the "Eighteen Benedictions"] and the *shema* [Deuteronomy 6:4]. So soon as the service is over, they shall occupy themselves a little with the Torah [the Pentateuch], the Psalms, or with works of charity. Their business must be conducted honestly, in their dealings both with Jew and Gentile. They must be gentle in their manners and prompt to accede to every honorable request. They must not talk more than is necessary; by this will they be saved from slander, falsehood, and frivolity. They shall give an exact tithe of all their possessions: they shall never turn away a poor man empty-handed, but must give him what they can, be it much or little. If he beg a lodging over night, and they know him not, let them provide him with the wherewithal to pay an innkeeper. Thus shall they satisfy the needs of the poor in every possible way....

If they can by any means contrive it, my sons and daughters should live in communities, and not isolated from other Jews, so that their sons and daughters may learn the ways of Judaism. Even if compelled to solicit from others the money to pay a teacher, they must not let the young of both sexes go without instruction in the Torah. Marry your children, O my sons and daughters, as soon as their age is ripe, to members of respectable families. [Boys of thirteen and girls of twelve were considered ready for marriage.] Let no child of mine hunt after money by making a low match for that object; but if the family is undistinguished only on the mother's side, it does not matter, for all Israel counts descent from the father's side. ...

I earnestly beg my children to be tolerant and humble to all, as I was throughout my life. Should cause for dissension present itself, be slow to accept the quarrel; seek peace and pursue it with all the vigor at your command. Even if you suffer loss thereby, forbear and forgive, for God has many ways of feeding and sustaining His creatures. To the slanderer do not retaliate with counterattack; and though it be proper to rebut false accusations, yet is it most desirable to set an example of reticence. You yourselves must avoid uttering any slander, for so will you win affection. In trade be true, never grasping at what belongs to another. For by avoiding these wrongs—scandal, falsehood, moneygrubbing—men will surely find tranquility and affection. And against all evils, silence is the best safeguard

Be very particular to keep your houses clean and tidy. [These ideas are interesting coming from a man who lived through the Black Death of 1349.] I was always scrupulous on this point, for every injurious condition and sickness and poverty are to be found in foul dwellings. Be careful over the benedictions; accept no divine gift without paying back the Giver's part; and His part is man's grateful acknowledgment. [Pay God for His blessings by blessing Him.]…

On holidays and festivals and Sabbaths seek to make happy the poor, the unfortunate, widows and orphans, who should always be guests at your tables; their joyous entertainment is a religious duty. Let me repeat my warning against gossip and scandal. And as you speak no scandal, so listen to none; for if there were no receivers there would be no bearers of slanderous tales; therefore the reception and credit of slander is as serious an offense as the originating of it. The less you say, the less cause you give for animosity, while [Proverbs 10:19] "in the multitude of words there wants transgression."

I beg of you, my sons and daughters, my wife, and all the congregation, that no funeral oration be spoken in my honor. Do carry my body on a bier, but in a coach. Wash me clean, comb my hair, trim my nails, as I was wont to do in my lifetime, so that I may go clean to my eternal rest, as I went clean to synagogue every Sabbath day. If the ordinary officials dislike the duty, let adequate payment be made to some poor man who shall render this service carefully and not perfunctorily. [The dead were washed by *Hebra Kaddisha*, "Holy Brotherhood."]

At a distance of thirty cubits from the grave, they shall set my coffin on the ground, and drag me to the grave by a rope attached to the coffin. [This is a symbolic punishment to atone for sins committed during one's lifetime and probably to anticipate the punishment of hell, *hibbut ha-keber.*] Every four cubits they shall stand and wait awhile, doing this in all seven times, so that I may find atonement for my sins. Put me in the ground at the right hand of my father, and if the space be a little narrow I am sure that he loves me well enough to make room for me by his side. If this be altogether impossible put me on his left, or near my grandmother, Yura. Should this also be impractical, let me be buried by the side of my daughter.

Jacob Marcus, *The Jew in the Medieval World: A Sourcebook*, 315-1791 [New York: JPS, 1938], pp. 309-316.

Lesson Three

Taking Leave
Our Evolving Relationship with the Departed

Is death painful for the soul? Does the soul of the deceased retain any attachment to this world, to its body, to its loved ones? This lesson discusses the Jewish view on, and some of the traditions associated with, the moment of passing, the preparation of the body for burial, the funeral, interment, and grave visitation. All of these inform us about the nature of the soul's continuing relationship with its life in this world and those that it loves.

JEWISH LEARNING INSTITUTE

Untethered

FIGURE 3.1

Soul Component	Function	Location After Body's Demise
Nefesh נֶפֶשׁ	physical/biological life	the grave
Ru'ach רוּחַ	emotions	*Gan Eden* (Paradise)

Rabbi Shne'ur Zalman of Liadi, *Tanya*, *Igeret Hakodesh*, Epistle 27 📖

כַּנּוֹדַע שֶׁחַיֵּי הַצַּדִּיק אֵינָם חַיִּים בְּשָׂרִים כִּי אִם חַיִּים
רוּחָנִיִּים, שֶׁהֵם אֱמוּנָה וְיִרְאָה וְאַהֲבָה . . .

וְהִנֵּה, בִּהְיוֹת הַצַּדִּיק חַי עַל פְּנֵי הָאֲדָמָה, הָיוּ שְׁלֹשָׁה מִדּוֹת אֵלּוּ בְּתוֹךְ כְּלִי וּלְבוּשׁ
שֶׁלָּהֶם, בִּבְחִינַת מָקוֹם גַּשְׁמִי, שֶׁהִיא בְּחִינַת נֶפֶשׁ הַקְּשׁוּרָה בְּגוּפוֹ. וְכָל תַּלְמִידָיו
אֵינָם מְקַבְּלִים רַק הֶאָרַת מִדּוֹת אֵלּוּ וְזִיוָן הַמֵּאִיר חוּץ לִכְלִי זֶה עַל יְדֵי דִּבּוּרָיו
וּמַחְשְׁבוֹתָיו הַקְּדוֹשִׁים. וְלָכֵן אָמְרוּ רַז"ל, שֶׁאֵין אָדָם עוֹמֵד עַל דַּעַת רַבּוֹ, וְכוּלֵי.

אֲבָל לְאַחַר פְּטִירָתוֹ, לְפִי שֶׁמִּתְפָּרְדִים בְּחִינַת הַנֶּפֶשׁ שֶׁנִּשְׁאֲרָה בְּקֶבֶר מִבְּחִינַת
הָרוּחַ שֶׁבְּגַן עֵדֶן שֶׁהֵן שָׁלֹשׁ מִדּוֹת הַלָּלוּ, לְפִיכָךְ יָכוֹל כָּל הַקָּרוֹב אֵלָיו לְקַבֵּל חֵלֶק
מִבְּחִינַת רוּחוֹ שֶׁבְּגַן עֵדֶן, הוֹאִיל וְאֵינָה בְּתוֹךְ כְּלִי וְלֹא בִּבְחִינַת מָקוֹם גַּשְׁמִי . . .

הִלְכָּךְ נָקֵל מְאֹד לְתַלְמִידָיו לְקַבֵּל חֶלְקָם מִבְּחִינַת רוּחַ רַבָּם הָעַצְמִיִּת, שֶׁהֵם
אֱמוּנָתוֹ וְיִרְאָתוֹ וְאַהֲבָתוֹ אֲשֶׁר עָבַד בָּהֶם אֶת ה', וְלֹא זִיוָם בִּלְבַד הַמֵּאִיר
חוּץ לַכְּלִי . . . כָּל אֶחָד כְּפִי בְּחִינַת הִתְקַשְּׁרוּתוֹ וְקִרְבָתוֹ אֵלָיו בְּחַיָּיו וּבְמוֹתוֹ
בְּאַהֲבָה רַבָּה, כִּי הַמַּמְשִׁיךְ כָּל רוּחָנִיּוּת אֵינָהּ אֶלָּא עַל יְדֵי אַהֲבָה רַבָּה.

As is known, the life of the *tsadik* is not physical but spiritual, and it consists of faith [in] and reverence and love [for God]....

While the *tsadik* is alive on earth, these three attributes, as they are comprised in the soul's *ru'ach* component, inhabit a defined physical space, for they are contained in their "vessel" and "garment"—the *nefesh* that is bound to the body. Consequently, all the *tsadik's* disciples receive but the glow of these attributes, a ray that is emitted from the vessel [i.e., the body] by means of the *tsadik's* holy words and thoughts. [Indeed, because a student can only relate to a reflection of the teacher's attributes, not his essence,] our sages, of blessed memory, said that it takes forty years for a

Rabbi Shne'ur Zalman of Liadi
(Alter Rebbe)
1745–1812

Chasidic rebbe, halachic authority, and founder of the Chabad movement. The Alter Rebbe was born in Liozna, Belarus, and was among the principal students of the Magid of Mezeritch. His numerous works include the *Tanya*, an early classic containing the fundamentals of Chabad Chasidism, and *Shulchan Aruch HaRav*, an expanded and reworked code of Jewish law.

student to fully plumb the depths of his master's teachings (Talmud, Avodah Zarah 5b).

After the *tsadik's* passing, however, the *nefesh* remains in the grave and separates from the *ru'ach* and its three attributes, which are now in *Gan Eden*. Therefore, whoever is close to the *tsadik* can receive directly from his *ru'ach* in *Gan Eden*, because the *ru'ach* is no longer contained in a vessel or confined to a specific physical space. . . .

Therefore, it is very easy for the *tsadik's* disciples to connect with the essence of their master's *ru'ach*—i.e., the faith, awe, and love with which he served God—and not merely a ray thereof, which is emitted beyond the vessel. . . . Each student connects and receives commensurate to his loving connection and closeness to the *tsaddik* during his lifetime and after his death. For the transmission of all things spiritual is always by means of great love.

Text 1b

Ibid., Epistle 28

כְּנוֹדָע, שֶׁכָּל עֲמָל הָאָדָם שֶׁעָמְלָה נַפְשׁוֹ בְּחַיָּיו לְמַעֲלָה בִּבְחִינַת הֶעְלֵם וְהֶסְתֵּר, מִתְגַּלֶּה וּמֵאִיר בִּבְחִינַת גִּילוּי מִלְמַעְלָה לְמַטָּה בְּעֵת פְּטִירָתוֹ.

It is known that all the effort of man that his soul toiled during his lifetime remains above in a hidden and concealed state. It becomes revealed and then radiates in a manifest way from above downwards at the moment of the person's passing.

In Transit

Text 2

Zohar 3:88a

וְלֵית לָה לְנַפְשָׁא קַשְׁיוּ בְּכֹלָּא כִּפְרִישׁוּ דִּילָה מִן גּוּפָא.

Nothing is as hard for the soul as its separation from the body.

Zohar

The seminal work of Kabbalah, Jewish mysticism. The Zohar is a mystical commentary on the Torah, written in Aramaic and Hebrew. According to Arizal, the Zohar contains the teachings of Rabbi Shimon bar Yocha'i who lived in the Land of Israel during the 2nd century. The Zohar has become one of the indispensable texts of traditional Judaism, alongside and nearly equal in stature to the Mishnah and Talmud.

QUESTION FOR DISCUSSION

Why would death be difficult and painful for the soul?

Text 3

Jerusalem Talmud

A commentary to the Mishnah, compiled during the 4th and 5th centuries. The Jerusalem Talmud predates its Babylonian counterpart by 100 years and is written in both Hebrew and Aramaic. While the Babylonian Talmud remains the most authoritative source for Jewish law, the Jerusalem Talmud remains an invaluable source for the spiritual, intellectual, ethical, historical, and legal traditions of Judaism.

Jerusalem Talmud, Mo'ed Katan 3:5 📖

כָּל תְּלָתָא יוֹמִין נַפְשָׁא טַיְיסָא עַל גּוּפָא, סְבִירָה דְּהִיא חָזְרָה לְגַבֵּיה. כֵּיוָן
דְּהִיא חַמְיָא דְּאִישְׁתַּנֵּי זִיוֵיהוֹן דְּאַפּוֹי, הִיא שַׁבְקָא לֵיה וְאָזְלָה לָה.

For three days, the soul hovers above the body, thinking that it can return to it. [After three days,] when it sees that the body's face has changed, it leaves the body and departs.

Text 4a

Zohar 1:218b–219a 📖

כָּל ז' יוֹמִין, נִשְׁמָתָא אָזְלָא מִבֵּיתֵיה לְקִבְרֵיה וּמִקִּבְרֵיה לְבֵיתֵיה וְאִתְאַבְּלַת עֲלוֹי
דְּגוּפָא . . . בָּתַר ז' יוֹמִין גּוּפָא הֲוֵי כְּמָה דַּהֲוָה, וְנִשְׁמָתֵיה עָאלַת לְדוּכְתָּא.

For seven days, the soul goes from the house where it lived to the grave, and from the grave back to the house, and mourns its body. . . . After seven days, the body is subjected to that which it is subjected, and the soul ascends to its place.

Text 4b

Zohar 2:199b

כָּל אִינוּן תְּלָתִין יוֹמִין, אִתְדָּנוּ נַפְשָׁא וְגוּפָא כְּחֲדָא, וּבְגִינֵי כַּךְ, אִשְׁתְּכַח נִשְׁמָתָא לְתַתָּא בְּאַרְעָא. . . . לְבָתַר, נִשְׁמָתָא סַלְקָא וְגוּפָא אִתְבְּלֵי בְּאַרְעָא.

For thirty days, the soul and the body are judged as one, and thus the soul is found below. . . . After that, the soul departs and the body erodes in the earth.

Text 4c

Talmud, Shabbat 152b–153a

כָּל שְׁנֵים עָשָׂר חֹדֶשׁ גּוּפוֹ קַיָּים, וְנִשְׁמָתוֹ עוֹלָה וְיוֹרֶדֶת. לְאַחַר שְׁנֵים עָשָׂר חֹדֶשׁ הַגּוּף בָּטֵל, וְנִשְׁמָתוֹ עוֹלָה, וְשׁוּב אֵינָהּ יוֹרֶדֶת.

For twelve months, the body still exists and the soul ascends and descends; after twelve months, the body becomes null and the soul rises and does not return.

Babylonian Talmud

A literary work of monumental proportions that draws upon the legal, spiritual, intellectual, ethical, and historical traditions of Judaism. The 37 tractates of the Babylonian Talmud contain the teachings of the Jewish sages from the period after the destruction of the 2nd Temple through the 5th century CE. It has served as the primary vehicle for the transmission of the Oral Law and the education of Jews over the centuries; it is the entry point for all subsequent legal, ethical, and theological Jewish scholarship.

Nefhesh = Componet of body
Reuhah — Componet of Soul — Released After death

Text 5

Maimonides, *Mishneh Torah*, Laws of Mourning 13:11

שְׁלֹשָׁה לִבְכִי, שִׁבְעָה לְהֶסְפֵּד, שְׁלֹשִׁים יוֹם לְתִסְפּוֹרֶת וְלִשְׁאָר הַחֲמִשָּׁה דְּבָרִים.

Three days for weeping, seven days for eulogies, and thirty days for observing the restrictions on haircuts and the other five matters.

Rabbi Moshe ben Maimon
(Maimonides, Rambam)
1135–1204

Halachist, philosopher, author, and physician. Maimonides was born in Cordoba, Spain. After the conquest of Cordoba by the Almohads, he fled Spain and eventually settled in Cairo, Egypt. There, he became the leader of the Jewish community and served as court physician to the vizier of Egypt. He is most noted for authoring the *Mishneh Torah*, an encyclopedic arrangement of Jewish law, and for his philosophical work, *Guide for the Perplexed*. His rulings on Jewish law are integral to the formation of halachic consensus.

Text 6

Talmud, Shabbat 152a–b

מֵת שֶׁאֵין לוֹ מְנַחֲמִין, הוֹלְכִין עֲשָׂרָה בְּנֵי אָדָם וְיוֹשְׁבִין בִּמְקוֹמוֹ.

הַהוּא דְּשָׁכִיב בְּשִׁבְבוּתֵיהּ דְּרַב יְהוּדָה, לֹא הָיוּ לוֹ מְנַחֲמִין. כָּל יוֹמָא, הֲוָה דְּבַר רַב יְהוּדָה בֵּי עֲשָׂרָה וְיָתְבֵי בְּדוּכְתֵּיהּ. לְאַחַר שִׁבְעָה יָמִים אִיתְחֲזֵי לֵיהּ בְּחֶילְמֵיהּ דְּרַב יְהוּדָה וְאָמַר לֵיהּ, "תָּנוּחַ דַּעְתָּךְ שֶׁהִנַּחְתָּ אֶת דַּעְתִּי".

If a person dies and leaves no [next of kin] to be comforted, ten people go and sit in his home.

A man died in Rabbi Yehudah's neighborhood. As there were no [mourners] to be comforted, Rabbi Yehudah assembled ten people every day and they sat in the deceased's home. After seven days, the dead man appeared to Rabbi Yehudah in a dream and said, "Let your mind be at rest, for you have set my mind at rest."

Torah requires us to return to dust
Mitzvot requires us to heed the wishes of the deceased

Bodily Affairs
Final Rites

Text 7a

Talmud, Mo'ed Katan 25a

הָעוֹמֵד עַל הַמֵּת בִּשְׁעַת יְצִיאַת נִשְׁמָה חַיָּיב לִקְרוֹעַ,
הָא לְמָה זֶה דוֹמֶה? לְסֵפֶר תּוֹרָה שֶׁנִּשְׂרָף.

One who is present at the time of a person's passing is required to tear his clothing. This is because [a person's passing] is likened to the burning of a Torah scroll.

Is our body ours to determine possession
No — it belongs to hashim
Tattoes are in the same category

Text 7b

Rabbi Yom Tov ben Avraham Asevilli, *Chidushei HaRitva*, ad loc.

וְהָרַמְבַּ"ן ז"ל פֵּירֵשׁ, שֶׁהַנֶּפֶשׁ בַּגּוּף כְּאַזְכָּרוֹת בִּגְוִילִין.

Nachmanides, of blessed memory, explains that the soul in the body is like the names of God inscribed on the parchment of a Torah scroll.

Rabbi Yomtov Asevilli (Ritva)
ca. 1250–1330

Spanish rabbi and Talmudist. Ritva was born in Seville. He is mostly known for his Talmudic commentary, which is extremely clear, and to this day, remains most frequently quoted and used.

Cremation denies the body to return to hashim in the way the Torah designates

Text 8

Rabbi Yechiel Michel Tucazinsky, *Gesher Hachayim* 5:1 📖

Rabbi Yechiel Michel Tukachinsky
1874–1955

Halachist. Rabbi Tukachinsky was born in Lithuania. In 1882, his family settled in Israel. He studied in the Ets Chaim Yeshivah, where he eventually became the dean. He published many books and articles on halachic issues, including *Hayomom Bikadur Ha'aretz*, an effort to locate the halachic dateline. His most famous work is *Gesher Hachayim*, a classic treatise on the laws of burial and mourning that examines life as a bridge between past and future.

כָּל מִתְעַסֵּק בְּמֵת צָרִיךְ לָדַעַת שֶׁיֵּשׁ לוֹ עֵסֶק עִם דָּבָר קָדוֹשׁ: גּוּפוֹ שֶׁל אָדָם הוּא לֹא רַק נַרְתֵּיק שֶׁל קְדוּשָּׁה שֶׁשָּׁמֵּשׁ לַנְּשָׁמָה הָעֶלְיוֹנָה, אֶלָּא שֶׁהוּא עַצְמוֹ נִתְקַדֵּשׁ גַּם בִּקְדוּשָּׁה עַצְמִית, בְּדוֹמֶה לְסֵפֶר תּוֹרָה.

All who handle the dead must be aware that they are involved with a holy entity. The human body is not only the "container" that served the exalted soul, but has itself become sanctified with an independent holiness, similar to a Torah scroll.

Text 9

Ibid., 5:4 📖

שְׁמִירַת הַמֵּת הִיא . . . מִשּׁוּם כְּבוֹדוֹ. שֶׁאִם יַנִּיחוּהוּ לְבַדּוֹ הֲרֵי זֶה כְּאִלּוּ עֲזָבוּהוּ כִּכְלִי אֵין חֵפֶץ עוֹד בּוֹ.

We maintain a watch over the dead . . . out of respect. For if we were to leave the body alone, it would appear as if we abandoned it like a utensil that we no longer desire.

Text 10

Rabbi Moshe Sofer, *Responsa Chatam Sofer, Yoreh De'ah* 353 📖

אֵין חִילוּק בֵּין סֵפֶר תּוֹרָה שָׁלֵם לְאוֹת אַחַת מִמֶּנּוּ, וְהוּא הַדִּין נַמֵּי עֶצֶם
מֵעַצְמוֹת הַקְּדוֹשִׁים שֶׁנִּבְרְאוּ בְּצֶלֶם אֱלֹקִים, אָסוּר לִנְהוֹג בָּהֶם מִנְהַג בִּזָּיוֹן.

Just as there is no difference between a complete Torah scroll and one letter from a Torah scroll [as both must be treated with utmost respect], it is forbidden to accord disrespect to even a single bone from sacred bodies that were created in God's image.

Rabbi Moshe Sofer
(*Chatam Sofer*)
1762–1839

A leading rabbinical authority of the 19th century. Born in Frankfurt am Main, *Chatam Sofer* ultimately accepted the rabbinate of Pressburg (now Bratislava), Slovakia. Serving as rabbi and head of the yeshivah that he established, Rabbi Sofer maintained a strong traditionalist perspective, opposing deviation from Jewish tradition. *Chatam Sofer* is the title of his collection of halachic responsa and his commentary to the Talmud.

Burial

Text 11

Ecclesiastes 12:5-7 📖

כִּי הֹלֵךְ הָאָדָם אֶל בֵּית עוֹלָמוֹ, וְסָבְבוּ בַשּׁוּק הַסֹּפְדִים . . .

וְיָשֹׁב הֶעָפָר עַל הָאָרֶץ כְּשֶׁהָיָה, וְהָרוּחַ תָּשׁוּב אֶל הָאֱלֹקִים אֲשֶׁר נְתָנָהּ.

Man goes to his everlasting home, and the mourners go about in the street. . . .

And the dust returns to the earth as it was, and the spirit returns to God Who gave it.

Text 12

Rabbi Chaim Vital, *Ets Hada'at Tov* 358 (Jerusalem 2008, edition) 🕮

Rabbi Chaim Vital
ca. 1542–1620

Lurianic Kabbalist. Rabbi Vital was born in Israel, lived in Safed and Jerusalem, and later in Damascus. He was authorized by his teacher, Rabbi Yitschak Luria, the Arizal, to record his teachings. Acting on this mandate, Vital began arranging his master's teachings in written form, and his many works constitute the foundation of the Lurianic school of Jewish mysticism. His most famous work is *Ets Chaim*.

"כִּי עָפָר אַתָּה וְאֶל עָפָר תָּשׁוּב" (בְּרֵאשִׁית ג, יט). כִּי גוּף הָאָדָם מִן הֶעָפָר הָיָה, וְדֶרֶךְ פִּקָדוֹן הוּפְקַד בְּיַד הָאָדָם. וּכְשֶׁמֵּת צָרִיךְ לְהַחְזִיר הַפִּקָדוֹן אֶל הֶעָפָר אֲשֶׁר מִמֶּנּוּ לוּקַח וּלְקוֹבְרוֹ.

"For dust you are, and to dust you will return" (Genesis 3:19). Man's body comes from the earth and is left with him as a deposit. Upon death, the deposit must be returned to the earth from where it came.

Text 13

Ruth 1:16–17 🕮

וַתֹּאמֶר רוּת: אַל תִּפְגְּעִי בִי לְעָזְבֵךְ לָשׁוּב מֵאַחֲרָיִךְ.

כִּי אֶל אֲשֶׁר תֵּלְכִי אֵלֵךְ, וּבַאֲשֶׁר תָּלִינִי אָלִין. עַמֵּךְ עַמִּי, וֵאלֹקַיִךְ אֱלֹקָי.

בַּאֲשֶׁר תָּמוּתִי אָמוּת, וְשָׁם אֶקָּבֵר.

Ruth responded, "Do not press me to leave you, to return [to Moab] rather than follow you.

"For wherever you go, I will go. Wherever you lodge, I will lodge. Your people shall be my people, and your God my God.

"Where you die, I will die, and there I will be buried."

Text 14

Deuteronomy 21:23

כִּי קָבוֹר תִּקְבְּרֶנּוּ בַּיּוֹם הַהוּא.

You shall surely bury him on the same day.

Text 15a

Talmud, Ta'anit 21a

מִצְוָה לְקַיֵּם דִּבְרֵי הַמֵּת.

It is a mitzvah to uphold the wishes of the deceased.

ARTICLE I: Funeral expenses & payment of debt

Text 15b

Maimonides, *Mishneh Torah*, Laws of Mourning 12:1

אֲבָל אִם צִוָּה שֶׁלֹּא יִקָּבֵר אֵין שׁוֹמְעִין לוֹ, שֶׁהַקְּבוּרָה מִצְוָה, שֶׁנֶּאֱמַר, "כִּי קָבוֹר תִּקְבְּרֶנּוּ".

If a person requested not to be buried, we disregard the request. This is because burial is a mitzvah, as it says (Deuteronomy 21:23), "You shall surely bury him."

Body on Loan

Text 16

Leviticus 19:28

וּכְתֹבֶת קַעֲקַע לֹא תִתְּנוּ בָּכֶם.

Do not place a tattoo on your bodies.

Grave Visitation

Text 17

Zohar 2:141b

נֶפֶשׁ דָּא אִשְׁתַּכְּחַת גּוֹ קִבְרָא . . . לְאִשְׁתַּכְּחָא גּוֹ חַיָּיא וּלְמִנְדַע
בְּצַעֲרָא דִלְהוֹן, וּבְשַׁעֲתָּא דִי אִצְטְרִיכוּ, בָּעֵאת רַחֲמֵי עֲלַיְיהוּ . . .

וְכַד אִצְטְרִיךְ לִבְנֵי עָלְמָא, כַּד אִינּוּן בְּצַעֲרָא וְאָזְלֵי לְבֵי קִבְרֵי, הַאי נֶפֶשׁ אִתְעֲרַת וְאִיהִי
אָזְלָא וּמְשַׁטְּטָא וְאִתְעֲרַת לְרוּחַ . . . וּכְדֵין קוּדְשָׁא בְּרִיךְ הוּא חַיִּיס עַל עָלְמָא.

The *nefesh* is present in the grave. . . . It is among the living and is acquainted with their pain. At a time of need, it pleads for mercy for them . . . .

When the inhabitants of the world are in need, when they are in sorrow and they go to the cemetery, the *nefesh* is awakened. It flies up and arouses the *ru'ach* [which, in turn, entreats God for mercy]. . . . The Holy One, blessed be He, then has mercy on the world.

Text 18

Rabbi Yehudah ben Shmuel of Regensburg, *Sefer Chasidim* 709–710 📖

קָהָל אֶחָד רָצוּ לָלֶכֶת לְמָקוֹם אֶחָד. בָּא מֵת לְאֶחָד בַּחֲלוֹם, וְאָמַר, "אַל תַּעַזְבוּ אוֹתָנוּ, כִּי יֵשׁ לָנוּ הֲנָאָה כְּשֶׁתֵּלְכוּ לְבֵית הַקְּבָרוֹת" . . .

בַּרְזִלַּי הַגִּלְעָדִי אָמַר (שְׁמוּאֵל ב, יט, לח) "אָמוּת בְּעִירִי". כִּי הֲנָאָה יֵשׁ לַמֵּתִים שֶׁאוֹהֲבִים הוֹלְכִים עַל קִבְרֵיהֶם וּמְבַקְשִׁים לְנִשְׁמָתָן טוֹבָה, מְטִיבִים לָהֶם בְּאוֹתוֹ עִנְיָן. וְגַם כְּשֶׁמְּבַקְשִׁים עֲלֵיהֶם, הֵם מִתְפַּלְּלִים עַל הַחַיִּים.

Rabbi Yehudah ben Shmuel Hachasid
1140–1217

Mystic and ethicist. Born in Speyer, Germany, he was a rabbi, mystic, and one of the initiators of Chasidei Ashkenaz, a Jewish German moralist movement that stressed piety and asceticism. Rabbi Yehudah settled in Regensburg in 1195. He is best known for his work Sefer Chasidim, on the ethics of day-to-day concerns.

There was once a community that wished to uproot and move to a different location. One of the deceased [of that community] appeared in a dream to a member of the community and said, "Please do not leave us, for we take pleasure when you visit the cemetery." . . .

Barzilai the Giladite said, "I would like to die in my own city" (II Samuel 19:38). He said this because the dead are delighted when we, their loved ones, visit their gravesites and request goodness for their souls; this improves their condition in heaven. And when we make requests, the departed pray for us.

Conclusion

Text 19

The Rebbe, Rabbi Menachem M. Schneerson,
Correspondence, 29 Sivan, 5718 [June 17, 1958] ▐▌

Blessing and Greeting:

I received your undated letters, in which you write about your emotional upsets in connection with the passing of your mother, and the questions which are troubling you in this connection, involving also questions in regard to the passing of your father, peace unto them. . . .

Another fundamental point to remember, which has a direct bearing on your letter, is that all believers in G-d believe also in the survival of the soul. Actually, this principle has even been discovered in this physical world, where science now holds, as an absolute truth, that nothing in the physical world can be absolutely destroyed. How much more so in the spiritual world, especially in the case of the soul, which, in no way, can be affected by the death and disintegration of the physical body. It would be silly and illogical to assume that, because a certain organ of the body ceases to function, affecting other physical organs of the body, the spiritual soul would also be affected thereby. The truth is that when the physical body ceases to function, the soul continues its existence, not only as before, but even on a higher level, inasmuch as it is no longer handicapped by the restraints of the physical frame.

Thirdly, the attachment of children to their parents, and the general attachment between close relatives during life

Rabbi Menachem Mendel Schneerson
1902–1994

The towering Jewish leader of the 20th century, known as "the Lubavitcher Rebbe," or simply as "the Rebbe." Born in southern Ukraine, the Rebbe escaped Nazi-occupied Europe, arriving in the U.S. in June 1941. The Rebbe inspired and guided the revival of traditional Judaism after the European devastation, impacting virtually every Jewish community the world over. The Rebbe often emphasized that the performance of just one additional good deed could usher in the era of Mashiach. The Rebbe's scholarly talks and writings have been printed in more than 200 volumes.

on this earth, is surely not a physical attachment by the respective physical bodies of the relatives. Essentially, the attachment is a spiritual one, due to the spiritual affinity between those concerned, and the qualities of the soul, including such spiritual things as character, kindness, goodness, etc., all of which are attributes of the soul, and not of the body. Therefore, also, every action on the part of a person in relation to a beloved person, and the desire to benefit that person, is not directed towards pleasing his physical body, his bones and tissue, for it is the spiritual pleasure that one is concerned with.

In view of the above, it is clear that even after the physical body has disintegrated and disappeared from view, it is still possible to bring joy and benefit to the soul, which, as noted above, not only survives, but does so on a higher level, and all the things which had previously brought joy and pleasure to one's parents, will continue to do so even after they are physically no longer here.

LEARNING EXERCISE

(a) Write down the point from today's lesson that resonated with you most.

_____

_____

_____

(b) Is there a deceased person with whom you wish to strengthen your bond of love? What step will you take to do so?

_____

_____

_____

Key Points

This lesson explored our continuing relationship with the deceased, burial, and grave visitation.

Continue your learning experience ONLINE

Visit www.myJLI.com/journey3

for insightful and inspiring videos, articles, and readings on these topics.

1. *Nefesh* and *ru'ach* are two of the soul's components. *Nefesh* powers physical life, while *ru'ach* drives ambitions, emotions, and feelings. After death, the *nefesh* remains with the body, while the *ru'ach* disengages and goes to *Gan Eden* (Paradise).

2. Once the *ru'ach* is no longer limited to material existence, it is accessible to all who wish to connect to it. Thus, when a person dies, our ability to spiritually connect with him or her is stronger and deeper than before.

3. Though the *nefesh* remains in the grave, it retains a connection with the higher levels of the soul. The gravesite is thus a port where we can commune with the departed souls and ask them to intercede before God on our behalf.

4. Over the course of a lifetime, the soul and body integrate and bond; their separation at death is therefore painful for the soul.

5. The soul departs the body in stages. These stages correspond to the prescribed periods of mourning. When we mourn, we are mourning not only for the deceased, but also *with* the deceased.

6. Dignity and sensitivity are the underlying principles that guide the care of a corpse and its preparation for burial. This is because even after death, the body retains its special status of having been the container for the soul.

7. Burial is of highest priority in Jewish tradition and culture. When God takes a person's soul, we are tasked to return it to the place from which God fashioned it.

8. Burial affirms two fundamental Jewish beliefs: (a) our bodies aren't ours—they belong to God; (b) there will be a resurrection of the dead in the Messianic era.

9. Cremation makes it impossible to fulfill the mitzvah of burial. Cremation is also a rejection of the holiness of the body, God's ownership of the body, and the belief in resurrection.

ADDITIONAL READINGS

SHE IS PURE

BY MIRIAM KARP

The years went on, the kids started to grow up. We gave away our last few disposable diapers, at long last. What a different phase, in so many ways. Little kids, little problems; big kids, big problems, the saying goes. It's true that as the children grew into more complex beings, their issues couldn't be solved with a lollypop and a kiss. I did miss the dizzy, delicious baby-on-the-hip days, much as it was a blur and hard to even believe that it had all transpired. But we savored and enjoyed the richness of our emerging people.

Finally, all the kids were in school—all day. I had time to branch out in new directions. A good friend regularly performed the *mitzvah* of *tahara*/purification, preparing a Jewish body for burial. I'd wanted to try this important task, but kept putting it off for… later. This wasn't one of the mitzvos that all observant people did such as keeping kosher, Shabbos, eating matzah on Passover, and so on. It was extra, voluntary—a *mitzvah* usually handled by more mature women, because of their freer schedules, and probably also because of their said maturity. As I rounded the corner on fifty, mortality wasn't a far off abstract notion that had little to do with me. My mom was struggling with dementia and decline. I had lost some close friends. So when Tamar asked if I might be willing to try this practice out, I gulped and hesitantly said yes.

"Good," she said briskly. "Malka told me you were thinking about it. The first time you mostly just watch, and the women will help guide you. How 'bout tomorrow morning? We need a fourth. Na'ama will pick up you up at 9:00. Okay?"

"Sure," I answered, sounding more confident than I was. Early the next morning, Na'ama honked right on time. She took side-roads for our half-hour trip,

avoiding rush hour traffic. We pulled into the funeral home parking lot, going around to the back. Na'ama punched the code to the rear door, and we entered the quiet building. Several empty caskets were in the hallway. I followed the women into a utilitarian room, with a cupboard, sinks, and a concrete floor. We washed our hands, put on plastic aprons and latex gloves. They examined the name of the deceased, left on a piece of paper on the counter. I recognized it—I had visited her several times during her month of decline and knew her somewhat. Would it be easier or harder to do this on someone I had known?

There was no time to think. Ruth opened the heavy door of the walk-in refrigerated room that adjoined our work room. We entered. Two *meisim*/newly deceased lay in that chilly room, covered with sheets. I recognized Rachel's bulky shape.

Suddenly, everyone else faded into the background. I was only aware of her and me.

I took a deep breath and followed the three women. They wheeled Rachel into the preparation room. I followed, a bit nervously.

I had been touched and intrigued when I first heard about this ritual, back in the early days of Chassidic immersion. Soon enough, Yankel and I were busily pouring all our energies into building a Jewish homestead. I was focused on pregnancies and nursing—busy with the kids and their constant needs. I was nurturing life, not yet physically or emotionally ready to deal with its end.

But now, I felt more or less ready, and somewhat obligated to try. Obligated because purifying the deceased was a sacred ritual, performed with care by

Jews all over the world. Some unknown *tahara* team had done it for my grandparents and in-laws, *alehem hashalom.* In our small community, we all shared the joys and responsibilities of Torah life, and every set of willing hands counted.

Alehem hashalom, may they rest in peace. According to Jewish law and tradition, the living helped the soul get ready to rest in peace, by preparing its earthly home—the body—with well-defined rituals of cleansing and dressing in simple shrouds.

These rituals were done with the utmost dignity, privacy, and respect. Rather than making an attractive façade for the funeral, they focused on purity and simplicity, each step suffused with deep Kabbalistic meaning.

I knew all this. In my head. But I still wasn't sure, could I really do it?

To be honest, I wasn't here just for altruistic reasons, beautiful and compelling as they were. Helping the dead was called *Chesed Shel Emes*—true kindness: you gave with no possibility of being paid back. I had my own reasons, beyond noble acts and shouldering my share of community responsibility; I wanted to expand my spiritual horizons.

Maybe I'd hone in on the real essence, become a truer wife and mother, waste less energy on trivialities; swallow and internalize a greater appreciation for the gift of life. Less kvetching even. Perhaps this encounter with mortality would make me a more sensitive artist and writer.

I was now a reputedly respectable figure, a rabbi's wife and Jewish educator busily mining the treasures of Jewish mysticism and living. Every now and then, I still longed for those *wow man* really intense experiences, like *far out—awesome—extreme;* albeit in a Jewish way. Surely helping a soul and its body in this transition would meet the bill. The burial committee was traditionally called the *Chevra Kadisha*—the holy society. With a name like that, I reckoned, they must be privy to some deep, mysterious truths.

The *tahara* turned out to be like most of Jewish life, where searching for rarified or transcendent "Spirituality" wasn't exactly it—was kind of off the mark.

Was it profound, quiet, hushed; *Spiritual?* Yes—and no.

The *tahara* was surprisingly prosaic. Earthy. Even ordinary. Na'ama, the group leader, a brisk and efficient woman, helped dispel my initial discomfort by referring to Rachel as "her." "Move her over here," she instructed. "Hold up her head."

There was nothing macabre about the scene, though my subconscious offered up images from different horror movies, accompanied by a Gothic organ's pitched tone. It wasn't a staged "religious service," with the choir marching quietly in perfect formation. We were about to help a real woman, a she, a person. We had a job to do.

Watching my experienced partners' faces, for a cue in this new universe, I felt both humbled and relieved: humbled by their ability to just step up, assess the situation, and figure out the best way to proceed, with earnest and every day kind of caring. Relieved to see them show signs of compassion, even distress, at some of the bodily signs of the suffering Rachel must have endured these last few months. It was hard for them too. But they each took a breath and continued.

The first glance at her was hard. The first touch was hard.

The other women started washing Rachel with washcloths, keeping as much of her face and body covered as possible at any one moment, respecting her privacy, even now. Initially I stood back, watching with hands folded. I knew it would be best to jump right in, so as they turned Rachel to wash her back, I reached out tentatively and held her hand to keep it from flopping over.

The words dead weight and rigor mortis echoed through my mind. Rachel's hand was cold, heavy, and stiff. I imagined holding a living hand that had the pulse of life flowing through it. This was different.

I helped more and more, as we proceeded, following my friends' spoken and intuited guidance. As we gently washed her body, a body that had lived and loved and borne children, it seemed almost like bathing an infant, with its total dependence, as we hovered protectively around.

Trying to talk only as necessary, we gave each other instructions in subdued, focused voices. The quiet was punctuated by coughs, sighs, the sound of water filling the buckets, the snap of latex gloves.

We took off whatever bandages we could, along with other substances that would block the purifying water, so it could cover her as completely as possible. Removing her frosted pink nail polish was like stripping away her earthly life. I imagined a kind nurse or grandchild sitting patiently with Rachel and applying this reassuring slick coat of certainty and vanity on her worn, fading hand.

That was all behind her now.

In a non-broken sequence, Na'ama, Ruth, and Malka poured cascading buckets of water from the *mikveh/* ritual bath from her head to toe. "*Tahara hee*—she is pure," they intoned. Over and over in almost a chant—rhythmically, asserting, defining. The sound of the water splashing against the metal table accenting the words.

Pausing at several points, Na'ama murmured several prayers and parts of Psalms, the familiar sounds of the ancient Hebrew washing over Rachel and clothing her in a cocoon of comfort. We listened, understanding the intent, even if we couldn't translate each word. Our wishes for this woman cushioned and cloaked her as well.

Then, we gently patted her dry. Ruth brushed her hair. I watched the wet grey-white hair spring into soft, fine curls. This tender act was touching, like giving a small child that final mother's touch.

Working together, we dressed Rachel in *tachrichim,* simple white linen garments: tunic, pants, gown, bonnet—each put on and tied in a special way.

We gently lowered her into the unadorned wooden casket. Fulfilling the Biblical declaration, "from the dust you came, to the dust you shall return," holes were drilled in the bottom of the casket, allowing the body contact with the dust of the earth.

Na'ama placed a shard of pottery on each of Rachel's eyes and on her mouth, symbolizing human frailty. Golden sand from the land of Israel was lightly sprinkled over her. We covered Rachel's face with a piece of the linen, and asked her to forgive us for any rough or disrespectful handling. We wished her a speedy journey to *Olam HaBah*—the world to come.

Lifting the heavy casket cover and positioning it onto its fastening pegs felt like an act of finality. Ruth opened the door to the refrigerated room. The whoosh and blast of cold air was startling, breaking the meditative mood. We wheeled Rachel inside, where she would wait for the next step of her voyage.

Stepping out of that quiet, windowless room into daylight, time, and schedules, we collected our purses and cell phones, and stepped back into our day; a sunny summer one.

The casual chatter on the drive home seemed strange after such intensity. But I soon relaxed, realizing the conversation offered a soothing transition. What we had shared did not really need to be put into words. Easing back to daily reality, I drew a blank when Malka asked me, "So, how was it for you?" I had to stop and think. How was what? Oh yeah. I just did a *tahara.* "It was okay," I said with a quiet smile, downplaying my inner relief that I'd made it through, which melded together with my sense of accomplishment.

I felt buoyed throughout the day. Catching up on the phone with Devora Leah, now a new mother, I told her, "I did my first *tahara.*"

She gasped. "Really?"

But, it wasn't a gasp type thing, not of horror, and not of an *Oh wow* mystical high. It was an ordinary, extraordinary thing to do.

Rachel's image flittered though my mind once or twice. Not morbid. Just an image of a friend I was glad to have helped.

Early Thursday, I awoke and remembered her. I said *Modeh Ani,* expressing thanks for the new day. No rote recital this time; I really felt it.

Rachel was in her place in G-d's universe—stripped down to her essence, purified of her worldly concerns. And I was thankful to be in mine: unfinished business, chaos, imperfection, and all.

WHY DOES JEWISH LAW FORBID CREMATION?

BY RABBI NAFTALI SILBERBERG

Question:

I'm in the process of making arrangements for my final resting place. In my family, some of my relatives have opted for a traditional Jewish burial, while others have chosen the route of cremation. While researching my options, I've discovered that Judaism is vehemently opposed to cremation. Can you please explain to me the origins and reasons for this stance?

Answer:

Before I respond to your question regarding the background of the Jewish prohibition against cremation, allow me to make some prefatory remarks:

In order to help clarify some of the issues, I am choosing to explain the topic "as is," i.e., as they appear in the "Big Books." Commenting on the particulars of one's experience may need additional questions clarified and is often best done in person with a rabbi more familiar with the particular person or family.

Thus, if anything that I will write will come across as insensitive, I beg your forgiveness in advance. That is clearly not my intention.

The laws I will attempt to present here are a distillation of rabbinic writings over the years. In terms of some of the deeper reflection on the human body and its role that I hope to provide—that is distilled from deep Chabad discourses, though I can hardly assert that my distillation of this lofty concept is categorically correct.

Jewish law ("Halachah") is unequivocal that the dead must be buried in the earth.[1]

As a deterrent measure,[2] cremated remains are not interred in a Jewish cemetery.[3] Furthermore, we are told that many of the traditional laws of mourning are not observed after the passing of an individual whose body was cremated.[4] *Kaddish,* however, is recited for such individuals, and it is certainly appropriate to give charity and do *mitzvot* in memory of their souls.[5]

Responsibility for the deceased's proper burial lies with the next of kin.[6] While ordinarily Jewish law requires the deceased's children to go to great lengths to respect the departed's wishes,[7] if someone requests to be cremated or buried in a manner which is not in accordance with Jewish tradition, we nevertheless

---

[1] Code of Jewish Law, Yorah Deah 348:3; 362:1.

[2] The rabbinic responsibility to institute ordinances to deter people from violating Biblical commands is referenced in Mishna, Avot 1:1; Talmud Yevamot 21a, based on Leviticus 18:30.

[3] Melamed L'hoil Vol 2 #114 (Responsa of Rabbi David Hoffman, 1843–1921, noted German authority on Jewish law). Whether or not there is an obligation to bury the ashes elsewhere, in order to prevent further disgrace, is the subject of dispute between halachic authorities.

[4] This is based on the principle (quoted in the Code of Jewish Law, Yoreh De'ah 345:5) that we do not mourn after individuals who have "strayed from the ways of the community" (Responsa Minchat Elazar, vol. 2 ch. 34).

[5] Chatam Sofer Responsa (by Rabbi Moses Sofer, 1762–1839, famed rabbi of Pressburg, Slovakia), vol. 3 (Even Ha'ezer 1) ch. 69.

[6] Code of Jewish Law, Yoreh Deah 348:2.

[7] E.g. Code of Jewish Law, Yoreh Deah 349:2.

provide him/her with a Jewish burial.[8] It is believed that since the soul has now arrived to the World of Truth, it surely sees the value of a proper Jewish burial, and thus administering a traditional Jewish burial is actually granting what the person truly wishes at the moment. Furthermore, if anyone, all the more so your father and mother, asks you to damage or hurt their body, you are not allowed to do so. For our bodies do not belong to us, they belong to G-d.

[It is important to note that according to Jewish law, a person is only held accountable for his/her actions when they are done willingly, and with full cognizance of their implications.[9] Therefore, all the above does not apply to an individual who was cremated against his will. After the Holocaust, many conscientious Jews gathered ashes from the extermination camp crematoria and respectfully buried them in Jewish cemeteries. Recently, too, I heard of an instance where a hospital mistakenly cremated a Jewish body. With rabbinic sanction the ashes were put into a coffin and given a proper Jewish burial.

Furthermore, an individual who was raised in a non-religious atmosphere and was never accorded a proper Jewish education cannot be held responsible for his or her lack of observance.[10] This general rule applies to individuals who opt to be cremated because their education and upbringing did not equip them with the knowledge necessary to make an informed choice in this area. This assumption impacts some of the legal results presented above.]

The Biblical Commandment

Man's soul comes from Above, "He breathed into his nostrils the soul of life,"[11] and when its earthly mission has been accomplished it rises back to G-d, returning to its source.

The body, on the other hand, was taken from the ground—"the L-rd G-d formed man of dust from the ground"[12]—and must therefore return to the earth. This is expressed in the words that G-d tells Adam, the first man,[13] "For dust you are, and to dust you will return."

This concept is reiterated in Deuteronomy,[14] where we are commanded to bury the dead: "You shall bury him on that day." The Jerusalem Talmud[15] explains that this requires us to bury the body in its entirety, not after it has been diminished through cremation or in any other manner: "You must bury him in entirety, not partially. From this verse we extrapolate that the command was not fulfilled if the person was partially buried."

Cremating a body destroys most of the body, making burial of the flesh impossible, and thus violates the biblical command.

Our Responsibilities Vis-à-Vis the Human Body

In Jewish law, the human body belongs to its Creator. It is merely on loan to the person, who is the guardian of the body, but he or she has no right to deface it in any way.[16] The body must be "returned" in its entirety, just as it was given.[17]

Additionally, Man was created in "G-d's image and likeness."[18] Any violation of the human body is considered, therefore, to be a violation of G-d Himself.[19]

This general principle and law governs many of our laws, like those prohibiting self-mutilation[20] or tattoos,[21] and requiring us to do our utmost to keep ourselves from danger by maintaining proper hy-

---

8 Code of Jewish Law, Yoreh Deah 348:3 (See Jerusalem Talmud Ketubot 11:1).

9 Talmud Nedarim 27a; Bava Kamma 28b; Avodah Zarah 54a; deduced from Deuteronomy 22:26.

10 Talmud Shabbat 68b; Maimonides, Laws of Mamrim 3:3.

11 Genesis 2:7.

12 Ibid.

13 Genesis 3:19. This is also the reason why Jewish law advocates the use of a wooden casket, which will fully disintegrate.

14 21:23.

15 Nazir 7:1.

16 See Maimonides, Laws of Murder 1:4; Ridvaz, Laws of Sanhedrin 18; Shulchan Aruch Harav (by Rabbi Schneur Zalman of Liadi) Laws of Body Damages 4.

17 Adapted from a letter by the Lubavitcher Rebbe, of righteous memory, dated 26 Nissan 5729 (1969).

18 Genesis 1:27.

19 See Genesis 9:6.

20 Deuteronomy 14:1.

21 Leviticus 19:28.

giene and the like.[22] This principle applies after death, too; any mutilation of the dead is prohibited.[23]

This is also one of the reasons why Jewish law does not permit autopsies[24] other than in the most extenuating of circumstances.[25]

Utmost respect for the sanctity of the human body is also the overriding concern which pervades the process of preparing the deceased for burial. The funeral is scheduled for the earliest possible time, ideally on the same day as the passing,[26] so that the body reaches its eternal rest as expeditiously as possible. The honor of caring for the dead is traditionally reserved for the most respected members of the community,[27] who are expected to maintain the highest levels of decorum, privacy, and respect throughout the entire process.

According to traditional Jewish sources, the merit of facilitating the proper burial of a Jewish corpse is immeasurable. Even the High Priest, who was even prohibited from attending the funerals of his next of kin, was *required* to preoccupy himself and personally bury a *met mitzvah,* an abandoned Jewish body that had no one to attend to its proper burial.[28]

No lengthy explanation is necessary to conclude that there can be no greater violation of our legal and moral responsibilities to the body's Owner than to cremate.

Delving Deeper into our Relationship with our Bodies

When the body becomes the soul's vehicle to do good deeds ("mitzvot") it—the body—is invested with permanent value and sanctity. The body is seen as sacred, as the temple of the soul, and the medium by which we do goodness in this world. According to Jewish law, an object which facilitated the fulfillment of a mitzvah must be accorded respect, and cannot be casually discarded. Examples: papers upon which are inscribed words of Torah, *tzitzit* fringes, or leather *tefillin* straps. Such articles must be buried with due respect. How much more does this idea apply to a body. In the words of the Talmud,[29] "even the wicked among [the Jewish people] are full of mitzvot"! Or, to quote the prophet Isaiah:[30] "And your nation are *all* righteous people."

On a deeper level, as Jews, we believe there is purpose to life, purpose to this world, purpose to the act of creation.

There are other belief systems that view the body and all the other physical trappings of this world, and the temptations they present, only as strategic challenges set in the soul's path, in order to overcome these challenges en route to a heavenly paradise. As such, the body has no intrinsic worth of its own, and once its function has been fully served, it retains no value whatsoever.

Jewish belief also recognizes the importance of the soul's reward earned through its life-journey,[31] but sees the refinement of the body and this physical

---

22 Maimonides, Laws of Murder 11:5; Code of Jewish Law, Yoreh De'ah 427:9-10.

23 Deduced from Deuteronomy 21:23. See Da'at Cohen, Responsa of Rabbi Abraham Isaac Kook (1864–1935, Israel's first Chief Rabbi).

24 The Talmud (Bava Batra 115a) relates: It once happened that a person sold his deceased father's estate, and then died himself. The other family members claimed that he was a minor at the time of death and was therefore unauthorized to sell the property. The rabbis did not allow them, however, to medically examine the body to determine his age. "You are not permitted to dishonor him," Rabbi Akiba said. From here we infer that it is forbidden to modify the body of the deceased in any manner even if it would lead to tangible results. The Talmud (Chullin 11b) also discusses the possibility of performing an autopsy on a murder victim to ascertain the state of the victim's health at the time of the murder. The result of this autopsy could have possibly affected the murderer's punishment. The Talmud objects on grounds of disrespect toward the dead and concludes that only in the theoretical event that the autopsy would actually serve to *save* the murderer (considering the premium Jewish law places on saving lives) would it be allowed.
See also Noda B'Yehudah Y.D. 210; Chatam Sofer Y.D. 336.

25 The Lubavitcher Rebbe explains in the previously cited letter (fn 16) that in those very rare cases "where an exception was made to the rule, it was because of special reasons, which in no way diminished the sanctity and inviolability of the body, as G-d's property, but only because under special circumstances, G-d Himself has permitted certain isolated exceptions, in which case it is the Owner's will that is being carried out, namely G-d's will."

26 Deuteronomy 21:23; Code of Jewish Law, Yoreh De'ah 357:1.

27 Kol Bo p. 175; Hadrat Kodesh 3a.

28 Maimonides, Laws of Mourning 3:6.

29 End of tractate Chagigah.

30 60:21.

31 Maimonides even considers the concept of the soul's reward to be a principle Jewish belief.

world as the paramount objective.[32] The soul was dispatched from its heavenly abode to infuse these otherwise mundane entities with holiness and purpose. While, the soul, too, is elevated to previously unimaginable heights through fulfilling its worldly mission,[33] it is the sanctification of the physical—both the body and the world at large—that constitutes the very reason for Creation.

The Penultimate Bodily Experience

Two of the most fundamental tenets of the Jewish faith are the belief in the ultimate redemption of the Jewish people—and of all of mankind—through a righteous messiah,[34] and the concept of the resurrection of the dead, an awaited time when all souls will return to their bodies.[35] These beliefs are so central to the Jewish worldview that Maimonides considers them to be two of the thirteen principles of the Jewish faith.[36]

The Messianic Era will be ushered in by a righteous scion of King David,[37] and will be characterized by world peace and harmony. "They shall beat their swords into plowshares and their spears into pruning hooks; nations shall not lift the sword against nation; neither shall they learn war anymore."[38] The Jewish people will be gathered from all corners of the earth and will be returned to the Promised Land,[39] where the Holy Temple will be rebuilt in Jerusalem.[40]

This era will be the culmination of G-d's master plan for Creation.[41] We will then be able to enjoy the fruits of our labor; we will then see the end-product of our millennia-long labor of permeating Creation with holiness and purpose. The curtain will be ripped aside, and the flesh, our very own bodies, will perceive G-d: "And the glory of the L-rd shall be revealed, and all flesh together shall see that the mouth of the L-rd spoke.[42]

These beliefs have sustained our nation throughout a 2,000-year exile fraught with pogroms, expulsions, and persecution. Just one generation ago countless Jews entered the gas chambers whilst singing *"Ani Ma'amin"* ("I believe...")—expressing their firm belief in a better time to come and their trust that they would be resurrected to witness that awaited day.

Cremation is an implied statement of rejection of the concept of resurrection. It is in effect a declaration that once the soul has departed the body, the lifeless body has served its purpose and now has no further value.[43]

Our Sages teach that those who deny the notion of the resurrection will not merit to be resurrected[44] within their own bodies, rather their souls will be enclothed in different bodies when that awaited day arrives.[45] Based on this idea, many authorities conclude that a person who opts for cremation is subject to this consequence as well.[46]

(However, this applies only to such instances where the cremation was done at the behest of the deceased; only in such instances can it be said that the person rejected the notion of the resurrection, etc. Not too long ago six million of our people were denied proper burial, most of them cremated. Without a doubt these holy martyrs will be at the forefront of those who will return during the Messianic Redemption.)

---

32 Tanya (by Rabbi Schneur Zalman of Liadi, 1745–1812, founder of Chabad chassidic movement), ch. 36.

33 See Likutei Torah (Rabbi Schneur Zalman of Liadi), Deuteronomy 29a.

34 Maimonides, Laws of Kings 11:1, based on Deuteronomy 30:3-5; ibid. 19:8; Numbers 24:17-18; and, to quote Maimonides, "from the words of the Prophets it is unnecessary to bring proof, for all their books are filled with this concept."

35 The Talmud, Sanhedrin 90b–91b, brings multiple scriptural proofs for the resurrection.

36 Introduction to his commentary on "Chapter *Chelek*" in tractate Sanhedrin.

37 Isaiah 11:1; Maimonides, Laws of Kings 11:1.

38 Micah 4:3.

39 Deuteronomy 30:3-4.

40 Maimonides, ibid.

41 Tanya, ch. 36.

42 Isaiah 40:5.

43 Achiezer Vol. 3 #72 (Responsa of Rabbi Chaim Ozer Grodzinski, early 20th century Lithuanian rabbi); Beit Yitzchok, Yoreh Deah Vol.2 #155.

44 Mishna, tractate Sanhedrin 10:1.

45 See Igrot Kodesh by the Lubavitcher Rebbe, vol. 1 p.142-153.

46 See Minchat Elazar responsa cited above in footnote 3.

Additional Prohibition and Concepts

A. We are commanded in the Torah[47] not to follow the practices of the non-Jews. Cremating the dead was (and, in fact, still is) a ritual observed by many pagan cultures, and thus is also a violation of this biblical prohibition.[48]

B. According to Kabbalah (Jewish mysticism), the soul does not depart the body immediately after death.[49] Such an abrupt departure would be intensely painful for the soul. The gradual decomposition of the body allows the soul the time to slowly depart the body and acclimate itself to its new heavenly abode.[50] The instant destruction of the body caused by cremation deprives the soul of this much-needed adjustment period.

C. Throughout our history, a traditional Jewish burial, known as *Kever Yisrael,* was always considered a highest priority. During times when many of their non-Jewish co-citizens regularly cremated their dead, the Jews were distinguishable by their commitment to bury their dead with dignity. This fact was already noted by Tacitus, the famed 1st century Roman historian.[51] Understanding the great importance of this mitzvah, the Israeli army is known to take great risks, venturing behind enemy lines to bring back to Israel the bodies of their fallen comrades.

It is safe to assume that the deceased's soul is certain to evoke heavenly mercy and blessings upon those individuals who ensured that its body was accorded its final proper respects.

To sum up:

Cremation
- is a transgression of a Biblical law to bury our dead,
- demonstrates a rejection of G-d's supreme "ownership" over all of Creation,
- violates our legal responsibility to return what was loaned to us (our bodies) in as wholesome a state as possible,
- constitutes a rejection of the Jewish belief of *tzelem Elokim* (created in G-d's image),
- constitutes a rejection of the Jewish belief in resurrection of the dead,
- (if done voluntarily, knowing fully the responsibilities) will cause the body not to be included among the Jewish People when the time of resurrection arrives,
- violates the biblical prohibition of following heathen practices,
- upends the soul's natural separation and acclimation process, thus causing it additional untold pain,
- deviates from Jewish history and our forebears' and contemporaries' selfless and heroic efforts to properly bury our dead, and
- declares, in effect, that once the soul has departed the body, the lifeless body has no further value.

May we soon merit seeing the day when this whole discussion is rendered inapplicable, for G-d will "conceal death forever, and the L-rd G-d shall wipe the tears off every face."[52]

Reprinted with permission from Chabad.org.

---

47 Leviticus 18:3.
48 See S'dei Chemed encyclopedia, "Mourning" entry.
49 Zohar I 122b.
50 Jerusalem Talmud Mo'ed Kattan 3:5.
51 Hist. 5:5.

52 Isaiah 25:8.

Lesson Four

In Heaven's Name
Heaven, Hell, and Reincarnation

In this lesson, we turn to sages and mystics for information on phenomena and states that no human eye has ever perceived: What really transpires in heaven and hell? Do Jews believe in reincarnation? Is there anything we can do to benefit the soul of a dearly departed one in the netherworld?

JLI

JEWISH LEARNING INSTITUTE

Born Twice

LEARNING EXERCISE 1

What I (think I) know about the Jewish view on afterlife and reincarnation:	What I would like to know about the Jewish view on afterlife and reincarnation:
1.	1.
2.	2.
3.	3.
4.	4.
5.	5.

Reward and Punishment

Physical vs. Spiritual

LEARNING EXERCISE 2

Rate the following entities in terms of how much pleasure you would receive from them (1 = most pleasurable; 10 = least pleasurable).

a Hawaiian cruise

1	2	3	4	5	6	7	8	9	10

a lifetime membership to an exclusive country club

1	2	3	4	5	6	7	8	9	10

a lifetime of meaning

1	2	3	4	5	6	7	8	9	10

love

1	2	3	4	5	6	7	8	9	10

social status

1	2	3	4	5	6	7	8	9	10

true joy

1	2	3	4	5	6	7	8	9	10

wealth

1	2	3	4	5	6	7	8	9	10

wisdom

1	2	3	4	5	6	7	8	9	10

Rabbi Moshe ben Maimon
(Maimonides, Rambam)
1135–1204

Halachist, philosopher, author, and physician. Maimonides was born in Cordoba, Spain. After the conquest of Cordoba by the Almohads, he fled Spain and eventually settled in Cairo, Egypt. There, he became the leader of the Jewish community and served as court physician to the vizier of Egypt. He is most noted for authoring the *Mishneh Torah*, an encyclopedic arrangement of Jewish law, and for his philosophical work, *Guide for the Perplexed*. His rulings on Jewish law are integral to the formation of halachic consensus.

Text 1a

Maimonides, Commentary on Mishnah, Introduction to *Chelek* 📜

הַיְּסוֹד הָאֶחָד עָשָׂר:

כִּי הוּא, הַשֵּׁם יִתְבָּרֵךְ, נוֹתֵן שָׂכָר לְמִי שֶׁעוֹשֶׂה מִצְוֹת הַתּוֹרָה. וְיַעֲנִישׁ לְמִי שֶׁעוֹבֵר עַל אַזְהָרוֹתֶיהָ.

The eleventh principle:

That God, blessed be He, gives reward to those who observe the commandments of the Torah and punishes those who transgress its prohibitions.

Text 1b

Maimonides, ibid. 📜

וְכִי הַשָּׂכָר הַגָּדוֹל הָעוֹלָם הַבָּא, וְהָעוֹנֶשׁ הֶחָזָק הַכָּרֵת.

The greatest reward is [to experience the pleasures of] the World to Come; the greatest punishment is to be cut off [from the World to Come].

Judism believes
Being denied From going into hell will deny the Soul
From going To heaven

A Life of Consequence

QUESTION FOR DISCUSSION

Why is the notion of divine reward and punishment a foundational Jewish belief?

The Torah is only interested in the here & now
The Torah is a book of instruction For your Life here on earth

Text 2

Rabbi Menachem Recanati, Exodus 29:1 📖

וְאַל יַעֲלֶה בְּדַעְתְּךָ כִּי הָעוֹנְשִׁים הַכְּתוּבִין בַּתּוֹרָה הֵם כְּמוֹ הַמַּעֲנִיש אֶת הָאָדָם עַל עָבְרוֹ עַל מִצְוַת הַמֶּלֶךְ לֹא כֵן, רַק הֵן דָּבָר טִבְעִי מַמָּשׁ, כִּי הַמְּבַטֵּל מִצְוָה מִמִּצְוֹת הַתּוֹרָה, אוֹתוֹ הַטּוֹב שֶׁהָיָה נִשְׁפַּע בְּסִבַּת עֲשִׂיָּיתָהּ הוּא נִמְנָע, כְּדִמְיוֹן מִי שֶׁאֵינוֹ זוֹרֵעַ שָׂדֵהוּ שֶׁאֵינוֹ קוֹצֵר, וּכְמִי שֶׁאֵינוֹ לוֹבֵשׁ בְּגָדִים שֶׁהוּא מִתְקָרֵר וּכְמוֹ שֶׁטֶּבַע הָאֵשׁ לְחַמֵּם וְטֶבַע הַמַּיִם לְהַרְטִיב וְהַלֶּחֶם לְהַשְׂבִּיעַ, כַּךְ טֶבַע כָּל מִצְוָה וּמִצְוָה לַעֲשׂוֹת אוֹתָם הַטּוֹבוֹת שֶׁנֶּאֶמְרוּ בָּהּ, אוֹ אוֹתָם הָעוֹנְשִׁים שֶׁנֶּאֶמְרוּ.

The punishments described in the Torah are not similar to the punishments meted for transgressing the decree of an earthly king. Rather, the Torah's punishments are natural consequences. One who fails to observe a Torah commandment is denied the good that naturally results from its observance. This is similar to one who doesn't sow, who then, obviously, cannot reap; or one who doesn't wear clothing and then becomes cold; or the nature of fire to cause heat; the nature of water to make

Rabbi Menachem ben Benyamin Recanati
ca. 1250–1310

Italian rabbi and kabbalist of note. He authored *Pirush Al Hatorah*, a mystical commentary on the Bible; *Pirush Hatefilot*, a commentary on the Sidur, and *Ta'amei Hamitzvot*, an explanation of the commandments. In addition, his halachic rulings are collected in his *Piskei Recanati*.

wet; and the nature of bread to satiate. Similarly, it is the nature of each mitzvah to elicit the positive consequences that are promised for its observance or the negative consequences for its transgression.

FIGURE 4.1

Profession	Process
Businessperson	Work – Money – Food
Farmer	Sow – Reap – Food

Mishnah

The first authoritative work of Jewish law that was codified in writing. The Mishnah contains the oral traditions that were passed down from teacher to student; it supplements, clarifies, and systematizes the commandments of the Torah. Due to the continual persecution of the Jewish people, it became increasingly difficult to guarantee that these traditions would not be forgotten. Rabbi Yehudah Hanasi therefore redacted the Mishnah at the end of the 2nd century. It serves as the foundation for the Talmud.

Text 3

Mishnah, Avot 4:2 📖

שֶׁשְּׂכַר מִצְוָה, מִצְוָה. וּשְׂכַר עֲבֵרָה, עֲבֵרָה.

The reward of a mitzvah is a mitzvah; the retribution for a sin is a sin.

Soul Catharsis
Soul Rehabilitation

LEARNING EXERCISE 3

What is the first word or idea that enters your mind when you hear the word "hell"?

_____

_____

Text 4

Talmud, Chagigah 15b

כִּי נָח נַפְשֵׁיה דְּאַחֵר, אָמְרִי "לֹא מִידָן לִידַיְינֵיה וְלֹא לְעָלְמָא דְּאָתֵי לֵיתֵי". לֹא מִידָן לִידַיְינֵיה, מִשּׁוּם דְּעָסַק בְּאוֹרַיְיתָא, וְלֹא לְעָלְמָא דְּאָתֵי לֵיתֵי, מִשּׁוּם דְּחָטָא.

אָמַר רַבִּי מֵאִיר, "מוּטָב דְּלִידַיְינֵיה וְלֵיתֵי לְעָלְמָא דְּאָתֵי".

When Acher died, the heavenly court declared: "Let him not be judged [in *Gehinom*] for his sins, nor let him enter Paradise." [Their reasoning was:] Let him not be judged, because he engaged in Torah study, nor let him enter Paradise, because he [so egregiously] sinned.

[Acher's former disciple] Rabbi Meir said: "Better that he be judged and then enter Paradise."

Babylonian Talmud

A literary work of monumental proportions that draws upon the legal, spiritual, intellectual, ethical, and historical traditions of Judaism. The 37 tractates of the Babylonian Talmud contain the teachings of the Jewish sages from the period after the destruction of the 2nd Temple through the 5th century CE. It has served as the primary vehicle for the transmission of the Oral Law and the education of Jews over the centuries; it is the entry point for all subsequent legal, ethical, and theological Jewish scholarship.

The Soul goes to hell to be refined before going to heaven

Text 5

Rabbi Shne'ur Zalman of Liadi, *Torah Or* 49b 📖

Rabbi Shne'ur Zalman of Liadi
(Alter Rebbe)
1745–1812

Chasidic rebbe, halachic authority, and founder of the Chabad movement. The Alter Rebbe was born in Liozna, Belarus, and was among the principal students of the Magid of Mezeritch. His numerous works include the *Tanya*, an early classic containing the fundamentals of Chabad Chasidism, and *Shulchan Aruch HaRav*, an expanded and reworked code of Jewish law.

עִנְיַן הַגֵּיהִנֹם הוּא כְּדֵי לְצָרֵף הַנֶּפֶשׁ מֵחוֹלַאַת הָרַע אֲשֶׁר בְּקִרְבָּהּ, כְּמוֹ מְצָרֵף לַכֶּסֶף, שֶׁהַפְּסוֹלֶת וְהַסִּיגִים נִשְׂרָפִים תּוֹךְ הַכּוּר וְנִשְׁאָר הַכֶּסֶף נָקִי מִכָּל סִיג. כָּךְ, כְּדֵי שֶׁתּוּכַל הַנֶּפֶשׁ לְקַבֵּל אוֹר עֹנֶג הָעֶלְיוֹן לִהְיוֹת נֶהֱנִים כוּ', צְרִיכָה לְהִתְבָּרֵר תְּחִלָּה בְּאֵשׁ שֶׁל גֵּיהִנֹם לְהַפְרִיד הָרַע מִן הַטּוֹב.

The purpose of *Gehinom* is to refine the soul and rid it of any negativity that it contracted. This is similar to the process of smelting silver, wherein the dross is burned away in a furnace, leaving the silver clean and without impurities. So, too, for the soul to be able to process the supernal pleasures, for it to be able to take delight [in God's radiance], it must first be refined in the "fires" of *Gehinom*, wherein the good is separated from the bad.

Sentencing Guidelines

Text 6

Mishnah, Sanhedrin 10:1

כָּל יִשְׂרָאֵל יֵשׁ לָהֶם חֵלֶק לָעוֹלָם הַבָּא, שֶׁנֶּאֱמַר, (יְשַׁעְיָה ס, כא) "וְעַמֵּךְ כֻּלָּם צַדִּיקִים, לְעוֹלָם יִירְשׁוּ אָרֶץ. נֵצֶר מַטָּעַי, מַעֲשֵׂה יָדַי לְהִתְפָּאֵר".

All of Israel has a portion in the World to Come, as it is stated (Isaiah 60:21), "Your people are all righteous; they shall inherit the land forever; they are the branch of My planting, the work of My hands, in which [I] take pride."

Text 7

Mishnah, Eduyot 2:10

מִשְׁפָּט רְשָׁעִים בְּגֵיהִנֹּם, שְׁנֵים עָשָׂר חֹדֶשׁ.

The wicked are judged in *Gehinom* for [a maximum of] twelve months.

Paradise

Close for Comfort

Text 8

Rabbi Don Yitschak Abarbanel
1437–1508

Biblical exegete and statesman. Abarbanel was born in Lisbon, Portugal and served as a minister in the court of King Alfonso V of Portugal. After intrigues at court led to accusations against him, he fled to Spain, where he once again served as a counselor to royalty. It is claimed that Abarbanel offered King Ferdinand and Queen Isabella large sums of money for the revocation of their Edict of Expulsion of 1492, but to no avail. After the expulsion, he eventually settled in Italy where he wrote a commentary on Scripture, as well as other venerated works.

Don Yitschak Abarbanel, Leviticus 26:3–46 📖

שֶׁהַגְּמוּל הָרוּחָנִי הוּא דָּבָר עָמוֹק וְקָשֶׁה עַל הַשֵּׂכֶל הָאֱנוּשִׁי לְצַיְּירוֹ וּלְהַשִּׂיגוֹ בִּהְיוֹתוֹ מְחוּבָּר לַגּוּף. כִּי כְּמוֹ שֶׁלֹּא יַשִּׂיג עִנְיַן הַמַּרְאִים, כֵּן הַנְּפָשׁוֹת בִּהְיוֹתָם עִם הַגְּשָׁמִים לֹא יַשִּׂיגוּ הַדְּבָרִים הָרוּחָנִיִּים.

The concept of spiritual reward is abstruse and difficult for human intellect (while still attached to the physical body) to visualize and grasp. Just as the blind person cannot grasp the concept of colors, so, too, the spirit, while still engaged with the physical, cannot grasp purely spiritual matters.

Text 9

Talmud, Berachot 17a 📖

הָעוֹלָם הַבָּא אֵין בּוֹ לֹא אֲכִילָה, וְלֹא שְׁתִיָּה, וְלֹא פְּרִיָּה וּרְבִיָּה, וְלֹא מַשָּׂא וּמַתָּן, וְלֹא קִנְאָה, וְלֹא שִׂנְאָה, וְלֹא תַּחֲרוּת. אֶלָּא צַדִּיקִים יוֹשְׁבִין וְעַטְרוֹתֵיהֶם בְּרָאשֵׁיהֶם וְנֶהֱנִים מִזִּיו הַשְּׁכִינָה.

In the hereafter there is no eating, drinking, procreation, commerce, jealousy, hatred, or competition. Rather, the righteous sit, their heads adorned by crowns, and they delight in the radiance of the divine presence.

Our Contribution

Text 10

Rabbi Shlomo ben Aderet, *Responsa* 5:49 📖

כְּשֶׁהוּא מוֹלִיד בֵּן צַדִּיק עוֹבֵד אֱלֹקִים, נִרְאֶה כְּאִילוּ מְסִיבוֹבוֹ

הוּא עוֹבֵד אֱלֹקִים, שֶׁהוּא הֱבִיאוֹ לָעוֹלָם לִהְיוֹת צַדִּיק . . .

וְעַל כֵּן רָאוּי בֶּאֱמֶת שֶׁיִּזְכֶּה הָאָב בִּזְכוּת הַבֵּן . . .

אָמְנָם, מִי שֶׁעוֹשָׂה צְדָקָה אוֹ תְּפִלָּה בְּעַד מִי שֶׁכְּבָר מֵת, מוֹעִיל

לַמֵּת . . . וְזֶהוּ מָה שֶׁנָּהֲגוּ יִשְׂרָאֵל בִּצְדָקוֹת, וְנִיחוֹת נָפֶשׁ.

When a child is righteous and serves God, it is seemingly on account of the parent that the child is doing so—it is the parent, after all, who brought this righteous individual into the world. . . . It is therefore appropriate that a child can accrue merits on behalf of a [deceased] parent. . . .

However, the charity or prayers of anyone on behalf of a departed person are helpful for the soul of the deceased. . . . This is why it is Jewish custom to give charity and [perform other actions to bring] comfort and pleasure to the soul.

A mitzvah is a connection to another

Rabbi Shlomo ben Aderet
1235–1310

Medieval Halachist, Talmudist, and philosopher. Rashba was born in Barcelona, Spain, and was a student of Nachmanides and Rabbi Yonah of Gerona. He was known as *El Rab d'España* ("the Rabbi of Spain") because of his fame as a rabbinical authority. More than 3,000 of his responsa are extant, dealing with varied questions on Halachah and religious philosophy, addressed to him from Spain, Portugal, Italy, France, Germany, and even from Asia Minor. Among his numerous students were the Ritva, Rabbeinu Bechaye, and the Re'ah.

FIGURE 4.2

Suggested *Mitzvot* to Benefit the Souls of Departed Loved Ones

1. Donate to charity. Especially in the first year, donate daily (even if only a small amount). A particularly opportune time to give charity is before lighting Shabbat candles.

2. Attend *Yizkor* services and pledge to give charity in memory of the deceased.

3. Study Torah.

4. Provide financial support to Torah students and scholars.

5. Sponsor a Torah class.

6. Sponsor or donate books to a Judaic library.

7. Write (or donate) a Torah scroll in the deceased's honor.

8. Any mitzvah done in the merit of the deceased is beneficial for the soul. Especially beneficial are good deeds whose observance the deceased encouraged in his or her will, or those that the deceased excelled in.

Yahrtzeit Customs

1. Light a 24-hour *yahrtzeit* candle.

2. Recite the *Kaddish* during all the day's prayers. If possible, lead the congregational prayers.

3. Visit the grave and recite chapters of Psalms.

4. Donate to charity.

5. Study Torah. The study of Mishnah is especially beneficial for the soul of the departed.

6. Receive an *aliyah* to the Torah on the Shabbat preceding the *yahrtzeit*.

7. A once widespread custom was to fast on the *yahrtzeit*. Today it is more common to sponsor a Kiddush for the congregation, and the blessings recited there serve as a merit for the soul.

8. Convene a gathering of relatives and friends to commemorate the deceased, and speak about and learn from the deceased's good deeds.

Kaddish

Text 11

Siddur (Nusach Ha'Arizal), Kaddish 📖

יִתְגַּדַּל וְיִתְקַדַּשׁ שְׁמֵהּ רַבָּא.

בְּעָלְמָא דִּי בְרָא כִרְעוּתֵהּ, וְיַמְלִיךְ מַלְכוּתֵהּ וְיַצְמַח פּוּרְקָנֵהּ וִיקָרֵב מְשִׁיחֵיהּ.
בְּחַיֵּיכוֹן וּבְיוֹמֵיכוֹן וּבְחַיֵּי דְכָל בֵּית יִשְׂרָאֵל, בַּעֲגָלָא וּבִזְמַן קָרִיב. וְאִמְרוּ אָמֵן.

יְהֵא שְׁמֵהּ רַבָּא מְבָרַךְ לְעָלַם וּלְעָלְמֵי עָלְמַיָּא.

יִתְבָּרַךְ וְיִשְׁתַּבַּח וְיִתְפָּאֵר וְיִתְרוֹמַם וְיִתְנַשֵּׂא, וְיִתְהַדָּר
וְיִתְעַלֶּה וְיִתְהַלָּל שְׁמֵהּ דְּקֻדְשָׁא בְּרִיךְ הוּא.

לְעֵלָּא מִן כָּל בִּרְכָתָא וְשִׁירָתָא, תֻּשְׁבְּחָתָא וְנֶחֱמָתָא, דַּאֲמִירָן בְּעָלְמָא. וְאִמְרוּ אָמֵן.

יְהֵא שְׁלָמָא רַבָּא מִן שְׁמַיָּא וְחַיִּים טוֹבִים עָלֵינוּ וְעַל כָּל יִשְׂרָאֵל. וְאִמְרוּ אָמֵן.

עוֹשֶׂה שָׁלוֹם בִּמְרוֹמָיו הוּא יַעֲשֶׂה שָׁלוֹם עָלֵינוּ וְעַל כָּל יִשְׂרָאֵל. וְאִמְרוּ אָמֵן.

Exalted and hallowed be His great name (congregation: *Amen*) throughout the world that He has created according to His will.

May He establish His kingship, give blossom to His redemption, and hasten [the coming of] His Messiah (*Amen*) in your lifetime and in your days, and in the lifetime of the entire House of Israel, speedily and soon. And say, Amen.

May His great Name be blessed forever and to all eternity.

Blessed and praised, glorified, exalted, and extolled, honored, upraised, and lauded be the Name of the Holy One, blessed be He (*Amen*), beyond all the blessings and songs, praises, and consolations that are uttered in the world, and say, Amen.

May there be abundant peace from heaven, and a good life for us and for all Israel; and say, Amen.

He Who makes peace in His heavens, may He make peace for us and for all Israel; and say, Amen.

Text 12

Rabbi Adin Even-Israel Steinsaltz, *HaSiddur Vehatefilah* 1:295 📖

Rabbi Adin Even-Israel Steinsaltz
1937–

Talmudist, author, and philosopher. Rabbi Even-Israel Steinsaltz is considered one of the foremost Jewish thinkers of the 20th century. Praised by *Time* magazine as a "once-in-a-millennium scholar," he has been awarded the Israel Prize for his contributions to Jewish study. He lives in Jerusalem and is the founder of the Israel Institute for Talmudic Publications, a society dedicated to the translation and elucidation of the Talmud.

כָּל אָדָם בְּיִשְׂרָאֵל הוּא בְּמוּבָן מְסוּיָּם אֶחָד מֵאֵלֶּה הַנּוֹשְׂאִים וּמְקַיְּמִים אֶת מַלְכוּת ה' בָּעוֹלָם, וְכִדְבְרֵי הַכָּתוּב "אַתֶּם עֵדַי נְאוּם ה'" (יְשַׁעְיָהוּ מג, י). מִשּׁוּם כַּךְ, חֶסְרוֹנוֹ שֶׁל כָּל אֶחָד מִיִּשְׂרָאֵל יוֹצֵר כִּבְיָכוֹל חָלָל וְחֶסֶר בְּמַלְכוּת ה' בָּעוֹלָם. וּכְדֵי לְהַשְׁלִים הַחִסָּרוֹן, אֶת פְּגַם הַמְּצִיאוּת, צְרִיכִים הָאֲחֵרִים לְהִתְגַּבֵּר בְּיֶתֶר שְׂאֵת, וּלְהַכְרִיז שׁוּב בְּשֵׁם עַצְמָם וּבְשֵׁם הַנִּפְטָרִים, "יִתְגַּדַּל וְיִתְקַדַּשׁ".

וְכַאן הוּא גַּם מָקוֹר הַהַכָּרָה כִּי אֲמִירַת הַקַּדִּישׁ הִיא עִלּוּי לְנִשְׁמַת הַמֵּת. חֶשְׁבּוֹן מַעֲשָׂיו וּפְעוּלָּתוֹ שֶׁל אָדָם הֵם בְּעִיקָר הַתַּמְצִית שֶׁל חַיָּיו, שֶׁל מַה שֶׁהִצְלִיחַ לַעֲשׂוֹת בִּזְמַן הֱיוֹתוֹ עַל הָאֲדָמָה. אוּלָם, חֶשְׁבּוֹן זֶה אֵינוֹ נִגְמָר תָּמִיד עִם הַמָּוֶת. הַהַעֲרָכָה הַשְּׁלֵמָה שֶׁל אָדָם קְשׁוּרָה לֹא רַק בַּמֶּה שֶׁהוּא עַצְמוֹ עָשָׂה, אֶלָּא גַּם בִּדְבָרִים שֶׁנּוֹצְרוּ וְצָמְחוּ מִכּוֹחוֹ וְעַל יָדוֹ. וּמִשּׁוּם כַּךְ, כַּאֲשֶׁר הַמַּמְשִׁיכִים הַחַיִּים (וּבְיֶתֶר שְׂאֵת – הַבָּנִים וְהַצֶּאֱצָאִים, שֶׁעַצָּם קִיּוּמָם הָיָה תָּלוּי בְּהוֹרֵיהֶם) עוֹשִׂים מַעֲשִׂים טוֹבִים – הֲרֵי הֵם מַשְׁלִימִים אֶת הַהַעֲרָכָה עַל הָאָדָם, שֶׁאַף שֶׁאֵינוֹ פּוֹעֵל יוֹתֵר בְּעַצְמוֹ בָּעוֹלָם, מַמְשִׁיכִים דְּבָרִים וְנַעֲשִׂים מִכּוֹחוֹ.

וּמִשּׁוּם כַּךְ, אֲמִירַת הַקַּדִּישׁ הִיא עִלּוּי לְנִשְׁמַת הַנִּפְטָר, שֶׁהֲרֵי בִּגְלָלוֹ וְלִשְׁמוֹ מַמְשִׁיכִים וּמוֹסִיפִים לִפְעוֹל בְּתוֹךְ הַמְּצִיאוּת.

Every member of the community of Israel is responsible for establishing and proclaiming God's sovereignty in this world. As the verse states, "You [Israel] are My witnesses, God proclaims" (Isaiah 43:10). Therefore, the absence of a Jewish person creates a void, as it were, in

God's sovereignty in the world. In order to fill this void, others need to intensify their work accordingly and proclaim—on behalf of themselves as well as the deceased—"May His name be exalted and hallowed!"

This is why reciting the *Kaddish* elevates the soul of the deceased. The aggregate of a person's actions and accomplishments in this world define his or her life. However, the tally of a person's achievements does not necessarily conclude at the moment of death. A complete evaluation of a person's accomplishments must also include all that is accomplished as a result of the person's inspiration and actions. Therefore, when those who remain alive (and especially the person's children and descendants, whose very existence is a credit to their forebears) do good deeds, they contribute to the deceased's balance of accomplishments. For although the deceased is no longer active in this world, his or her actions continue to inspire positive deeds and actions.

The recitation of *Kaddish* elevates the soul because God is being exalted in this world due to and in the name of the deceased.

Reincarnation

The Many Lives of a Soul

QUESTION FOR DISCUSSION

How do you feel about reincarnation? Are you fascinated and pleased by the idea? Does it disturb you? Or does it leave you indifferent?

Splitting the Adam

Text 13

Rabbi Chaim Vital, *Sha'ar Hagilgulim*, Introduction 11 📖

כִּי תְּחִלָּה יֵשׁ נְשָׁמָה אַחַת אָב לְכֻלָּם, וְהוּא אָדָם הָרִאשׁוֹן כּוֹלֵל כֻּלָּם. וְאַחַר כָּךְ נִכְלָלוֹת כֻּלָּם בְּג׳ אָבוֹת: אַבְרָהָם, יִצְחָק, וְיַעֲקֹב. וְאַחַר כָּךְ נִכְלָלוֹת כֻּלָּם לִשְׁנֵים עָשָׂר שְׁבָטִים, וְאַחַר כָּךְ נֶחֱלָקִים לְע׳ נָפֶשׁ. וְאַחַר כָּךְ אֵלּוּ הָע׳ נֶפֶשׁ נֶחֱלָקִים עַד ס׳ רִבּוֹא נִצוֹצוֹת גְּדוֹלִים.

It all began with one master soul: the soul of Adam, which included the souls of all future souls. Subsequently, this master soul passed on to Abraham, Isaac, and Jacob, and then was divided among the twelve tribes. The soul was then further subdivided among the seventy souls [of the descendants of Jacob that went to Egypt], and then among the 600,000 [who left Egypt].

Rabbi Chaim Vital
ca. 1542–1620

Lurianic Kabbalist. Rabbi Vital was born in Israel, lived in Safed and Jerusalem, and later in Damascus. He was authorized by his teacher, Rabbi Yitschak Luria, the Arizal, to record his teachings. Acting on this mandate, Vital began arranging his master's teachings in written form, and his many works constitute the foundation of the Lurianic school of Jewish mysticism. His most famous work is *Ets Chaim*.

Text 14

Ibid., Introduction 16

עוֹד צָרִיךְ שֶׁתֵּדַע, כִּי הָאָדָם צָרִיךְ לְקַיֵּם כָּל הַתַּרְיַ"ג מִצְוֹת,
בְּמַעֲשֶׂה, וּבְדִבּוּר, וּבְמַחְשָׁבָה . . . וְאִם לֹא קִיֵּם כָּל הַתַּרְיַ"ג בִּשְׁלֹשָׁה
בְּחִינוֹת הַנִּזְכָּר, מְחוּיָּב לְהִתְגַּלְגֵּל עַד שֶׁיַּשְׁלִים אוֹתָם.

עוֹד דַּע, כִּי הָאָדָם מְחוּיָּב לַעֲסוֹק בַּתּוֹרָה בְּד' מַדְרֵגוֹת, שֶׁסִּימָנָם פַּרְדֵּ"ס,
וְהֵם, פְּשָׁט, רֶמֶז, דְּרוּשׁ, סוֹד. וְצָרִיךְ שֶׁיִּתְגַּלְגֵּל עַד שֶׁיַּשְׁלִים אוֹתָם.

Furthermore, you must know that every person must fulfill all of the 613 *mitzvot*—in action, speech, and thought.... If a soul does not fulfill all 613 *mitzvot*, it is reincarnated until it completes them all.

Moreover you must know that every person must study all four of the Torah's dimensions—*peshat, remez, derush,* and *sod* (literal, allusion, exegetic, and mystical)—and is reincarnated until this is accomplished.

Mechanism of Reincarnation

Text 15

Ibid., Introduction 14 ▮

דַּע, כִּי אַף עַל פִּי שֶׁתִּמְצָא כָּתוּב אֶצְלֵינוּ בִּמְקוֹמוֹת רַבִּים כִּי פְּלוֹנִי נִתְגַּלְגֵּל בִּפְלוֹנִי, וְאַחַר כַּךְ בִּפְלוֹנִי וְכוּ', אַל תִּטְעֶה לוֹמַר כִּי הַנְּשָׁמָה הָרִאשׁוֹנָה עַצְמָהּ הִיא הַמִּתְגַּלְגֶּלֶת תָּמִיד. אֲבָל הָעִנְיָן הוּא, כִּי הִנֵּה כַּמָּה שָׁרָשִׁים לְאֵין קֵץ נִתְחַלְּקוּ נִשְׁמוֹת בְּנֵי אָדָם, וּבְשׁרֶשׁ אֶחָד מֵהֶם יֵשׁ כַּמָּה נִצוֹצוֹת נְשָׁמוֹת לְאֵין קֵץ, וּבְכָל גִּלְגּוּל וְגִלְגּוּל נִתְקָנִים קְצָת נִצוֹצוֹת מֵהֶם, וְאוֹתָם נִצוֹצוֹת שֶׁלֹּא נִתַּקְנוּ, חוֹזְרִים לְהִתְגַּלְגֵּל לְהִתַּקֵן. וְאוֹתָם שֶׁכְּבָר נִתַּקְנוּ, אֵינָם מִתְגַּלְגְּלִים, אָמְנָם עוֹלִים וְעוֹמְדִים בַּמַּדְרֵגָה הָרְאוּיָה לָהֶם.

Although we've written in many places [in this treatise] that so-and-so's soul was reincarnated in so-and-so, and then was reincarnated again in so-and-so, etc., do not err to think that it is the first soul itself that is being reincarnated over and over. Rather, every human soul is divided into an innumerable number of roots. Furthermore, every root is divided into an infinite amount of sparks. In every reincarnation, some of the sparks are rectified. The sparks that were rectified ascend [to *Gan Eden*] and dwell in the level appropriate for them. However, those sparks that were not rectified are reincarnated in order to be rectified.

Who Was I?

Text 16

Rabbi Moshe Cordovero, *Shi'ur Komah* 84 ◼

אֵין מִי שֶׁיֵּדַע מִצַּד מְצִיאוּת עַצְמוּתוֹ אוֹ יַרְגִּישׁ בְּעַצְמוֹ שֶׁהוּא מְגוּלְגָּל
אוֹ בִּלְתִּי מְגוּלְגָּל אֶלָּא מִי שֶׁנִּמְסַר לָהֶם עַל צַד הַקַּבָּלָה . . .

וְאִם תֹּאמַר, בַּמֶּה יֵדַע הָאָדָם אֶת הַדָּבָר שֶׁעַל אוֹתוֹ דָּבָר בָּא, אִם
מִצְוָה אוֹ עֲבֵירָה, כְּדֵי שֶׁיִּזָּהֵר עַצְמוֹ אוֹ יְתַקֵּן עַצְמוֹ? הָעִנְיָן הַזֶּה
הוּא מוּטְבָּע בִּסְגוּלָּה בָּאָדָם בְּסוֹד רְדִיפַת הַנְּשָׁמָה וְחֶשְׁקָהּ בְּעִנְיָן
הַמִּצְוָה אוֹ יִצְרוֹ מְפַתֵּהוּ עַל אוֹתָהּ עֲבֵירָה שֶׁהִכְשִׁילוֹ קוֹדֶם.

Rabbi Moshe Cordovero
(Ramak)
1522–1570

Prominent Kabbalist. Ramak belonged to the circle of Jewish mystical thinkers who flourished in 16th century Safed. The name Cordovero indicates that his family originated in Córdoba, Spain. His most famous Kabbalistic work is *Pardes Rimonim.*

It is impossible to deduce or intuit whether one possesses a reincarnated soul or not, unless one is the recipient of a mystical tradition in this regard. . . .

If you wonder, how then will we know the purpose for which we entered this world, which mitzvah we need to scrupulously perform or which transgression we must especially avoid? The answers to these questions are naturally engrained in us. We feel a natural affinity and longing to do a certain mitzvah. Or, our inclination will work especially hard to entice us to do that sin which we stumbled on in the past [incarnation].

Lesson Conclusion

Text 17

Rabbi Eliyahu of Vilna, Commentary on Song of Songs 1:3 📖

כִּי עִיקָר עוֹלָם הַבָּא הוּא לְהָשִׁיב הַנְּשָׁמָה לִמְקוֹרָהּ לִידָבֵק בַּשְּׁכִינָה, וּבְוַדַּאי יוֹתֵר טוֹב מִזֶּה כְּשֶׁהַשְּׁכִינָה דְּבֵקָה לְמַטָּה כַּאֲשֶׁר הָיְתָה כַּוָּנַת הַבְּרִיאָה.

The primary reward in the hereafter is the soul returning to its Source and uniting with God. Certainly, however, it is even greater when the soul can connect with God *here in this world* [through the study of Torah and the performance of *mitzvot*], for that is the purpose of Creation.

Rabbi Eliyahu of Vilna
(Vilna Ga'on, Gra)
1720–1797

Talmudist, halachist, and Kabbalist. The Vilna Ga'on was one of the greatest scholars of his day. In addition to Talmud, he excelled in all aspects of Torah study, including Kabbalah, and was proficient in secular subjects as well. He left a tremendous legacy, both from his vast writings on the Tanach, Talmud, and Shulchan Aruch, and from the many students that he inspired to Torah and scholarship.

Text 18

Rabbi Menachem Mendel of Lubavitch, *Derech Mitsvotecha* 138a 📖

וְכָךְ הָיָה נִשְׁמַע הַלָּשׁוֹן מִמּוֹרֵינוּ וְרַבֵּינוּ נִשְׁמָתוֹ עֵדֶן בִּדְבֵיקוּתוֹ, שֶׁהָיָה אוֹמֵר בְּזֶה הַלָּשׁוֹן:

אִיךְ וְוִיל זֶע גָאר נִיסְט. אִיךְ וְוִיל נִיט דַאיין גַּן עֵדֶן. אִיךְ וְוִיל נִיט דַאיין עוֹלָם הַבָּא כו׳. אִיךְ וְוִיל מֶער נִיט אַז דִיךְ אַלֵיין.

When our master and teacher [Rabbi Shne'ur Zalman of Liadi] would enter a state of spiritual ecstasy, he would be heard exclaiming:

"I want nothing at all! I don't want Your Paradise, I don't want Your World to Come. . . . I want nothing but You alone."

Rabbi Menachem Mendel Schneersohn of Lubavitch
(*Tsemach Tsedek*)
1789–1866

Chasidic rebbe and noted author. The *Tsemach Tsedek* was the third leader of the Chabad Chasidic movement and a noted authority on Jewish law. His numerous works include halachic responsa, Chasidic discourses, and Kabbalistic writings. Active in the plight of Russian Jewry, he worked to alleviate the plight of the Cantonists, Jewish children kidnapped to serve in the Czar's army. He passed away in Lubavitch, leaving seven sons and two daughters.

LEARNING EXERCISE 4

A. Write down the point from today's lesson that resonated with you most.

_____

_____

_____

_____

B. Identify a good deed you can do in memory of a beloved deceased parent, relative, or friend.

_____

_____

_____

_____

C. Identify a mitzvah to which you feel a strong connection, the one that might constitute the reason that your soul re-entered this world.

_____

_____

_____

_____

Key Points

1. Physical pleasures pale in comparison to spiritual pleasures, and the spiritual pleasures of this world pale in comparison to their heavenly counterparts.

2. Rewards and punishments of the afterlife are natural consequences of our actions. Afterlife is the full, unhindered experience of our actions.

3. *Mitzvot* forge an intimate relationship with God. In the afterlife, the soul experiences the effects of its actions: its relationship with God. This is the greatest possible pleasure for the soul—also known as Paradise (*Gan Eden*).

4. Inappropriate behavior diminishes the soul's capacity to experience spiritual pleasures. *Gehinom* ("hell") is a painful yet cleansing process that enables the soul to experience Paradise. Every soul ultimately reaches Paradise.

5. In *Gan Eden*, souls are constantly ascending to higher levels. Good deeds performed in a person's memory elevate the soul to higher levels than it can attain on its own.

6. Each soul is comprised of 613 sparks, corresponding to the 613 *mitzvot*. When a person performs a mitzvah, he or she rectifies the corresponding spark. After death, the rectified sparks return to their Source and the remaining sparks spin off and reincarnate, giving them the opportunity to attain completion

7. Generally speaking, the souls of our era are reincarnated, yet we cannot know or feel our incarnation history.

8. Reincarnation gives each of us a unique role to play within the general human mission.

9. What we do in the here and now is more important than the pleasure (or pain) our soul experiences in the afterlife. Living in this world in order to receive rewards in the next world shifts our focus from where it belongs.

This lesson explored the afterlife, heaven, hell, and reincarnation.

Continue your learning experience ONLINE

Visit www.myJLI.com/journey4

for insightful and inspiring videos, articles, and readings on these topics.

Appendix A

Text 1

Leviticus 26:3–6 🔊

אִם בְּחֻקֹּתַי תֵּלֵכוּ וְאֶת מִצְוֹתַי תִּשְׁמְרוּ וַעֲשִׂיתֶם אֹתָם.

וְנָתַתִּי גִשְׁמֵיכֶם בְּעִתָּם, וְנָתְנָה הָאָרֶץ יְבוּלָהּ, וְעֵץ הַשָּׂדֶה יִתֵּן פִּרְיוֹ.

וְהִשִּׂיג לָכֶם דַּיִשׁ אֶת בָּצִיר וּבָצִיר יַשִּׂיג אֶת זָרַע, וַאֲכַלְתֶּם לַחְמְכֶם לָשֹׂבַע, וִישַׁבְתֶּם לָבֶטַח בְּאַרְצְכֶם.

וְנָתַתִּי שָׁלוֹם בָּאָרֶץ וּשְׁכַבְתֶּם וְאֵין מַחֲרִיד, וְהִשְׁבַּתִּי חַיָּה רָעָה מִן הָאָרֶץ, וְחֶרֶב לֹא תַעֲבֹר בְּאַרְצְכֶם.

If you follow My statutes and observe My commandments and perform them:

I will give your rains in their time, the land will yield its produce, and the tree of the field will give forth its fruit.

Your threshing will last until the vintage, and the vintage will last until the sowing; you will eat your food to satiety, and you will live in security in your land.

And I will grant peace in the land, and you will lie down with no one to frighten [you]; I will remove wild beasts from the land, and no army will pass through your land.

Text 2

Don Yitschak Abarbanel, Leviticus 26:3–46 📖

שֶׁהַגְּמוּל הָרוּחָנִי הוּא דָּבָר עָמוֹק וְקָשֶׁה עַל הַשֵּׂכֶל הָאֱנוֹשִׁי לְצַיְּירוֹ

וּלְהַשִּׂיגוֹ בִּהְיוֹתוֹ מְחוּבָּר לַגּוּף. כִּי כְּמוֹ שֶׁלֹּא יַשִּׂיג הַסּוּמָא עִנְיָן הַמַּרְאִים,

כֵּן הַנְּפָשׁוֹת בִּהְיוֹתָם עִם הַגְּשָׁמִים לֹא יַשִּׂיגוּ הַדְּבָרִים הָרוּחָנִיִּים.

וְהִנֵּה, הַתּוֹרָה הָאֱלֹקִית לֹא נִיתְּנָה לַחֲכָמִים לְבַד, כִּי אִם לְכָל הָעָם מִקָּצֶה, הַקְּטַנִּים

עִם הַגְּדוֹלִים. וְלָכֵן . . . הוּצְרְכָה לְיַעֲדָם בִּגְמוּלִים גַּשְׁמִיִּים שֶׁיְּצַיְּירוּם כָּל אָדָם.

The concept of spiritual reward is very abstruse and difficult for human intellect to visualize and grasp while it is still attached to the physical body. Just as the blind person cannot grasp the concept of colors, so, too, the spirit, while still engaged with the physical, cannot grasp purely spiritual matters.

Now, the divine Torah was not given to the wise exclusively, but to the entire nation, the small and the great alike. Therefore . . . the Torah needed to promise physical incentive that can be envisioned by all.

Appendix B

Maimonides, Commentary on the Mishnah, Introduction to *Chelek* 🔊

שִׂים בְּדַעְתְּךָ כִּי נַעַר קָטָן הֱבִיאוּהוּ אֵצֶל הַמְלַמֵּד לְלַמְּדוֹ תּוֹרָה. וְזֶהוּ
הַטּוֹב הַגָּדוֹל לוֹ . . . אֶלָּא שֶׁהוּא, לְמִיעוּט שְׁנוֹתָיו וְחֻלְשַׁת שִׂכְלוֹ, אֵינוֹ
מֵבִין מַעֲלַת אוֹתוֹ הַטּוֹב . . . וּלְפִיכָךְ בְּהֶכְרֵחַ יִצְטָרֵךְ הַמְלַמֵּד . . . שֶׁיְזָרֵז
אוֹתוֹ עַל הַלִּמוּד בִּדְבָרִים שֶׁהֵם אֲהוּבִים אֶצְלוֹ לְקַטְנוּת שְׁנוֹתָיו. וְיֹאמַר
לוֹ: "קְרָא וְאֶתֵּן לְךָ אֱגוֹזִים אוֹ תְּאֵנִים, וְאֶתֵּן לְךָ מְעַט דְּבַשׁ" . . .

וּכְשֶׁיַּגְדִּיל וְיֶחֱזַק שִׂכְלוֹ וְיֵקַל בְּעֵינָיו אוֹתוֹ הַדָּבָר שֶׁהָיָה אֶצְלוֹ נִכְבָּד
מִלְּפָנִים, וְחָזַר לֶאֱהוֹב זוּלָתוֹ . . . יֹאמַר לוֹ מְלַמְּדוֹ: "קְרָא וְאֶקַּח לְךָ מִנְעָלִים
יָפִים אוֹ בְּגָדִים חֲמוּדִים" . . . וּכְשֶׁיִּהְיֶה דַעְתּוֹ שְׁלֵמָה . . . יֹאמַר לוֹ רַבּוֹ:
"לְמוֹד כְּדֵי שֶׁתִּהְיֶה רֹאשׁ וְדַיָּין, וִיכַבְּדוּךְ בְּנֵי אָדָם וְיָקוּמוּ מִפָּנֶיךָ" . . .

וְכָל זֶה מְגוּנֶּה . . . שֶׁאֵין לָשׁוּם תַּכְלִית הַחָכְמָה לֹא לְקַבֵּל כָּבוֹד מִבְּנֵי אָדָם
וְלֹא לְהַרְוִיחַ מָמוֹן . . . וְלֹא תִהְיֶה אֶצְלוֹ תַּכְלִית לִמוּד הַחָכְמָה אֶלָּא לָדַעַת
אוֹתָהּ בִּלְבַד . . . וְאוּלָם זֶה טוֹב לָהֶם, עַד שֶׁיִּהְיֶה לָהֶם כֹּחַ וְהֶרְגֵּל וְהִשְׁתַּדְּלוּת
בַּעֲשִׂיַּית הַתּוֹרָה, וּמִזֶּה יִתְעוֹרְרוּ לָדַעַת הָאֱמֶת וְיַחְזְרוּ עוֹבְדִים מֵאַהֲבָה.

וְזֶה הוּא מַה שֶּׁאָמְרוּ ז"ל (פְּסָחִים נ, ב) "לְעוֹלָם יַעֲסוֹק אָדָם בַּתּוֹרָה
וַאֲפִילוּ שֶׁלֹּא לִשְׁמָהּ, שֶׁמִּתּוֹךְ שֶׁלֹּא לִשְׁמָהּ בָּא לִשְׁמָהּ".

Imagine a young child who is brought to a teacher to learn Torah, which is the child's greatest good . . . but due to youth and immaturity, the child does not appreciate this. . . . So the teacher needs to . . . motivate the child with age-appropriate incentives. So the teacher should say, "Read your lesson, and I will give you nuts, figs, or honey." . . .

When the child grows older, and the sweets are no longer attractive . . . the teacher should say, "Read your lesson, and I will buy you nice shoes or attractive clothes." . . . Then, as the child's mind reaches full maturity . . . the teacher should say, "Study, and you will become a leader and scholar, and people will respect you and rise in your honor." . . .

Now all this is shameful. . . . For the purpose of wisdom is not to receive honor from people, nor to bring monetary profit. . . . We should study wisdom for no purpose other than to know it. . . . Yet this is for the children's good, for it gives them the motivation and gets them in the habit of studying and observing the Torah, and from this they will be roused to know the truth and to do it out of love.

Thus, our sages have said (Talmud, Pesachim 50b): "We should study and observe the Torah even if not for its own sake; because doing it for ulterior motives will bring us to do it for its own sake."

Appendix C

Rabbi Yitschak ben Moshe of Vienna, *Or Zaru'a*, vol. 2, Shabbat 50 📖

מַעֲשֶׂה בְּרַבִּי עֲקִיבָה, שֶׁרָאָה אָדָם אֶחָד שֶׁהָיָה עָרוֹם וְשָׁחוֹר כְּפֶחָם, וְהָיָה טוֹעֵן עַל רֹאשׁוֹ כְּטוֹעֵן עֲשָׂרָה טְעוֹנִין וְהָיָה רָץ כִּמְרוּצַת הַסּוּס. גָּזַר עָלָיו רַבִּי עֲקִיבָה, וְהֶעֱמִידוֹ. וְאָמַר לְאוֹתוֹ הָאִישׁ, "לָמָּה אַתָּה עוֹשֶׂה עֲבוֹדָה קָשָׁה כָּזֹאת? אִם עֶבֶד אַתָּה וַאֲדוֹנְךָ עוֹשֶׂה לְךָ כָּךְ, אֲנִי אֶפְדֶּה אוֹתְךָ מִיָּדוֹ. וְאִם עָנִי אַתָּה, אֲנִי מַעֲשִׁיר אוֹתְךָ".

אָמַר לוֹ, "בְּבַקָּשָׁה מִמְּךָ אַל תְּעַכְּבֵנִי, שֶׁמָּא יִרְגְּזוּ עָלַי אוֹתָם הַמְמוּנִּים עָלַי".

אָמַר לוֹ, "מַה זֶּה וּמַה מַּעֲשֶׂיךָ?"

אָמַר לוֹ, "אוֹתוֹ הָאִישׁ מֵת הוּא. וּבְכָל יוֹם וָיוֹם שׁוֹלְחִים אוֹתִי לַחְטוֹב עֵצִים וְשׂוֹרְפִין אוֹתִי בָּהֶם".

וְאָמַר לוֹ, "בְּנִי, מַה הָיְתָה מְלַאכְתְּךָ בָּעוֹלָם שֶׁבָּאתָ מִמֶּנּוּ?"

אָמַר לוֹ, "גַּבַּאי הַמַּס הָיִיתִי וְהָיִיתִי מֵרָאשֵׁי הָעָם, וְנוֹשֵׂא פָנִים לַעֲשִׁירִים וְהוֹרֵג עֲנִיִּים".

אָמַר לוֹ, "כְּלוּם שָׁמַעְתָּ מִן הַמְּמוּנִּים עָלֶיךָ אִם יֵשׁ לְךָ תַּקָּנָה?"

אָמַר לוֹ, "בְּבַקָּשָׁה מִמְּךָ אַל תְּעַכְּבֵנִי, שֶׁמָּא יִרְגְּזוּ עָלַי בַּעֲלֵי פוּרְעָנוּת, שֶׁאוֹתוֹ הָאִישׁ אֵין לוֹ תַּקָּנָה. אֶלָּא שָׁמַעְתִּי מֵהֶם דָּבָר שֶׁאֵינוֹ יָכוֹל לִהְיוֹת, שֶׁאִילְמָלֵי הָיָה לוֹ לָזֶה הֶעָנִי בֵּן שֶׁהוּא עוֹמֵד בַּקָּהָל וְאוֹמֵר 'בָּרְכוּ אֶת ה' הַמְבוֹרָךְ' וְעוֹנִין אַחֲרָיו 'בָּרוּךְ ה' הַמְבוֹרָךְ לְעוֹלָם וָעֶד', אוֹ יֹאמַר 'יִתְגַּדַּל' וְעוֹנִין אַחֲרָיו 'יְהֵא שְׁמֵיהּ רַבָּא מְבָרַךְ', מִיָּד מַתִּירִין אוֹתוֹ הָאִישׁ מִן הַפּוּרְעָנוּת. וְאוֹתוֹ אִישׁ לֹא הִנִּיחַ בֵּן בָּעוֹלָם, וְעָזַב אִשְׁתּוֹ מְעוּבֶּרֶת וְאֵינוֹ יוֹדֵעַ אִם תֵּלֵד זָכָר, מִי מְלַמְּדוֹ? שֶׁאֵין לְאוֹתוֹ הָאִישׁ אָהוּב בָּעוֹלָם".

בְּאוֹתָהּ שָׁעָה קִיבֵּל עָלָיו רַבִּי עֲקִיבָה לֵילֵךְ וּלְחַפֵּשׂ אִם הוֹלִיד בֵּן כְּדֵי שֶׁיְּלַמְּדוֹ תּוֹרָה וְיַעֲמִידוֹ לִפְנֵי הַצִּבּוּר. אָמַר לוֹ, "מַה שְּׁמֶךָ?" אָמַר לוֹ "עֲקִיבָה".

"וְשֵׁם אִנְתְּתָךְ?" אָמַר לוֹ, "שׁוֹשְׁנִיבָא".

"וְשֵׁם קַרְתָּךְ?" אָמַר לוֹ, "לוּדְקְיָא".

מִיָּד נִצְטַעֵר רַבִּי עֲקִיבָה צַעַר גָּדוֹל וְהָלַךְ וְשָׁאַל עָלָיו. כֵּיוָן שֶׁבָּא לְאוֹתוֹ מָקוֹם שָׁאַל עָלָיו. אָמְרוּ לוֹ, "יִשְׁתַּחֲקוּ עַצְמוֹתָיו שֶׁל אוֹתוֹ הָרָשָׁע". שָׁאַל עַל אִשְׁתּוֹ, אָמְרוּ לוֹ, "יִמָּחֶה זִכְרָהּ מִן הָעוֹלָם". שָׁאַל עַל הַבֵּן, אָמְרוּ, "הֲרֵי עָרֵל הוּא, אֲפִילוּ מִצְוַת מִילָה לֹא עָסַקְנוּ".

מִיָּד נָטְלוּ רַבִּי עֲקִיבָה וּמִלְּאוֹ וְהוֹשִׁיבוֹ לְפָנָיו, וְלֹא הָיָה מְקַבֵּל תּוֹרָה עַד שֶׁיָּשַׁב עָלָיו מ' יוֹם בְּתַעֲנִית. יָצְתָה בַּת קוֹל וְאָמְרָה לוֹ, "רַבִּי עֲקִיבָה, לֵךְ וְלַמֵּד לוֹ". הָלַךְ וְלִמְּדוֹ תּוֹרָה, וּקְרִיאַת שְׁמַע, וי"ח בְּרָכוֹת, וּבִרְכַּת הַמָּזוֹן, וְהֶעֱמִידוֹ לִפְנֵי הַקָּהָל וְאָמַר, "בָּרְכוּ אֶת ה' הַמְבוֹרָךְ!" וְעָנוּ הַקָּהָל, "בָּרוּךְ ה' הַמְבוֹרָךְ לְעוֹלָם וָעֶד!" "יִתְגַּדַּל!" "יְהֵא שְׁמֵיהּ רַבָּא".

בְּאוֹתָהּ שָׁעָה, מִיָּד הִתִּירוּ הַמֵּת מִן הַפֻּרְעָנִיּוֹת. מִיָּד בָּא לְרַבִּי עֲקִיבָה בַּחֲלוֹם וְאָמַר, "יְהִי רָצוֹן מֵה' שֶׁתָּנוּחַ דַּעְתְּךָ בְּגַן עֵדֶן, שֶׁהִצַּלְתָּ אוֹתִי מִדִּינָהּ שֶׁל גֵּיהִנָּם".

Rabbi Akiva once saw a man, naked and darkened by coal dust, carrying an extremely heavy load of firewood on his head and running at a rapid pace. Rabbi Akiva commanded the man to stop. Rabbi Akiva said to him, "Why are you running with such a heavy load? If you are a slave, I shall free you! If you are poor and must exert yourself to such an inhuman extent, let me give you money and make you wealthy!"

"Please," the man entreated Rabbi Akiva, "Let me continue my work, lest my overseers become angry with me!"

Rabbi Akiva asked, "And what is your work?"

The man replied, "I am a dead man. Each day, I am sent to collect wood for a giant fire into which I am then cast."

Rabbi Akiva asked, "What was your occupation in this world?"

The man answered, "I was a tax collector. I took bribes from the rich, and I had the poor executed."

Rabbi Akiva inquired, "My son, have you not heard in the other worlds that something might be done to help you and alleviate your suffering?"

Rabbi Yitschak ben Moshe of Vienna
ca. 1180–1250

Student of the German tosafists. His fame stems primarily from his influential halachic work and commentary to the Talmud, *Or Zaru'a*, which was subsequently quoted by many halachic authorities. His son Rabbi Chaim wrote a compendium of his father's work, which for many generations was the only widely used version of the *Or Zaru'a*. In the 19th century, the original work was found and published. Among his students was the Maharam of Rothenburg.

"Please," he cried, "Allow me to resume my work. My taskmasters will be angry with me and punish me further. They say that I have no way of being redeemed. Had I had a child who would stand up in public and cause others to praise God through prayers or *Kaddish*, then they could release me from this punishment. But I left behind a wife who was pregnant, and I'm not sure if she gave birth to a child. And even if she did, there is no one who would teach my child Torah, for I have no friend left in the world."

At that moment, Rabbi Akiva resolved to seek out and teach this man's child and teach him Torah and stand him before the congregation. "What is your name?" he asked.

"My name is Akiva, my wife's name is Shoshniba, and I am from the town of Ludkiya," said the man.

Rabbi Akiva felt extremely pained because of this soul, and he traveled until he came to that very town and inquired about him.

"May his bones be ground to dust in hell!" the villagers answered.

"Where is this man's wife?"

The villagers answered, "May her memory be blotted out from this world!"

"Where is this man's child?"

"He is uncircumcised, and no one will circumcise him!"

Rabbi Akiva took the man's son, circumcised him, and began to teach him Torah. But the boy would not accept his teaching. Rabbi Akiva fasted for forty days on his behalf until a heavenly voice said, "Rabbi Akiva, you may now teach him."

Rabbi Akiva taught him Torah, and to recite the *Shema*, the silent prayer, and the Grace after Meals. He placed the child before the congregation, and he led them in prayers and in the reciting of *Kaddish*.

Then the soul was spared from his punishment. He came to Rabbi Akiva in a dream and said, "May God grant you a peaceful portion in heaven because you have spared me from the punishments of hell."

ADDITIONAL READINGS

DEFEATING DEATH

BY RABBI JONATHAN SACKS

Only now, reaching *Nitzavim-Vayelech*, can we begin to get a sense of the vast, world-changing project at the heart of the Divine-human encounter that took place in the lifetime of Moses and the birth of Jews/Hebrews/Israel as a nation.

To understand it, recall the famous remark of Sherlock Holmes. "I draw your attention," he said to Dr Watson, "to the curious incident of the dog at night." "But the dog did nothing at night," said Watson. "That," said Holmes, "is the curious incident." Sometimes to know what a book is about you need to focus on what it does *not* say, not just on what it does.

What is missing from the Torah, almost inexplicably so given the background against which it is set, is a *fixation with death*. The ancient Egyptians were obsessed with death. Their monumental buildings were an attempt to defy death. The pyramids were giant mausoleums. More precisely, they were portals through which the soul of a deceased pharaoh could ascend to heaven and join the immortals. The most famous Egyptian text that has come down to us is The Book of the Dead. Only the afterlife is real: life is a preparation for death.

There is nothing of this in the Torah, at least not explicitly. Jews believed in *olam haba*, the world to come, life after death. They believed in *techiyat hametim*, the resurrection of the dead. There are six references to it in the second paragraph of the Amidah alone. But not only are these ideas almost completely absent from Tanakh. They are absent at the very points where we would expect them.

The book of Kohelet/Ecclesiastes is an extended lament at human mortality. *Havel havalim hakol havel*: Everything is worthless because life is a mere fleeting breath. Why did the author of Ecclesiastes not mention the world to come and life-after-death? The book of Job is a sustained protest against the apparent injustice of the world. Why did no one answer Job: "You and other innocent people who suffer will be rewarded in the afterlife"? We believe in the afterlife. Why then is it not mentioned—merely hinted at—in the Torah? That is the curious incident.

The simple answer is that obsession with death ultimately devalues life. Why fight against the evils and injustices of the world if this life is only a preparation for the world to come? Ernest Becker in his classic *The Denial of Death* argues that fear of our own mortality has been one of the driving forces of civilization. It is what led the ancient world to enslave the masses, turning them into giant labour forces to build monumental buildings that would stand as long as time itself. It led to the ancient cult of the hero, the man who becomes immortal by doing daring deeds on the field of battle. We fear death; we have a love-hate relationship with it. Freud called this *thanatos*, the death instinct, and said it was one of the two driving forces of life, the other being *eros*.

Judaism is a sustained protest against this worldview. That is why "No one knows where Moses is buried" (Deut. 34: 6) so that his tomb should never become a place of pilgrimage and worship. That is why in place of a pyramid or a temple such as Ramses II built at Abu Simbel, all the Israelites had for almost five centuries until the days of Solomon was the *mishkan*, a portable sanctuary, more like a tent than a temple. That is why, in Judaism, death defiles and why the rite of the Red Heifer was necessary to purify people from contact with it. That is why the holier you are—if you are a cohen, more so if you are the High Priest—the less you can be in contact or under the same roof as a dead person. God is not in death but in life.

Only against this Egyptian background can we fully sense the drama behind words that have become so familiar to us that we are no longer surprised by them, the great words in which Moses frames the choice for all time:

> See, I have set before you today life and good, death and evil … I call heaven and earth as witnesses today against you, that I have set before you life and death, the blessing and the curse; therefore choose life, that you and your children may live. (Deut. 30: 15, 19)

Life is good, death is bad. Life is a blessing, death is a curse. These are truisms for us. Why even mention them? Because they were not common ideas in the ancient world. They were revolutionary. They still are.

How then do you defeat death? Yes there is an afterlife. Yes there is *techiyat hametim*, resurrection. But Moses does not focus on these obvious ideas. He tells us something different altogether. You achieve immortality by being part of a covenant—a covenant with eternity itself, that is to say, a covenant with God.

When you live your life within a covenant something extraordinary happens. Your parents and grandparents live on in you. You live on in your children and grandchildren. They are part of your life. You are part of theirs. That is what Moses meant when he said, near the beginning of this week's parsha:

> It is not with you alone that I am making this covenant and oath, but with whoever stands with us here today before the Lord our God as well as those not with us here today. (Deut. 29: 13–14)

In Moses' day that last phrase meant "your children not yet born." He did not need to include "your parents, no longer alive" because their parents had themselves made a covenant with God forty years before at Mount Sinai. But what Moses meant in a larger sense is that when we renew the covenant, when we dedicate our lives to the faith and way of life

of our ancestors, they become immortal in us, as we become immortal in our children.

It is precisely because Judaism focuses on this world, not the next, that it is the most child-centred of all the great religions. They are our immortality. That is what Rachel meant when she said, "Give me children, or else I am like one dead" (Gen. 30: 1). It is what Abraham meant when he said, "Lord, God, what will you give me if I remain childless?" (Gen. 15: 2). We are not all destined to have children. The rabbis said that the good we do constitutes our *toledot*, our posterity. But by honouring the memory of our parents and bringing up children to continue the Jewish story we achieve the one form of immortality that lies this side of the grave, in this world that God pronounced good.

Now consider the two last commands in the Torah, set out in parshat *Vayelech*, the ones Moses gave at the very end of his life. One is *hakhel*, the command that the king summon the nation to an assembly every seven years:

> At the end of every seven years … Assemble the people—men, women and children, and the stranger living in your towns—so that they can listen and learn to fear the Lord your God and follow carefully all the words of this law (Deut. 31: 12).

The meaning of this command is simple. Moses is saying: It is not enough that your parents made a covenant with God at Mount Sinai or that you yourselves renewed it with me here on the plains of Moab. The covenant must be perpetually renewed, every seven years, so that it never becomes history. It always remains memory. It never becomes old because every seven years it becomes new again.

And the last command? "Now write down this song and teach it to the Israelites and make them sing it, so that it may be a witness for me against them" (Deut. 31: 19). This, according to tradition, is the command to write [at least part of] a Sefer Torah. As Maimonides puts it: "Even if your ancestors have left you a

Sefer Torah, nonetheless you are commanded to write one for yourself."

What is Moses saying in this, his last charge to the people he had led for forty years, was: It is not sufficient to say, our ancestors received the Torah from Moses, or from God. You have to take it and make it new in every generation. You must make the Torah not just your parents' or grandparents' faith but your own. If you write it, it will write you. The eternal word of the eternal God is your share in eternity.

We now sense the full force of the drama of these last days of Moses' life. Moses knew he was about to die, knew he would not cross the Jordan and enter the land he had spent his entire life leading the people toward. Moses, confronting his own mortality, asks us in every generation to confront ours.

Our faith—Moses is telling us—is not like that of the Egyptians, the Greeks, the Romans, or virtually every other civilization known to history. We do not find God in a realm beyond life—in heaven, or after death, in mystic disengagement from the world or in philosophical contemplation. We find God in life. We find God in (the key words of Devarim) love and joy. To find God, he says in this week's parsha, you don't have to climb to heaven or cross the sea (Deut. 30: 12–13). God is here. God is now. God is life.

And that life, though it will end one day, in truth does not end. For if you keep the covenant, then your ancestors will live in you, and you will live on in your children (or your disciples or the recipients of your kindness). Every seven years the covenant will become new again. Every generation will write its own Sefer Torah. The gate to eternity is not death: it is life lived in a covenant endlessly renewed, in words engraved on our hearts and the hearts of our children.

And so Moses, the greatest leader we ever had, became immortal. Not by living forever. Not by building a tomb and temple to his glory. We don't even know where he is buried. The only physical structure he left us was portable because life itself is a journey. He didn't even become immortal the way Aaron did, by seeing his children become his successors. He became immortal by making us his disciples. And in one of their first recorded utterances, the rabbis said likewise: Raise up many disciples.

To be a leader, you don't need a crown or robes of office. All you need to do is to write your chapter in the story, do deeds that heal some of the pain of this world, and act so that others become a little better for having known you. Live so that through you our ancient covenant with God is renewed in the only way that matters: in life. Moses' last testament to us at the very end of his days, when his mind might so easily have turned to death, was: Choose life.

www.rabbisacks.org
Reprinted with permission of the author.

KADDISH: THE UNANSWERED CRY

BY RABBI KENNETH CHELST, PhD

The Kaddish is a prayer whose utterance reflects the saga of the Jewish nation as a whole as well as the depths of emotion of the lonely Jew of faith. How powerful is the image of the Jews of the Kovno Ghetto reciting in one voice the Kaddish for their beloved, the 10,000 innocent martyrs killed by the Nazis only days before.[1] No less moving is the image of the young orphan arising in the midst of a crowded synagogue, striving to maintain a link with his parents and the past through the Kaddish. Yet the utterance of this prayer also forces the orphan to repeatedly confront the stark reality of his loss.

Prayer is a central component of the Jewish religious experience, conveying through its words and symbolism a unique relationship between man and God in general and Jew and God in particular. In the cauldron of Jewish history, certain prayers have taken on an overpowering significance that transcends their individual words. The *Shema's* strength lies in the simplicity of its acceptance of One God. In contrast, the power of the Kaddish lies in its complex message that may conflict with the emotions of the day. It is a message of acceptance of God's will when life's vagaries seem difficult to accept. It is a statement of the unity of God's universe when to the mourner the world is a chaotic black hole. It is a prayer of hope focused on the future for a mourner having difficulty coming to grips with the present and immediate past. It is a prayer for the lonely mourner and also a prayer for the Jewish nation as we oscillate between the peaks and valleys of our historical experiences. It is a prayer whose recital fulfills the commandment of "I shall be sanctified amongst the children of Israel"[2] and simultaneously reminds us that others have ful-

filled this commandment by giving their lives. And it is also a prayer to console God over the loss of the irreplaceable Jew who is an entire legion in God's small army.[3]

The Kaddish is believed to have been instituted in response to the destruction of the First Temple.[4] As we explore its words and phrases, it will be obvious how the Kaddish assumed its role as a prayer of national tragedy and destiny. Only later was a second dimension added, that of a mourner's prayer of personal anguish. Unfortunately, as in the Kovno Ghetto, the personal and national tragedies have often been intertwined.

Structure and Phraseology

The structure of the Kaddish is that of an archetypal prayer of special holiness. Like *Borechu* and *Kedusha*, it begins with an individual's request for a glorification of the name of God.[5] The congregation then responds by praising God. The individual continues by adding his own words of praise. The introductory words of Kaddish, *Yisgadal v'yiskadash shmai rabah*,[6] [Let His great name be magnified and sancti-

---

[1] The scene in the Kovno Ghetto was replayed all over Eastern Europe in the 1930s and 1940s. I mention this ghetto because of a responsum by Rabbi Ephraim Oshry, who lived in Kovno. He held that Kaddish had to be recited even for individuals whose souls had been purified in the crucible of Nazi atrocities. In his book of responsa, he describes the scene when the entire community began to say Kaddish. Rabbi Ephraim Oshry, *Responsa MiMa'amakim* (Out of the Depths), 2:6.

[2] Leviticus 22:32. See Rabbi Dr. Norman Lamm, *Kedusha VeKaddish*, which appears in the proceedings of the Fifth Congress on Oral Law (New York, 1984).

[3] S. Y. Agnon *"Petichah LeKaddish,"* in *Samuch VeNireh*; T. B. Berachot 3a; and Rabbi M. Luban, *"The Kaddish: Man's Reply to Evil,"* in Studies in Torah Judaism, edited by L. Stitskin. (New York: Yeshiva University Press, 1969).

[4] Rabbi Yechiel Epstein, *Aruch HaShulchan, Orach Chaim* 55:1. This opinion is supported in part by the aggadah at the beginning of T.B. Berachot 3a, which describes Cod's mourning the Temple's destruction and His being consoled by the recital of the Kaddish. See also David De Sola Pool, *The Kaddish,* for a linguistic assessment of the age of the Kaddish.

[5] Rabbi Dr. N. Lamm, *Kedusha VeKaddish*, finds the basis for this "initiation and response" in the verse "For I will proclaim the name of the Lord, ascribe greatness unto our Cod" (Deuteronomy 32:3).

[6] There is a halachic debate as to the proper pronunciation of the first two words of the Kaddish. In addition, there are a number of other words and phrases in the Kaddish that are the subject of conflicting opinions and different customs. For a discussion of these issues, see Rabbi Yisroel Meir HaCohen (Chofetz Chaim) *Mishneh Berurah* 56:1-4. The most complete discussion of Kaddish is found in Rabbi David Assaf, *The Kaddish, Its Basis, Meaning and Laws* (Israel, 1966). The pronunciation reflected here is that found in the Philip Birnbaum, *HaSiddur HaShalem* (New York: Hebrew Publishing Company). Similarly, I do not explore here the different customs with regard to frequency of Kaddish recital. The message I wish to convey is independent of the specific variances in custom and pronunciation. The transliteration used in the text comes from Rabbi Maurice Lamm,

---

fied], are simply a hope and request to glorify God's great name. The first two words were drawn from the Messianic vision of Ezekiel[7] referring to a time when God's glory will be apparent to all. Implicit in the request is recognition that God's glory is diminished because of the evil actions of each individual and that positive actions can restore God's glory. In short, the Kaddish begins as both a prayer of hope for the future and a statement of responsibility to change the present. Faced with God's hiding His face as the Temple burned to the ground, the Jew assumed a responsibility to bring God back to earth and to sustain a hopeful vision of this return even when blinded by Temple ruins and human ashes. Face to face with evil, the Jew responded by reaffirming his faith in a just God.[8]

The next phrase, *b'olmo dee'vro chirusai v'yamlich malchusai* [in the world created according to His will], contains an implicit acceptance of the will of God by referring to a world created by God's will and that God continues to rule. How difficult it must have been at the time of the Temple's destruction to accept that the powers that be were One power; that an all-powerful God had decreed the destruction of God's own Temple as a moral lesson to us. And yet, it was the acceptance of this fact that allowed the Jewish nation to survive this catastrophe and prevented our national identity from dissolving in a philosophical quagmire of doubt.

The concluding section of this opening request contains the phrase *b'chaiyechon u'vyomechon, u'vchaiyai d'chol bais yisroel ba'agolah u'vizman koriv* [in your lifetime and in your days and in the lifetime of all of the House of Israel, quickly and in the near future]. In contrast to the opening words of the Kaddish, in the impersonal third person, the focus here shifts to the very personal second person- "in your lifetime."[9] This phrase affirms both the life of an individual as well as the life of the Jewish nation. It is an implicit

prayer for long life:[10] the sanctification of God's name does not demand death but should be accomplished by living a sanctified existence. Confronted with mass destruction and loss of life after the destruction of the Temple, we were expected to reaffirm the value of life. The final three words of this request, "quickly and in the near future," state the urgency of our vision of God's glorification. Implicitly, these words demand that the listeners respond immediately in order to speed this vision into reality.

The congregation is then expected to respond with the phrase *Amen, y'hai shmai rabah m'vorach, l'olam u' lolmai olmaya* [Amen, Let God's great name[11] be blessed forever and ever]. An "Amen" equates the respondent with the individual making the blessing and consequently should not be said in a voice louder than the original blessing.[12] In contrast, *y'hai shmai rabah* stands on its own foundation and should always be said in a loud voice,[13] no matter how softly the initiator said the preceding words. It is this congregational response to the request that is crucial; without it, all the other words and symbolism lose their force. *Y'hai shmai rabah* is not just a reactive affirmation of the initiator's words; it is an active attempt to bring God into every dimension of this world. According to the Talmud, it is a phrase that "when said with complete feeling, negative heavenly decrees are torn to shreds."[14] In short, this phrase is the essence of the Kaddish and is often used in the Talmud to refer to the entire Kaddish.

This phrase has a Hebrew equivalent which is the second verse of the *Shema Yisroel*. Tradition records that this verse, *Boruch shem kevod malchuso l'ol-*

The Jewish Way in Death and Mourning (New York: Jonathan David Publishers, 1969). This book also contains a beautiful discussion of the meaning of Kaddish.

7 Ezekiel 38:23.

8 Rabbi M. Luban, *The Kaddish*.

9 Rabbi Yechiel M. Tuckachinsky, *Gesher HaChaim*, 1:321. See also footnote 8 on the same page.

10 Rabbi Oshry, *Responsa MiMa'amakim*, 3:8. Rabbi Oshry cites sources that describe a custom of adding references to specific individuals in this phrase. During the Babylonian Exile, "in the lives of the heads of Exile" was added and during the time of Maimonides, "in the lifetime of Maimonides" was added.

11 T.B. Berachot 3a; see Tosefot there. Rashi in the *Machzor Vitry* interprets the word *"rabah"* as a verb meaning "to complete." In Rashi's opinion the congregational response has two components: a prayer that God's name be completed (through the destruction of Amalek) and that His name be blessed in the World to Come.

12 T.B. Berachot 45a.

13 T.B. Shabbat 119b, Tosefot ad loc., and Rabbi Joseph Caro *Shulchan Aruch, Orach Chaim* 56:1. However, Kaddish should not be said in so loud a voice as to sound ridiculous.

14 T.B. Shabbat 119b.

am va'ed, was Jacob's immediate response when his sons declared the first *Shema Yisroel* as he lay on his deathbed. Interestingly, this verse is always read silently except on Yom Kippur.[15]

After the congregation completes its response, the initiator continues with a series of words in praise of God and then concludes with the statement that God is beyond man's ability to praise and console Him, *l'aila min kol birchasa v'shirasa, tushbechasa, v'nechamasa, da'amiron b'olmo* [(He is) above all blessings, hymns, praises, and consolation that we can say in this world]. Thus the Kaddish reflects the enigma of Jewish existence. It begins with a prayer to bring God's glory down to earth and concludes with the recognition that the complete glory of God can never be captured in this world.

Different Forms

When the congregation responds with the second "Amen," the basic Kaddish has been completed. If the Kaddish ends at this point, it has been labeled the Half-Kaddish, although, in fact, it is the completed form of the original Kaddish. This form is recited by the cantor at transition points in the prayers. In the morning prayer this Half-Kaddish appears before *Borechu* and after *Tachanun.* In the afternoon and evening prayers, it is recited immediately before the *Shemoneh Esray,* the silent prayer that is the heart of each service.

The Kaddish fulfills this important transitional role by reminding us of the importance of glorifying and exalting God. It is appropriate that as we switch from one phase of a prayer service to another, we are reminded of why we are praying in the first place. This transitional Kaddish suggests that we contemplate what we have just said and prepare for what we are about to say.[16]

There are four major additions to the basic Kaddish and are recited on different occasions or at different points in the daily prayers.

1. Mourner's (or Orphan's Kaddish) concludes with two sentences, one in Aramaic, the other in Hebrew, both of which are a prayer that God, the source of all peace, grant us and all of Israel peace. These two sentences appear at the end of every form of Kaddish except the Half-Kaddish. The concluding Hebrew sentence is also recited at the end of *Shemoneh Esray.* In these days of intermittent war and death, this has become an oft-repeated prayer of hope.

2. Rabbis' Kaddish contains the added paragraph that begins with *al yisroel v 'al rabonon* [for Israel and for its rabbis]. It is recited after learning part of the Oral Law to honor of our teachers of Jewish law and their families. Interestingly, the prayer begins with a praise of Jews in general because they support the Torah.[17] This form of Kaddish appears in the morning prayer service after the recital of a section of the Oral Law that deals with the order of service in the Temple.

3. Complete Kaddish contains the added phrase that begins *tiskabel tzelosehone* [accept their prayers], which is a request that the congregation's previous prayers be accepted by God. It generally appears at the conclusion of services, just before *Aleinu* in the morning, afternoon, and evening prayers.

4. The Burial Kaddish and the Kaddish recited after completion of a Tractate of the Talmud is essentially identical to the Rabbis' Kaddish from *y'hai shmai rabah* onward. However, the introductory paragraph of this Kaddish is unique. It explicitly refers to the future resurrection of the dead and the rebuilding of the Temple and Jerusalem.[18]

The Orphan's Kaddish

The origin of the custom that an orphan recites Kaddish for a departed parent is not totally clear. The earliest reference to the impact of Kaddish recital on a departed soul appears in a Midrash about Rabbi Aki-

---

15 T.B. Pesachim 56a. See also Rabbi Dr. Norman Lamm, *The Shema: Spirituality and Law in Judaism* (Philadelphia: Jewish Publication Society, 2000), Chapters 3 and 9.

16 Rabbi Dr. Reuven Bulka, private communication.

17 Rabbi Assaf, *The Kaddish,* 132. Also see De Sola Pool, *The Kaddish,* for a discussion of the intimate link between Kaddish and the study of the Oral Law.

18 See Rabbi Nosson Scherman, *Kaddish* (New York: Mesorah Publications Ltd., 1980) 56–60 for a discussion of different opinions with regard to the recital of this Kaddish.

va.[19] In the story, Rabbi Akiva confronts the terribly suffering soul of a dishonest tax collector. He informs Rabbi Akiva that his suffering would cease if a son of his would recite *Borechu* or Kaddish and the congregation would respond by sanctifying God's name. In response Rabbi Akiva seeks out this man's son and educates him until the boy is ready to stand before the congregation and lead the prayers from *Yishtabach* onward. The son's actions relieve the father's suffering and enable his soul to rest in peace. The Kaddish referred to in this Midrash is that recited by the cantor as part of the regular services and not what we have come to label as the Orphan's Kaddish.[20]

Recitation of the Orphan's Kaddish at the end of the daily prayers is a custom that was known to the early *Rishonim* and is cited by Rabbi Moses Isserles in his comments on the *Shulchan Aruch*.[21] This custom was probably begun in order to facilitate the recital of Kaddish for a deceased parent by a child who was either not of age or sufficiently educated to lead the congregation in prayer and could therefore not lead the recital of the many instances of Kaddish said by the cantors.[22]

The relationship between the recital of Kaddish and the departed soul has been the subject of much homiletical discourse. The common message is that a person's primary responsibility is to live a life that sanctifies God's name and that each person during the course of his life has committed acts that have detracted from the glory of God. By having his son[23]

lead others to glorify God's name in public, the negative effects are compensated for and erased and the soul of the deceased is elevated to a higher plane in the World To Come. For the child who died too young to have impinged on God's glory, there is little need for the Kaddish to right his wrongs. For the Jewish martyr, whose death sanctified God's name, earlier wrongs have been atoned for. The Kaddish recited in their memory by mourners is a statement of the deceased's lost opportunities to further glorify God's name; it enables their souls to rise to an even higher sphere in the World To Come.[24]

In any case it is important to understand that the Kaddish is not a direct prayer for the dead in the traditional sense. No mention of death or the deceased is made in the standard Kaddish. Instead, the mourner affects the soul of the deceased by causing others to sanctify God.

Just as for Israel in general, the Kaddish conveys a number of messages to the mourner:

1. It forces the mourner to publicly confront the death of a relative.

2. The mourner is asked to accept the fact that the death of a relative was God's will and was not an accident of life.

3. By affirming the relationship between the Kaddish and the deceased, the mourner reaffirms that there is reward and punishment in the World To Come.

---

19 Sec ibid., xxi-xxii, for the complete story in English. Rabbi Isaac of Vienna in his book *Or Zarua* provides one of the earliest known references that links the recital of Kaddish to the Midrash about Rabbi Akiva.

20 Rabbi Tuckachinsky, *Gesher HaChaim*, 316.

21 Rabbi Moshe Isserles, comments on *Shulchan Aruch, Yoreh Deah*, 376:4.

22 Ibid. The preferred way to sanctify God's name is to do so by leading the congregation in prayer.

23 With regard to a daughter reciting Kaddish, see Assaf, *The Kaddish*, 171–173 and the associated footnotes for a discussion of earlier sources on this issue. My father-in-law, Rabbi Isaac Simon, was the highest Judaic studies teacher in Maimonides School in Brookline, MA for almost thirty years. When he died in 1984 leaving only daughters, Rabbi Joseph B. Soloveitchik discussed the issue in the Maimonides synagogue and with my wife, Tamy, during *shiva*. Later that summer, I visited the Rav and presented a written summary of his recent remarks on the subject of women reciting Kaddish. The Rav edited and authorized the following for inclusion in this work. "Although the Jewish woman's role is not in the synagogue, a daughter could recite Kaddish in honor

of a deceased parent if there were no sons to recite Kaddish. She could recite Kaddish even if she were the only one saying Kaddish in the synagogue and the congregation could answer her Kaddish but was not required to do so. The Rav reminisced about a visit decades earlier to Vilna in which he saw a young woman recite Kaddish after the evening services. His curiosity piqued, he checked around and discovered that this woman's actions were consistent with the prevailing custom in Vilna." Joyce Steg Kosowsky, who said Kaddish for her mother in 2000, attributed that decision to her recollection of Rabbi Soloveitchik's discussion with Tamy Simon Chelst, during the June 1984 *shiva* week for Rabbi Simon.

24 Rabbi Oshry, *Responsa MiMa'amakim*, 1:16. This responsum was written after a mass slaughter of children. Rabbi Oshry authorized the recital of Kaddish for any child who was at least thirty days old at the time of death.

4. The Kaddish reminds the orphan that the commandment "Honor Thy Father and Mother"[25] extends beyond life itself. More important, the Kaddish provides an opportunity to continue to fulfill this commandment.

5. Implicit in the recital of the Kaddish is a statement of a belief in the coming of the Messiah and the resurrection of the dead.[26]

6. The concluding prayer for peace reminds the orphan that by the end of the year, when the deceased will have certainly found peace with God, the mourner's personal anguish will also have been healed by God.

These are intellectual concepts that over time impinge on the emotions of the orphan. As the orphan stands by the graveside and the loved one is lowered into the ground to the final resting place, with the coffin then completely covered with the dust of the earth, the enormity of the orphan's anguish reaches new depths with the cry of his first Kaddish.[27]

This Kaddish is a primordial cry of pain. The orphan cannot hear the Kaddish's complex message as he tries to recall hearing his parent's words. Nor can he envision God's glory filling this earth, as he stares through his tears at the small mound of earth in front of him. The first Kaddish recited is unlikely to convey an intellectual message to the mourner. Instead, it forces and allows the mourner to express his overwhelming grief. This Kaddish only makes the loss and grief more concrete and therefore more painful, but ultimately this verbalization is a prerequisite for coming to grips with the loss. During the seven-day mourning period, as the mourner recites the Kaddish and articulates indirectly his loss, the other messages contained in the Kaddish begin to pierce through the

cloud of tears. The mourner begins to see the message of acceptance and hope. Later, during the eleven-month period[28] of Kaddish recital, the Kaddish tells the mourner that it is too soon to forget the loss.

Loneliness and Guilt

After the loss of a close relative, the mourner experiences a loss of companionship. In many ways the laws of Jewish mourning address this loss and thus enable the mourner to face and ultimately accept it. Jewish customs of mourning provide extended opportunities for relatives, friends, and acquaintances to help fill the void with expressions of concern and sympathy. In addition, these laws reaffirm the importance of friendship in other ways. The mourner is obligated by Jewish Law to pay less attention to personal appearance and to refrain from certain social activities. However, some of these obligations cease when friends begin to become upset with the mourner's appearance and lack of social involvement.[29]

Besides the loss of companionship, the mourner experiences a spiritual loss: two souls whose destinies were interwoven have suddenly been separated. This cannot be assuaged merely by expressions of sympathy. Nor can friendship rebind the two souls. Rather, the institution of Kaddish, by placing the mourner in the position of publicly proclaiming God's greatness

---

[25] Rabbi Caro, *Shulchan Aruch, Yoreh Deah* 240:9.

[26] Rabbi Tuckachinsky, *Gesher HaChaim,* 321. Rabbi Tuckachinsky relates the word *b'chayechon* to the future resurrection of the dead. The Sefardic liturgy, which is also used in Hasidic congregations, includes four additional words, *"v'yatzmach purkonai vi'koraiv m'shichai,"* an explicit prayer for the early coming of the Messiah.

[27] Ibid ., 327. The first Kaddish, according to some opinions, may even be said prior to the burial, especially if the burial is delayed several days from the time of death.

[28] Ibid., 376 and Rabbi Isserles, *Yoreh Deah* 376:4. The Kaddish should be recited for a twelve-month period, but the custom is for only eleven months. Death begins a process of atonement for past sins which is completed as the flesh decays and returns to dust (T.B. Sanhedrin 46a). Our sages have established that for twelve months the body survives to serve as an intermittent resting place for the soul that is wandering between heaven and earth (T.B. Shabbat 152b). However, there is another Midrash that states that a wicked person, after dying, spends a full twelve months in Gehennom atoning for his sins *(Mishnah, Eduyot* 2:10). Therefore, the sages limited the recital of Kaddish to eleven months so as not to imply that a parent was a wicked individual.

[29] Rabbi Caro, *Shulchan Aruch, Yoreh Deah* 390:4. A mourner for a parent is not allowed to cut his or her hair even after the first thirty-day mourning period. The mourner must wait until the hair is so long that friends would be angry with him over his appearance *(Shulchan Aruch, Yoreh Deah* 380:25). Similarly, this mourner was prohibited from joining a business caravan until enough time had elapsed so that his friends would be upset over his lack of involvement and ask him to come along. (In the time of the Talmud, a caravan often involved celebrations along the route, much the same way a modern business convention mixes business with pleasure.) This unique time standard for limiting mourning observances conveys a message about the importance of friendships and warns the mourner against allowing friendships to deteriorate because of a too-long and intense period of personal grief.

and holiness for the benefit of the departed loved one's soul, reaffirms daily that these bonds still exist. The bonds may have been weakened, but Kaddish, along with acts of charity, prayer, religious study, and other dedicated actions, can still bind together the souls of the mourner and the deceased.

In rebinding the two souls, the Kaddish enables the mourner to deal with a sense of guilt that often accompanies the loss of a relative, especially a parent. During the introspective seven-day mourning period known as *shiva*, the orphan mourns not having done more for the parent, measuring his own performance against some unachieved ideal, and yearning for a little more time to express love and respect for the parent. He cries over lost opportunities for visiting a distant parent, of trips never made that perhaps should have been.

The Kaddish is instructive in this regard: it tells the mourner that love and honor do have meaning after life ceases to exist. Kaddish, when said with heart and soul, is the highest expression of love and honor, since the orphan cannot even expect a simple parental smile or hug in return. And the twice or thrice daily[30] trip to the synagogue is a continuing expression of the orphan's willingness to give of himself for the parent. To a world that views death with finality and accompanies the body to its grave with thoughts of "it is too late," the Kaddish is one way of reminding us that for the deceased's soul it is not too late as long as children and friends act to glorify God in his or her honor.

The Synagogue Experience

To strengthen the souls' bonds through the recital of Kaddish, the mourner will need help: the involve-ment of the nation of Israel as represented by the minyan around him. The orphan cries out *Yis'gadal v'yis'kadash,* asking that God be publicly sanctified and that his words link him with the departed. But without the minyan's response, the Kaddish cannot sanctify, cannot link. To the mourner the minyan is a physical reminder of the eternal nature of the soul. Just as the nation of Jews can never be totally physically destroyed, so too, no individual soul can ever totally vanish.

How sad it is that in so many of our synagogues this cry of Kaddish, which demands and pleads for a response, often remains unanswered. The *Kedusha* in the cantor's repetition of the *Shemoneh Esray* is accorded universal respect. Yet the Kaddish, which the Talmud places on an equal or higher plane,[31] is all too often ignored, drowned out by a chorus of talkers. The holiness intrinsic in the *Kedusha* derives from man's attempt to uplift himself by praising God in the language of angels. (It opens with the words "Let us sanctify Your name just as is done in the heavens above.") In contrast, the Kaddish is an attempt to bring God's glory down to earth by praising God in words of our own choosing[32] and in what was at the time the vernacular, Aramaic.[33] How little is demanded of us to respond with but seven words[34] and an occasional *Amen* or *Brich Hu;* yet how difficult it seems to be to interrupt our worldly conversations to bring God into our world. And the unanswered Kaddish remains an impassioned plea in a vacuum, making no sound, a Jewish body of words without its soul.

---

[30] The custom concerning the number of times an orphan recites Kaddish during the three daily prayers varies from community to community. When the custom of an orphan's Kaddish began, only one individual would recite the Kaddish at any one time and there were detailed rules as to who had priority. As a result, an orphan might have recited the Kaddish infrequently. In many German congregations, the custom is still to have only one individual recite the Kaddish at any one time. Sometimes an effort is made to add to the number of times the Kaddish is recited during services in order to provide each mourner with his own opportunity to recite at least one Kaddish. Rabbi Moshe Feinstein in *Iggerot Moshe, Yoreh Deah* 1:254 reviews the custom and states that the present basic minimum requirement is to recite one Kaddish each day in honor of the departed soul.

[31] T.B. Berachot 21b and *Mishneh Berurah* 56:6.

[32] Rabbi Tuckachinsky, *Gesher HaChaim,* 314–316.

[33] T.B . Berachot 3a. Tosefot ad loc. discuss two reasons for the use of Aramaic: so that the angels will not understand and therefore not be jealous, and so that the masses will understand. The comments above attempt to integrate these two reasons. For a more detailed discussion of this issue, see *Tefillat HaKaddish* by Rabbi Binyamin S. Jacobson (Israel, 1964), 13. Also see Rabbi M. Luban's *The Kaddish,* which states that Aramaic is a symbol of exile and Jewish confrontation with a hostile environment, and De Sola Pool, *The Kaddish.*

[34] There is a fundamental debate among the early post-Talmudic sages as to whether the congregation must also say the first word *yisborach* from the series of praises that follow. Sec Rabbi Caro, *Orach Chaim* 56:3, and the *Mishneh Berurah* ad loc. for a discussion of the various opinions.

Picture the Kovno ghetto survivor arising to recite the Kaddish on the *yahrzeit* of not just one relative but of an entire community. He asks us to sanctify God in the memory of those who died because they were Jews. Their deaths were the ultimate sanctification of God, and the Kaddish is the torch passed on to us to continue the task of sanctifying God's name. The survivor's Kaddish of acceptance, hope, and rebinding of souls is also living testimony that our faith cannot be consumed in ovens. How tragic that too often "the Jews of noisy, spiritual silence" near and around him in the synagogue are too busy to hear his testimony and reaffirm its truth.

Think of the mourner who has not set foot in a synagogue for years except perhaps on the High Holy Days. Now, because of a beloved parent, he attends services on a daily basis. His first recitals of Kaddish result in a tongue-twisting distortion of unfamiliar Aramaic and Hebrew words; only later will the Kaddish flow naturally. For him, the Kaddish is not only an attempt to link his soul with the deceased's; the Kaddish also represents the last strand that ties his soul to traditional Judaism. The recital of Kaddish and the warmth and unity of the congregational response provide an opportunity to reinforce this weak link. Tragically, the unheard and unanswered Kaddish, instead of hallowing this synagogue experience, leaves behind a hollow-sounding Kaddish. For this Kaddish Jew, the living, binding strand shrivels up and dies at the end of the Kaddish year.

Experience the emptiness of the mourner in a large synagogue in which decorum is the norm but in which few of the congregants appreciate the message of the Kaddish cry. The Kaddish cry draws little response because it is viewed as the mourner's personal prayer and not a plea for action. Those who respond do so out of habit or courtesy in an empty, perfunctory fashion that takes the life out of the emotion-filled words of the mourner's Kaddish.

Observe the private, self-conscious mourner who is accustomed to keeping his feelings to himself. For him, the public recital of Kaddish can be disconcerting. Wherever he travels and in whatever synagogue he finds himself, when the time for Kaddish recital occurs, he must rise and bare his soul to all those present, letting strangers know that in the recent past he has lost a close relative. As a result, instead of saying the Kaddish with the slow stately dignity it deserves, he rapidly mumbles his way through the Kaddish in the hope that no one will really notice him. This mumbling becomes a mumble jumble when each mourner scattered throughout the synagogue races through the Kaddish to the arrhythmic beat of a different heart. No wonder that the confused listener finds that to answer the Kaddish, he must become a world-class juggler, juggling simultaneously in his mouth three or more phrases, an *Amen* for the mourner nearby, a *Y'hai shmai rabah* for the mourner in the back, and a *Brich Hu* for the one standing off to the right. How sad, too, that in the process of making the Kaddish unheard, the private mourner has himself made the Kaddish undone.

Some synagogues have a custom that all mourners stand in one place when reciting the Kaddish. This custom significantly alleviates the problems noted above by enabling the mourners to recite the Kaddish in unison. In addition, the group provides a critical mass useful in attracting the attention of the remaining congregants. This custom is a classic illustration of the principle cited in Proverbs, "In a multitude of people is found the glory of the King"—*B'rov am hadras melech.*[35]

Finally, picture a Sabbath morning after two or more hours of religious services. The Jewish mourner rises again to recite the Kaddish. It is a lonely experience for him.

To be surrounded by
friends, neighbors, and acquaintances
in a crowded synagogue.

To shout, no, to cry
for the sanctification of God's name.

To strive, to strain,
to uplift ties with a parent's soul.

---

[35] Proverbs 14:28.

Instead of a chorus of voices engulfing the
orphan saying,
"Let God's Great Name Be Blessed,"
there is a spiritual silence that is deafening.

The Kaddish has now become a true
Orphan Kaddish.
The Kaddish is the Orphan
with no one to hear and respond to its cry.

And in this seeming spiritual vacuum,
the orphan hears all too clearly
the echo of his own lonely, muffled voice
reflecting off the walls of the synagogue:

Let God's great name be blessed forever and ever.
Y'hai shmai rabah m'vorach l'olam u'lolmai olmaya.

Mourner's Kaddish
Let His great name be magnified and sanctified (Amen)

In the world created according to His will,
and may He establish His Kingdom
in your lifetime and in your days
and in the lifetime of all of the House of Israel,
quickly and in the near future, and say Amen.

May His great name be blessed
forever and for all eternity.

Blessed, praised, glorified, exalted,
uplifted, honored, elevated and extolled,
be His Holy Name, Blessed is He

(He is) above[36] all blessings, hymns,
praise and consolation,
that we can say in this world, and say Amen.

May heaven be the source of abundant peace
and life for us and all of lsrael,
and say Amen.

May He who makes peace in the heavens above,
grant peace to us and all of lsrael,
and say Amen.

Graveside Kaddish
Let His great name be magnified and sanctified,
in the world that He will renew in the future,

and where He will bring the dead to life
and raise them up to an everlasting life,

and rebuild the city of Jerusalem
and erect His Temple in it,

and uproot foreign worship from the Land,
and return the worship of heaven to its Land,

and establish the kingship of the Holy One,
Blessed is He,

with sovereignty and glory,
in your lifetime and in your days.

and in the lifetime of all of the House of lsrael,
quickly and in the near future, and say Amen.

May His great name be blessed
forever and for all eternity.

Blessed, praised, glorified, exalted,
uplifted, honored, elevated and extolled,
Be His Holy Name, Blessed is He

(He is) above all blessings, hymns, praise
and consolation,
that we can say in this world, and say Amen.

May Heaven be the source of abundant peace
and good life for us and all of Israel, and say Amen.

May He who creates peace in the heavens above,
mercifully grant peace to us and all of Israel, and
say Amen.

Kaddish: The Unanswered Cry [Michigan, 2015], pp. 7–27.
Reprinted with permission of the author.

---

[36] During the ten days from the New Year until the Day of Atonement,
a word is added that changes the meaning to "far beyond."

THE REINCARNATED PRINCE

BY RABBI TUVIA BOLTON

Some three hundred years ago, the name of Rabbi Israel Baal Shem Tov spread throughout Europe as one who was willing to do anything, even perform miracles like Elijah and Moses, in order to help another, especially a fellow Jew.

One evening a middle-aged couple came with a desperate request; they wanted a child. Despite their prayers, good deeds and various remedies and treatments, they had failed to conceive a child in all the years of their marriage.

The Baal Shem Tov closed his eyes, put his face into his hands, lowered his head to the desk before him and his consciousness soared to the spiritual realms.

Minutes later he sat upright, looked at them sadly and said: "There is nothing I can do. Continue praying, continue your good deeds. May G-d have mercy, but it is beyond my ability to help you."

The woman burst into bitter tears; her husband turned his face aside and wept silently, his body shaking.

"No, no!" she cried. "I won't believe it. I will not accept no for answer. I know that when a *tzaddik* (righteous person) decrees, G-d must fulfill. I want a child!" Her cry pierced the walls and broke the holy master's heart.

He lowered his head again for many long minutes then looked up and said: "Next year you will have a child."

The couple was speechless. The man began trembling, took the Baal Shem Tov's hand and kissed it as his wife showered thanks and blessings. They backed out the door, bowing, weeping and praising G-d and His servant the holy Rabbi Israel.

Sure enough, two months later the woman conceived, and nine months thereafter gave birth to a beautiful baby boy.

The couple's joy increased day by day as the child grew. Their baby was beautiful! His eyes sparkled with life and his every smile filled their lives with warmth and happiness. At the age of one year, it was obvious he was something special; he was already walking and talking. As he approached the age of two they began looking for a tutor to begin teaching him Torah. They planned to take him to the Baal Shem Tov; they would show him what his blessing had brought.

But on the morning of his second birthday the child didn't wake up.

The neighbors came running when they heard the screams, but nothing could be done. As miraculously as the boy had come, so mysteriously and tragically had he departed this world.

The funeral was enough to make the heavens cry. After the week of mourning they returned to the Baal Shem Tov to inform him of the tragedy. But the Baal Shem Tov understood better than they could possibly have imagined.

"Your child," he said to the grieving parents, "contained a lofty soul that had made a huge sacrifice to save thousands of people. But this soul needed you to achieve its *tikkun* ('rectification') and become spiritually complete. That day, when you came to me, I looked into the heavens and saw that it was impossible for you to have children; but when I heard your cries and saw the depth of your pain, I realized that this special soul was destined to be yours for the short span of its return to physical life. Sit down, dear friends, I have a story to tell you."

* * *

Several hundred years ago lived a king who was childless. He was rich and powerful, but he desperately desired a son to carry on the lineage. He ordered that all his subjects hold daily prayers in their houses of worship that G-d should grant their sovereign an heir.

One of his advisors suggested that the reason the king was childless was because his Jewish subjects did not pray for him sincerely enough. The only way to make them do that, said this advisor, was to oppress them.

The next day the king issued a public proclamation stating that if the queen was not blessed with a child in the next three months, all the Jews would be expelled from his kingdom. With all the neighboring countries closed to Jewish settlement, the poor Jews had nowhere to go. Their cries and prayers rose from every synagogue in the land.

A call resounded through the heavens for a soul willing to descend into the spiritually desolate environment of the royal palace in order the save the Jews of that land. Finally, one very holy soul agreed to make the sacrifice.

Shortly thereafter, the queen became pregnant and soon gave birth to a son. The king was overjoyed and showered the Jews of his realm with presents and favors.

At the age of two, the child could already read and write, and when he was five years old he had surpassed all his teachers and learned all they had to teach. A master teacher—a priest whose fame as a genius and scholar had spread far and wide—was brought from afar to teach the prodigy.

This new tutor was of a different caliber altogether. It seemed that he had mastered every form of wisdom in the world and his very presence radiated a thirst for knowledge. The young genius could not get enough of his new teacher. He became more attached to him than even to his own father the king. He spent every moment of the day and most of the night with the tutor, absorbing more and more wisdom and learning. And the more he absorbed, the more he desired.

But the priest demanded his times of privacy. He had an agreement with the king that for two hours of every day he would lock himself in his room and no one, not even the king himself, was allowed to enter or disturb him in any way. It was on this condition that he accepted the task of teaching the prince.

But the prince was curious. He could not tolerate the idea that his beloved master was withholding something from him. He had to know everything!

One day, the young prince managed to hide himself in his teacher's room before the priest's daily two hours of seclusion. The priest entered the room, locked the door securely behind him, and searched the room thoroughly. Somehow he failed to discover the prince's hiding place and he proceeded in his strange daily ritual.

First he removed all the crosses from the walls and from around his neck, and put them in a box outside his window. Then he took out a large white woolen shawl with strings at the corners, wrapped it completely around his head and body, and began weeping like a baby.

Then he took out two small black boxes with long black straps attached to them, tied one to his left upper arm and the other above the middle of his forehead. After that he began to pray, swaying, singing and crying for over an hour. Finally, he took out a large Hebrew text and began reading from it in a sing-song voice, swaying back and forth all the time.

Suddenly, he stopped and listened intently. The faint but unmistakable sound of another person in the room had caught his ear. The priest was terrified. He jumped from his chair, hurriedly removed the black boxes and shawl, stuffed them in a drawer, and began to search the room. It did not take long for him to discover his young pupil, who had been observing everything with rapt fascination.

The priest begged the boy not to reveal what he saw. If the king found out he would certainly be beheaded. But the prince's curiosity had been aroused. He swore that he would never tell anyone what he saw in the room, but only if the priest would explain what he had just done and teach him what it was all about.

So the priest had no choice but to reveal that he was a Jew, doing was what Jews have been doing for thousands of years: praying and studying the Torah and fulfilling its commandments. He had been compelled to hide his faith during one of the many decrees of forced conversions that Jews were subjected to in those times; now he was forced to assume the guise of an alien religion on the pain of death.

"You must teach me your ancient wisdom!" the prince insisted. "I knew that you were hiding something from me. In everything that you taught me, I always sensed that there was something more there, something deeper and truer, that you were withholding from me!" In vain did the "priest" plead that he would be subjecting them both to mortal danger. "If you refuse to teach me," the prince threatened, "I'll tell everyone what I saw in this room."

For several years they learned Torah together, until the boy announced that he wanted to convert to Judaism. His desire became so strong that teacher and pupil made up a story about going to Rome to further their studies. Instead of traveling to Rome, they escaped to another country where the boy converted and never returned to the palace again.

* * *

"The prince became a great and famous sage," the Baal Shem Tov concluded his story, "living a life of saintliness and good deeds. When he passed on from this world and his soul ascended to the heavens, it was the most luminous soul that had returned from earth in many generations. Only one blemish dimmed its shinning perfection: the lingering effect of the fact that it had been conceived, borne, and fed for two years in the spiritually negative environment of the royal palace. All it lacked to attain the true heights of its glorious potential was for it to be conceived and return to earth, given birth to and weaned in the holy atmosphere of a righteous home.

"When I saw the depth of your holy desire for a child, I know that you were worthy parents for this righteous soul."

Reprinted with permission from Chabad.org.

Lesson Five

The Mourning After
Grief and Consolation

Bereavement: It is pointless to attempt to describe the feeling. Those who've experienced it know and remember it all too well. For those fortunate enough not to have experienced it, no words will enable them to relate to the depth of the loss, pain, and agony. The Jewish perspective on mourning and its associated rituals provide the survivors with a healthy channel for the crushing grief and the necessary tools to—when the time is right—reemerge and cope with "life after death."

JLI

JEWISH LEARNING INSTITUTE

Introduction

Text 1

George A. Bonanno, PhD, *The Other Side of Sadness: What the New Science of Bereavement Tells Us About Life After Loss* [Basic Books, New York: 2009], pp. 1–2

George A. Bonanno, PhD.

Psychologist. Dr. Bonanno is a professor of clinical psychology at Columbia University. His research focuses on how people cope with potentially traumatic events. He is author of the *Other Side of Sadness: What the New Science of Bereavement Tells Us About Life After Loss.*

Heather Lindquist was in the kitchen cleaning up after lunch when she heard a dull thud. It sounded as if it came from the hallway, and it was just a little too loud to ignore. "Boys!" she yelled. "What are you up to?" There was no answer. She found her two boys playing quietly on the couch in the living room. They giggled. "You jokers," she said with a smile. "What was that sound?" They shrugged. "Where is your father?" Without waiting for an answer, she ran toward the hallway. She cried out in fear when she found her husband, John, writhing on the floor. John had severe asthma. He was taking a new medication, and it had seemed to be working, but suddenly he had collapsed in the worst attack he'd ever had. Heather tried everything she could think of to save her husband's life. Then she called an ambulance. The rest was a blur. John died of cardiac arrest on the way to the hospital.

Heather was thirty-four years old. Her boys were five and seven. At that moment, John's death felt like the worst thing that could ever have happened to her. . . .

Heather Lindquist had lived her entire life in the same quiet suburban community in northern New Jersey. She and John had been high school sweethearts. They married and purchased a small ranch-style house. They had children. They got a dog. The schools were good and the community was stable. Heather thought that the television was on more than it should be, but other than that, everything seemed in order. Then John died and she had to rethink it all.

Now she was a single parent. She had to find new ways to earn money and also find extra time to be with her boys. And somehow she had to contain everyone's anguish. She found strength she didn't know she had. It was lonely and painful at times. But Heather found meaning and vigor and even joy in the idea that she was going to make it.

"I expected to collapse. I really did. That's what I wanted to do. That would have been the easiest thing to do," Heather explained. "But . . . I couldn't. Each day I got up and did what I had to. The days passed and somehow it was OK. The boys were great. They were upset in the beginning, of course. We all were. They hung in there. And we stayed together. I love those boys so much. John would have been proud of them."

Faith – Belief in Something that gives you Strength To get
Fantasy – An Escape From your Challenge   Through your
                                                                    Struggle

Religion is There To give a person Strength To Face
Problems + Challenges

Text 2

Fran Schumer, "After a Death, the Pain That Doesn't Go Away," *The New York Times*, September 28, 2009

In 2004, Stephanie Muldberg of Short Hills, N.J., lost her son Eric, 13, to Ewing's sarcoma, a bone cancer. Four years after Eric's death, Ms. Muldberg, now 48, walked around like a zombie. "I felt guilty all the time, guilty about living," she said. "I couldn't walk into the deli because Eric couldn't go there any longer. I couldn't play golf because Eric couldn't play golf. My life was a mess.

"And I couldn't talk to my friends about it, because after a while they didn't want to hear about it. 'Stephanie, you need to get your life back,' they'd say. But how could I? On birthdays, I'd shut the door and take the phone off the hook. Eric couldn't have any more birthdays; why should I?"

QUESTIONS FOR DISCUSSION

1. Heather and Stephanie reacted differently to their respective losses. Is one response healthier than the other?

2. Is Heather in denial? Is Stephanie overreacting?

3. Why did the two women react differently?

4. Do you know someone who did or did not deal well with loss? Why was that person equipped or ill-equipped to cope with his or her grief?

Mourning and Consolation
Space to Grieve

Text 3

Plato, *Phaedo*, p. 61

"Tell this to Evenus, Cebes," [Socrates said,] "and bid him be of good cheer; say that I would have him come after me if he be a wise man, and not tarry; and that today I am likely to be going, for the Athenians say that I must."

Simmias said: "What a message for such a man! Having been a frequent companion of his I should say that, as far as I know him, he will never take your advice unless he is obliged."

"Why," said Socrates, "is not Evenus a philosopher?"

"I think that he is," said Simmias.

"Then he, or any man who has the spirit of philosophy, will be willing to die; but he will not take his own life, for that is held to be unlawful. . . . The day may come when you will understand . . . why, [though] a man is better dead, he is not permitted to be his own benefactor, but must wait for the hand of another."

Plato
428/427–348/347 BCE

Classical Greek Athenian philosopher. Plato was the founder of the Academy in Athens, the first institution of higher learning in the Western world. He developed a rigorous and systemic method of intellectual examination, and his ideas have been enormously influential on philosophical, mathematical, and scientific thinking. Along with his teacher Socrates and his student Aristotle, he is one of the foundational figures in Western philosophy.

Text 4a

Nachmanides, Deuteronomy 14:1–2 📖

Rabbi Moshe ben Nachman
(Nachmanides, Ramban)
1194-1270

Scholar, philosopher, author and physician. Nachmanides was born in Spain and served as leader of Iberian Jewry. In 1263, he was summoned by King James of Aragon to a public disputation with Pablo Cristiani, a Jewish apostate. Though Nachmanides was the clear victor of the debate, he had to flee Spain because of the resulting persecution. He moved to Israel and helped reestablish communal life in Jerusalem. He authored a classic commentary on the Pentateuch and a commentary on the Talmud.

וְלֹא יֶאֱסֹר הַכָּתוּב הַבֶּכִי, כִּי הַטֶּבַע יִתְעוֹרֵר לִבְכּוֹת בְּפֵירוּד הָאוֹהֲבִים וְנִדּוּדָם, אַף בַּחַיִּים.

The Torah does not disallow [mourners] to cry, because it is human nature to be moved to tears when taking leave of loved ones, even if they are still alive [and merely traveling to a distant location].

Text 4b

Maimonides, *Guide for the Perplexed*, 3:41 📖

Rabbi Moshe ben Maimon
(Maimonides, Rambam)
1135-1204

Halachist, philosopher, author, and physician. Maimonides was born in Cordoba, Spain. After the conquest of Cordoba by the Almohads, he fled Spain and eventually settled in Cairo, Egypt. There, he became the leader of the Jewish community and served as court physician to the vizier of Egypt. He is most noted for authoring the *Mishneh Torah*, an encyclopedic arrangement of Jewish law, and for his philosophical work, *Guide for the Perplexed*. His rulings on Jewish law are integral to the formation of halachic consensus.

כִּי לְבַעֲלֵי הָאֵבֶל, מְנוּחָה בִּבְכִיָּה וְעוֹרְרָם אֶבְלָם, עַד שֶׁיֵּחָלְשׁוּ כֹחוֹת הַגּוּפָנִים מִסְּבוֹל הַמִּקְרֶה הַהוּא הַנַּפְשִׁי, כְּמוֹ שֶׁלְּבַעֲלֵי הַשִּׂמְחָה מְנוּחָה בְּמִינֵי הַשְׂחוֹק.

Mourners find comfort in crying and in wallowing in their sorrow, to the point that the body is weakened by the intense emotions, in the same manner as happy persons find contentment in various forms of amusements.

Text 4c

Rabbi David ibn Zimra, *Responsa*, 3:555 📖

שְׁאֵלָה: עַל אֶחָד מִגְּדוֹלֵי הַדּוֹר שֶׁמֵּת לוֹ בֵּן וְלֹא הוֹרִיד
עָלָיו דִּמְעָה אַחַת, אִם זוֹ מִדָּה טוֹבָה אוֹ לֹא?

תְּשׁוּבָה: זוֹ מִדָּה רָעָה, מוֹרָה עַל קוֹשִׁי הַלֵּב וְעַל רוֹעַ תְּכוּנַת
הַנֶּפֶשׁ, וְהִיא מִדַּת אַכְזָרִיּוּת, וְהוּא דֶּרֶךְ הַפִּילוֹסוּפִים הָאוֹמְרִים
כִּי זֶה הָעוֹלָם הַכֹּל הוּא מַעֲשֵׂה תַּעְתּוּעִים . . .

אֲבָל אֲנַחְנוּ מְקַבְּלֵי הַתּוֹרָה יֵשׁ לָנוּ לְהַאֲמִין וְלָדַעַת כִּי הָעוֹלָם
הַזֶּה עִנְיָן נִכְבָּד מְאֹד לַמִּסְתַּפְּקִים מִמֶּנּוּ כָּרָאוּי וְלַמִּתְנַהֲגִים
בּוֹ כַּשּׁוּרָה, וּבוֹ יַשִּׂיג הָאָדָם חַיֵּי הָעוֹלָם הַבָּא . . .

וְהַבּוֹכֶה וּמִתְאַבֵּל וּמוֹרִיד דְּמָעוֹת עַל קְרוֹבִים, וְכָל שֶׁכֵּן עַל אָדָם כָּשֵׁר, מִדַּת
חֲסִידִים וּנְבִיאִים וְאַנְשֵׁי מַעֲשֶׂה הִיא . . . וְלֹא לְחִנָּם אָמְרוּ רַזַ"ל, "שְׁלֹשָׁה לַבֶּכִי,
ז' לַהֶסְפֵּד, שְׁלֹשִׁים לְגִיהוּץ וְתִסְפּוֹרֶת", וְאִם הָיָה הַדָּבָר בִּלְתִּי נָאוֹת לֹא הָיוּ
מְתַקְּנִין לוֹ ג' יָמִים. וְכֵן אַבְרָהָם אָבִינוּ עָלָיו הַשָּׁלוֹם כְּתִיב בֵּיהּ, "לִסְפֹּד לְשָׂרָה
וְלִבְכֹּתָהּ" (בְּרֵאשִׁית כג, ב), וְכֵן יַעֲקֹב, וְכֵן דָּוִד הַמֶּלֶךְ, וְרַבִּים כָּאֵלֶּה אֵין מִסְפָּר.

Question:

One of the great men of the generation lost a son and did not shed a single tear. Is this a praiseworthy reaction?

Answer:

Such behavior is offensive and objectionable; it demonstrates heartlessness, distasteful character, and cruelty. This is the way of the philosophers who maintained that this world is worthless [and, as such, death is not a major concern and not worth bewailing]. . . .

We who have received the Torah believe that this world is of great value for those who properly utilize their time here

Rabbi David ibn Zimra (Radvaz)
1479–1573

Noted halachist. Radvaz was born in Spain and immigrated to Safed, Israel upon the expulsion of the Jews from Spain in 1492. In 1513, he moved to Egypt and served as rabbi, judge, and head of the yeshivah in Cairo. He also ran many successful business ventures and was independently wealthy. In 1553, he returned to Safed where he would later be buried. He authored what would later become a classic commentary to Maimonides' code of law, and wrote many halachic responsa, of which more than ten thousand are still extant.

and behave appropriately. It is only through our actions in this world that we merit the World to Come. . . .

Crying, mourning, and shedding tears after the passing of a relative, and especially for an honorable person, is the way of the pious, the prophets, and people of good deeds. . . . It is not for naught that our sages tell us, "Three days for weeping, seven for eulogies, and thirty for observing the restrictions on wearing new clothing and getting haircuts [etc.]." If weeping were improper, the sages would not have instituted a three-day period for this. We see that our father Abraham came to "eulogize Sarah and weep for her" (Genesis 23:2), and we also find that Jacob, King David, and innumerable others mourned the passing of loved ones.

Text 5

Maimonides, *Mishneh Torah*, Laws of Mourning 1:1 ▐

מִצְוַת עֲשֵׂה לְהִתְאַבֵּל עַל הַקְּרוֹבִים.

We are commanded to mourn [the passing of] next of kin.

The Mourning Process

FIGURE 5.1

Key Jewish Mourning Observances[*]

Aninut	From the moment of passing until the interment

This is the most intense phase of mourning. At this point, we do not even attempt to comfort or console the mourners. During this period, the next of kin are absolved from all "positive" *mitzvot* (i.e., obligations to do something, such as pray or don *tefilin*). Nothing should detract or distract from the mourners' pain and the interment arrangements.

Sometime during the *aninut* stage, the mourners tears their outer garments as a sign of mourning.

Shiva	A seven-day mourning period, commencing with interment

The mourners stay in the house of mourning and do not work. The mourners sit on low stools, wear their torn garments, and do not wear leather footwear. During shiva, it is a mitzvah to visit the mourners and attempt to comfort them.

Sheloshim	A thirty-day mourning period, commencing with interment

After "getting up" from shiva and resuming the everyday routines of life, certain mourning practices are continued until thirty days elapse from the time of burial. These include refraining from wearing new clothes, getting a haircut or shaving, and participating in festive events.

Twelve months	A twelve-month mourning period, commencing with interment

After the passing of a parent, some of the *sheloshim* mourning practices (such as not participating in festive events) are continued by the children until twelve months have passed. It is customary to have a candle burning in the home of the deceased during the twelve-month period.

---

[*] *Important notes:*

1. The list enumerated here is a brief overview of some of the primary mourning practices (*aveilut*) mandated by Torah law. It should not be taken as a practical guidance for the observances of *aveilut*, as the actual laws are quite detailed, and some of them vary from situation to situation.

2. Almost all mourning practices are suspended on Shabbat and biblical holidays.

Text 6

Genesis 37:31–34 📖

וַיִּקְחוּ אֶת כְּתֹנֶת יוֹסֵף וַיִּשְׁחֲטוּ שְׂעִיר עִזִּים וַיִּטְבְּלוּ אֶת הַכֻּתֹּנֶת בַּדָּם. וַיְשַׁלְּחוּ אֶת כְּתֹנֶת הַפַּסִּים וַיָּבִיאוּ אֶל אֲבִיהֶם וַיֹּאמְרוּ, "זֹאת מָצָאנוּ. הַכֶּר נָא הַכְּתֹנֶת בִּנְךָ הִוא אִם לֹא".

וַיַּכִּירָהּ, וַיֹּאמֶר, "כְּתֹנֶת בְּנִי. חַיָּה רָעָה אֲכָלָתְהוּ. טָרֹף טֹרַף יוֹסֵף".

וַיִּקְרַע יַעֲקֹב שִׂמְלֹתָיו וַיָּשֶׂם שַׂק בְּמָתְנָיו וַיִּתְאַבֵּל עַל בְּנוֹ יָמִים רַבִּים.

The [brothers] slaughtered a goat and took Joseph's tunic and dipped it in its blood. They sent the colored tunic and brought it to their father, and they said, "We have found this; identify whether it is your son's tunic or not."

Jacob recognized it and said, "It is my son's tunic; a wild beast has devoured him. Joseph has been torn to pieces."

Jacob rent his garments and put sackcloth on his loins, and he mourned his son for many days.

Finding Comfort

Text 7

Talmud, Mo'ed Katan 27b

"אַל תִּבְכּוּ לְמֵת וְאַל תָּנֻדוּ לוֹ" (יִרְמְיָהוּ כב, י). "אַל תִּבְכּוּ
לְמֵת" יוֹתֵר מִדַּאי, "וְאַל תָּנֻדוּ לוֹ" יוֹתֵר מִכַּשִּׁיעוּר.

הָא כֵּיצַד? שְׁלֹשָׁה יָמִים לִבְכִי, וְשִׁבְעָה לַהֶסְפֵּד, וּשְׁלֹשִׁים לַגִּיהוּץ וְלַתִּסְפּוֹרֶת.

מִכָּאן וְאֵילָךְ אָמַר הַקָּדוֹשׁ בָּרוּךְ הוּא, "אִי אַתֶּם רַחְמָנִים בּוֹ יוֹתֵר מִמֶּנִּי".

"Neither cry for the dead nor bemoan him" (Jeremiah 22:10). "Neither cry for the dead" more than necessary, "nor bemoan him" more than what is prescribed.

What does this mean? Three days for weeping, seven days for eulogies, and thirty days for [the prohibition against wearing] new clothing and getting haircuts.

More than this, God says: "You are not more compassionate than I am."

Babylonian Talmud

A literary work of monumental proportions that draws upon the legal, spiritual, intellectual, ethical, and historical traditions of Judaism. The 37 tractates of the Babylonian Talmud contain the teachings of the Jewish sages from the period after the destruction of the 2nd Temple through the 5th century CE. It has served as the primary vehicle for the transmission of the Oral Law and the education of Jews over the centuries; it is the entry point for all subsequent legal, ethical, and theological Jewish scholarship.

QUESTION FOR DISCUSSION

What ideas have we learned in previous lessons that might serve as consolation to a mourner?

Text 8a

Traditional Ashkenazic Text for Comforting Mourners

הַמָּקוֹם יְנַחֵם אֶתְכֶם בְּתוֹךְ שְׁאָר אֲבֵלֵי צִיּוֹן וִירוּשָׁלָיִם.

May God console you among the other mourners of Zion and Jerusalem.

QUESTION FOR DISCUSSION

Are there any ideas or questions that enter your mind as you read this text?

Text 8b

The Rebbe, Rabbi Menachem M. Schneerson, *Igrot Kodesh* 25:5

כְּמוֹ שֶׁבְּנוֹגֵעַ לְצִיּוֹן וִירוּשָׁלַיִם שָׁלְטָה יַד הָרוֹמִים, וְקוֹדֶם לָכֵן יַד הַבַּבְלִים,
רַק בְּבֵית הַמִּקְדָּשׁ הַבָּנוּי מֵעֵצִים וַאֲבָנִים כֶּסֶף וְזָהָב, אֲבָל בֵּית הַמִּקְדָּשׁ
הַפְּנִימִי שֶׁבַּלֵּב כָּל אֶחָד וְאַחַת שֶׁל יִשְׂרָאֵל אֵין יַד הָאוּמוֹת יְכוֹלָה לִשְׁלוֹט בּוֹ
וְנִצְחִי הוּא, כַּךְ הוּא גַם בְּנוֹגֵעַ לְאֵבֶל הַיָּחִיד, אֲשֶׁר יַד הַמָּוֶת שׁוֹלֶטֶת אַךְ וְרַק
בְּהַגּוּף וְעִנְיָנָיו, אֲבָל הַנְּשָׁמָה נִצְחִית הִיא, רַק שֶׁעָלְתָה לְעוֹלָם הָאֱמֶת.

In regard to Zion and Jerusalem, the Romans—and before them, the Babylonians—were given dominion only over the wood and stone, silver and gold of the Temple's physical manifestation, but not over its inner spiritual essence, contained within the heart of each and every Jew. Over, this, the nations have no dominion, and it stands eternally. So too, regarding the mourning of the individual, death dominates only the physical body and concerns of the deceased person. The soul, however, is eternal; it has merely ascended to the World of Truth.

Rabbi Menachem Mendel Schneerson
1902–1994

The towering Jewish leader of the 20th century, known as "the Lubavitcher Rebbe," or simply as "the Rebbe." Born in southern Ukraine, the Rebbe escaped Nazi-occupied Europe, arriving in the U.S. in June 1941. The Rebbe inspired and guided the revival of traditional Judaism after the European devastation, impacting virtually every Jewish community the world over. The Rebbe often emphasized that the performance of just one additional good deed could usher in the era of Mashiach. The Rebbe's scholarly talks and writings have been printed in more than 200 volumes.

Text 9

Rabbi Aron Moss, "Why Do We Tear Our Clothes After a Death?" www.Chabad.org

Rabbi Aron Moss

Rabbi and author. Rabbi Moss is a teacher of Kabbalah, Talmud, and practical Judaism in Sydney, Australia. He serves as rabbi of the Nefesh Synagogue and authors a popular weekly syndicated article on modern Jewish thought.

Often, within [their] pain, the mourners have an underlying belief that "it isn't true"—that their loved one hasn't really gone. This is not just denial; in a way they are right. Death is not an absolute reality. Our souls existed before we were born, and they continue to exist after we die. The souls that have passed on are still with us. We can't see them, but we sense they are there. We can't hear them, but we know that they hear us. On the surface, we are apart. Beyond the surface, nothing can separate us.

So we tear our garments. This has a dual symbolism. We are recognizing the loss, that our hearts are torn. But ultimately, the body is also only a garment that the soul wears. Death is when we strip off one uniform and take on another. The garment may be torn, but the essence of the person within it is still intact.

From our worldly perspective, death is indeed a tragedy, and the sorrow experienced by the mourners is real. But as they tear their garments, we hope that within their pain they can sense a glimmer of a deeper truth: that souls never die.

Healing Truths

Stuck in Grief

QUESTION FOR DISCUSSION

What sort of painful feelings and emotions accompany the loss of a loved one?

Anger and Injustice

FIGURE 5.2

(a) A ninety-year-old dies peacefully in his sleep.

(b) A twenty-year-old dies from leukemia.

QUESTION FOR DISCUSSION

How might reactions to these scenarios differ?

QUESTION FOR DISCUSSION

What ideas have we learned in previous lessons that might mitigate feelings of anger and injustice?

Text 10

Avot DeRabbi Natan 14:6 📖

כְּשֶׁמֵּת בְּנוֹ שֶׁל רַבָּן יוֹחָנָן בֶּן זַכַּאי, נִכְנְסוּ תַלְמִידָיו לְנַחֲמוֹ.

נִכְנַס רַבִּי אֱלִיעֶזֶר וְיָשַׁב לְפָנָיו. וְאָמַר לוֹ, "רַבִּי, רְצוֹנְךָ אוֹמֵר דָּבָר אֶחָד לְפָנֶיךָ". אָמַר לוֹ, "אֱמוֹר".

אָמַר לוֹ, "אָדָם הָרִאשׁוֹן הָיָה לוֹ בֵּן וּמֵת וְקִיבֵּל עָלָיו תַּנְחוּמִין. וּמִנַּיִן שֶׁקִּבֵּל עָלָיו תַּנְחוּמִין? שֶׁנֶּאֱמַר (בְּרֵאשִׁית ד, א), 'וַיֵּדַע אָדָם עוֹד אֶת אִשְׁתּוֹ'. אַף אַתָּה קַבֵּל תַּנְחוּמִין".

אָמַר לוֹ, "לֹא דַי לִי שֶׁאֲנִי מִצְטַעֵר בְּעַצְמִי, אֶלָּא שֶׁהִזְכַּרְתָּ לִי צַעֲרוֹ שֶׁל אָדָם הָרִאשׁוֹן".

נִכְנַס רַבִּי יְהוֹשֻׁעַ וְאָמַר לוֹ, "רְצוֹנְךָ אוֹמֵר דָּבָר אֶחָד לְפָנֶיךָ". אָמַר לוֹ, "אֱמוֹר".

אָמַר לוֹ, "אִיּוֹב הָיוּ לוֹ בָּנִים וּבָנוֹת, וּמֵתוּ כּוּלָם בְּיוֹם אֶחָד, וְקִיבֵּל עֲלֵיהֶם תַּנְחוּמִין. אַף אַתָּה קַבֵּל תַּנְחוּמִין. וּמִנַּיִן שֶׁקִּבֵּל אִיּוֹב תַּנְחוּמִין? שֶׁנֶּאֱמַר (אִיּוֹב א, כא), 'ה' נָתַן וַה' לָקַח, יְהִי שֵׁם ה' מְבוֹרָךְ'".

אָמַר לוֹ, "לֹא דַי לִי שֶׁאֲנִי מִצְטַעֵר בְּעַצְמִי, אֶלָּא שֶׁהִזְכַּרְתָּ לִי צַעֲרוֹ שֶׁל אִיּוֹב".

נִכְנַס רַבִּי יוֹסֵי וְיָשַׁב לְפָנָיו. אָמַר לוֹ, "רַבִּי, רְצוֹנְךָ אוֹמֵר דָּבָר אֶחָד לְפָנֶיךָ". אָמַר לוֹ, "אֱמוֹר".

אָמַר לוֹ, "אַהֲרֹן הָיוּ לוֹ שְׁנֵי בָנִים גְדוֹלִים, וּמֵתוּ שְׁנֵיהֶם בְּיוֹם אֶחָד, וְקִבֵּל עֲלֵיהֶם תַּנְחוּמִין. שֶׁנֶּאֱמַר (וַיִּקְרָא י, ג), 'וַיִּדֹּם אַהֲרֹן'. אֵין שְׁתִיקָה אֶלָּא תַּנְחוּמִין. וְאַף אַתָּה קַבֵּל תַּנְחוּמִין."

אָמַר לוֹ, "לֹא דַי לִי שֶׁאֲנִי מִצְטַעֵר בְּעַצְמִי, אֶלָּא שֶׁהִזְכַּרְתַּנִי צַעֲרוֹ שֶׁל אַהֲרֹן."

נִכְנַס רַבִּי שִׁמְעוֹן וְאָמַר לוֹ, "רַבִּי, רְצוֹנְךָ אוֹמֵר דָּבָר אֶחָד לְפָנֶיךָ". אָמַר לוֹ, "אֱמוֹר."

אָמַר לוֹ, "דָּוִד הַמֶּלֶךְ הָיָה לוֹ בֵן וּמֵת, וְקִבֵּל עָלָיו תַּנְחוּמִין. וְאַף אַתָּה קַבֵּל תַּנְחוּמִין. וּמִנַּיִן שֶׁקִּבֵּל דָּוִד תַּנְחוּמִין? שֶׁנֶּאֱמַר (שְׁמוּאֵל ב, יב, כד), 'וַיְנַחֵם דָּוִד אֵת בַּת שֶׁבַע אִשְׁתּוֹ וַיָּבֹא אֵלֶיהָ וַיִּשְׁכַּב עִמָּהּ וַתֵּלֶד בֵּן וַיִּקְרָא אֶת שְׁמוֹ שְׁלֹמֹה'. אַף אַתָּה רַבִּי קַבֵּל תַּנְחוּמִין."

אָמַר לוֹ, "לֹא דַי שֶׁאֲנִי מִצְטַעֵר בְּעַצְמִי, אֶלָּא שֶׁהִזְכַּרְתַּנִי צַעֲרוֹ שֶׁל דָּוִד הַמֶּלֶךְ."

נִכְנַס רַבִּי אֶלְעָזָר בֶּן עֲרָךְ. כֵּיוָן שֶׁרָאָהוּ, אָמַר לְשַׁמָּשׁוֹ, "טוֹל לְפָנַי כֵּלִי, וְלֵךְ אַחֲרַי לְבֵית הַמֶּרְחָץ, לְפִי שֶׁאָדָם גָּדוֹל הוּא וְאֵינִי יָכוֹל לַעֲמוֹד בּוֹ."

נִכְנַס וְיָשַׁב לְפָנָיו וְאָמַר לוֹ, "אֶמְשׁוֹל לְךָ מָשָׁל. לְמָה הַדָּבָר דּוֹמֶה? לְאָדָם שֶׁהִפְקִיד אֶצְלוֹ הַמֶּלֶךְ פִּקָּדוֹן. בְּכָל יוֹם וְיוֹם הָיָה בּוֹכֶה וְצוֹעֵק וְאוֹמֵר, 'אוֹי לִי, אֵימָתַי אֵצֵא מִן הַפִּיקָּדוֹן הַזֶּה בְּשָׁלוֹם?'

"אַף אַתָּה רַבִּי, הָיָה לְךָ בֵּן. קָרָא תוֹרָה מִקְרָא נְבִיאִים וּכְתוּבִים מִשְׁנָה הֲלָכוֹת וְאַגָּדוֹת, וְנִפְטַר מִן הָעוֹלָם בְּלֹא חֵטְא. וְיֵשׁ לְךָ לְקַבֵּל עָלֶיךָ תַּנְחוּמִים כְּשֶׁהֶחֱזַרְתָּ פִּקְדוֹנְךָ שָׁלֵם."

אָמַר לוֹ, "רַבִּי אֶלְעָזָר בְּנִי, נִחַמְתַּנִי כְּדֶרֶךְ שֶׁבְּנֵי אָדָם מְנַחֲמִין."

When the son of Rabbi Yochanan ben Zakai passed away, his students entered to offer condolences.

Rabbi Eliezer entered and sat before him. "Master! If it pleases you, I will say one thing," he said.

"Speak," Rabbi Yochanan responded.

Rabbi Eliezer said, "Adam had a son who died, and he allowed himself to be consoled. How do we know that he was consoled? For it is stated (Genesis 4:1), 'Adam was

Avot DeRabbi Natan

A commentary on, and an elaboration of, the mishnaic tractate Avot, bearing the name of Rabbi Natan, one of the sages of the Mishnah. The work exists in two very different versions, one of which appears in many editions of the Talmud.

intimate again with his wife.' You, too, should allow yourself to be consoled."

Rabbi Yochanan answered, "Not only am I pained because of my own loss, now you have caused me to be pained for Adam too!"

Rabbi Yehoshua entered. "If it pleases you, I will say one thing," he said.

"Speak," Rabbi Yochanan responded.

Rabbi Yehoshua said, "Job had sons and daughters, and they all died in a single day, yet he allowed himself to be consoled. You, too, should allow yourself to be consoled. How do we know that he was consoled? For Job said, 'God has given and God has taken; may God's name be blessed' (Job 1:21)."

Rabbi Yochanan answered, "Not only am I pained because of my own loss, now you have caused me to be pained for Job too!"

Rabbi Yosei entered and sat before him. "Master! If it pleases you, I will say one thing," he said.

"Speak," Rabbi Yochanan responded.

Rabbi Yosei said, "Aaron had two illustrious sons, and they both died in a single day, yet he allowed himself to be consoled. For it is stated, 'Aaron was silent' (Leviticus 10:3); his silence implied that he [was without grievance and] accepted consolation. You, too, should allow yourself to be consoled."

Rabbi Yochanan answered, "Not only am I pained because of my own loss, now you have caused me to be pained for Aaron too!"

Rabbi Shimon entered. "Master! If it pleases you, I will say one thing," he said.

"Speak," Rabbi Yochanan responded.

Rabbi Shimon said, "King David had a son who died, and he allowed himself to be consoled. You, too, should allow yourself to be consoled. How do we know that King David was consoled? For it is stated (II Samuel 12:24), 'David comforted Bathsheba his wife, and he was intimate with her and she bore a son, and he called his name Solomon.' You, too, Master, should allow yourself to be consoled."

Rabbi Yochanan answered, "Not only am I pained because of my own loss, now you have caused me to be pained for King David too!"

Rabbi Elazar ben Arach entered. When Rabbi Yochanan saw him, he told his attendant, "Take my clothing and [be prepared to] follow me to the bathhouse. For Rabbi Elazar is a great person and I will not be able to hold out [in the face of his comforting words]."

Rabbi Elazar entered. He sat down before him and said: "I would like to share a parable. Your situation can be compared to that of a man to whom the king entrusted an article for safekeeping. Every day, the man would cry and shout, 'Woe is to me! When will I be able to return the deposited item undamaged and be relieved of the incredible responsibility I bear?'

"Master, you had a son. He read the Torah, Prophets, and Holy Writings, and studied the Mishnah, the laws, and the ethical teachings. He passed from this world without sin. You should be consoled because you returned your deposit in perfect condition."

Rabbi Yochanan responded, "Rabbi Elazar, my son, you have comforted me in a most humane fashion."

QUESTIONS FOR DISCUSSION

1. Why wasn't Rabbi Yochanan comforted by the words of his first four students?

2. Why did he take comfort from the words of Rabbi Elazar ben Arach?

Guilt

QUESTION FOR DISCUSSION

What ideas have we learned in previous lessons that can mitigate feelings of guilt?

Text 11

Rabbi Aharon of Karlin (cited in Rabbi Gavriel Zinner, *Nitei Gavriel*, Laws of Mourning 2:291) 📖

כְּשֶׁהַבֵּן אוֹמֵר קַדִּישׁ עַל אָבִיו אוֹ אִמּוֹ הֲרֵי זֶה כְּמוֹ שֶׁשָּׁלַח לָהֶם פְּרִיסַת שָׁלוֹם, כְּשֶׁלּוֹמֵד פֶּרֶק מִשְׁנָיוֹת בַּעֲדָם הֲרֵי זֶה כְּמוֹ שֶׁשָּׁלַח לָהֶם אִגֶּרֶת, וּכְשֶׁמְּקַיֵּים מִצְווֹת וּמַעֲשִׂים טוֹבִים לְטוֹבַת נִשְׁמָתָם הֲרֵי זֶה כְּמוֹ שֶׁשָּׁלַח לָהֶם חֲבִילָה שְׁלֵימָה.

When children say *Kaddish* for their parents, it is like sending them regards. When they learn a chapter of Mishnah on their behalf, it is like sending them a letter. And when they fulfill *mitzvot* and good deeds for the benefit of their souls, it is like sending them an entire parcel.

Rabbi Aharon of Karlin
1736–1772

Chasidic rebbe. Rabbi Aharon was a disciple of Rabbi Dov Ber of Mezeritch. He was known as Rabbi Aharon the Great, and was one of the pioneers of Chasidism in Lithuania. He is known for his ecstatic and unrestrained fervor during his prayers and for his caring for the needy. He is the composer of the Shabbat hymn *Kah echsof*.

Comforting the Bereaved

Text 12

Maimonides, *Mishneh Torah*, Laws of Mourning 14:1 📖

מִצְוַת עֲשֵׂה שֶׁל דִּבְרֵיהֶם לְבַקֵּר חוֹלִים וּלְנַחֵם אֲבֵלִים . . .

וְאֵלּוּ הֵן גְּמִילוּת חֲסָדִים שֶׁבְּגוּפוֹ שֶׁאֵין לָהֶם שִׁעוּר.

אַף עַל פִּי שֶׁכָּל מִצְוֹת אֵלּוּ מִדִּבְרֵיהֶם, הֲרֵי הֵן בִּכְלָל

"וְאָהַבְתָּ לְרֵעֲךָ כָּמוֹךָ" (וַיִּקְרָא יט, יח).

The sages obligated us to visit the sick and console mourners. . . . These are deeds of kindness that one carries out in person and have no limit.

Although these are rabbinic ordinances, they fall under the purview of the biblical commandment to "love your fellow as yourself" (Leviticus 19:18).

QUESTIONS FOR DISCUSSION

1. Have you ever experienced discomfort or unease at a shiva house? If yes, why?

2. Have you ever said something to a mourner that was especially effective or ineffective?

Text 13

Talmud, Berachot 6b 📖

אַגְרָא דְּבֵי טַמְיָא שְׁתִּיקוּתָא.

The reward for visiting the home of mourning is for the silence.

Text 14

Talmud, Mo'ed Katan 28b 📖

אֵין מְנַחֲמִין רַשָּׁאִין לוֹמַר דָּבָר עַד שֶׁיִּפְתַּח אָבֵל.

The comforters may not say anything until the mourner opens the conversation.

Text 15

Midrash, *Kohelet Rabah* 12:13 📖

סוֹף דִּיבּוּרוֹ שֶׁל אָדָם, הַכֹּל מַשְׁמִיעִין אֶת מַעֲשָׂיו, "כָּשֵׁר הָיָה פְּלוֹנִי זֶה", "יְרֵא שָׁמַיִם הָיָה פְּלוֹנִי זֶה". . .

שֶׁבְּשָׁעָה שֶׁאָדָם נִפְטַר מִן הָעוֹלָם, הַקָּדוֹשׁ בָּרוּךְ הוּא אוֹמֵר לְמַלְאֲכֵי הַשָּׁרֵת: רְאוּ מַה הַבְּרִיּוֹת אוֹמְרוֹת עָלָיו: כָּשֵׁר הָיָה, יְרֵא שָׁמַיִם הָיָה פְּלוֹנִי זֶה, מִיַּד מִטָּתוֹ פּוֹרַחַת בָּאֲוִיר.

The final word regarding a person is that of the people proclaiming his deeds, saying, "So-and-so was upright," "So-and-so was God-fearing." . . .

Kohelet Rabah

A Midrashic text on the Book of Ecclesiastes. Midrash is the designation of a particular genre of rabbinic literature. The term "Midrash" is derived from the root d-r-sh, which means "to search," "to examine," and "to investigate." This particular Midrash provides textual exegeses and develops and illustrates moral principles. It was first published in Pesaro, Italy, in 1519, together with four other Midrashic works on the other four biblical *megilot*.

When a person departs the world, God says to the ministering angels: "See what people are saying about him." [If they say] that he had been upright and God-fearing, his soul immediately ascends to Paradise.

LEARNING EXERCISE

(a) **Write down the point from today's lesson that resonated with you most on a personal level.**

_____

_____

_____

_____

(b) **If you are currently grieving the loss of a loved one, identify an idea you can focus on that will help you heal and live a fuller life.**

_____

_____

_____

_____

Key Points

1. Everyone reacts to and deals with grief differently. No two people are psychologically alike, and no two circumstances of death and bereavement are the same.

2. It is a mitzvah to mourn the loss of a loved one. Acceptance is an important first step of mourning. This is exemplified by tearing one's garment, which is a tangible expression of loss.

3. Processing a loss is critical to the healing process. This is accomplished by shiva, a mandatory period of grieving.

4. The Torah validates and encourages mourning, but only for a prescribed period of time, after which the mourner is enjoined to transition back to normal life. When one knows that the soul lives on and is not diminished by death, death loses its all-annihilating force, and one can slowly find the strength to move on.

5. Mourners commonly feel anger and a sense of injustice, especially when the deceased's life was cut too short. We can cope with these feelings in knowing that (a) life is a deposit, and God decides when to give it and when it must be returned, and (b) for this soul and its unique mission, this constituted a full life.

6. Mourners commonly feel guilt due to what they perceive as a lost opportunity to right wrongs they have committed against the deceased. However, it is never too late to improve our relationship with the deceased—though our physical relationship has ended, we can still give him or her spiritual gifts.

7. The most basic principle of comforting a mourner is simply being there. Our presence offers comfort and lessens the loneliness that often accompanies mourning.

8. Proper shiva etiquette includes (a) not offering comfort until the mourner opens the conversation, (b) not attempting to lighten the mood, (c) not philosophizing or teaching, (d) not saying or asking anything that is intrusive, and (e) discussing positive qualities and achievements of the departed.

This lesson explored mourning, consolation, and providing comfort to the bereaved.

Continue your learning experience ONLINE

Visit www.myJLI.com/journey5

for insightful and inspiring videos, articles, and readings on these topics.

Appendix A

Ed. Note: On May 13, 2011, someone posted on Reddit.com: "My friend just died. I don't know what to do." The following poignant response penned by "GSnow" has since gone viral.

Alright, here goes. I'm old. What that means is that I've survived (so far) and a lot of people I've known and loved did not. I've lost friends, best friends, acquaintances, co-workers, grandparents, mom, relatives, teachers, mentors, students, neighbors, and a host of other folks. I have no children, and I can't imagine the pain it must be to lose a child. But here's my two cents.

I wish I could say you get used to people dying. I never did. I don't want to. It tears a hole through me whenever somebody I love dies, no matter the circumstances. But I don't want it to "not matter." I don't want it to be something that just passes. My scars are a testament to the love and the relationship that I had for and with that person. And if the scar is deep, so was the love. So be it. Scars are a testament to life. Scars are a testament that I can love deeply and live deeply and be cut, or even gouged, and that I can heal and continue to live and continue to love. And the scar tissue is stronger than the original flesh ever was. Scars are a testament to life. Scars are only ugly to people who can't see.

As for grief, you'll find it comes in waves. When the ship is first wrecked, you're drowning, with wreckage all around you. Everything floating around you reminds you of the beauty and the magnificence of the ship that was, and is no more. And all you can do is float. You find some piece of the wreckage and you hang on for a while. Maybe it's some physical thing. Maybe it's a happy memory or a photograph. Maybe it's a person who is also floating. For a while, all you can do is float. Stay alive.

In the beginning, the waves are 100 feet tall and crash over you without mercy. They come 10 seconds apart and don't even give you time to catch your breath. All you can do is hang on and float. After a while, maybe weeks, maybe months, you'll find the waves are still 100 feet tall, but they come further apart. When they come, they still crash all over you and wipe you out. But in between, you can breathe, you can function. You never know what's going to trigger the grief. It might be a song, a picture, a street intersection, the smell of a cup of coffee. It can be just about anything ... and the wave comes crashing. But in between waves, there is life.

Somewhere down the line, and it's different for everybody, you find that the waves are only 80 feet tall. Or 50 feet tall. And while they still come, they come further apart. You can see them coming. An anniversary, a birthday, or Christmas, or landing at O'Hare. You can see it coming, for the most part, and prepare yourself. And when it washes over you, you know that somehow you will, again, come out the other side. Soaking wet, sputtering, still hanging on to some tiny piece of the wreckage, but you'll come out.

Take it from an old guy. The waves never stop coming, and somehow you don't really want them to. But you learn that you'll survive them. And other waves will come. And you'll survive them too. If you're lucky, you'll have lots of scars from lots of loves. And lots of shipwrecks.

Appendix B

Sarah Kershaw, "What Hurricane Katrina Has Taught Us about Human Resilience," *The Washington Post*, August 26, 2015

Prompted in large part by the Sept. 11th terrorist attacks in 2001—although early research on resilience was inspired by the stories of breast cancer survivors—a large body of work has emerged examining the concept and experience of resilience. Psychologists and other social scientists have identified multiple factors that influence what happens to people after catastrophic events.

One key to understanding responses is the nature of the event itself.

"Not all events are created equal," said Roxane Cohen Silver, a professor of psychology at the University of California, Irvine.

Individuals and communities tend to experience more negative consequences and have an especially hard time recovering from man-made disasters like the terrorist attacks on New York and Washington, the Boston marathon bombing or the massive BP oil spill in the Gulf of Mexico in 2010, researchers say. But natural disasters like hurricanes, earthquakes, floods and wildfires can be different....

Some of the questions that can determine how survivors will respond and recover include: Was the event an "act of God" or Mother Nature—an anticipated disaster linked to geography, like hurricanes along the Gulf and Atlantic coasts and wildfires in California? Or was it entirely unexpected, like the 2012 shooting inside a movie theater in

Aurora, Colo. that killed 12 people and injured more than 70 others in a place that most people would assume is safe?

Was there someone to blame, like Osama bin Laden or other terrorists, or the different shooters who killed 32 people in 2007 at Virginia Tech; the 20 children and six adults in 2012 at Sandy Hook Elementary school in Newtown, Conn.; and the nine people gunned down in June while worshipping in their church in Charleston, S.C.?

With blame, and possibly a sense of injustice, comes anger, a potential obstacle to recovery from trauma and resilience. (The opposite, forgiveness, can be one of the strongest signs of resilience, experts say, but it is often extremely difficult for victims to practice.)

Appendix C

The Rebbe, Rabbi Menachem M. Schneerson, *Igrot Kodesh* 25:4–5 ▌

בְּהִתְבּוֹנְנוּת רִאשׁוֹנָה תָּמוּהַּ הַקֶּשֶׁר שֶׁבֵּין שְׁנֵי הָעִנְיָנִים. אֶלָּא שֶׁכְּאָמוּר בָּזֶה הוּא עִקַּר הַנֶּחָמָה בְּתָכְנָה הַפְּנִימִי, אֲשֶׁר כְּמוֹ שֶׁאֲבֵלוּת צִיּוֹן וִירוּשָׁלַיִם הֲרֵי מְשֻׁתֶּפֶת הִיא לְכָל בְּנֵי וּבְנוֹת יִשְׂרָאֵל בְּכָל מָקוֹם שֶׁהֵם, אַף כִּי נִרְגָּשׁ הַדָּבָר יוֹתֵר אֵצֶל הַיּוֹשֵׁב בִּירוּשָׁלַיִם וְרוֹאֶה כֹּתֶל הַמַּעֲרָבִי וּבֵית מִקְדָּשֵׁנוּ בְּחוּרְבָּנוֹ מֵאֵלּוּ הַנִּמְצָאִים בְּרָחוֹק מָקוֹם, אֲבָל גַּם אֶצְלָם גָּדוֹל הַכְּאֵב וְהַצַּעַר. וְכֵן הוּא גַּם בְּאֵבֶל הַיָּחִיד וְהַמִּשְׁפָּחָה, אֲשֶׁר מֵהַנֶּחָמָה בָּזֶה הִיא שֶׁכָּל הָעָם מִשְׁתַּתֵּף בְּצַעֲרוֹ, שֶׁהֲרֵי בִּסְגָנוֹן חֲכָמֵינוּ ז"ל כָּל בְּנֵי יִשְׂרָאֵל הֵם קוֹמָה אַחַת שְׁלֵימָה.

At first glance, the connection [between the mourner to whom this blessing is directed and the mourners of Jerusalem's destruction] appears to be quite puzzling. In truth, however, they are connected. For the main consolation embodied by this phrase is in its inner content, namely: The grief over Zion and Jerusalem is common to all the sons and daughters of our people, Israel, wherever they may be (although it is more palpable to those who dwell in Jerusalem and actually see the Western Wall and the ruins of our Holy Temple than to those who are far away from it; nonetheless, even those who are far experience great pain and grief over the destruction). So too is the grief of a single individual Jew or Jewish family shared by the entire nation. For, as the sages have taught, all of the Jewish people comprise one integral organism.

ADDITIONAL READINGS

THE *SHIVA*: A FORM OF GROUP PSYCHOTHERAPY

BY IRWIN W. KIDORF, PhD

The reasons for the perpetuation of religious rituals through the centuries present a continuously challenging question for those interested in such matters. Many have suggested analogies between religious rites and the obsessive-compulsive behavior of the neurotic. "Psychoanalysts who turned their attention to religious rituals were struck by the similarity of the private compulsive rituals they observed in their patients to the socially patterned ceremonies they found in religion. They expected to find that the religious rituals followed the same mechanism as the neurotic compulsions."[1]

It seems, however, that there are differences between the person in the throes of neurosis and the religious traditionalist following the tenets of his religion. One way of exploring this difference is to examine the ritual with the aim of seeking its dynamics; perhaps in this way one may find a more meaningful explanation of the perpetuation of the ceremony in question.

Erich Fromm differentiates religious ritual from compulsive behavior, pointing out that the latter is irrational, based on the repression of irrational impulses, while the former can be considered rational. He defines ritual as a shared action expressing common strivings and rooted in common values. "The rational differs from the irrational ritual primarily in its function; it does not ward off repressed impulses, but expresses strivings recognized as valuable by the individual."[2]

Elsewhere, I have applied a psychoanalytic framework as a means of analysing traditional Jewish mourning customs. I made a comparison between the Freudian theory of mourning and this phase of religious observance.[3] In the present paper, I shall explore the dynamics of a particular rite of traditional Jewish mourning custom, the *Shiva*. In trying to understand this particular ceremony, which is inherent in Jewish mourning, I shall point out relationships between the dynamics involved and those involved in group psychotherapy.

The term *Shiva* is derived from the Hebrew word for "seven." According to traditional Jewish observance, a person who has suffered the loss of a close relative (parent, child, sibling, spouse) must spend the first seven days following burial in deep mourning. There are minor exceptions, such as the intervention of the Sabbath or religious holidays, but essentially this is the rule. During this period, men do not shave and women are required to refrain from wearing make-up or adorning themselves with glittering jewelry. The wearing of leather shoes or slippers is prohibited. In general, as might be expected, frivolity and levity are not encouraged. Certain prescribed prayers, in addition to the normally required thrice daily prayers, are recited. The mourners sit on low benches or stools, even for meals, and the meals themselves are prepared in a plain manner. The period of the *Shiva* is a time to receive visitors and well-wishers. Indeed, according to tradition, it is considered of special merit to visit and comfort the bereaved during this week. The rites and customs as I have described them are

---

[1] Fromm, Erich, Psychoanalysis and Religion. New Haven, Yale University Press, 1950, p. 107.
[2] *Ibid*., p. 108.

[3] Kidorf, Irwin W., "Jewish Tradition and the Freudian Theory of Mourning," Journal of Religion and Health, 1963, 2, 248–252.

those observed according to Orthodox Jewish traditions; they are modified in some ways by Conservative and Reform Jews. Mourning observance does not come to an abrupt end when the *Shiva* period has passed. Somewhat less restrictive mourning rites continue for thirty days following the funeral, and the observant Orthodox Jew continues to attend daily services at the synagogue during the whole first year after the bereavement.

Why has the custom of observing the *Shiva* lasted from its beginnings until the present? Aside from purely religious factors, it appears that this ceremony does satisfy many needs of people in mourning. Analysis of the ritual brings to light dynamics that appear to parallel the dynamics underlying the process of group psychotherapy.

In each case, we are dealing with a group of people who have come together with a common problem, bringing with them their own back grounds, feelings, and attitudes.

The presence of visitors, the overt, acceptable signs of mourning, and in fact the entire atmosphere encourage catharsis of feeling on the part of the participants. While it is true that this is at the surface level, it does bring about amelioration of the surface-level aspects of the problem, which is quite often, of course, one of the goals for the early stages of most types of psychotherapy. With the alleviation of the immediate problem (i.e., at the surface level) therapeutic intervention into deeper levels is so much more facilitated. In addition, one may say that the house in which the *Shiva* is observed lends itself rather easily to a setting for psychodrama. The presence of visitors can often promote a kind of role-playing on the part of the mourners. Grief, an emotion that is often difficult to express, especially for people who tend to over-control, can thus be acted out in a socially approved manner and in a relatively benign, even encouraging, environment.

The mourners, sitting together as a group through an extended period, have an opportunity to project their feelings from themselves as individuals to the group as a whole. Because this is essentially an "in group"

(i.e., a family), regression can be facilitated, probably to the lowering of defenses that might ordinarily be maintained in a group of strangers. In successful group therapy, these defenses are eventually overcome; in the *Shiva* group, the process is speeded up. Thus there is a difference only in time, with regard to this aspect, between the two kinds of groups. The type of regression that occurs in the *Shiva* group is, of course, most frequently in the service of the ego. The opportunity to cry, to express deeper feelings, to discuss and thereby attempt to resolve the ambivalent feelings that are almost universally aroused on learning of the death of someone close—all these primary processes can take place. Again, there is catharsis.

The *Shiva*-observing group is essentially a leaderless group, although a nominal leader may be, in a sense, appointed tacitly by the group. For example, the closest in relationship to the deceased, or the oldest in the family, or the one for whom, for one reason or another, the family has the greatest respect, assumes (or, as noted, is tacitly appointed to) a kind of leader role. However, often enough, as is the case where there is no definite leader, this role is circulated among the various members of the group.

Because of the almost naked expression of feeling, facilitated by an atmosphere that lends itself to a partial breakdown of defenses as described earlier, there is, of course, some danger of a breakdown of the *Shiva* group. The physical properties of the group, which are by definition subject to external control, will cause the individuals to remain together, but the matter in question is one of psychological or emotional withdrawal of individual group members. Psychotherapists who have had any experience at all with therapy groups will recognize this as a not uncommon phenomenon. However, toward the end of the *Shiva* period comes the realization that the "groupness" is coming to an end; the members will, in reality, return to their own families, their own ways of life, and will, in effect, be scattered again. If one thinks in terms of a group ego, it may be hypothesized that the ego functions begin anew. The threat aroused by the imminence of breaking apart serves as the catalyst. The realities of the "outside world," which, in a sense, have been ignored, suppressed, or even repressed during the week of rather intense mourning, now must be faced. There arrives the realization among the various members that they will not be able to submerge themselves within the group; that is, they will no longer have the group on which to draw for support. There comes, then, a reunification of the group.

Parenthetically, one may say, in learning-theory terms, that with the end of the *Shiva* period in sight, a kind of end-spurt occurs. One sees this often in individual as well as in group therapy, both when approaching the end of a previously specified number of sessions and even occasionally toward the end of the therapy hour itself.

As in successful group (or individual) psychotherapy, the members who have worked through the stages of catharsis, regression, and the return of ego functioning have now reached a new level of maturity and are, therefore, in a better position to think rationally and deal constructively with their specific environments.

As is often the case with brief, intensive psychotherapy, the immediate problem is usually ameliorated, if only temporarily. The remainder of the traditional mourning ritual can serve to aid the individual mourner.[4] As shown, the effect on the group as a group as well as on the individual members can, as a result of optimally utilizing the *Shiva* period, be most beneficial. Exploring the dynamics of this rite, then, does provide clues as to the efficacy and goal-directiveness of the rite, and perhaps explains its perpetuation.

Journal of Religion and Health, Vol. 5, No. 1 (Jan., 1966), pp. 43–46.

THE FAMILY'S CONNECTION WITH THE SOUL
FROM THE CORRESPONDENCE OF THE LUBAVITCHER REBBE

By the Grace of G-d
5 Tammuz 5743
Brooklyn, NY

Blessing and Greeting:

I have just received your letter of 3 Tammuz.

To begin with a blessing, may G-d grant that henceforth you and all your family should have only goodness and benevolence—in the kind of good that is revealed and evident.

At the same time, you must make every effort to regain the proper state of mind, despite the pain.

You should remember the teaching and instruction of the Torah which is called Toras Chayim, Guide in Life, and Toras Emes, the Torah of Truth, meaning that what it teaches is not just to ease the mind, but the actual truth. Thus, the Torah, taking into account human nature/feelings in a case of bereavement, and the need to provide an outlet for the natural feelings of sorrow and grief, prescribes a set of regulations and period of mourning.

At the same time the Torah sets limits in terms of the duration of the periods of mourning and the appropriate expression, such as shiva (the first seven days), shloshim (thirty days), etc. If one extends the intensity of mourning which is appropriate for shiva into shloshim, it is not proper, for although shloshim is part of the overall mourning period, it is so in a lesser degree. And since the Torah says that it is not proper to overdo it, it does no good for the neshama [soul] of the dearly departed. On the contrary, it is pain-

---

[4] *Ibid.*

ful for the neshama to see that it is the cause for the conduct that is not in keeping with the instructions of the Torah.

A second point to bear in mind is that a human being cannot possibly understand the ways of G-d. By way of a simple illustration: An infant cannot possibly understand the thinking and ways of a great scholar or scientist—even though both are human beings, and the difference between them is only relative, in terms of age, education and maturity. Moreover, it is quite possible that the infant may someday surpass the scientist, who also started life as an infant. But the difference between a created human being and his Creator is absolute.

Therefore, our Sages declare that a human being must accept everything that happens, both those that are obviously good and those that are incomprehensible, with the same positive attitude that "all that G-d does is for the good," even though it is beyond human truths is that the neshama is part of G-dliness and is immortal. When the time comes for it to return to Heaven, it leaves the body and continues its eternal life in the spiritual World of Truth.

It is also a matter of common sense that whatever the direct cause of the separation of the soul from the body (whether a fatal accident, or a fatal illness, etc.), it could affect only any of the vital organs of the physical body, but could in no way affect the spiritual soul.

A further point, which is also understandable, is that during the soul's lifetime on earth in partnership with the body, the soul is necessarily "handicapped"—in certain respects—by the requirements of the body (such as eating and drinking, etc.). Even a tzaddik [holy man], whose entire life is consecrated to Hashem, cannot escape the restraints of life in a material and physical environment. Consequently, when the time comes for the soul to return "home," it is essentially a release for it, as it makes its ascent to a higher world, no longer restrained by a physical body and physical environment. Henceforth the soul is free to enjoy the spiritual bliss of being near to Hashem in the fullest measure. This is surely a comforting thought!

It may be asked: if it is a "release" for the soul, why has the Torah prescribed periods of mourning, etc. But there is really no contradiction. The Torah recognizes the natural feeling of grief that is felt by the loss of a near and dear one, whose passing leaves a void in the family, and the physical presence and contact of the beloved one will be sorely missed. So the Torah has prescribed the proper periods of mourning to give vent to these feelings and to make it easier to regain the proper equilibrium and adjustment.

However, to allow oneself to be carried away by these feelings beyond the limits set by the Torah—in addition to its being a disservice to one's self and all around, as well as to the neshama, as mentioned above—would mean that one is more concerned with one's own feelings than with the feelings of the dear neshama that has risen to new spiritual heights of eternal happiness. Thus, paradoxically, the overextended feeling of grief, which is due to the great love of the departed one, actually causes pain to the loved one, since the neshama continues to take an interest in the dear one left behind, sees what is going on (even better than before), rejoices with them in their joys, etc.

One thing the departed soul can no longer do, and that is, the actual fulfillment of the mitzvoth, which can be carried out only jointly by the soul and body together in this material world. But this, too, can at least partly be overcome when those left behind do a little more mitzvoth and good deeds in honor and for the benefit of the dear neshama.

More could be said on the subject, but I trust the above will suffice to help you discover within you the strength that G-d has given you, not only to overcome this crisis, but also to go from strength to strength in your everyday life and activities in full accord with the Torah.

In your case, there is an added G-d-given capacity, having been blessed with lovely children, long may they live, with a strong feeling of motherly responsibility to raise each and all of them to a life of Torah, chuppah [marriage], and good deeds, with even greater attention and care than before, and in this, as in all good things, there is always room for improvement.

Now to conclude with a blessing, may G-d grant you much Yiddishe nachas [Jewish happiness] from each and all your children, raising them to Torah, chuppah, and good deeds in good health and peace of mind, and in comfortable circumstances.

With blessing,

[Signature]

P.S. I do not know if you were aware of it when writing your letter on 3 Tammuz. But it is significant that you wrote the letter on the anniversary of the beginning of the geula [redemption] of my father-in-law of saintly memory—an auspicious time for geula from all distractions and anxieties, to serve Hashem wholeheartedly and with joy.

COMFORTING THE BEREAVED (NICHUM AVEILIM)

BY RABBI MAURICE LAMM

A sacred obligation devolves upon every Jew to comfort the mourners, whether he is related to them or not, and whether he was a close friend or a passing acquaintance. In Judaism, exercising compassion by paying a condolence call is a mitzvah, considered by some of our greatest scholars to be biblically ordained. The Bible records that God visited Isaac: "And it came to pass after the death of Abraham, that God blessed Isaac, his son" (Genesis 25:11). The sages infer from this verse that God Himself, as it were, was comforting the bereaved Isaac.

It is a man's duty to imitate God: as God comforts the bereaved, so man must do likewise. Consolation is considered a God-like action which all the children of Israel must perform. When, following the destruction of Jerusalem and the decimation of the Jewish people, Isaiah proclaimed God's message: "Comfort ye, comfort ye my people" (Isaiah 40:1), it indicated not merely a recommendation from on high, but a specific mandate obliging the prophet to bring consolation to his people.

The fundamental purpose of the condolence call during shiva is to relieve the mourner of the intolerable burden of intense loneliness. At no other time

is a human being more in need of such comradeship. *Avelut* means withdrawal, the personal and physical retreat from social commerce and the concern for others. It is the loss that he alone has suffered. All the traditions of mourning express this troubled loneliness in diverse ways, covering the spectrum of social life—from the excessive growing of hair in indifference to social custom, to the avoidance of greetings, the minimum social courtesy.

Recognizing this state of mind, the visitor comes to the house of mourning, silently, to join the bereaved in his loneliness, sorrowfully to sit alongside him, to think his thoughts and to linger on his loss. The warmth of such human presence is inestimable. Practiced as the tradition prescribes it, true consolation is the distillation of empathy. The sum effect of the visitation of many friends and relatives, some long forgotten, others members of a community who may rarely have paid the mourner any attention at all, is the softening of loneliness, the relief of the heavy burden of internalized despair, and the affirmation that the world at-large is not a hateful and angry place, but a warm and friendly one. It is a beckoning with open arms for the mourner to return to society. Comforting the mourners, says Maimonides, is *gemillat chasadim*, a genuine kindness to both the dead and the living.

The purpose of the condolence call is not to convince the mourner of anything at all. This is the time for accompanying him on his very own path, not for argumentation or debate. It is the time for the contemplation of disaster. While the mourner himself may wish to discuss it, it is not the prime purpose of this visit to relieve his fears for the future or his guilt for the past. It is not proper, say the sages (indeed it borders on sacrilege), to impress upon the mourner the inevitability of death, as though to doubt the true purpose and justice of a decree that God issued, but would change if only He were free to do so. It is not seemly, perhaps it is even entirely useless, to assure the mourner that others have suffered similar tragedies, or worse fates, as though by right he should be less despairing. "It could have been worse," is cold consolation. This is a time for subjectivity, for an intensely personal evaluation of life, and the mourners should not be deprived of even this indulgence. Some of the importuning of visitors that "life must go on," and that the mourner should be "thankful that worse did not occur," are well-meaning, but hollow and sometimes annoying expressions.

The strategy of true compassion is presence and silence, the eloquence of human closeness. Sad, muttered words are clumsy openers of the heart compared with the whisper of soft eyes. The comradeship demonstrated by the expression on the face speaks volumes that the ancient bards could not match with mere words, no matter how beautiful. It fulfills at once the mourner's desperate need for both companionship and privacy. It was, therefore, an old custom, unfortunately lost to our generations, for visitors to sit silently on the earth with, and like, the mourner. How magnificent an expression of compassion!

The first principle of comforting the mourners, found in the major codes of Jewish law, is that one should remain silent and allow the mourner to speak first. In many Jewish communities in olden days, the congregants accompanied the mourner as he walked home from synagogue on the Sabbath or holiday, and there they sat with him. How warm the mere physical presence of other human beings! How it relieves the sharp sting of tragedy! The classic mourner, Job, visited by three friends, sat with them for seven days and none uttered a sound. Ecclesiastes wisely notes that there "is a time to keep silent and a time to speak." The Midrash (Kohelet Rabbah on 3:5) records that the wife of Rabbi Mana died. His colleague, Rabbi Abin, came to pay a condolence call. Asked Rabbi Mana, "Are there any words of Torah you would like to offer us in our time of grief?" Rabbi Abin replied, "At times like this the Torah takes refuge in silence!"

It is in this spirit that Maimonides cautions visitors that they not speak overly much as, somehow, words have the tendency to generate a spirit of frivolity so contrary to the spirit of shiva. Indeed, the Talmud notes this when it remarks perceptively, "True reward comes to one who is silent in the house of mourning, and voluble in the wedding hall!"

It is true, of course, that it is exceedingly difficult to comfort with warmth and hope and compassion, while sitting relatively silent. Perhaps, that is the reason for the parting phrase of comfort, "May God comfort you among the other mourners of Zion and Jerusalem." For only God can truly comfort, even as He consoled Isaac after his father Abraham's death, and as He has comforted, through the ages, the other mourners of Zion after the tragic destruction of the ancient Temple, and has comforted the exiled, and those who suffered in pogroms and crusades. If the visitor feels uncomfortable in the tension of silence, he may of course converse with the mourner, but— little and wisely.

The Jewish Way in Death and Mourning [New York: J. David Publishers, 1999], pp. 132–135.
Reprinted with permission of the publisher.

THE BLESSING OF A BROKEN HEART*

BY SHERRI MANDELL

The Shiva and the Faces of God

It is as if I have left my body. My husband and I have become one body, one soul, joined together in our pain, alone with our pain together. That first night we sleep a few hours, wake at 4:00 A.M. and go out to the terrace off our bedroom. The birds are singing, it is growing light, the sky is streaked with purple and pink, and we wrap our arms around each other and cry together.

My husband remembers friends of his who died young. I remember waking up with Koby when he was a baby early in the morning, nursing him. The birds sang loudly, sweeping across the sky. It was a secret, magic time, a time alone with my baby when the true beauty of the world was revealed to me.

This morning I hear the birds again. The sound is so loud, it seems like a texture, something you can touch, like a thick blanket over us. The sound is a sign telling me that the ordinary life we knew is being transformed; intangible sound has suddenly become material, tangible. We are not just one form but can be transformed; matter transmuting itself into spirit and back. Death is a permutation, a change of form. Rimbaud wrote about different senses merging in poetry. Touch and sound have merged, as synesthesia is made manifest for me.

The moon still in the sky looks like the opening of a tunnel, calling me to believe that my son is on a journey to a land I cannot yet know. I want to hold his hand, and yank him back to me. I want to say to him: Did you take a jacket? Did you take water? Did you eat? I want to take care of him.

My husband and I stand together in a kind of tenderness that we haven't felt in years, perhaps never. We are fully present for each other. Koby has given the gift of a bond that feels necessary, urgent, a life support system that will keep us alive.

Later that day, Gavi asks me: "Who is Koby's mommy, now?"

I wonder what to answer. It's true that I am still Koby's mommy, but I am no longer the one who takes care of him. I answer, "God is his mommy."

"Oh good," answers Gavi. "Then he can see a falling star whenever he wants."

My child believes in the goodness of the world. My child believes in magic. My child believes in God. ...

During the seven days of mourning, the *shiva*, I live in the land of pain. My friends fear I won't return to myself, that I won't have the strength to go on. Seth worries about me because my eyes swing in their sockets; I can't eat. My friends beg me to eat. They rub my shoulders and my back. They try to spoon baby food into my mouth. The doctor comes and checks my tongue, my blood pressure. He tells me I must eat. But food is for people who are alive, and I am not. I get up and go downstairs and cry out in my pain. I sit on the floor and am cradled by thousands of people who reach out to me. My children join me on the floor; they are in their rooms with friends; they play upstairs, I don't know who is taking care of them but I see them eating. I see adults surrounding them. I speak to them and hold them, but they prefer to be with their friends. My pain is a flame that they can feel in my hands, see in my eyes.

Seven days of mourning. The mirrors are covered. Vanity is a luxury in the midst of such pain. One

---

* Sherri Mandell wrote her memoir *The Blessing of a Broken Heart* after enduring the horrific murder of her eldest son, Koby. Mandell, an American-born writer raising her family in Israel, sent her 13-year-old son off to school on May 8, 2001. But Koby never made it to school that day. Instead, he skipped school to go hiking with his friend Yosef. The two boys' bodies were found the next day, bludgeoned to death in a cave near Koby's home in Tekoa. Palestinian terrorists were blamed for the attacks, although the murderers were never found. Mandell later founded the Koby Mandell Foundation, which offers healing retreats for bereaved mothers and widows as well as a camp for children whose parents or siblings have been killed by terrorists.

wants to forget the material world, be transformed into a spirit so that one can merge with the dead. This world seems like a world of shadow. The body is insubstantial. I don't want to perform my rituals of vanity—the quick dab of eye makeup, lipstick. I don't bathe. I wear the same ripped shirt all week. Breathing is all I can manage. Most people can't tolerate a mourner's silence, and rush to fill it, but Jewish mourning laws dictate that a person paying a *shiva* call should be silent until the mourner speaks. If the mourner says nothing, the person visiting should say nothing as well. Neither should greet each other. The first three days, when the pain is most intense, the mourner is like an egg, without a mouth, dwelling in silence. The point of the *shiva* is not to comfort a mourner for her loss but to stand with her in the time of her grief. As Rabbi Maurice Lamm notes, the main purpose of the *shiva* is to relieve the mourner of his loneliness. A person expresses compassion for the mourner through his presence and silence. Job sat with his friends for seven days and none uttered a sound. For only God can comfort. That is why, when departing a *shiva*, many traditional Jews state these words: "May God comfort you among the mourners of Zion and Jerusalem." But I am not silent. I need to talk about Koby. I cannot contain the pain of silence.

And there are people who come and offer me words that ease my loneliness. Not formulaic statements like 'he's in a better place', or 'thank God you have your other children', but words that tell me that they can stand with us in this place of sorrow. I need to speak. I need people to talk to me. I ask my friend to put a sign on a door—this is a house of *shiva* and all conversation should be about Koby. I refuse to listen to anything trite, anything mundane. I tell people: only Koby, only Koby.

There are many people who offer me wisdom, and I hold on to their words like a rope that I can climb. The women bend down to me, sitting on the floor, putting their faces to mine. Their faces are so beautiful—their eyes open, their voices soft and strong. Today I know that each person is created in the image of God, because I see and hear God in their faces, the faces of God. I know all of these women are God coming to comfort me, their arms wrapped around me; their eyes looking into mine. They reach into their souls and give me divine pieces of themselves; love and compassion—they feed me with their words. Israeli women are unafraid of suffering; they know death as a companion. They say:

"Your son will not be forgotten. We will not let him be forgotten . . ."

"We will be with you. You will never be alone, never . . ."

"He is our son too; we are crying with you . . ."

"He is with God and he is basking in God's love and you will bask in our love . . ."

"Your son is like a boat, a beautiful boat sailing and when it goes over the horizon you won't be able to see it, but it's still there, sailing along the open waters . . ."

And this: "My brother was killed and my mother suffered but after the terrible pain, there were gifts. My mother was a Holocaust survivor, her parents and brothers and sisters were killed in the war. She made a new life here in Israel. Then my brother was killed in a terrorist attack on a bus in 1979." I remember this. I once stayed at this woman's house for *Shabbat,* and all night, the picture of the handsome young man in the photograph looked down at me, and I felt he had died. In the morning, I asked her, and she told me that her brother had died when he was twenty-six. She says: "My mother had great blessings in her life, even with her misfortune, and so will you. God takes away, but he also gives. You will receive. God will give you *bracha.*"

These words move me, and I want to believe them. But I don't understand them.

The mothers who have lost children to terrorism arrive. One, who lost her teenage son in an attack when he was hiking in Wadi Kelt, says: "You will go on. You will live." She gives me practical advice: "Don't make a shrine for your son. Pack up his things and put them away. Use his room. You don't need to keep out his pictures everywhere."

She is an attractive woman, her hair styled in a fashionable, short cut. She is wearing makeup, earrings. I look at her and realize: You can still be alive after your son is dead.

A woman who lost her nineteen-year-old son in a drive-by shooting says: "He is not gone. He will live inside of you now. We miss their physical bodies but we are still tied to them. You will never forget him."

I reach out for their hands like branches that will pull me across a raging river. One of my friends tells me: "You are all soul, you are letting us see your soul."

The politicians arrive. Israel is a small country with a history of conflict, and there is a custom of politicians attending the funeral or the *shiva* of each person killed by terror or war, each person killed by a national enemy. I tell the President, Moshe Katzav—I need a father to comfort me. He stares at me without seeing me. The chief rabbi, the ministers, the mayors . . . none of them have the right words of comfort for me.

"What do we do with the pain?" my husband asks a rabbi who, years ago, lost his eleven-year-old child in a bus accident. The rabbi answers: "You must use it to grow."

Another rabbi says that ours is a heartbreaking test, but we need to turn to God, that only God can give us comfort. Outside of the house, my friend Valerie tells me, the rabbis cry like babies.

Because no matter how much we try to intellectualize or interpret the pain, to will it away, the pain crouches on our heart like a beast who is waiting to crush us, to chew us to bits until we are nothing, dust that the wind can blow away. I wake up each morning crying and I go to sleep in tears. My body is a poor companion now. It is too material. I want to peel it away, find the soul inside and merge with my son.

I look at the women who wrap their arms around me, who give me their bodies to cry on. They are my Yemenite and Moroccan and Portuguese and American mothers. There is so much love in that *shiva*, so much

love; the love lifts me up and keeps me afloat like I am a body being carried. ...

The Broken Glass

. . . I cry and grieve, but at the same time, I have not shut down my capacity for feeling joy and awe at the world. On the contrary, it is as if my palate of emotion has expanded. Now when I feel joy it is more exquisite because I know that love needs to be held on to, gathered close, appreciated because it is so precious. Being home when my children return from school is a moment of gratitude for me.

My heart now feels like a heart of truth, a heart that yearns for eternity. It's a heart that is broken like the goblet at a Jewish wedding ceremony.

At my own wedding, I had learned the meaning of breaking the glass. I knew that it meant that even in the greatest of happiness, we need to remember our obligations to God—not to get too carried away in our joy. It reminds us that we are always dependent on God's mercy. It reminds us that we can't have complete happiness because of the destruction of the Temple, the place of God's dwelling, in Jerusalem. It reminds us that perfect joy is not possible in this world.

Back then, I understood the meaning of the broken glass in an abstract way. Now I have lived the broken glass. God himself seeks out broken vessels for use (*Leviticus Rabah* 7:2). As it says in Psalm 147, verse 3, "God is the healer of shattered hearts." Now I understand that there is a shattering first. Then there will be a healing. It is out of destruction that the Resurrection will come. The Messiah was born on the day that the Temple was destroyed. It is out of pain that the Messiah will be born. In this world, pain and beauty coexist. In the World-to-Come, as I understand it, the pain will be gone. We won't need answers to our suffering, because we will no longer have questions.

In the book *Made in Heaven*, Aryeh Kaplan teaches us that a human being can be likened to glass—vulnerable. But glass, when it is broken, can be re-melted and re-blown. It can be made whole again. So, too, even after a person dies, his life is not over. He too can be restored, made whole. And so, too, can our hearts. Though I will never again be that same innocent bride, and I will never again look at a wedding without pain in my heart, I have become a different person, one who is more vulnerable, more open and, I hope, has more compassion. I pray that one day I will meet my son in the World-to-Come. All of the broken fragments of the world will be mended, and I will know that as Rabbi Menachem Mendel of Kotsk, a nineteenth century Chassidic rabbi, said: There is nothing so whole as a broken heart.

The Blessing of a Broken Heart [London: Toby Press, 2009], pp. 51–56, 97–98.
Reprinted with permission of the author and publisher.

Lesson Six

The Ultimate Destination
The Kabbalah of Life, Death, and Resurrection

Life, death, afterlife—where does it all lead? What is the ultimate endgame? The metaphysics of death are rooted in what transpired in the Garden of Eden at the beginning of time. To understand the end, we need to first explore the beginning. Let us begin . . .

JLI

JEWISH LEARNING INSTITUTE

The Fatal Glitch
The Genesis of Mortality

Text 1a

Genesis 2:16–17 🕮

וַיְצַו ה' אֱלֹקִים עַל הָאָדָם לֵאמֹר: "מִכֹּל עֵץ הַגָּן אָכֹל תֹּאכֵל. וּמֵעֵץ הַדַּעַת טוֹב וָרָע לֹא תֹאכַל מִמֶּנּוּ, כִּי בְּיוֹם אֲכָלְךָ מִמֶּנּוּ מוֹת תָּמוּת".

God commanded man, saying, "Of every tree of the garden you may freely eat. But of the Tree of Knowledge of Good and Evil you shall not eat, for on the day that you eat thereof, you shall surely die."

Text 1b

Ibid., 3:6–7 🕮

וַתֵּרֶא הָאִשָּׁה כִּי טוֹב הָעֵץ לְמַאֲכָל, וְכִי תַאֲוָה הוּא לָעֵינַיִם, וְנֶחְמָד הָעֵץ לְהַשְׂכִּיל. וַתִּקַּח מִפִּרְיוֹ וַתֹּאכַל וַתִּתֵּן גַּם לְאִישָׁהּ עִמָּהּ וַיֹּאכַל.

וַתִּפָּקַחְנָה עֵינֵי שְׁנֵיהֶם וַיֵּדְעוּ כִּי עֵירֻמִּם הֵם, וַיִּתְפְּרוּ עֲלֵה תְאֵנָה וַיַּעֲשׂוּ לָהֶם חֲגֹרֹת.

The woman saw that the tree was good for food and that it was a delight to the eyes, and the tree was desirable to make one wise; she took of its fruit and ate, and she gave also to her husband with her, and he ate.

The eyes of both of them were opened, and they knew that they were naked, and they sewed fig leaves and made themselves girdles.

Text 1c

Ibid., 3:19 📖

בְּזֵעַת אַפֶּיךָ תֹּאכַל לֶחֶם עַד שׁוּבְךָ אֶל הָאֲדָמָה כִּי מִמֶּנָּה לֻקָּחְתָּ. כִּי עָפָר אַתָּה וְאֶל עָפָר תָּשׁוּב.

By the sweat of your brow you shall eat bread, until you return to the ground; for you were taken therefrom. For dust you are, and to dust you will return.

Text 2

Isaiah 25:8 📖

בִּלַּע הַמָּוֶת לָנֶצַח וּמָחָה ה' אֱלֹקִים דִּמְעָה מֵעַל כָּל פָּנִים.

God shall conceal death forever, and He shall wipe the tears off every face.

Misalignment

Text 3

Rabbi Ovadiah Sforno, Genesis 2:25 ▯

כִּי אָז הָיוּ כָל פְּעוּלוֹתֵיהֶם וְכָל אֵיבָרֵיהֶם לַעֲשׂוֹת רְצוֹן קוֹנָם בִּלְבַד,
לֹא לְהַשִּׂיג תַּעֲנוּגוֹת נִפְסָדוֹת כְּלָל, בְּאוֹפֶן שֶׁהָיְתָה פְּעוּלַּת הַזִּיוּוּג
אֶצְלָם כִּפְעוּלַּת הָאֲכִילָה וְהַשְׁתִיָּה הַמְסַפֶּקֶת, וּבְכֵן הָיָה עִנְיָן
אֵיבָרִים הָהֵם אֶצְלָם כְּמוֹ עִנְיָן הַפֶּה וְהַפָּנִים וְהַיָּדַיִם אֶצְלֵנוּ.

Rabbi Ovadiah Sforno
1475–1550

Biblical exegete, philosopher, and physician. Sforno was born in Cesena, Italy. After gaining a thorough knowledge of Talmud and the sciences, he moved to Rome where he studied medicine and taught Hebrew to the German scholar Johannes Reuchlin. Sforno eventually settled in Bologna where he founded and directed a yeshivah until his death. His magnum opus is a biblical commentary focused on the simple interpretation of text, with an emphasis on philology and philosophy.

At that time [before the sin of the Tree of Knowledge], all of Adam and Eve's pursuits and all of their limbs were aimed solely to please their Creator, not to engage in temporal pleasures. They viewed marital intercourse no differently than purposeful eating and drinking. They viewed their reproductive organs much as we view our mouths, faces, and hands.

Text 4

The Rebbe, Rabbi Menachem M. Schneerson,
Sefer Hama'amarim Melukat 2:277–278

דְּהַמִּיתָה בָּעוֹלָם שֶׁנַּעֲשְׂתָה עַל יְדֵי חֵטְא עֵץ הַדַּעַת הִיא מְסוּבֶּבֶת מֵהַחֵטְא עַצְמוֹ.

וְהָעִנְיָן הוּא, דְּעִנְיַן הַחִיּוּת הוּא בִּקְדוּשָׁה דַּוְקָא, מַה שֶּׁאֵין כֵּן הָרַע וְהַטּוּמְאָה (הֵיפֶּךְ הַקְּדוּשָׁה) הֵם מָוֶת, וְלָכֵן, מִכֵּיוָן שֶׁעַל יְדֵי חֵטְא עֵץ הַדַּעַת נִתְעָרֵב רַע בָּהָאָדָם, מָוֶת רוּחָנִי, מִזֶּה נִשְׁתַּלְשֵׁל בּוֹ גַּם מִיתָה כִּפְשׁוּטָהּ.

Death was introduced to the world as a direct result of the sin of the Tree of Knowledge.

Life is associated exclusively with holiness. Unholiness, on the other hand, is synonymous with death. As a result of the sin of the Tree of Knowledge, unholiness—spiritual death—became part of the human being's identity. This resulted in physical death.

Rabbi Menachem Mendel Schneerson
1902–1994

The towering Jewish leader of the 20th century, known as "the Lubavitcher Rebbe," or simply as "the Rebbe." Born in southern Ukraine, the Rebbe escaped Nazi-occupied Europe, arriving in the U.S. in June 1941. The Rebbe inspired and guided the revival of traditional Judaism after the European devastation, impacting virtually every Jewish community the world over. The Rebbe often emphasized that the performance of just one additional good deed could usher in the era of Mashiach. The Rebbe's scholarly talks and writings have been printed in more than 200 volumes.

QUESTION FOR DISCUSSION

According to the text we just read, what is the connection between self-consciousness (ego) and death?

You Only Live Twice
The Thirteenth Principle

Text 5

Maimonides, Commentary on Mishnah, Introduction to *Chelek* 📖

Rabbi Moshe ben Maimon
(Maimonides, Rambam)
1135–1204

Halachist, philosopher, author, and physician. Maimonides was born in Cordoba, Spain. After the conquest of Cordoba by the Almohads, he fled Spain and eventually settled in Cairo, Egypt. There, he became the leader of the Jewish community and served as court physician to the vizier of Egypt. He is most noted for authoring the *Mishneh Torah*, an encyclopedic arrangement of Jewish law, and for his philosophical work, *Guide for the Perplexed*. His rulings on Jewish law are integral to the formation of halachic consensus.

וּתְחִיַּת הַמֵּתִים יְסוֹד מִיסוֹדוֹת תּוֹרַת מֹשֶׁה רַבֵּינוּ, אֵין דָּת וְאֵין קֶשֶׁר עִם הָאוּמָּה הַיְהוּדִית לְמִי שֶׁאֵינוּ מַאֲמִין בְּכַךְ.

The resurrection of the dead is a foundation of the Torah of Moses; one cannot maintain a connection to the Jewish religion without this belief.

QUESTION FOR DISCUSSION

Based on the Kabbalistic understanding of reincarnation, as discussed in Lesson Four, how would you reconcile the resurrection of the dead with the concept of reincarnation?

Text 6

Rabbi Chaim Vital, *Sha'ar Hagilgulim*, Introduction 4 📖

אִם בַּפַּעַם הָא׳ . . . לֹא זָכָה לְתַקֵּן אוֹתָהּ (הַנֶּפֶשׁ) כּוּלָהּ וּמֵת . . . בְּעֵת תְּחִיַּת הַמֵּתִים אֵין לוֹ לַגוּף הָא׳ אֶלָּא אוֹתוֹ הַחֵלֶק הַפְּרָטִי (שֶׁל הַנֶּפֶשׁ) אֲשֶׁר תִּיקֵן הוּא בַּחַיִּים.

וְלָכֵן כְּשֶׁמִּתְגַּלְגֶּלֶת הַנֶּפֶשׁ הַזֹּאת בְּגוּף אַחֵר לְהַשְׁלִים תִּיקוּנָהּ . . . בְּחִינַת הַחֲלָקִים שֶׁל הַנֶּפֶשׁ שֶׁנִּתַּקְנוּ בְּגוּף הַזֶּה הַשֵּׁנִי . . . הֵם לְזֶה הַגוּף הַב׳ בִּזְמַן הַתְּחִיָּה.

I f the first time [a soul descended into a body] . . . it passed away before it was fully rectified . . . at the time of resurrection, that body will possess the portion of the soul it rectified while alive.

When the same soul reincarnates into another body to complete its rectification . . . the portion of the soul that was rectified in the second body . . . will vivify the second body when it arises at the resurrection.

Rabbi Chaim Vital
ca. 1542–1620

Lurianic Kabbalist. Rabbi Vital was born in Israel, lived in Safed and Jerusalem, and later in Damascus. He was authorized by his teacher, Rabbi Yitschak Luria, the Arizal, to record his teachings. Acting on this mandate, Vital began arranging his master's teachings in written form, and his many works constitute the foundation of the Lurianic school of Jewish mysticism. His most famous work is *Ets Chaim*.

LEARNING EXERCISE 1

What are the superficial purposes of the items in this list, and what are their true and holy purposes?

	Superficial Purpose	True Purpose
Food	*pleasure*	*nourishment, energy, health*
Sleep		
Socializing		
Vacation		
Work		

Text 7

The Rebbe, Rabbi Menachem M. Schneersohn, *Igrot Kodesh* 2:67–68 📖

וְהִנֵּה טַעַם הַבְּרִיאָה בִּכְלַל וּבְרִיאַת הָאָדָם בִּפְרָט וְתַכְלִיתָם הוּא מִפְּנֵי שֶׁנִּתְאַוָּה הַקָּדוֹשׁ בָּרוּךְ הוּא לִהְיוֹת לוֹ דִּירָה בַּתַּחְתּוֹנִים דַּוְקָא. הַיְינוּ שֶׁהַתַּחְתּוֹנִים (בְּמַעֲלָה וּמַדְרֵיגָה, כִּי לֹא שַׁיָּיךְ לְפָנָיו יִתְבָּרֵךְ מַעֲלָה וּמַטָּה בְּמָקוֹם. וְהֵם) הַיֵּשׁ וְהַחוֹמֶר, יִהְיוּ בִּבְחִינַת בִּיטוּל, שֶׁעַל יְדֵי זֶה שׁוֹרֶה וּמִתְגַּלֶּה בָּהֶם אוֹר ה' אֵין סוֹף בָּרוּךְ הוּא. וּבִיטוּל זֶה הוּא תַּכְלִית וִיסוֹד הַתּוֹרָה וְהַמִּצְוָה . . . וְזֶהוּ שֶׁהַתּוֹרָה וְהַמִּצְוֹת נִיתְּנוּ לְמַטָּה, בִּדְבָרִים גַּשְׁמִיִּים וְלַנְּשָׁמָה כְּשֶׁהִיא מְלוּבֶּשֶׁת בְּגוּף גַּשְׁמִי דַּוְקָא.

The reason God created the entire world, and the human being in particular, is because He "desired a home in the lower realms." That is, God wished that the "lower realms," namely, the physicality of this world, should become subservient to and a vehicle for expressing God. The purpose of Torah and *mitzvot* is to effect this transformation. . . . This is the reason why Torah and *mitzvot* are performed with physical objects by a soul vested in a physical body.

Resurrection of the Living

Text 8

Ezekiel 37:1–14

הָיְתָה עָלַי יַד ה', וַיּוֹצִאֵנִי בְרוּחַ ה' וַיְנִיחֵנִי בְּתוֹךְ הַבִּקְעָה, וְהִיא מְלֵאָה עֲצָמוֹת. וְהֶעֱבִירַנִי עֲלֵיהֶם סָבִיב סָבִיב, וְהִנֵּה רַבּוֹת מְאֹד עַל פְּנֵי הַבִּקְעָה, וְהִנֵּה יְבֵשׁוֹת מְאֹד.

וַיֹּאמֶר אֵלַי, "בֶּן אָדָם, הֲתִחְיֶינָה הָעֲצָמוֹת הָאֵלֶּה? . . . הִנָּבֵא עַל הָעֲצָמוֹת הָאֵלֶּה; וְאָמַרְתָּ אֲלֵיהֶם, הָעֲצָמוֹת הַיְבֵשׁוֹת שִׁמְעוּ דְּבַר ה'. כֹּה אָמַר אֲדֹנָ-י ה' לָעֲצָמוֹת הָאֵלֶּה, הִנֵּה אֲנִי מֵבִיא בָכֶם רוּחַ וִחְיִיתֶם" . . .

וְנִבֵּאתִי כַּאֲשֶׁר צֻוֵּיתִי. וַיְהִי קוֹל כְּהִנָּבְאִי, וְהִנֵּה רַעַשׁ, וַתִּקְרְבוּ עֲצָמוֹת עֶצֶם אֶל עַצְמוֹ. וְרָאִיתִי וְהִנֵּה עֲלֵיהֶם גִּדִים, וּבָשָׂר עָלָה, וַיִּקְרַם עֲלֵיהֶם עוֹר מִלְמָעְלָה . . . וַתָּבוֹא בָהֶם הָרוּחַ וַיִּחְיוּ, וַיַּעַמְדוּ עַל רַגְלֵיהֶם חַיִל גָּדוֹל מְאֹד מְאֹד.

וַיֹּאמֶר אֵלַי, "בֶּן אָדָם, הָעֲצָמוֹת הָאֵלֶּה כָּל בֵּית יִשְׂרָאֵל הֵמָּה, הִנֵּה אֹמְרִים, יָבְשׁוּ עַצְמוֹתֵינוּ וְאָבְדָה תִקְוָתֵנוּ, נִגְזַרְנוּ לָנוּ. לָכֵן הִנָּבֵא וְאָמַרְתָּ אֲלֵיהֶם, כֹּה אָמַר אֲדֹנָ-י ה', הִנֵּה אֲנִי פֹתֵחַ אֶת קִבְרוֹתֵיכֶם וְהַעֲלֵיתִי אֶתְכֶם מִקִּבְרוֹתֵיכֶם, עַמִּי, וְהֵבֵאתִי אֶתְכֶם אֶל אַדְמַת יִשְׂרָאֵל . . . וְנָתַתִּי רוּחִי בָכֶם וִחְיִיתֶם".

God took hold of me and by His spirit carried me out and set me down in the midst of a valley; it was full of bones. He led me around the bones; there were many bones on the surface of the valley, and they were exceedingly dry.

God said to me: "Son of man, can these bones become alive? . . . Prophesy over these bones, and say to them, 'O dry bones, hear the word of God! So says God to these bones: Behold, I will cause spirit to enter into you, and you shall live!'" . . .

I prophesied as I was commanded. There was a noise as I prophesied and then a commotion. The bones came together, one bone to its neighbor. And as I looked, sinews and flesh came upon the bones, and skin covered them from above. . . . The spirit then entered them and they came alive. They then stood on their feet, an exceedingly great army.

Then God said to me, "Son of man, these bones are [a symbol for] the house of Israel; behold they say, 'Our bones have become dried up, our hope is lost, we are cut off.' Therefore, prophesy and say to them: 'So says God: Behold, My people, I will open your graves and bring you up from them and bring you to the land of Israel. . . . I will put My spirit within you, and you shall live.'"

Lesson and Course Conclusion

Text 9

Midrash, *Bamidbar Rabah* 19:3 🕮

Bamidbar Rabah

An exegetical commentary on the first seven chapters of the book of Numbers and a homiletic commentary on the rest of the book. The first part of *Bamidbar Rabah* is notable for its inclusion of esoteric material; the second half is essentially identical to *Midrash Tanchuma* on the book of Numbers. It was first published in Constantinople in 1512, together with four other midrashic works on the other four books of the Pentateuch.

אָמַר שְׁלֹמֹה: "עַל כָּל אֵלֶּה עָמַדְתִּי, וּפָרָשָׁה שֶׁל פָּרָה אֲדוּמָּה חָקַרְתִּי וְשָׁאַלְתִּי וּפִשְׁפַּשְׁתִּי. 'אָמַרְתִּי, אֶחְכָּמָה, וְהִיא רְחוֹקָה מִמֶּנִּי' (קֹהֶלֶת ז, כג)".

Solomon said: I was able to arrive at the reason for all these [other enigmatic commandments]. The law of the red heifer, however, I investigated, queried, and searched, and I [finally] admitted: "I am determined to be wise, yet this is distant from me" (Ecclesiastes 7:23).

Text 10

Ibid., 19:4 🕮

עַל כָּל דָּבָר וְדָבָר שֶׁהָיָה אוֹמֵר הַקָּדוֹשׁ בָּרוּךְ הוּא לְמֹשֶׁה, אוֹמֵר לוֹ טוּמְאָתוֹ וְטָהֳרָתוֹ. כֵּיוָן שֶׁהִגִּיעַ לְפָרָשַׁת "אֱמוֹר אֶל הַכֹּהֲנִים" אָמַר לוֹ מֹשֶׁה, "רִבּוֹנוֹ שֶׁל עוֹלָם! אִם נִטְמָא זֶה, בַּמֶּה תְּהֵא טָהֳרָתוֹ?"

לֹא הֱשִׁיבוֹ. בְּאוֹתָהּ שָׁעָה, נִתְכַּרְכְּמוּ פָּנָיו שֶׁל מֹשֶׁה.

כֵּיוָן שֶׁהִגִּיעַ לְפָרָשַׁת פָּרָה אֲדוּמָּה אָמַר לוֹ הַקָּדוֹשׁ בָּרוּךְ הוּא, "בְּאוֹתָהּ שָׁעָה שֶׁאָמַרְתִּי לְךָ 'אֱמוֹר אֶל הַכֹּהֲנִים', וְאָמַרְתָּ לִי, 'אִם נִטְמָא בַּמֶּה תְּהֵא טָהֳרָתוֹ?' לֹא הֱשַׁבְתִּיךָ זוֹ טָהֳרָתוֹ: 'וְלָקְחוּ לַטָּמֵא מֵעֲפַר שְׂרֵפַת הַחַטָּאת' (בְּמִדְבָּר יט, יז)".

In all matters of ritual impurity that God taught Moses, He would tell him both the manner of contamination and the manner of purification. When God arrived at the Torah portion of *Emor* [which discusses the laws regarding one who comes in contact with a dead body], Moses said to Him: "Master of the universe! If one is thus contaminated, how may he be purified?"

God did not respond. At that moment, Moses's face changed colors.

When God came to the section of the red heifer, He said to Moses: "When I told you the portion of Emor, you asked Me, 'If one is thus contaminated, how may he be purified?' At the time, I did not respond. This is how such a person becomes pure: 'They shall take for the impure person of the ashes of the burnt heifer' (Numbers 19:17)."

Text 11

The Rebbe, Rabbi Menachem M. Schneerson, *Sefer Hasichot* 5748 1:311–312 📖

בִּיטוּל הָרוֹשֶׁם דִּפְעוּלַת הַמִּיתָה (הַתּוֹכֶן דְּפָרָשַׁת פָּרָה) בְּתַכְלִית
הַשְׁלֵימוּת, הוּא – כְּפְשׁוּטוֹ מַמָּשׁ – עַל יְדֵי זֶה שֶׁ"הָקִיצוּ וְרַנְּנוּ שׁוֹכְנֵי
עָפָר" (יְשַׁעְיָהוּ כו, יט), שֶׁאָז, אֵין צוֹרֶךְ בְּהֶסְבֵּר שִׂכְלִי וְהִשְׁתַּדְּלוּת בְּנוֹגֵעַ
לַפְּעוּלָה עַל רֶגֶשׁ הַלֵּב, מִכֵּיוָן שָׁרוֹאִים בָּעֵינַיִים שֶׁ"הָקִיצוּ . . שׁוֹכְנֵי
עָפָר", וְשׁוֹמְעִים בָּאָזְנַיִים קוֹל רִינָתָם, "הָקִיצוּ וְרַנְּנוּ שׁוֹכְנֵי עָפָר".

The complete eradication of death's effect will occur, in a literal way, when "those that dwell in dust will arise and joyfully sing" (Isaiah 26:19). At that time, there will be no need to rationalize death or to emotionally process such rationalizations. For our eyes will see the awakening of those who dwell in dust, and our ears will hear the sound of their joyful singing.

Text 12

The Rebbe, Rabbi Menachem M. Schneersohn, *Igrot Kodesh* 25:5 📖

אֲשֶׁר כְּמוֹ שֶׁבַּוַדַּאי וּבְוַדַּאי יִבְנֶה הַשֵּׁם חָרְבוֹת צִיוֹן וִירוּשָׁלַיִם וִיקַבֵּץ נִדְחֵי יִשְׂרָאֵל מִכָּל קַצְוֵי תֵבֵל עַל יְדֵי מָשִׁיחַ צִדְקֵנוּ וִיבִיאֵם בְּרִנָּה לִרְאוֹת בְּשִׂמְחָתָהּ שֶׁל צִיוֹן וִירוּשָׁלַיִם, כָּךְ הוּא לְלֹא סָפֵק בְּנוֹגֵעַ לְאָבֵל הַיָּחִיד, אֲשֶׁר יְקַיֵּים ה' דְּבָרוֹ וְהָקִיצוּ וְרַנְּנוּ שׁוֹכְנֵי עָפָר, וְתִגְדַּל הַשִּׂמְחָה, שִׂמְחָה אֲמִתִּית, בְּהִפָּגְשָׁם כּוּלָם יַחַד בְּעֵת תְּחִיַּת הַמֵּתִים.

We have perfect confidence that God will rebuild the ruins of Zion and Jerusalem; He will gather the dispersed remnants of Israel from the ends of the earth through our righteous Mashiach, and He will bring them in gladness to witness the joy of Zion and Jerusalem. We are equally confident that the same is true with regard to our personal bereavement: God will fulfill His promise that "those that dwell in the dust shall awake and joyfully sing." Great indeed will be the happiness and rejoicing then, when all will meet together after the resurrection of the dead.

LEARNING EXERCISE 2

1. Write down the point from today's lesson that resonated with you most.

    _____

    _____

    _____

2. Identify an activity you can do to help you stay aligned with "life," i.e., that which is truly meaningful.

    _____

    _____

    _____

Key Points

1. Death entered the human condition as a result of Adam and Eve's eating from the Tree of Knowledge. From this we learn that death is a consequence of human error, and that immortality is the ideal state of existence. When we fix this error, we will again become immortal.

2. In the Messianic Era, not only will death be abolished, but the souls of all those who perished will be reunited with their bodies. Every body will be resurrected, including those that possessed reincarnated souls. This is a cardinal principle of Jewish faith.

3. Before the sin, the body was an extension of the soul, and their desires were perfectly in synch; in a broader sense, there was no separation between the physical world (the "body") and its Godly purpose (the "soul"). The sin of eating from the tree was an act of spiritual death—the separation of body and soul due to misaligned values. This resulted in physical death.

4. Our job is to see beyond the superficial layers of things and instead focus on their inner truth and purpose—their "life." This brings body and soul back in synch, thus precluding spiritual and physical death.

5. The resurrection is a message of hope. Even at times we feel lifeless, we have the capacity to be "resurrected" at any moment, nationally and personally.

6. The ability to heal from loss defies all logic and reason. Nevertheless, the law of the Red Heifer empowers us to heal, to a degree, from pain, anguish, and grief. The hole in our hearts will be completely healed with the resurrection of the dead, when we will be reunited with our loved ones.

Appendix A

Zohar, *Midrash Hane'elam*, 1:139a 📖

בֵּית הַמִּקְדָּשׁ קוֹדֵם לְקִבּוּץ גָּלֻיּוֹת, קִבּוּץ גָּלֻיּוֹת קוֹדֵם לִתְחִיַּת הַמֵּתִים, וּתְחִיַּת הַמֵּתִים הוּא אַחֲרוֹן שֶׁבְּכֻלָּם.

מְנָא לֵיהּ? דִּכְתִיב (תְּהִילִים קמז, ב-ג) "בּוֹנֵה יְרוּשָׁלַיִם ה' נִדְחֵי יִשְׂרָאֵל יְכַנֵּס, הָרוֹפֵא לִשְׁבוּרֵי לֵב וּמְחַבֵּשׁ לְעַצְּבוֹתָם". זוֹ הִיא תְּחִיַּת הַמֵּתִים שֶׁהִיא הָרְפוּאָה לִשְׁבוּרֵי לֵב עַל מֵתֵיהֶם. בּוֹנֵה יְרוּשָׁלַיִם תְּחִלָּה, וְאַחֲרָיו נִדְחֵי יִשְׂרָאֵל יְכַנֵּס, וְ"הָרוֹפֵא לִשְׁבוּרֵי לֵב" אַחֲרוֹן עַל הַכֹּל.

תְּנַן מ' שָׁנָה קוֹדֵם הַקִּבּוּץ גָּלֻיּוֹת לִתְחִיַּת הַמֵּתִים.

The [rebuilding of the] Holy Temple will precede the ingathering of exiles [to the Land of Israel], and the ingathering will precede the resurrection of the dead—which will be the last of them all.

What is the Scriptural support for this? It is stated (Psalms 147:2–3), "God is the builder of Jerusalem; He will gather the exiles of Israel; He heals the brokenhearted and bandages their wounds." "Heals the brokenhearted" refers to the resurrection that will heal those whose hearts are broken over their loved ones who have died. [The order of the verse indicates that] God will first build Jerusalem, then gather the exiles of Israel, and only then will He heal the brokenhearted.

It was taught that the ingathering of exiles precedes the resurrection by forty years.

Zohar

The seminal work of Kabbalah, Jewish mysticism. The Zohar is a mystical commentary on the Torah, written in Aramaic and Hebrew. According to Arizal, the Zohar contains the teachings of Rabbi Shimon bar Yocha'i who lived in the Land of Israel during the 2nd century. The Zohar has become one of the indispensable texts of traditional Judaism, alongside and nearly equal in stature to the Mishnah and Talmud.

Appendix B

Midrash, *Bereishit Rabah* 28:3 📖

אַדְרִיָאנוֹס שְׁחִיק עֲצָמוֹת שָׁאַל אֶת רַבִּי יְהוֹשֻׁעַ בֶּן חֲנַנְיָא, אָמַר לֵיהּ,
"מֵהֵיכָן הַקָדוֹשׁ בָּרוּךְ הוּא מֵצִיץ אֶת הָאָדָם לֶעָתִיד לָבֹא?"

אָמַר לֵיהּ, "מִלוּז שֶׁל שִׁדְרָהּ".

אָמַר לֵיהּ, "מִנַיִן אַתָּה יוֹדֵעַ?"

אָמַר לֵיהּ, "אַיְתִיתֵיהּ לְיָדִי וַאֲנָא מוֹדַע לָךְ".

טָחֲנוֹ בְּרֵחַיִם וְלֹא נִטְחַן, שְׂרָפוֹ בָּאֵשׁ וְלֹא נִשְׂרָף, נְתָנוֹ בַּמַיִם וְלֹא נִמְחָה, נְתָנוֹ עַל
הַסַדָן וְהִתְחִיל מַכֶּה עָלָיו בַּפַּטִישׁ, נֶחֱלַק הַסַדָן וְנִבְקַע הַפַּטִישׁ וְלֹא חָסַר כְּלוּם.

Bereishit Rabah

An early rabbinic commentary on the Book of Genesis. This Midrash bears the name of Rabbi Oshiya Rabah (Rabbi Oshiya "the Great") whose teaching opens this work. This Midrash provides textual exegeses and stories, expounds upon the biblical narrative, and develops and illustrates moral principles. Produced by the sages of the Talmud in the Land of Israel, its use of Aramaic closely resembles that of the Jerusalem Talmud. It was first published in Constantinople in 1512 together with four other Midrashic works on the other four books of the Pentateuch.

Emperor Hadrian, may his bones be pulverized, asked Rabbi Yehoshua ben Chanania, "From which part of the body will God recreate man at the time of the resurrection?"

"From the *luz* bone located in the vertebral column" answered the rabbi.

"How do you know this?"

"Bring me a *luz* and I will show you." He ground it in a mortar, but it was not crushed; he burnt it in fire, but it was not burned; he put it in water, but it did not dissolve; he placed it on a board and beat it with a hammer, the board split, and the hammer was pierced, and the *luz* remained whole.

Appendix C

Talmud, Sanhedrin 91a-b

אָמַר לֵיה אַנְטוֹנִינוֹס לְרַבִּי: גּוּף וּנְשָׁמָה יְכוֹלִין לִפְטוֹר עַצְמָן מִן הַדִּין. כֵּיצַד? גּוּף אוֹמֵר, "נְשָׁמָה חָטָאת. שֶׁמִּיּוֹם שֶׁפֵּירְשָׁה מִמֶּנִי הֲרֵינִי מוּטָל כְּאֶבֶן דּוֹמֵם בְּקֶבֶר". וּנְשָׁמָה אוֹמֶרֶת, "גּוּף חָטָא. שֶׁמִּיּוֹם שֶׁפֵּירַשְׁתִּי מִמֶּנוּ הֲרֵינִי פּוֹרַחַת בָּאֲוִיר כְּצִפּוֹר".

אָמַר לֵיה: אֶמְשׁוֹל לְךָ מָשָׁל.

לְמָה הַדָּבָר דּוֹמֶה? לְמֶלֶךְ בָּשָׂר וָדָם שֶׁהָיָה לוֹ פַּרְדֵּס נָאֶה וְהָיָה בּוֹ בִּכּוּרוֹת נָאוֹת, וְהוֹשִׁיב בּוֹ שְׁנֵי שׁוֹמְרִים אֶחָד חִיגֵּר וְאֶחָד סוּמָא.

אָמַר לוֹ חִיגֵּר לְסוּמָא, "בִּכּוּרוֹת נָאוֹת אֲנִי רוֹאֶה בַּפַּרְדֵּס, בֹּא וְהַרְכִּיבֵנִי וּנְבִיאֵם לְאָכְלָם". רָכַב חִיגֵּר עַל גַּבֵּי סוּמָא וֶהֱבִיאוּם וַאֲכָלוּם.

לְיָמִים בָּא בַּעַל פַּרְדֵּס. אָמַר לָהֶן, "בִּכּוּרוֹת נָאוֹת הֵיכָן הֵן?"

אָמַר לוֹ חִיגֵּר, "כְּלוּם יֵשׁ לִי רַגְלַיִם לְהַלֵּךְ בָּהֶן?"

אָמַר לוֹ סוּמָא, "כְּלוּם יֵשׁ לִי עֵינַיִם לִרְאוֹת?"

מַה עָשָׂה? הִרְכִּיב חִיגֵּר עַל גַּבֵּי סוּמָא וְדָן אוֹתָם כְּאֶחָד.

אַף הַקָּדוֹשׁ בָּרוּךְ הוּא מֵבִיא נְשָׁמָה וְזוֹרְקָה בַּגּוּף וְדָן אוֹתָם כְּאֶחָד.

Antoninus said to Rebbi, "The body and the soul can both exculpate themselves from judgment. The body can plead: 'It is the soul that has sinned, for since it left me, I lie in the grave like an inanimate stone.' The soul can say: 'It is the body that has sinned, for since the day I departed it, I fly about in the air like a bird [and commit no sin].'"

Rebbi said, "I will reply with a parable. This may be compared to a king who owned an orchard filled with splendid figs. He appointed two watchmen to guard the figs, one lame and the other blind.

"[One day] the lame watchman said to the blind one, 'I see beautiful figs in the orchard. Put me on your shoulders, and I will guide you to them, so that we can pick them and eat them.' [The blind watchman agreed, and they carried through with the thieving plan.]

"Sometime after, the orchard's owner arrived and inquired, 'Where are the beautiful figs?'

"The lame man replied, 'Have I feet to go?'

"The blind man replied, 'Have I eyes to see?'

"What did the owner do? He placed the lame watchman on the blind one's shoulders and judged them together.

"So, too, will God bring the soul, and place it in the body, and judge them together."

Appendix D

Adapted from Rabbi Shalom Dovber of Lubavitch,
Sefer Hama'amarim 5759, pp. 30–31 🕮

וְהִנֵּה כְּשֶׁיִּתְבּוֹנֵן הָאָדָם בְּכָל זֶה, אֵיךְ שֶׁבְּכָל דָּבָר יֵשׁ אוֹר וְחִיּוּת הָאֱלֹקִי, וְהָעִיקָר הוּא הָאוֹר הָאֱלֹקִי שֶׁבּוֹ, וְהַנִּבְרָאִים בֶּאֱמֶת בְּטֵלִים לְהָאוֹר הָאֱלֹקִי שֶׁבָּהֶם וּלְשָׁרְשָׁם וְלִמְקוֹרָם הַמְחַוֶּה כו', עַל יְדֵי זֶה יִתְעוֹרֵר בְּרָצוֹן וּתְשׁוּקָה וְאַהֲבָה גְדוֹלָה לֶאֱלֹקוּת, שֶׁזֶּה יִהְיֶה כָּל חֶפְצוֹ וּמְגַמָּתוֹ רַק בֶּאֱלֹקוּת לְבָד, וְלֹא יִרְצֶה בַּחִיצוֹנִיּוּת וְגַשְׁמִיּוּת הָעוֹלָם שֶׁהֵם מֵתֵי מֵת מִצַּד עַצְמָם, הֹוִים וְנִפְסָדִים כו', רַק יִרְצֶה בְּהַחִיּוּת הָאֱלֹקִי שֶׁהוּא הָעִיקָר כו', וּמִכָּל שֶׁכֵּן שֶׁאֵין צָרִיךְ לְהַפְרִיד אֶת הַדָּבָר הַגַּשְׁמִי. דְּהֲרֵי נִתְבָּאֵר לְעֵיל דְּהַגַּשְׁמִי בָּטֵל בֶּאֱמֶת אֶל הָאוֹר וְהַחִיּוּת הָאֱלֹקִי, אָמְנָם עַל יְדֵי שֶׁהָאָדָם מְחַשֵּׁב אֶת הַגַּשְׁמִי לְדָבָר בִּפְנֵי עַצְמוֹ, דְּהַיְנוּ בְּמַה שֶּׁרוֹצֶה לֵהָנוֹת הַדָּבָר הַגַּשְׁמִי עַל יְדֵי זֶה מוֹרִיד וּמַפְרִיד אוֹתוֹ. דְּגַם אֶת הָעוֹלָם נָתַן בְּלִבּוֹ שֶׁל אָדָם כו', וְלָכֵן חֵטְא עֵץ הַדַּעַת גָּרַם פֵּירוּד בִּכְלָלוּת הָעוֹלָם, כְּמוֹ כֵן כָּל אֶחָד וְאֶחָד עַל יְדֵי שֶׁרוֹצֶה לֵהָנוֹת מֵהַדָּבָר הַגַּשְׁמִי מִצַּד עַצְמוֹ הֲרֵי הוּא מַפְרִיד אוֹתוֹ, וּלְהֵיפֶךְ כְּשֶׁרוֹצֶה בְּהָאֱלֹקוּת שֶׁל הַדָּבָר הַגַּשְׁמִי הֲרֵי הוּא מַעֲלֶה אוֹתוֹ, וְהַיְנוּ שֶׁיִּהְיֶה נִרְאֶה וְנִגְלֶה בּוֹ אֵיךְ שֶׁהוּא בָּטֵל כו'. . .

When we contemplate how every created thing contains a soul—i.e., Godly life and purpose, which constitutes the primary quality of that thing—and that all created matter is subordinate to its Godly source and purpose, we will be aroused to a great love for God and an intense desire to connect to Him. We will have no desire for the physical externality of anything, for it is intrinsically death, as it is in a constant state of deterioration and decomposition, as opposed to the object's eternal Godly core. We will desire only the divine purpose inherent in all our worldly endeavors—eating, drinking, commerce, and so forth. Our intention will be solely to gain energy to study Torah and serve God.

"God placed the world in the heart of man" (Ecclesiastes 3:11). This means that it is within the human being's power

Rabbi Shalom Dovber Schneersohn (Rashab)
1860- 1920

Chasidic rebbe. Rabbi Shalom Dovber became the 5th leader of the Chabad movement upon the passing of his father, Rabbi Shmuel of Lubavitch. He established the Lubavitch network of *yeshivot* called Tomchei Temimim. He authored many volumes of Chasidic discourses and is renowned for his lucid and thorough explanations of Kabbalistic concepts.

to impact the world. Therefore, if we view the physical element of a thing as an independent and significant entity, meaning that we desire to derive pleasure from the physicality of the object, we lower the object and separate it from its divine core and Godly purpose. This is what happened when Adam and Eve ate from the Tree of Knowledge, and they caused "separation" in the entire world. On the other hand, when we desire something in order to fulfill its Godly purpose, we elevate that object and reveal how it is in synch with its divine purpose.

ADDITIONAL READINGS

ETERNITY & CORPOREAL EXISTENCE

BY RABBI DOVBER PINSON

Physical existence, in its distinct shape, form, and dimension, is by its very definition temporary and provisional. The concept of death is universal and all-invasive. Death is present throughout all of nature: nothing can escape death. The natural course of all life is birth, maturity, then death. No creation can go unscathed from death's grip; nobody leaves this realm of existence alive. Nobody lives forever, no one goes through life without at some point relinquishing physical form.

Whereas in the Torah and in later Talmudic writings there are recorded instances where human beings ascend to heaven, without experiencing, as it were, any form of corporeal death—most notably the prophet Elijah—as a whole, at the end of life the body melts down and slowly disintegrates. In fact, the Torah statement "earth you are and to earth you will return" is not only a prediction or an inevitable conclusion of life, it is very much a part of life itself. Part of the cycle of life is birth, the emergence of one life, death, the returning of the elements, and then rebirth and resurrection. The Baal Shem Tov once declared that he had the spiritual power to enter paradise with body and soul in unison. However, he did not do so, for he desired to go through the natural process of "earth returning to earth."

Just as death is part of the life cycle, so is the idea of physical and even bodily deathlessness. In the most elementary manner, corporeal immortality can be interpreted as the body living on as part of the whole. Earth rejoins earth, and the individual elements of the body rearrange themselves and become part of entire ecosystem. Yet, in this arrangement there is also the idea of bodily resurrection, implying an eventual revival of body and a perpetuation of that same body in its distinct shape and form. There will

come a time of re-creation, an ingathering of the elements, or, if you will, a reconstruction of the DNA, and bodies of old will once again resurface to roam the earth, to and relive again.

On some level, resurrection can be interpreted as a metaphor for the reviving spirit. Just as a lifeless body is frigid and cold, so too is the human intellect. Intellect can be cold, detached, and apathetic. However, when a person meditates and enlivens his or her intellect, imbuing it with holy passion and divine rapture, this is a kind of resurrection. Likewise, if through deviation and transgression one detaches the self from the Source of life, becoming spiritually insensitive and lifeless, when that person re-engages, reintegrates, and embarks on the path of *teshuvah,* he or she is in a sense experiencing internal resurrection.

While these life lessons are certainly appreciated, clearly the notion of resurrection in the Torah is intended to be taken quite literally. Recognizing the intrinsic value of the human body—and for that matter all physicality—viewing the body as a potential instrument and vehicle for soul expression, it becomes axiomatic that the body is not something to be disregarded or overlooked. Undoubtedly, the body too has a place in a world of ultimate goodness and spirituality. Bodily resurrection is so much a part of Torah that, according to many opinions, resurrection is one of the fundamental principles of Torah.

Resurrection & Olam Habah

The Ramban, the thirteenth-century legalist and mystic also known as Nachmanides, equates the period of resurrection with the ultimate state of *olam habah,* the "World to Come." The peak of goodness and spiritual delight will be experienced in a time when body and soul are joined as one in total harmony and unison.

With realities mirroring each other, the universal law of cause and effect is a truth in the world of spirit as well. Mankind labors intensely and is challenged to transform physicality into spirituality, simply by taking tangible objects and hallowing them. The effect, the result of this action, is a complete material transformation. The ultimate "thing" transformation will become apparent in the state of *olam habah*, when the body will also participate in the greatest/ deepest of spiritual revelations, when the body will become an equal partner in receiving, absorbing, and then projecting the Infinite's light.

To phrase it differently, if *individual* immortality is the goal, then mere soul eternity is not satisfactory. A human being is the total package, soul/ mind/ body: exclusion of any one of these dimensions renders the immortality incomplete. Soul immortality is not individual immortality, since elements of the individual are still absent from the equation. In addition, rewards—which are the consequence and effect of actions—should be given to those who deserve them, which in this case are the perpetuators of the actions. Since it was the conglomeration of the body and soul that worked on engendering physical transformation, in all fairness, the result of the labor, the reward, also must be felt by both the soul and body. If the body is left out of the picture, the reward is incomplete and inadequate.

What's more, it is the inevitable natural progression from physical deed to physical effect that is called reward. The spiritual laws of cause and effect ensure that the extension of physical deed is physical reward.

In stark contrast to *gan eden*, where souls exist in bodiless states, resurrection, which is a reward and the end result of physical actions and material transformation, will be experienced when the soul and body are joined as one. The way to stimulate physical transformation is through the *mitzvot*. *Mitzvot* are the spiritual tools that were handed over to help humankind tap into the vast energies of soul and through which the awesome engaged power can in-

spire the total reorientation of physicality. The soul's latent powers are made apparent by the *mitzvot*; once these forces are unleashed, one has the amazing Godlike ability to create and recreate, to take a something—a physical object—and recreate it as a "no-thing," a wing-like spiritual entity.

Though some people are more attuned to the *mitzvot* than others, still, as the Talmud testifies, "All people of the nation of Israel are satiated with *mitzvot* as a pomegranate is filled with seeds"—that is to say, if not quantitatively then qualitatively. In other words, most people have at least one area in life that they excel in. Most people have, at the very minimum, one *mitzvah* that is their specialty, and it is through this glimmer of articulated soul that they achieve physical transformation—and thus they will eventually feel the inevitable ramifications of their action in resurrection.

Olam habah is not reserved for the elite; rather, all moral, good, and decent human beings will experience its blessings. It is through the spark of goodness accreting into one individualized self that each person will be ultimately resurrected. Just as in life, through the entire gamut of the soul, where only one or two aspects of the soul became a person's particular element, and through that individuated spark which a person lived, the same will occur in the afterlife and in the time of resurrection. Each body will be re-birthed with the sparks of the soul that had become theirs, and theirs alone.

In this way, reincarnation does not preclude resurrection, and these two are not mutually exclusive. Every time a soul incarnates, a new and unexplored dimension of the soul becomes apparent. Each person manifests a new aspect of the soul, and it is with this individualized spark of the soul that the body will experience revivification and resurrection.

In truth, even those souls that may have departed this world in an imperfect state, with the individualized aspect of soul unarticulated and not actualized, can attain *tikkun*, and that is through the assistance of those who survived them. Souls enclothed within bodies have the wonderful ability, through thoughts, deeds, and actions, to bring about a *tikkun* for souls that have already left this world. Embodied souls, through the power of their good deeds, have the capacity to inspire spiritual elevation for bodiless souls—so much so, in some instances, *olam habah* will not be experienced by becoming enlivened by one's own soul, which never attained *tikkun*—this comes about instead through other avenues. Occasionally, souls that are unable to shake off the dust to achieve *olam habah* on their own accord gain entry by receiving sparks from other souls, and these sparks become their own source of reanimation.

Reality Beyond Opposites

Once resurrection occurs, bodies will endure, either for a very long period and then at some juncture in time pass on, or, as others suggest, the bodies will live forever. In the latter view, the body will enter a world beyond duality, plurality, and separation, and exist perennially in absolute oneness.

Today, life as we know it is defined and further pushed on to a more evolved and developed complexity by its constant state of tension and friction. The articulation of human thought, whether in science or philosophy, literature or psychology, is dependent on opposition and contrasting theories. First there is a thesis, then an antithesis, and finally a greater or deeper thesis or synthesis that reconciles or calls forth a new paradigm. Later on, this too is challenged, bringing forth an ever deeper understanding. There are continuous ups and downs, ascents and descents, evolution and devolution.

In a world of "many," a universe of opposites, there is nonstop rhythm and fluctuation. Each living body has basic four modifications: birth, growth, maturity, and eventual death. In this cycle of life, the culmination of death gives rise to a new life, which experiences the same cycle all over again.

In the world of the living as well as in the world of abstractions, there is a continuous cycle: any other reality would seem boring by comparison, without desire or strife. And yet, in the time of redemption and perfect harmony, when the world will be healed of its fragmentation and splinteredness, life will be defined differently; it will be a life without opposites. In a universe of oneness there can only be one continuous, eternal state.

Life, though it is hard today to fathom, will be a seamless whole, comprising a relentless progression forward and upward. There will be no need for descents or setbacks, antithetical hypotheses or countercultural revolutions to inspire further development. Ultimately, on a most profound level, death as a concept and death as a reality will become something of the past, and a new cosmic order will emerge where life develops, evolves, and expands endlessly, without any lapses, whether temporal or permanent, partial or complete.

Body as a Reflection of Soul

Speaking of resurrection, some inspired authorities contend that to live forever is part of mankind's original lot, that it is part of our genetic make up, the DNA of the human being. Mortality is the distortion of a higher truth and a foreign invasion of the body's reality. Humans, in this line of thinking, were created to survive incessantly. The original, primordial, prototypical human beings, Adam and Eve, were deemed able to live throughout eternity, where the physical properties of their bodies were "refined" in such a way that they had the potential to live eternally. Apparently, as we know, they had other plans. In the time of resurrection, the original, distilled version of body will be reinstated, and humankind will live on everlastingly. Some sources add that in the time of resurrection, bodies will be even more refined than the original bodies of Adam and Eve.

Paradoxical as it may seem, in the state of *olam habah* bodies will continue to exist, though they will no longer be needed to properly—or even improperly—function. There will come a time when the body can survive, be sustained and even nourished, from *within*, without the need to consume any externalities. Eating, drinking, and all the other bodily activities will become something of the past. Yet, though the body will appear superfluous, it will nonetheless continue to live on.

The reason for this is twofold. Since it was a body in conjunction with soul that ushered in this perfect era, it was the collaboration of body and soul effort that brought about the epoch of *olam habah*—and the body will therefore get to experience the fruit of its labor. The deeper underlying reason for this is due to the physical structure of body that, as ungraceful and clumsy as it occasionally may appear, possesses a wonderful spiritual significance.

The construct of the body is not merely a random formation secured simply by the evolution of nature, genetics, and other environmental factors—there is also a deep profundity and meaning to it. "From my flesh I see God": from the flesh, by taking a deeper look at the body, one is allowed a glimpse of soul and a vision of its Creator. The body tells us much about our souls, and much about everything else in life, including revealing to us our Creator and the purpose of our being.

Outward is a reflection of inward. The inner dynamic of the soul expresses itself in the outer manifestations of body. Body and soul are mirror images of each other. The structure of the body is analogous and represents the spiritual structure of the soul. Since the soul is a spark of God, a part of the All, the soul contains images of the totality. All of reality is contained within the soul; all forces and energies, whether they are physically based or spiritually oriented, are enclosed within. The body, in turn, which is the vehicle for soul expression, is the physically manifested reflection of the inner structure of all worlds and all realities.

Having confirmed the body's significance, we can understand how it will endure even in a period when it ceases to function in its present state. To be sure, especially in that time, the body will achieve its maximum potentiality and will self-generate the energy it needs to be sustained and nourished, so much so that it will actually offer spiritual nourishment to the soul. As opposed to today, where, in the hierarchy of created reality, the soul gives life to the body, in a future redeemed, revealed world, the reverse will occur and body will give life to soul.

At the time of resurrection, the best of mankind will live on, and will live on under the most favorable conditions possible. Illness, disease, and all other maladies will be obliterated. It will be a time when body and soul will be completely in sync, aligned with each other. Life will be lived harmoniously and pleasantly integrated. In this time, the Infinite will be felt as present within the finite—a time when the essence of the Creator, that essence beyond and transcendent of both the physical and spiritual, will be apparent in all of reality, both in the dimensionless and dimensional, the spiritual and the material.

"Body" After Death

Aside from the future collective resurrection, which brings about bodily immortality, there are certain rare situations where even bodies presently, for better or worse, are preserved for extended periods of time, long after their souls have departed. There are bodies that are less susceptible to decay. One notable example in the Torah is the body of Moses, whose eyes did not falter and whose strength did not leave him even in death. This phenomenon is not an isolated occurrence; rather it is something that can occur to all those who wholeheartedly direct their neutral, amoral bodies for either the positive or the negative.

On some level, all souls experience "bodily" immortality, and there is body-like continuance in death for each person. As discussed earlier, in addition to the *guf gas,* there is a mental projected body, referred to as the *guf dak.* In its anatomy, there is included an immediate body, which is felt and easily observable, and a distilled, refined body, which some refer to as the astral or psychological body or etheric form. This latter form is commonly known as the *tzelem,* the surrounding ether or aura.

Our internal reality is projected onto our immediate surroundings. Formulated as a collective projection, this image mirrors the likeness of the material form. This "body," being a vehicle of consciousness can either be mental, emotional, or spiritual, depending essentially on the reality we choose to live our lives in. Once the soul/ consciousness leaves material form, it initially enters the distilled astral body, which in turn can be projected to one's beloved, even after death.

For the living, the appearance of the soul of a departed one in this ethereal "body" that can be observed or felt as a presence, as if that person were in the room—or even as a "something" that can be "seen," if not with the physical eyes then with the third eye.

Beyond bodiless projection in *guf dak,* there are pious and integrated individuals who were and are able to project an autocopy of themselves, of their *guf dak,* into a distant location, even during life and while they are vested with a *guf gas.* Physically, they can exist in one locality and project a manifestation of themselves in another, perhaps even distant, place. This phenomenon is referred to as astral projection, or out-of-body travel. The celebrated Chassidic Rebbe, R. Zusiya of Hanipoli, once remarked that he saw in his home the face of his revered brother, R. Elimelech of Lizhensk.

Those in total control, who are full masters of their internal and external reality, have the power to detach their *tzurah,* substantial ethereal body, from their *chomer,* which is the form of their material body, dispatching it at will. Sending the image to another place allows a "person" to be in two different places at once, to exist in a condition of bilocation.

In rare instances, one's own image can be reflected back to the person himself. Doppelgangers or autoscopic, self-seeing hallucinations are the preferred terms used to describe a situation where one sees one's own body as an apparition. History is replete with prominent figures who have experienced an apparition of their own body, a kind of mirror image of themselves.

While chemical imbalance is indeed the grounds for many such cases, found in those who suffer from brain tumors, strokes, migraine headaches—and this may in fact be the root cause of such visions—in some situations the physical is merely the effect, where the cause may be a possible authentic interaction with the metaphysical and supernatural. Occasionally, the image can communicate truth to the person, indicating a phenomenon that is more than simply a hallucination. The prophetic experience consists of the prophet's original self going into a state of suspended animation, as the prophet falls to the ground, whereupon he apprehends a mirror image of himself that is vibrant, alive, and pulsating, transmitting prophetic insight.

The experience is not reserved for the prophets alone, for there are, as R. Moshe Cordovero writes, "some of the pious that attain an observation of their own image." All and all, this most extraordinary of phenomena is sometimes viewed as an occurrence that rises from within, a physical reality rooted in the inner workings of the brain, and at times it is seen as a spiritual occurrence with physical manifestations. In the former, physicality is the cause; in the latter, it is the effect. Though the differences may be difficult to discern, they ought not to be confused.

Jewish Wisdom on the Afterlife: the Mysteries, the Myths, and the Meanings [New Jersey: Q&A Books, 2006], pp. 177–187.
Reprinted with permission of the author.

ON THE RESURRECTION

BY RABBI ARYEH KAPLAN

In order to understand the significance of the Resurrection *(Techiyas Hameisim)* it would be instructive to look at the first two blessings of the Amidah *(Shemoneh Esrei)*, a prayer that is recited three times daily by every Jew.

The first blessing of the Amidah deals with our relationship to God; indeed, one can say that it establishes our relationship with God for the rest *of* this fundamental prayer. Thus the first blessing speaks of God as, "the Great Mighty, Awesome, Highest God, Who bestows bountiful kindness, Who is Master of all, Who recalls the love of the Patriarchs and will bring a redeemer to their children's children ..."

The second blessing begins with the words, "You are eternally Mighty, O God, You bring the dead back to life ..." The second blessing of this most important prayer thus deals with the Resurrection. From this alone, one would see that it is a key teaching of Judaism.

The Meaning of Life

The first two blessings of the Amidah actually deal with the two most important concerns of man regarding his own existence. The two primary questions that a person can ask are:

(1) What is the meaning of life?

(2) What happens after life in this world ends?

The first blessing of the Amidah brings us into contact with the answer to the first question. The meaning of life is defined by God's existence and our relationship to Him. If a person can establish a relationship to the One Author of all existence, then his own existence will have meaning.

However, no matter how meaningful life would be, if it would all end with death, its meaning would only be temporary. Therefore, the second blessing of the Amidah gives us the answer to the second question,

"What happens after life in this world ends?" It also teaches that when one finds meaning in life, it is permanent, not temporary. Although life in this world may be temporary, there is another life, beyond the Resurrection, which will be permanent.

Influence of the Patriarchs

A key teaching of Judaism is that the actions of the Patriarchs, Abraham, Isaac, and Jacob, continue to serve as a spiritual inheritance to their descendants today. Every Jew is to some degree markedly influenced by the past acts of the Patriarchs.

Again, this is evident in the first blessing of the Amidah, which begins with the words, "Blessed are You, O Lord our God, God of our fathers, God of Abraham, God of Isaac, and God of Jacob ... " Here, we attempt to elevate our own conception of God to that of the Patriarchs.

In order to understand this, it would be useful to repeat a teaching of the Baal Shem Tov (founder of Chassidism). He asks, why does the Amidah begin by saying, "Our God, God of our fathers"? The first term implies that we have discovered His existence by our own efforts—He is "our God." The expression, "God of our fathers," however, implies that we were taught about His existence. Thus, the two phrases seem to contradict each other. The Baal Shem Tov explains that every person must develop his own perception of God, since it is something that cannot be communicated totally to another. Hence, we speak of Him as "our God." But still, one must be able to determine whether one's perception of God is authentic, and one must therefore relate it to the perceptions of past generations. We thus add, "God of our fathers." Both are needed: the person's individual perception, and the historical perception of past generations. And since the paradigm of perception of the Divine was that of the Patriarchs, Abraham Isaac and Jacob when we say, "God of Abraham, God of Isaac, and God of Jacob," we acknowledge that our ultimate goal would be to reach their level of spiritual perception.

Four Degrees of Closeness to God

Moreover, in the last four words of the blessing of the Patriarchs, we establish an increasingly closer relationship with the Divine. In these words we address God as: "King, Helper, Rescuer, and Shield." Each of these words relates to a degree of closeness to God.

First, we speak to God as our "King." A king rules over his subjects, and in a general sense, is concerned with their welfare. However, the king is not available to help each subject on an individual basis, except in the most general terms. Therefore, a person who relates to God as "King" is quite distant from Him.

The next level is that of a helper (*ozer*). Imagine a situation where you are in financial straits and need a loan. You could not go to the king for it, but you could go to someone to whom you feel close. Such a person is your "helper." The relationship between a person and a "helper," then, is much closer than his relationship to a king.

The third level is that of rescuer (*moshia*). A helper can send assistance from a distance, but a rescuer must be right there on the spot. If a person is drowning, then his rescuer must be close enough to jump in and save him. So the level of rescuer is closer than that of the helper.

Finally, the fourth level is that of shield (*magen*). A rescuer can be a few hundred feet away when the person needs him. However, when an arrow is shot at a person, hi s shield must be directly in front of him, to intercept the arrow. Therefore, when a person has a conception of God as his "Shield," his perception is that of God right in front of him and surrounding him from all sides, protecting him from all danger.

The first person to attain this fourth level was Abraham. God explicitly told him, "Do not fear, Abram, I am your Shield" (Genesis 15:1). We recognize that Abraham reached the ultimate of this level of closeness to God when we conclude the first blessing, "Blessed are You, O Lord, Shield of Abraham." We strive to attain this degree of closeness with God, using Abraham as the paradigm.

This was also the level attained by King David, and hence, the *Haftarah* blessings contain a section which concludes, "Blessed are You, O Lord, Shield of David." David was on this level when he said, "I have placed the Lord before me at all times" (Psalms 16:8).

In any case, after completing the first blessing of the Amidah, one may wonder why the relationships that the Patriarchs had with God should be significant, since they belong to a generation that is dead and buried. If the Patriarchs are dead and we are alive, how can we relate to their spiritual experiences?

The second blessing of the Amidah therefore speaks of the Resurrection. It teaches that death is not a permanent situation, and that the experiences of the Patriarchs are as alive today as they were during their actual lifetimes.

Two Conceptions of the Resurrection

There are two basic opinions regarding the Resurrection, those of the Rambam (Maimonides), and the Ramban (Nachmanides).

The Rambam's opinion is that when a person dies, he immediately goes to *Olam Haba* (the "World to Come" or the "Future World"), so called because it comes after life in this world. Thus, according to the Rambam, the "World to Come" promised in Torah literature involves only the soul, and is completely spiritual.

According to the Rambam then, the Resurrection, of necessity, involves a *temporary* return to the physical plane. Some advance a possible reason for the Resurrection, that the righteous will be able to see the Messianic world with physical eyes. In any case, according to the Rambam, the resurrected dead will die once again and will return to the "World to Come."

The Ramban, on the other hand, maintains that the World to Come is the world that will exist after the Resurrection, and that it will be a world that includes both body and soul. This is also the opinion of the *Zohar* and of most of the major Kabbalists. According to this opinion, a whole person consists of body and soul, and therefore, a person cannot attain maximum perception of the Divine without his body as well as his soul. Thus, the Resurrection is a key element in God's ultimate reward for mankind. It is seen as the inception of the World to Come.

This opinion states that when a person dies, his soul goes to the "World of Souls" (*Olam Haneshamos)*. There it has a certain degree of perception of the Divine, and it waits there until the Resurrection. It is only after the Resurrection, however, in the World to Come, that this perception reaches its ultimate.

The Meaning of Death

The first mention of death in the Torah is in relation to the Tree of Knowledge, where God tells Adam, " And from the Tree of Knowledge of Good and Evil, do not eat from it, for on the day you eat from it, you will be bound to die" (Genesis 2: 17). Hence, on the simplest level, death is seen as punishment for Adam's original sin.

It is significant that in the very next verse, God says, "It is not good for man to be alone, I will make him a helpmate as his counterpart" (ibid. 2: 18). On a simple level, this means that once the possibility of death exists, God must make arrangements for the continuation of the species. When the possibility of death came into existence, then Adam would have to have a wife if mankind was not to become extinct with his death.

However, this can also be understood on a much deeper level. From a number of Midrashic sources, we see that the spiritual realm is looked upon as masculine, while the physical world is feminine. Thus, in the overall scheme of creation, the spiritual realm fertilizes the physical while the physical realm acts as the womb, through which God's purpose is brought to fruition.

Life, of course, is the connection of the body and the soul. Since the body, as part of the physical realm, is feminine and the soul masculine, death is a separation of the masculine from the feminine. Hence, after the possibility of death came into existence in the world, God said, "It is not good for man to be alone"—it is not good for the soul, the masculine

component of the body-soul unit, to be isolated from bodily existence through death.

Thus, there are two male-female relationships that a person can have. One is immortality, while the other is marriage. Either one can guarantee the existence of the species. If man was to lose immortality, then he would have to marry and beget children.

The Tree of Knowledge was closely related to the male-female relationship; indeed, "knowledge" to some degree defines the male-female relationship. In Hebrew, "knowledge" is *daas,* a word which connotes "togetherness" and "unity." Thus, the Torah says "Adam knew his wife, Eve..." (ibid. 4:1).

Therefore, before eating of the Tree of Knowledge, "the man and the woman were naked, but they were not ashamed of themselves" (ibid. 2:25). Since the male-female relationship was perfect there was no cause for shame (see Ramban, etc.). And indeed, in the Torah we see that the relationship between man and woman was damaged by eating from the Tree of Knowledge, as God told Eve, "To your husband will be your desire, and he will dominate you" (ibid. 3:16).

If life itself is a male-female relationship, then after man ate from the Tree of Knowledge and damaged this relationship, death was inevitable. It was for this reason that death was punishment for the first sin.

The World to Come, however, is seen as a time when all the effects of Adam's sin will be eradicated. Thus, the relationship between body and soul will also be perfected. Therefore, it will (according to the Ramban and the Kabbalists) be a time when man will live immortally with body and soul together.

The Mystery of Life

One can look at the entire Amidah as being the vehicle through which a person perfects his life. In the Amidah one develops a relationship with God and with life, and then asks God to provide everything needed for the good life.

Indeed, that is one reason that the Amidah has eighteen blessings. The Amidah is called the *Shemoneh*

Esrei, which literally means "eighteen." The Hebrew word for "life" is *chai*, which has a numerical value of eighteen (see *Avodas Hakodesh)*.

This may be yet another reason why the Resurrection is the second blessing of the Amidah. Living in the physical world, we may see ourselves as spiritually dead. Therefore, as soon as we develop a close relationship with God in the first blessing, we ask that He resurrect us spiritually. This is then accomplished through the eighteen (which equals *chai*, life) blessings of the Amidah. By drawing ourselves close to God, we can experience a taste of the World to Come.

The Aryeh Kaplan Reader [New York: Mesorah Publications, 1983], pp. 184–188.
Reprinted with permission of the publisher.

SWALLOWED UP FOREVER

BY YAAKOV BRAWER, PhD

From every incident in a person's life, one can acquire profound insight into the service of the Creator. So says the holy Baal Shem Tov. Fortified by this idea, I began my descent in the morgue elevator of the Department of Anatomy and Cell Biology at McGill University.

As the director of a neuroscience course, I was responsible for the annual inventory of brain prosections used in the student laboratory. These were stored in containers at the back of "the cold room," a sort of walk-in refrigerator, which also happened to house some forty cadavers awaiting the scalpels of the first year medical students.

I am uncomfortable with these yearly expeditions. The departmental morgue is no place for a nice *Chassidisher Yid* (Chassidic Jew). In fact, in my opinion, it is no place for anyone. Why then, did providence arrange things so that I had to go there? What sage wisdom in the service of my Creator was I supposed to attain in that dismal place?

I completed the inventory with customary dispatch and happily left the cold room to its silent occupants. While ascending in the elevator, I began to wonder if there might not be exceptions to the Baal Shem Tov's maxim. Later that day, however, the meaning behind the trip to the morgue dawned on me in the form of a question: What is the difference between the denizens of the morgue, and the students, colleagues, technicians, and secretaries scurrying about on the floors above?

Lest the reader dismiss this thought as the morbid musing of a crackpot, I must emphasize that it is firmly rooted in Chassidic teaching. Indeed, it represents one of the most perplexing paradoxes in Chassidic literature, namely that anything destined to die and deteriorate is dead and deteriorated, while it is yet alive. I had wrestled with this conundrum in the past without success and I had long since shelved it away in a remote region of my brain reserved for intractable enigmas. The morgue experience, however, recast the question in visual imagery that demanded reconsideration. How was it possible to relate, much less equate those young, happy, healthy, rambunctious students with the inhabitants of the cold room?

Life as an Add-On
It is, of course, clear from the Torah perspective, that life and death define states considerably more complex and subtle than the simplistic physical notions held by the secular world. A creature does not necessarily have to be biologically defunct in order to be properly identified by Torah as "dead." Conversely, departed souls of the so-called dead, experience life far more intensely than do their earthly "living" counterparts.

What, then, is life? Inasmuch as G-d is not only the ultimate but the sole reality, life, quite simply, is

G-dliness or Divinity. The degree to which an entity partakes of and is identified with G-dliness determines the extent to which it is alive. The divine soul, for example, is intrinsically and eternally alive because its very being is an uninterrupted extension of pure G-dliness. The body, on the other hand, is dissociated from the Divine source of its own existence, and its life is thus bestowed from without, as it were. Bodies, unlike souls, are not innately G-dly and are not, therefore, inherently alive.

The life of the body is a little like the weight of an object. Although we regard weight as an innate characteristic, it is really an alien property imposed externally by the gravitational force of the earth. Indeed, in space, an object has no weight. Since the body, per se, is not transparent to G-dliness, its life is only borrowed. It is an external feature bestowed provisionally in order to afford the body limited existence in this world. The fact that bodies are animated indirectly by transcendent levels of G-dliness precludes their awareness of the Divine source of their own being, which results in a powerful impression of independence.

This state of affairs pertains to the entire realm of *kelipot* ("shells"), which comprise most things and creatures in this material world. The process that gives rise to, and sustains the world of *kelipah* (also referred to as the *sitra achra*, "other side") differs fundamentally from the manner in which Divinity channels life to creations in the domain of holiness, such as souls or sacrosanct angelic beings. G-d extends life to the side of holiness by means of ten divine attributes or *sefirot*, whereas *kelipot* are animated through the agency of eleven *sefirot* referred to in the language of Kabbalah as the "eleven crowns of impurity."

The reason the realm of Kelipah requires an "extra" *sefirah* becomes clear once we understand the necessity for *sefirot* altogether. We can best appreciate the significance of *sefirot* by drawing an analogy to the soul.

The soul, as an emanation of G-dliness, is a simple (uncompounded) unified essence, which is, nonetheless, capable of expressing itself in a variety of specific ways. The attributes (*sefirot*) of the soul, such as wisdom, understanding, kindness, etc., are the particular abilities through which the soul-essence achieves this diversity of self-expression. Similarly, G-dliness transcends particularization, definition or limitation, whereas the creations that it animates are finite and multifarious. It is through the agency of *sefirot* that the infinite, unitary, supernal source of all life (G-dliness) can be expressed in distinct modes in order to sustain and vitalize a multiplicity of finite beings.

In the realm of holiness, G-dliness fuses with the *sefirot* and thereby acquires definitive characteristics such as kindness, or justice. A well-known analogy for this process is light passing through a colored glass. Although the light remains light, it has acquired the restrictive property of "color." Similarly, Divine Will shining though each of the ten *sefirot* represents a direct and continuous extension of G-dliness (life) that has acquired the limiting features necessary to engender a variety of finite creations.

In contrast, G-dliness (life) is detached from the "other side," and thus relates to the *sefirot* of *sitra achra* at a distance, so to speak. Its influence encompasses them but is not invested within them. The Divine light that indirectly vitalizes the *sitra achra* is thus accounted as an eleventh "separate" *sefirah*.

Since G-dliness is the very soul or life force of *sefirot*, the *sefirot* of the *sitra achra*, in a sense, have no soul, and they can, therefore, be considered "dead." It follows that the *kelipot* that derive from these *sefirot* are also "dead," even while they cavort about in this world.

A Practical Application

Because life is a peripheral rather than an integral feature of the body, it is hardly surprising that the body, as well as all other manifestations of *kelipah*, must eventually die in actual fact. A practical consequence of this is that bodily pleasures and worldly terrors are transient and insubstantial, and we must not be seduced by the former or immobilized by fear of the latter.

A powerful recent object lesson is the sudden, inexplicable demise of the Soviet Union. Anyone who watched the West quiver in fear when Khrushchev banged his shoe on the table at the U.N., or who cowered beneath his grade-school desk during an air raid drill, knows the monster that was the Soviet Union. The USSR was fully capable of destroying the entire world on a whim. Then, one day, for no apparent reason, it utterly vanished. It did not gradually deteriorate, it did not collapse under the weight of its own success, and it was not a casualty of strategic or political miscalculation. At the height of its influence, it just disintegrated.

Although the world was stunned by the totally unexpected dissolution of the USSR, students of Chassidut should not have been surprised. The USSR was, after all, a *kelipah*, immense, obstreperous, and intimidating, but a *kelipah* nonetheless, and *kelipot*, as we know, have no life. Thus, once the USSR had fulfilled whatever role the Almighty had in mind for it, in accordance with its true nature, it simply ceased to exist.

This is all good and well, but it only partially addresses our original paradox, which is that anything destined to die and deteriorate is dead and deteriorated (*nifsad* in Hebrew), while it is yet alive. We can now understand that since *kelipot* are not essentially and intrinsically alive, the designation "dead" accurately describes their status even while they exist in this world. But what do we do with the term "deteriorated"? Although an entity can be considered dead even before it palpably expires, how can something be deteriorated before it deteriorates? Deterioration, unlike death, refers to a purely physical condition.

Furthermore, despite the fact that *kelipah* is founded on a mirage, the misery that *kelipot*, such as the USSR, are able to inflict on humanity during their earthly tenure is disturbingly authentic.

So, although the morgue experience had inspired me to focus attention on this classic riddle anew, my insight was no keener than when I had first encountered it years before. After a week of abortive mental gymnastics I was ready to abandon the question once

again, when, while setting my alarm clock one evening, the answer suddenly crystallized.

Being vs. Becoming

My alarm clock is of the electrical digital variety on which the time is set by pushing a button that drives the number display. When the desired time is reached, one simply releases the button. As I gazed absently at the hours speeding by, I was jolted by a phenomenal discovery. Time designations are fictitious. It is never three o'clock, nor is it ever four o'clock, midnight or noon. Because the movement of the number display never ceases, the time may approach twelve or depart from twelve but it never is twelve. Even if it were possible to determine the exact position on a clock that indicates noon, since the second hand never stops at that position, it is never noon.

To put it another way, we can ask the question: for how long is it noon? for one second? one hundredth of a second? one thousandth of second? Clearly it is noon for no measurable time, which is to say, it is never noon. The verb to "be," of which the word "is" is the third person singular present form, confers upon its subject the status of reality. This verb, therefore, can not apply to any entity governed by time. Since time-locked creations are in a state of incessant becoming, they never "are." An entity ceases "becoming" only when it escapes the inexorable course of time and achieves a final, immutable stable state. It can then be said to "be."

This then, explains why anything destined to die and deteriorate is dead and deteriorated while it is yet alive. The permanent, eternal, stable state of a *kelipah* is nonexistence. That is its reality, and its entire earthly duration is directed toward this condition. Once it totally deteriorates, all change ceases. It is no longer under the influence of time, which is to say that it is no longer becoming what it is ultimately supposed to be, but rather it now simply "is."

Intuitively, we appreciate this even without the foregoing explication. We know, for example, that the Almighty liberally stocks life with obstacles and trials with the express intention that we overcome them. The reality of obstacles, therefore, the end to which they are conceived, is negation. Evil exists only to be vanquished and darkness is created only to be dispelled.

Now that we understand why the physical integrity of *kelipah* is as illusory as is its life force, we can properly appreciate our own condition. Just as the reality of *kelipah* is death and disintegration, so is the reality of the Jewish people life, on both the spiritual and physical plane.

The Divine soul is a direct uninterrupted emanation of G-dliness, and since G-dliness is eternal, any concept of death is inapplicable to the soul. Moreover, the death of the body is merely a transient condition, just as life is a temporary phase for *kelipah*. The consummation of G-d's purpose in creating the universe is *z'man techiah*, the time of resurrection of the dead. At this point physical change will cease as the Divine Will that drove existence toward perfection is realized. We will then be what we have been in the process of becoming these thousands of years, and what we were intended to be from the outset.

What About the World?
There is yet one remaining loose end. When that glorious day arrives, in what sort of world will we live? Our world, at present is described in the Tanya as a world "filled with *kelipah* and *sitra achra*," the ultimate stable state of which is nonexistence. What then, will remain of the physical universe, and more specifically, our home planet when G-d's supreme purpose is realized?

Obviously, the universe, including our world, will continue to exist if for no other reason than that we (body and soul) will need a place to live. Moreover, inasmuch as the physical universe is the ultimate expression of G-d's creative ability, simple common sense dictates that it is neither ephemeral nor illusory. Indeed, the Torah (Isaiah, 45:18) tells us as much: "Not for dissolution did He create it, but to be inhabited."

In fact, the eternal nature of the universe is even now apparent in the immutability of natural law and in the constant endless pattern of celestial movement.

Throughout the natural order one detects the infinitude that is the signature of the Almighty. The limitlessness of G-d's generative power is even discernible in living beings. Although individuals die, the species to which they belong are perpetuated without end.

It would appear then, that the world as a manifestation of G-d's supernal Will is very much "alive" and will remain so. How do we reconcile this with the fact that the ingredients of worldly existence consist mostly of kelipah?

Understanding Kelipah
The problem is easily resolved once we refine our concept of *kelipah*.

The term *kelipah* literally means a "shell" or a "rind." To what extent does the shell represent the reality of a nut? Clearly, the shell is a minor, if necessary component. We do not buy walnuts because we are enamored of their shells. Yet although the significant feature of a nut is obviously the fruit, it is the shell that endows the nut with its characteristic appearance.

Similarly, *kelipot* do not constitute the reality of anything in this world. They are merely external garments that conceal the particular expressions of G-d's creative will that bring worldly beings into existence. By masking the Divine light that is the true essence of created beings, *kelipot* simulate a schism between Creator and creation. Indeed, the effect of *kelipah* may be so powerful that not only is the unity of G-d with creation obscured, but the very existence of Justice and a Judge may appear doubtful. When confronted with the apparent triumph of emphatic evil, it is not always easy to remember that *kelipah* is only a deceptive, lifeless husk.

Although the world is indeed filled with *kelipot*, since they constitute only the most superficial dimension of any given creation, they really do not add up to much at all. Moreover, it is only this superficial exterior that has no connection with life and for which nullity is its absolute terminal condition.

Indeed, the temporary (hence, unreal) death and deterioration experienced by the body serves to free it of its *kelipah* aspect, such that at *techiat hamai-tim* (the resurrection of the dead), the body will be reestablished in its essential pure condition. In the case of the righteous, who have purified their bodies of the dross of *kelipah* through their divine service, the body does not undergo deterioration altogether. When, following the advent of Moshiach, the veneer of *kelipah* dissipates, G-d's living creative will will be revealed as the underlying reality of all being.

It was in order to learn this lesson, that Providence sent me year after year to the morgue, until I finally caught on. How can I be so certain? Simple. A few months following this episode, the department built cabinets for the brain prosections adjacent to the student laboratory, and I have never had to return.

Reprinted with permission from Chabad.org.

THE REFUSAL TO BE COMFORTED

BY RABBI JONATHAN SACKS

The deception has taken place. Joseph has been sold into slavery. His brothers have dipped his coat in blood. They bring it back to their father, saying: "Look what we have found. Do you recognise it? Is this your son's robe or not?" Jacob recognised it and replied, "It is my son's robe. A wild beast has devoured him. Joseph has been torn to pieces." We then read:

> Jacob rent his clothes, put on sackcloth, and mourned his son for a long time. His sons and daughters tried to comfort him, but he refused to be comforted. He said, "I will go down to the grave mourning for my son." (37: 34–35)

Why did Jacob refuse to be comforted? There are laws in Judaism about the limits of grief—*shiva, she-loshim*, a year. There is no such thing as a bereavement for which grief is endless. The *Gemara* (*Moed Katan* 27b) says that G-d says to one who weeps beyond the appointed time, "You are not more compassionate than I."

A *midrash* gives a remarkable answer. "One can be comforted for one who is dead, but not for one who is still living." Jacob refused to be comforted because he had not yet given up hope that Joseph was still alive. That, tragically, is the fate of those who have lost members of their family (the parents of soldiers missing in action, for example), but have as yet no proof that they are dead. They cannot go through the normal stages of mourning because they cannot

abandon the possibility that the missing person is still capable of being rescued. Their continuing anguish is a form of loyalty; to give up, to mourn, to be reconciled to loss is a kind of betrayal. In such cases, grief lacks closure. To refuse to be comforted is to refuse to give up hope.

On what basis did Jacob continue to hope? Surely he had recognized Joseph's blood-stained coat and said, explicitly, "A wild beast had devoured him. Joseph has been torn to pieces"? Do these words not mean that he had accepted that Joseph was dead?

The late David Daube made a suggestion that I find convincing. The words the sons say to Jacob—*haker na*, "do you recognise this?"—have a quasi-legal connotation. Daube relates this passage to another, with which it has close linguistic parallels:

> If a man gives a donkey, an ox, a sheep or any other animal to his neighbour for safekeeping and it dies or is injured or is taken away while no one is looking, the issue between them will be settled by the taking of an oath before the Lord that the neighbour did not lay hands on the other person's property . . . If it [the animal] was torn to pieces by a wild animal, he shall bring the remains as evidence and he will not be required to pay for the torn animal. (Shemot 22: 10–13)

The issue at stake is the extent of responsibility borne by a guardian (*shomer*). If the animal is lost through negligence, the guardian is at fault and must make good the loss. If there is no negligence, merely force majeure, an unavoidable, unforeseeable accident, the guardian is exempt from blame. One such case is where the loss has been caused by a wild animal. The wording in the law—*tarof yitaref*, "torn to pieces"—exactly parallels Jacob's judgment in the case of Joseph: *tarof toraf Yosef*, "Joseph has been torn to pieces."

We know that some such law existed prior to the giving of the Torah. Jacob himself says to Laban, whose flocks and herds have been placed in his charge, "I did not bring you animals torn by wild beasts; I bore the loss myself" (Bereishit 31: 39). This implies that guardians even then were exempt from responsibility for the damage caused by wild animals. We also know that an elder brother carried a similar responsibility for the fate of a younger brother placed in his charge (i.e. when the two were alone together). That is the significance of Cain's denial when confronted by G-d as to the fate of Abel: "Am I my brother's guardian [*shomer*]?"

We now understand a series of nuances in the encounter between Jacob and his sons, when they return without Joseph. Normally they would be held responsible for their younger brother's disappearance. To avoid this, as in the case of later biblical law, they "bring the remains as evidence." If those remains show signs of an attack by a wild animal, they must—by virtue of the law then operative—be held innocent. Their request to Jacob, *haker na*, must be construed as a legal request, meaning, "Examine the evidence." Jacob has no alternative but to do so, and in virtue of what he has seen, acquit them. A judge, however, may be forced to acquit someone accused of the crime because the evidence is insufficient to justify a conviction, yet he may hold lingering private doubts. So Jacob was forced to find his sons innocent, without necessarily believing what they said. Jacob did not believe it, and his refusal to be comforted shows that he was unconvinced. He continued to hope that Joseph was still alive. That hope was even-

tually justified. Joseph was still alive, and eventually father and son were re-united.

The refusal to be comforted sounded more than once in Jewish history. The prophet Jeremiah heard it in a later age:

This is what the Lord says:

"A voice is heard in Ramah,
Mourning and great weeping,
Rachel weeping for her children
And refusing to be comforted,
Because her children are no more."
This is what the Lord says:
"Restrain your voice from weeping,
And your eyes from tears,
For your work will be rewarded," says the Lord.
"They will return from the land of the enemy.
So there is hope for your future," declares the Lord,
"Your children will return to their own land."
(Jeremiah 31: 15–17)

Why was Jeremiah sure that Jews would return? Because they refused to be comforted—meaning, they refused to give up hope.

So it was during the Babylonian exile, in one of the great expressions of all time of the refusal to be comforted:

By the rivers of Babylon we sat and wept,
As we remembered Zion . . .
How can we sing the songs of the Lord in a
strange land?
If I forget you, O Jerusalem,
May my right hand forget [its skill],
May my tongue cling to the roof of my mouth
If I do not remember you,
If I do not consider Jerusalem my highest joy.
(Psalm 137: 1–6)

It is said that Napoleon, passing a synagogue on Tisha B'Av, heard the sounds of lamentation. "What are the Jews crying for?" he asked one of his officers. "For Jerusalem," he replied. "How long ago did they lose it?" "More than 1,700 hundred years ago." "A people who can mourn for Jerusalem so long, will one day have it restored to them," he is reputed to have replied.

Jews are the people who refused to be comforted because they never gave up hope. Jacob did eventually see Joseph again. Rachel's children did return to the land. Jerusalem is once again the Jewish home. All the evidence may suggest otherwise: it may seem to signify irretrievable loss, a decree of history that cannot be overturned, a fate that must be accepted. Jews never believed the evidence because they had something else to set against it—a faith, a trust, an unbreakable hope that proved stronger than historical inevitability. It is not too much to say that Jewish survival was sustained in that hope. Where did it come from? From a simple—or perhaps not so simply—phrase in the life of Jacob. He refused to be comforted. And so—while we live in a world still scarred by violence, poverty and injustice—must we.

www.rabbisacks.org
Reprinted with permission of the author.

GLOSSARY

Achzari. Cruel.

Al yisroel v 'al rabonon. "For Israel and for our rabbis." Excerpt of "Rabbi's Kaddish" prayer.

Alehem hashalom. May they rest in peace.

Aleinu. (lit. it is our duty); Concluding prayer of each of the daily services.

Aliyah. The honor of being called up to recite one of the blessings over the Torah.

Amen, y'hai shmai rabah m'vorach, l'olam u' lolmai olmaya. (Aramaic) "Amen. May His great Name be blessed forever and ever." Congregational response to the Kaddish prayer.

Ani ma'amin. (lit. I believe); formulaic beginning of Maimonides' Thirteen Principles of Faith.

Aninut. Mourning period following the moment of death until the burial.

Arba canfoth. (lit. four corners); see Tzitzit.

Avelut. Mourning.

Averah. Sin.

B'chaiyechon u'vyomechon, u'vchaiyai d'chol bais yisroel ba'agolah u'vizman koriv. (Aramaic) "In your lifetime and in your days and in the lifetime of all of the House of Israel, quickly and in the near future." Excerpt of Kaddish prayer.

B'olmo dee'vro chirusai v'yamlich malchusai. (Aramaic) "In the world He created according to His will." Excerpt of Kaddish prayer.

B'rov am hadras melech. "In a multitude of people is found the glory of the King" (Proverbs 14:28).

Binah. (lit. "comprehension"); the second of the ten *sefirot*; the second stage of the intellectual process of Chabad that develops abstract conceptions, giving them breadth and depth.

Borechu. In the liturgy, the formal call to prayer and the beginning of the section of Shema and its blessings.

Boruch shem kevod malchuso l'olam va'ed. "Blessed is the Name of His glorious kingdom forever and ever." In the liturgy, directly follows the Shema.

Brich Hu. (Aramaic) "Blessed be He." Congregational response to the Kaddish prayer.

Chai. Life.

Chaluka d'rabanan. (Aramaic) Garment of the sages.

Chassidisher Yid. (Yiddish) Chasidic Jew.

Chassidut. Chasidic philosophy.

Chesed Shel Emes. (lit. true kindness); Usually a reference to kindness conferred upon the deceased, e.g., care of the body and burial.

Cheshbon. Accounting or assessment.

Chevra Kadisha. (lit. holy society) The society that attends to the burial of the deceased and oversees the management of the community cemetery.

Chibut HaKever (Hibbut ha-keber). (lit. beating of the grave); a form of Gehinom in which a soul is metaphorically beaten and shaken.

Chuppah. Marriage canopy.

Cohanim. Members of the Jewish priestly class, descended from Aaron, charged with sacrificial, ministerial, and other sacred functions.

Daas. (lit. knowledge); the third of the ten *sefirot*; the third stage of the intellectual process, which guides emotion.

Derush. Exegesis.

Din. Judgment.

Eglah Arufah. Slaughtered calf as a communal atonement for an unsolved murder.

Emor. The eighth Torah portion in the book of Leviticus.

Eros. In Greek mythology, the god of love.

Farbrengen. (Yiddish) A gathering of Chasidim characterized by singing and inspiring talk.

Gan Eden. Garden of Eden, Paradise.

Gehinom (Gehinnom). Purgatory, the spiritual realm in which the souls are cleansed from the blemishes brought about by their conduct while on Earth.

Gemillat chasadim. Acts of goodness and kindness.

Gerogerot. Dried figs.

Guf dak. Ethereal body.

Guf gas. Dense body.

Haftarah. Reading from the Prophets at the conclusion of the weekly Torah reading.

Haker na. "Do you recognize this?" (Genesis 37:32).

Hakhel. The year following the Sabbatical year, at the beginning of which all Jews would gather in the Temple to hear the king read selections from Deuteronomy.

Halachah. Jewish law.

Havel havalim hakol havel. "Vanity of vanities, all is vanity" (Ecclesiastes 1:2).

Hebra Kaddisha. See Chevra Kadisha.

Kaddish. Brief prayer recited in the synagogue by a mourner or prayer leader.

Kaf HaKela. A form of Gehinom in which a soul is metaphorically slung with a slingshot.

Kar. Cold.

Kedusha (Kedushah). (a) Holiness; (b) part of the Shemoneh Esrei liturgy.

Kelipah (pl., kelipot). (lit. shell); The representation of evil or impure spiritual forces in Jewish mysticism.

Kever Yisrael. Traditional Jewish burial.

Kiddush. Blessing recited over a cup of wine expressing the sanctity of the Sabbath or of a festival.

Kinot. Elegies.

Korath ruah. Pleasure.

L'aila min kol birchasa v'shirasa, tushbechasa, v'nechamasa, da'amiron b'olmo. (Aramaic) "[He is] above all blessings, hymns, praises, and consolation that we can say in this world." Excerpt of Kaddish prayer.

Limen. (Latin) threshold.

Luz. Bone at the top of the spine that, according to Jewish tradition, cannot be destroyed.

Machpeila. The burial site of Adam, Eve, the Patriarchs, and most of the Matriarchs in Hebron, Israel.

Magen. Shield.

Malbush. Garb.

Matzah. Unleavened bread eaten on Passover.

Meisim. Deceased/newly deceased ones.

Mi. Hebrew prepositional prefix that means "from" indicated by the letter mem.

Miccol. Than all.

Miknehu. His cattle.

Mikveh. Ritual bathing pool in which a person immerses as part of the transition to ritual purity.

Mishkan. The tabernacle or temporary Sanctuary in which the Divine Presence dwelled during the Jews' journeys through the desert.

Mitzvah (pl. mitzvot, mitzvoth). The Torah's commandments.

Modeh Ani. "I acknowledge." Opening words of the prayer of thanksgiving recited immediately upon waking in the morning.

Moshia. Rescuer.

Moshiach. (lit. "the anointed one"); the Messiah.

Nefesh HaBehamis. Animal soul.

Nefesh. (a) Spirit; (b) lowest of the five levels of the human soul.

Neshamah. (a) Soul; (b) the third of the five levels of the human soul.

Nichum aveilim. Comforting the bereaved.

Nifsad. In a state of deterioration.

Nitzavim-Vayelech. Ninth and tenth Torah portions of the book of Deuteronomy, often read together.

Nivul. Degradation.

Olam Haba (Olam HaBah). World to Come.

Olam Haneshamos. World of Souls.

Oneg. Pleasure or delight.

Or ein sof. God's infinite light.

Or. Light.

Ozer. Helper.

Peshat. The plain meaning (of a scriptural passage).

Remez. Hermeneutics.

Rishonim. Post-Talmudic authorities who flourished from the mid-eleventh to the mid-sixteenth centuries.

Rosh Hashanah. The Jewish New Year holiday.

Ru'ach. (lit. wind); The second lowest of the five levels of the human soul.

Ruach ha'kodesh. Divine inspiration.

Sefirah (pl. sefirot). Divine attributes or emanations that are manifested in each of the four spiritual worlds and are the source of the corresponding ten faculties of the soul.

Sein-zum-tode. (German) Being-toward-death; in Heidegger's thought, refers to a mode of being in which death can guide one toward gaining an authentic perspective.

Sephirah. See Sefirah.

Shabbat. The Sabbath, the divinely-ordained day of rest on the seventh day of the week.

Shanah. Year.

Shechinah (Sh'chinah). The manifestation of the divine presence; God's feminine manifestation.

Shema (Sh'ma). Verses from the Bible declaring, among other things, one's faith in God, recited by Jews every morning and evening.

Shema Yisroel. "Hear O Israel." The opening words of the Shema prayer.

Shemoneh Esrei (Shemoneh Esray). (lit. eighteen); the most important prayer of the daily liturgy.

Shetut. Folly.

Shiva. (lit. seven); The seven-day mourning period following the burial of a deceased next of kin.

Shloshim (sheloshim). (lit. thirty); The thirty-day mourning period following the burial of a deceased next of kin.

Shomer. Guardian.

Sitra achra. (Aramaic) (lit. the other side); Forces of evil.

Sod. Esoteric meaning (of a scriptural passage).

Sukkahs. Huts or booths roofed with vegetation in which the festival of Sukkot is observed.

Sukkot. Festival of seven days (eight in the Diaspora) beginning on 15 Tishrei, taking its name from the temporary dwelling (sukkah) in which one lives during this period.

Tachanun. (lit. supplication); part of the weekday morning and afternoon liturgy.

Tachrichim. Shrouds.

Tahara hee. "She is pure."

Tahara. Purification.

Tanakh. The bible; acronym for Torah (i.e., the Five Books of Moses), Nevi'im (Prophets), and Ketuvim (the Writings).

Tarof toraf Yosef. "Joseph has been torn to pieces" (Genesis 37:33).

Tarof yitaref. Torn to pieces.

Techiyat hametim (techiat hamaitim, techiyas hameisim). Resurrection of the dead.

Tefillah. Prayer.

Tefillin. Small black leather cubes containing parchment scrolls inscribed with biblical passages, wrapped on the arm and head of adult men during weekday morning prayers.

Teshuvah. Repentance, the return to one's true essence.

Thanatos. (Greek) Personification of death in Greek mythology.

Tikkun. Rectification.

Tisha B'Av. (lit. ninth of Av); day of fasting and mourning commemorating the destruction of the first and the second Temples.

Tiskabel tzelosehone. (Aramaic) "Accept the prayers." Excerpt of Kaddish prayer.

Toledot. Descendants

Torah. (lit. instruction, teaching); Pentateuch, also the totality of Jewish teaching and practice.

Toras Chayim. A living Torah.

Toras Emes. A Torah of Truth.

Tsadik (tzaddik, pl. tsadikim/tzaddikim). A righteous person.

Tzelem Elokim. The image of God.

Tzelem. Shadow.

Tzitzit (tzitzith). Ritual fringed four-corner garment.

Yahrtzeit. (Yiddish: lit. time of year); Anniversary of someone's passing.

Yiddishe nachas. (Yiddish) Jewish pride and joy.

Yisgadal v'yiskadash shmai rabah. (Aramaic) "Let His great name be magnified and sanctified."

Introductory words of the Kaddish prayer.

Yishtabach. Prayer in the morning liturgy.

Yizkor. Prayer for the souls of departed loved ones recited on certain festival days.

Z'man techiah. The time of resurrection of the dead.

Zaidy. (Yiddish) Grandfather.

ACKNOWLEDGMENTS

"It is better to go to a house of mourning than to go to a house of feasting,
for that is the end of every man,
and the living shall take to heart."
—Ecclesiastes 7:2

Sooner or later, we are all touched by the passing of a loved one, a person to whom we are attached by the strongest bonds of blood and love. The specter of our own mortality weighs on our hearts and minds, as well. King Solomon, the wisest of all men, advises us against escapism and denial, against seeking oblivion from our pain, heartbreak, and existential angst in a "house of feasting." Go to the house of mourning, he says, but be careful to "take to heart": have the spiritual clarity to view death as a lesson for life.

The Rohr Jewish Learning Institute (JLI) has assumed the daunting and formidable task of creating a course that attempts to shed some of the Torah's light on the darkest moments of the human experience. *Journey of the Soul* speaks to the heart, the mind, and the soul—each in its own language. It explores attitudes toward death and mortality in Jewish traditional thought, focusing on the Kabbalistic perspective, and how these perspectives profoundly influence our choices and actions in the here and now.

We extend our appreciation to **Rabbis Mordechai Dinerman** and **Naftali Silberberg,** who direct the JLI Curriculum Department and the Flagship editorial team; to **Rabbi Dr. Shmuel Klatzkin,** JLI's senior editor; and to **Rabbi Zalman Abraham,** charged with JLI strategic branding and marketing, who skillfully provides the vision for branding JLI course offerings.

We are grateful to **Rabbis Yanky Raskin** and **Shmuel Super,** and **Chava Shapiro** for their assistance in developing and writing this course, and to **Rochel Holzkenner** for her careful review of the lesson drafts. We thank the staff of **Machon Shmuel: The Sami Rohr Research Institute** and **Rabbi Eli Raksin** for their meticulous research that greatly aided in the preparation of this course.

The JLI editorial board provided many useful suggestions to enhance the course and ensure its suitability for a wide range of students. Many thanks to **Rabbis Yisroel Mangel, Sholom Raichik,** and **Avrohom Sternberg** for their careful review of this course.

We are pleased to be able to offer this course for credits from the American Psychological Association (APA), the American Council for Continuing Medical Education (ACCME), and the California Board of Behavioral Sciences (CBBS). We are indebted to **Dr. Casey Skvork** for his dedicated collaboration, and to **William Wears** of the Washington School of Psychiatry for his patient guidance through the accreditation process. Special thanks to **Mindy Wallach** for coordinating the accreditation and to **Shulamis Nadler** for her administrative assistance.

We acknowledge **Miriam Levy-Haim** and **Zeldy (Nemanov) Friedman** for managing the many components of course production. We extend a warm *mazal tov* to Zeldy on her recent marriage; in the merit of her important work, may she and her husband be showered with much blessing and happiness.

We are grateful to **Mendel Schtroks** for designing the textbooks with taste, eloquence, and patience, and **Mendel Sirota** for directing book production. **Miriam Levy-Haim** and **Rachel Witty** enhanced the quality and professionalism of the course with their copyediting and proofreading.

Moshe and **Getzy Raskin** head the production team charged with producing the videos for this course. The video scripts were masterfully created by **Rabbi Yaakov Paley. Mushka Lisker** and **Mushka Pruss** designed the course's PowerPoints.

We acknowledge the hard work and efforts of JLI's support staff and administration, whose contributions to this course were critical, but whose names are too many to enumerate.

We are immensely grateful for the encouragement of JLI's visionary chairman and vice-chairman of Merkos L'Inyonei Chinuch—Lubavitch World Headquarters, **Rabbi Moshe Kotlarsky.** Rabbi Kotlarsky has been highly instrumental in building the infrastructure for the expansion of Chabad's international network and is the architect of scores of initiatives and services to help Chabad representatives across the globe succeed in their mission. We are blessed to have the unwavering support of JLI's principal benefactor, **Mr. George Rohr,** who is fully invested in our work and continues to be instrumental in JLI's monumental expansion.

The commitment and sage direction of JLI's dedicated executive board— **Rabbis Chaim Block, Hesh Epstein, Ronnie Fine, Yosef Gansburg, Shmuel Kaplan, Yisrael Rice,** and **Avrohom Sternberg**—and the countless hours they devote to the development of JLI is what drives the vision, growth, and flourishing of the organization.

Finally, JLI represents an incredible partnership of more than 900 *shluchim* and *shluchot,* who give of their time and talent to further Jewish adult education. We thank them for generously sharing feedback and making suggestions that steer JLI's development and growth. They are our most valuable critics and our most cherished contributors.

Inspired by the call of the **Lubavitcher Rebbe,** of righteous memory, it is the mandate of the Rohr JLI to encourage all Jews throughout the world to experience and participate in their precious heritage of Torah learning. May this course succeed in fulfilling this sacred charge.

On behalf of the Rohr Jewish Learning Institute,

Rabbi Efraim Mintz, Executive Director
Rabbi Yisrael Rice, Chairman, Editorial Board

18 Elul, 5775

The **Rohr Jewish Learning Institute**

An affiliate of
Merkos L'Inyonei Chinuch
The Educational Arm of
The Chabad Lubavitch Movement
822 Eastern Parkway, Brooklyn, NY 11213

Rabbi Shraga Sherman
Merion Station, PA

Rabbi Avraham Steinmetz
S. Paulo, BR

Rabbi Avrohom Sternberg
New London, CT

Rabbi Aryeh Weinstein
Newtown, PA

Rabbi Motti Wilhelm
Portland, OR

Multimedia Development

Moshe Raskin
Director

Mrs. Mushka Lisker
Mushka Pruss
Mrs. Rivkah Rapoport
Mrs. Chava Shapiro
Rabbi Chesky Edelman
Getzy Raskin

Administration

Mrs. Chana Dechter

Affiliate Support

Rabbi Mendel Sirota
Mrs. Fraydee Kessler
Mrs. Mindy Wallach

Online Division

Rabbi Mendy Elishevitz
Director

Rabbi Yisroel Silman
Creative Director

Rabbi Elchonon Korenblit
Ram Rabins
Mrs. Rochie Rivkin
Avi J. Levy

Marketing and Branding

Rabbi Zalman Abraham
Director

Mrs. Shevi Rivkin
Raizel Shurpin
Graphic Design

Rabbi Yossi Klein
Marketing for Results

Rabbi Yaakov Paley
Writer

Marketing Committee

Rabbi Simcha Backman
Glendale, CA

Rabbi Ronnie Fine
Montreal, QC

Rabbi Ovadia Goldman
Oklahoma City, OK

Rabbi Mendy Halberstam
Miami Beach, FL

Rabbi Reuven New
Boca Raton, FL

Rabbi Yehuda Shemtov
Yardley, PA

Marketing Consultants

JJ Gross
New York, NY

Warren Modlin
MednetPro, Inc.
Alpharetta, GA

Alan Rosenspan
Alan Rosenspan & Associates
Sharon, MA

Gary Wexler
Passion Marketing
Los Angeles, CA

Publication Design

Rabbi Zalman Abraham
Mendel Schtroks

Printing

Shimon Leib Jacobs
Point One Communications
Montreal, QC

Distribution

Mary Stevens
Nixa, MO

Accounting

Musie Karp
Mrs. Shaina B. Mintz
Mrs. Shulamis Nadler

JLI Departments

Rabbi Levi Kaplan
Director of Operations

Rabbi Dubi Rabinowitz
Administrator

JLI Flagship

Rabbi Yisrael Rice
Chairman
S. Rafael, CA

Rabbi Mordechai Dinerman
Rabbi Naftali Silberberg
Editors-in-Chief

Rabbi Yanky Tauber
Course Editor

Rabbi Dr. Shmuel Klatzkin
Senior Editor
Dayton, OH

Rabbi Yanky Raskin
Associate Editor

Rabbi Shmuel Super
Rabbi Eliezer Raksin
Research Fellows

Mrs. Zeldy Friedman
Administrative Assistant

Rabbi Mendel Sirota
Production Manager

Miriam Levy-Haim
Mrs. Rachel Witty
Proofreaders

Department of Continuing Education

Mrs. Mindy Wallach
Director

Musie Karp
Registrar

Mrs. Shulamis Nadler
Service and Support

JLI International Desk

Rabbi Avrohom Sternberg
Chairman
New London, CT

Rabbi Dubi Rabinowitz
Director
Brooklyn, NY

Chava Farkash
Administrative Assistant

Mendel Schtroks
Content Manager

Rabbi Yosef Yitzchok Noiman
Administrator, JLI Israel
In Partnership with
Tzeirei Agudat Chabad

Rabbi Eli Wolf
Administrator, JLI in the CIS
In Parternship with the Federation of Jewish
Communities of the CIS

Rabbi Avraham Golovacheov
Regional Respresentative
German Division

Rabbi Nochum Schapiro
Regional Respresentative
Australia

Beis Medrosh L'Shluchim
in partnership with
Shluchim Exchange

Rabbi Mendy Yusewitz
Director

Rabbi Mendel Margolin
Producer

Steering Committee
Rabbi Simcha Backman
Rabbi Mendy Kotlarsky
Rabbi Efraim Mintz

JLI Academy

Rabbi Hesh Epstein
Chairman

Rabbi Yossi Klein
Director

JLI Teens
in partnership with
CTeeN: Chabad Teen Network

Rabbi Chaim Block
Chairman
San Antonio, TX

Rabbi Elya Silfen
Director

Rabbi Michoel Shapiro
Editor in Chief

Mrs. Nechi Gudelsky
Program Administrators

Rohr JLI Faculty

ALABAMA

BIRMINGHAM
Rabbi Yossi Friedman
205.970.0100

ARIZONA

CHANDLER
Rabbi Mendel Deitsch
480.855.4333

FLAGSTAFF
Rabbi Dovie Shapiro
928.255.5756

ORO VALLEY
Rabbi Ephraim Zimmerman
520.477.8672

PHOENIX
Rabbi Zalman Levertov
Rabbi Yossi Friedman
602.944.2753

SCOTTSDALE
Rabbi Yossi Levertov
480.998.1410

ARKANSAS

LITTLE ROCK
Rabbi Pinchus Ciment
501.217.0053

CALIFORNIA

AGOURA HILLS
Rabbi Moshe Bryski
Rabbi Shlomo Bistritsky
818.991.0991

BEL AIR
Rabbi Chaim Mentz
310.475.5311

BEVERLY HILLS
Rabbi Chaim I. Sperlin
310.734.9079

BRENTWOOD
Rabbi Boruch Hecht
Rabbi Mordechai Zaetz
310.826.4453

BURBANK
Rabbi Shmuly Kornfeld
818.954.0070

CARLSBAD
Rabbi Yeruchem Eilfort
Mrs. Nechama Eilfort
760.943.8891

CENTURY CITY
Rabbi Tzemach Cunin
310.860.1260

CHATSWORTH
Rabbi Yossi Spritzer
818.718.0777

CONTRA COSTA
Rabbi Dovber Berkowitz
925.937.4101

CORONADO
Rabbi Eli Fradkin
619.365.4728

ENCINO
Rabbi Joshua Gordon
Rabbi Aryeh Herzog
818.784.9986

FOLSOM
Rabbi Yossi Grossbaum
916.608.9811

GLENDALE
Rabbi Simcha Backman
818.240.2750

HUNTINGTON BEACH
Rabbi Aron Berkowitz
714.846.2285

IRVINE
Rabbi Alter Tenenbaum
Rabbi Elly Andrusier
949.786.5000

LA JOLLA
Rabbi Baruch Shalom Ezagui
858.455.5433

LAGUNA BEACH
Rabbi Elimelech Gurevitch
949.499.0770

LOMITA
Rabbi Eli Hecht
Rabbi Sholom Pinson
310.326.8234

LONG BEACH
Rabbi Abba Perelmuter
562.621.9828

LOS ANGELES
Rabbi Leibel Korf
323.660.5177

MARINA DEL REY
Rabbi Danny Yiftach-Hashem
Rabbi Dovid Yiftach
310.859.0770

NORTH HOLLYWOOD
Rabbi Nachman Abend
818.989.9539

NORTHRIDGE
Rabbi Eli Rivkin
818.368.3937

PACIFIC PALISADES
Rabbi Zushe Cunin
310.454.7783

PALO ALTO
Rabbi Yosef Levin
Rabbi Ber Rosenblatt
650.424.9800

PASADENA
Rabbi Chaim Hanoka
626.564.8820

RANCHO MIRAGE
Rabbi Shimon H. Posner
760.770.7785

RANCHO PALOS VERDES
Rabbi Yitzchok Magalnic
310.544.5544

RANCHO S. FE
Rabbi Levi Raskin
858.756.7571

REDONDO BEACH
Rabbi Yossi Mintz
Rabbi Zalman Gordon
310.214.4999

S. BARBARA
Rabbi Mendel Loschak
CHAPTER FOUNDED BY
RABBI YOSEF LOSCHAK, OBM
805.683.1544

S. CLEMENTE
Rabbi Menachem M. Slavin
949.489.0723

S. DIEGO
Rabbi Motte Fradkin
858.547.0076

S. FRANCISCO
Rabbi Peretz Mochkin
415.571.8770

S. LUIS OBISPO
Rabbi Chaim Leib Hilel
805.706.0256

S. MONICA
Rabbi Boruch Rabinowitz
310.394.5699

S. RAFAEL
Rabbi Yisrael Rice
415.492.1666

SOUTH LAKE TAHOE
Rabbi Mordechai Richler
530.314.7677

STOCKTON
Rabbi Avremel Brod
209.952.2081

STUDIO CITY
Rabbi Yossi Baitelman
818.508.6633

THOUSAND OAKS
Rabbi Chaim Bryski
805.493.7776

TUSTIN
Rabbi Yehoshua Eliezrie
714.508.2150

VENTURA
Rabbi Yakov Latowicz
Mrs. Sarah Latowicz
805.658.7441

YORBA LINDA
Rabbi Dovid Eliezrie
714.693.0770

COLORADO
ASPEN
Rabbi Mendel Mintz
970.544.3770

DENVER
Rabbi Mendel Popack
720.515.4337

Rabbi Yossi Serebryanski
303.744.9699

FORT COLLINS
Rabbi Yerachmiel Gorelik
970.407.1613

HIGHLANDS RANCH
Rabbi Avraham Mintz
303.694.9119

LONGMONT
Rabbi Yakov Dovid Borenstein
303.678.7595

VAIL
Rabbi Dovid Mintz
970.476.7887

WESTMINSTER
Rabbi Benjy Brackman
303.429.5177

CONNECTICUT
FAIRFIELD
Rabbi Shlame Landa
203.373.1118

GREENWICH
Rabbi Yossi Deren
Rabbi Menachem Feldman
203.629.9059

MILFORD
Rabbi Schneur Wilhelm
203.878.4569

NEW LONDON
Rabbi Avrohom Sternberg
860.437.8000

STAMFORD
Rabbi Yisrael Deren
Rabbi Levi Mendelow
203.3.CHABAD

WEST HARTFORD
Rabbi Yosef Gopin
Rabbi Shaya Gopin
860.659.2422

WESTPORT
Rabbi Yehuda L. Kantor
Mrs. Dina Kantor
203.226.8584

DELAWARE
WILMINGTON
Rabbi Chuni Vogel
302.529.9900

FLORIDA
BAL HARBOUR
Rabbi Dov Schochet
305.868.1411

BOCA RATON
Rabbi Zalman Bukiet
Rabbi Moishe Denburg
Rabbi Arele Gopin
561.417.7797

BOYNTON BEACH
Rabbi Yosef Yitzchok Raichik
561.732.4633

BRADENTON
Rabbi Menachem Bukiet
941.388.9656

CAPE CORAL
Rabbi Yossi Labkowski
239.541.1777

CORAL SPRINGS
Rabbi Yankie Denburg
954.471.8646

DELRAY BEACH
Rabbi Sholom Ber Korf
561.496.6228

EAST BOCA RATON
Rabbi Ruvi New
561.417.7797

FLEMING ISLAND
Rabbi Shmuly Feldman
904.290.1017

FORT LAUDERDALE
Rabbi Yitzchok Naparstek
954.568.1190

FORT MYERS
Rabbi Yitzchok Minkowicz
Mrs. Nechama Minkowicz
239.433.7708

HALLANDALE BEACH
Rabbi Mordy Feiner
954.458.1877

HOLLYWOOD
Rabbi Leizer Barash
954.965.9933

Rabbi Leibel Kudan
954.801.3367

KENDALL
Rabbi Yossi Harlig
305.234.5654

LAKELAND
Rabbi Moshe Lazaros
863.510.5968

LAKE MARY
Rabbi Yanky Majesky
407.878.3011

MAITLAND
Rabbi Sholom Dubov
Rabbi Levik Dubov
470.644.2500

OCALA
Rabbi Yossi Hecht
352.291.2218

ORLANDO
Rabbi Yosef Konikov
407.354.3660

ORMOND BEACH
Rabbi Shmuel Konikov
386.672.9300

PALM BEACH GARDENS
Rabbi Dovid Vigler
561.624.2223

PALMETTO BAY
Rabbi Zalman Gansburg
786.282.0413

PLANTATION
Rabbi Pinchas Taylor
954.644.9177

PONTE VEDRA BEACH
Rabbi Nochum Kurinsky
904.543.9301

SARASOTA
Rabbi Chaim Shaul Steinmetz
941.925.0770

SATELLITE BEACH
Rabbi Zvi Konikov
321.777.2770

SOUTH PALM BEACH
Rabbi Leibel Stolik
561.889.3499

SOUTH TAMPA
Rabbi Mendy Dubrowski
813.287.1795

Share the **Rohr JLI** experience with friends and relatives worldwide

SUNNY ISLES BEACH
Rabbi Alexander Kaller
305.803.5315

WESTON
Rabbi Yisroel Spalter
954.349.6565

WEST PALM BEACH
Rabbi Yoel Gancz
561.659.7770

VENICE
Rabbi Sholom Ber Schmerling
941.493.2770

GEORGIA
ALPHARETTA
Rabbi Hirshy Minkowicz
770.410.9000

ATLANTA
Rabbi Yossi New
Rabbi Isser New
404.843.2464

ATLANTA: INTOWN
Rabbi Eliyahu Schusterman
Rabbi Ari Sollish
404.898.0434

GWINNETT
Rabbi Yossi Lerman
678.595.0196

MARIETTA
Rabbi Ephraim Silverman
770.565.4412

IDAHO
BOISE
Rabbi Mendel Lifshitz
208.853.9200

ILLINOIS
CHAMPAIGN
Rabbi Dovid Tiechtel
217.355.8672

CHICAGO
Rabbi Meir Hecht
312.714.4655

Rabbi Dovid Kotlarsky
773.495.7127

Rabbi Yosef Moscowitz
773.772.3770

Rabbi Levi Notik
773.274.5123

CHICAGO-HYDE PARK
Rabbi Yossi Brackman
773.955.8672

ELGIN
Rabbi Mendel Shemtov
847.440.4486

GLENVIEW
Rabbi Yishaya Benjaminson
847.998.9896

HIGHLAND PARK
Mrs. Michla Schanowitz
847.266.0770

NAPERVILLE
Rabbi Mendy Goldstein
630.778.9770

NORTHBROOK
Rabbi Meir Moscowitz
847.564.8770

OAK PARK
Rabbi Yitzchok Bergstein
708.524.1530

PEORIA
Rabbi Eli Langsam
309.692.2250

ROCKFORD
Rabbi Yecheskel Rothman
815.596.0032

SKOKIE
Rabbi Yochanan Posner
847.677.1770

VERNON HILLS
Rabbi Shimmy Susskind
847.984.2919

WILMETTE
Rabbi Dovid Flinkenstein
847.251.7707

INDIANA
INDIANAPOLIS
Rabbi Mendel Schusterman
317.251.5573

KANSAS
OVERLAND PARK
Rabbi Mendy Wineberg
913.649.4852

KENTUCKY
LOUISVILLE
Rabbi Avrohom Litvin
502.459.1770

LOUISIANA
METAIRIE
Rabbi Yossie Nemes
Rabbi Mendel Ceitlin
504.454.2910

MARYLAND
BALTIMORE
Rabbi Elchonon Lisbon
410.358.4787

Rabbi Velvel Belinsky
CLASSES IN RUSSIAN
410.764.5000

BEL AIR
Rabbi Yekusiel Schusterman
443.353.9718

BETHESDA
Rabbi Bentzion Geisinsky
Rabbi Sender Geisinsky
301.913.9777

COLUMBIA
Rabbi Hillel Baron
Rabbi Yosef Chaim Sufrin
410.740.2424

FREDERICK
Rabbi Boruch Labkowski
301.996.3659

GAITHERSBURG
Rabbi Sholom Raichik
301.926.3632

OLNEY
Rabbi Bentzy Stolik
301.660.6770

OWINGS MILLS
Rabbi Nochum H. Katsenelenbogen
410.356.5156

POTOMAC
Rabbi Mendel Bluming
301.983.4200

Rabbi Mendel Kaplan
301.983.1485

ROCKVILLE
Rabbi Moishe Kavka
301.836.1242

MASSACHUSETTS
CAPE COD
Rabbi Yekusiel Alperowitz
508.775.2324

LONGMEADOW
Rabbi Yakov Wolff
413.567.8665

NEWTON
Rabbi Shalom Ber Prus
617.244.1200

MILFORD
Rabbi Mendy Kievman
508.473.1299

SUDBURY
Rabbi Yisroel Freeman
978.443.3691

SWAMPSCOTT
Mrs. Layah Lipsker
781.581.3833

MICHIGAN
ANN ARBOR
Rabbi Aharon Goldstein
734.995.3276

GRAND RAPIDS
Rabbi Mordechai Haller
616.957.0770

WEST BLOOMFIELD
Rabbi Elimelech Silberberg
248.855.6170

MINNESOTA
MINNETONKA
Rabbi Mordechai Grossbaum
952.929.9922

S. PAUL
Rabbi Shneur Zalman Bendet
651.998.9298

MISSOURI
CHESTERFIELD
Rabbi Avi Rubenfeld
314.258.3401

S. LOUIS
Rabbi Yosef Landa
314.725.0400

MONTANA
BOZEMAN
Rabbi Chaim Shaul Bruk
406.585.8770

NEVADA
SUMMERLIN
Rabbi Yisroel Schanowitz
Rabbi Tzvi Bronchtain
702.855.0770

NEW JERSEY
BASKING RIDGE
Rabbi Mendy Herson
908.604.8844

CHERRY HILL
Rabbi Mendy Mangel
856.874.1500

CLINTON
Rabbi Eli Kornfeld
908.623.7000

FAIR LAWN
Rabbi Avrohom Bergstein
718.839.5296

FANWOOD
Rabbi Avrohom Blesofsky
908.790.0008

FORT LEE
Rabbi Meir Konikov
201.886.1238

FRANKLIN LAKES
Rabbi Chanoch Kaplan
201.848.0449

HASKELL
Rabbi Mendy Gurkov
201.696.7609

HILLSBOROUGH
Rabbi Shmaya Krinsky
908.874.0444

HOLMDEL
Rabbi Shmaya Galperin
732.772.1998

MADISON
Rabbi Shalom Lubin
973.377.0707

MANALAPAN
Rabbi Boruch Chazanow
Rabbi Levi Wolosow
732.972.3687

MOUNTAIN LAKES
Rabbi Levi Dubinsky
973.551.1898

MULLICA HILL
Rabbi Avrohom Richler
856.733.0770

NORTH BRUNSWICK
Rabbi Levi Azimov
732.398.9492

OLD TAPPAN
Rabbi Mendy Lewis
201.767.4008

ROCKAWAY
Rabbi Asher Herson
Rabbi Mordechai Baumgarten
973.625.1525

TEANECK
Rabbi Ephraim Simon
201.907.0686

TENAFLY
Rabbi Mordechai Shain
Rabbi Yitzchak Gershovitz
201.871.1152

TOMS RIVER
Rabbi Moshe Gourarie
732.349.4199

WEST ORANGE
Rabbi Mendy Kasowitz
973.486.2362

WOODCLIFF LAKE
Rabbi Dov Drizin
201.476.0157

NEW YORK
BEDFORD
Rabbi Arik Wolf
914.666.6065

BINGHAMTON
Mrs. Rivkah Slonim
607.797.0015

BRIGHTON BEACH
Rabbi Zushe Winner
Rabbi Moshe Winner
718.946.9833

BROOKLYN HEIGHTS
Rabbi Mendy Hecht
Rabbi Ari Raskin
347.378.2641

BROOKVILLE
Rabbi Mendy Heber
516.626.0600

CEDARHURST
Rabbi Zalman Wolowik
516.295.2478

CHESTNUT RIDGE
Rabbi Chaim Tzvi Ehrenreich
845.356.6686

COMMACK
Rabbi Mendel Teldon
631.543.3343

DIX HILLS
Rabbi Yaakov Saacks
631.351.8672

EAST HAMPTON
Rabbi Leibel Baumgarten
Rabbi Mendy Goldberg
631.329.5800

FOREST HILLS
Rabbi Yossi Mendelson
917.861.9726

GREAT NECK
Rabbi Yoseph Geisinsky
516.487.4554

KINGSTON
Rabbi Yitzchok Hecht
845.334.9044

LARCHMONT
Rabbi Mendel Silberstein
914.834.4321

LONG BEACH
Rabbi Eli Goodman
516.897.2473

NYC KEHILATH JESHURUN
Rabbi Elie Weinstock
212.774.5636

NYC MIDTOWN
Mrs. Raizy Metzger
212.758.3770

OSSINING
Rabbi Dovid Labkowski
914.923.2522

PORT WASHINGTON
Rabbi Shalom Paltiel
516.767.8672

RIVERDALE
Rabbi Levi Shemtov
718.549.1100

ROCHESTER
Rabbi Nechemia Vogel
585.271.0330

ROSLYN
Rabbi Yaakov Reiter
516.484.8185

Share the **Rohr JLI** experience with friends and relatives worldwide

Sea Gate
Rabbi Chaim Brikman
718.266.1736

Southampton
Rabbi Chaim Pape
917.627.4865

Stony Brook
Rabbi Shalom Ber Cohen
631.585.0521

Suffern
Rabbi Shmuel Gancz
845.368.1889

Westbury
Rabbi Mendy Brownstein
516.850.4486

NORTH CAROLINA
Asheville
Rabbi Shaya Susskind
828.505.0746

Caryy
Rabbi Yisroel Cotlar
919.651.9710

Chapel Hill
Rabbi Zalman Bluming
919.630.5129

Charlotte
Rabbi Yossi Groner
Rabbi Shlomo Cohen
704.366.3984

Greensboro
Rabbi Yosef Plotkin
336.617.8120

Raleigh
Rabbi Pinchas Herman
Rabbi Lev Cotlar
919.637.6950

Wilmington
Rabbi Moshe Lieblich
910.763.4770

NORTH DAKOTA
Fargo
Rabbi Yonah Grossman
701.212.4164

OHIO
Beachwood
Rabbi Shmuli Friedman
Rabbi Moshe Gancz
216.370.2887

Blue Ash
Rabbi Yisroel Mangel
513.793.5200

Columbus
Rabbi Areyah Kaltmann
Rabbi Levi Andrusier
614.294.3296

OKLAHOMA
Oklahoma City
Rabbi Ovadia Goldman
405.524.4800

Tulsa
Rabbi Yehuda Weg
918.492.4499

OREGON
Portland
Rabbi Moshe Wilhelm
Rabbi Mordechai Wilhelm
503.977.9947

Salem
Rabbi Avrohom Yitzchok Perlstein
503.383.9569

PENNSYLVANIA
Ambler
Rabbi Shaya Deitsch
215.591.9310

Bala Cynwyd
Rabbi Shraga Sherman
610.660.9192

Lafayette Hill
Rabbi Yisroel Kotlarsky
347.526.1430

Lancaster
Rabbi Elazar Green
717.368.6565

Newtown
Rabbi Aryeh Weinstein
215.497.9925

Philadelphia: Center City
Rabbi Yochonon Goldman
215.238.2100

Pittsburgh
Rabbi Yisroel Altein
412.422.7300 ext. 269

Pittsburgh: South Hills
Rabbi Mendy Rosenblum
412.278.3693

Wynnewood
Rabbi Moishe Brennan
610.529.9011

RHODE ISLAND
Warwick
Rabbi Yossi Laufer
401.884.7888

SOUTH CAROLINA
Columbia
Rabbi Hesh Epstein
Rabbi Levi Marrus
803.782.1831

TENNESSEE
Chattanooga
Rabbi Shaul Perlstein
423.490.1106

Memphis
Rabbi Levi Klein
901.766.1800

TEXAS
Arlington
Rabbi Levi Gurevitch
817.451.1171

Bellaire
Rabbi Yossi Zaklikofsky
713.839.8887

Dallas
Rabbi Mendel Dubrawsky
Rabbi Moshe Naparstek
972.818.0770

Houston
Rabbi Dovid Goldstein
713.774.0300

Rabbi Moishe Traxler
713.774.0300

Houston: Rice University Area
Rabbi Eliezer Lazaroff
713.522.2004

League City
Rabbi Yitzchok Schmukler
713.398.2460

Missouri City
Rabbi Mendel Feigenson
832.758.0685

Plano
Rabbi Mendel Block
Rabbi Yehudah Horowitz
972.596.8270

S. Antonio
Rabbi Chaim Block
Rabbi Levi Teldon
210.492.1085

The Woodlands
Rabbi Mendel Blecher
281.719.5213

UTAH
Salt Lake City
Rabbi Benny Zippel
801.467.7777

VERMONT
Burlington
Rabbi Yitzchok Raskin
802.658.5770

VIRGINIA
Alexandria/Arlington
Rabbi Mordechai Newman
703.370.2774

Share the **Rohr JLI** experience with friends and relatives worldwide

FAIRFAX
Rabbi Leibel Fajnland
703.426.1980

NORFOLK
Rabbi Aaron Margolin
Rabbi Levi Brashevitzky
757.616.0770

RICHMOND
Rabbi Shlomo Pereira
804.740.2000

TYSONS CORNER
Rabbi Chezzy Deitsch
CHAPTER FOUNDED BY
RABBI LEVI DEITSCH, OBM
703.829.5770

WASHINGTON
LYNNWOOD
Rabbi Berel Paltiel
425.741.9633

MERCER ISLAND
Rabbi Elazar Bogomilsky
206.527.1411

OLYMPIA
Rabbi Cheski Edelman
360.584.4306

SPOKANE COUNTY
Rabbi Yisroel Hahn
509.443.0770

WISCONSIN
KENOSHA
Rabbi Tzali Wilschanski
262.359.0770

MADISON
Rabbi Avremel Matusof
608.231.3450

MEQUON
Rabbi Menachem Rapoport
262.242.2235

MILWAUKEE
Rabbi Mendel Shmotkin
414.961.6100

WAUKESHA
Rabbi Levi Brook
925.708.4203

PUERTO RICO
CAROLINA
Rabbi Mendel Zarchi
787.253.0894

ARGENTINA
CAPITAL FEDERAL
Rabbi Mendy Gurevitch
54.11.4545.7771

PALERMO NUEVO
Rabbi Mendy Grunblatt
54.11.4772.1024

AUSTRALIA
AUSTRALIAN CAPITAL TERRITORY
CANBERRA
Rabbi Shmuel Feldman
614.3167.7805

DOUBLE BAY
Rabbi Yanky Berger
Rabbi Yisroel Dolnikov
612.9327.1644

DOVER HEIGHTS
Rabbi Motti Feldman
612.9387.3822

NORTH SHORE
Rabbi Nochum Schapiro
Mrs. Fruma Schapiro
612.9488.9548

SOUTH HEAD
Rabbi Benzion Milecki
612.9337.6775

QUEENSLAND
BRISBANE
Rabbi Levi Jaffe
617.3843.6770

SOUTH AUSTRALIA
GLENSIDE
Rabbi Yossi Engel
618.8338.2922

VICTORIA
BENTLEIGH EAST
Rabbi Mendel Raskin
613.9570.6707

CAULFIELD NORTH
Rabbi Menachem Stern
614.4850.4301

CAULFIELD SOUTH
Rabbi Peretz Schapiro
613.9532.9180

ELSTERNWICK
Rabbi Chaim Cowen
614.3330.8584

Rabbi Motty Liberow
613.9533.0090

MALVERN
Rabbi Zev Slavin
614.0476.6759

Rabbi Shimshon Yurkowicz
613.9822.3600

MELBOURNE
Rabbi Sholem Gorelik
614.5244.8770

Rabbi Mendel Groner
613.9532.7299

Rabbi Dovid Gutnick
614.3038.4948

MOORABBIN
Rabbi Elisha Greenbaum
614.0349.0434

ST. KILDA EAST
Rabbi Moshe Kahn
613.9522.8217

Rabbi Dovid Leib Shmerling
613.9526.3874

WESTERN AUSTRALIA
PERTH
Rabbi Shalom White
618.9275.2106

BRAZIL
RIO DE JANEIRO
Rabbi Yehoshua Binyomin Goldman
Rabbi Avrohom Tsvi Beuthner
55.21.2294.3138

S. PAULO
Rabbi Avraham Steinmetz
55.11.3081.3081

CANADA
ALBERTA
CALGARY
Rabbi Mordechai Groner
403.238.4880

EDMONTON
Rabbi Ari Drelich
Rabbi Mendy Blachman
780.851.1515

BRITISH COLUMBIA
RICHMOND
Rabbi Yechiel Baitelman
604.277.6427

VANCOUVER
Rabbi Yitzchok Wineberg
604.266.1313

VICTORIA
Rabbi Meir Kaplan
250.595.7656

MANITOBA
WINNIPEG
Rabbi Shmuel Altein
204.339.8737

NOVA SCOTIA
HALIFAX
Rabbi Mendel Feldman
902.422.4222

LAWRENCE/EGLINTON
Rabbi Menachem Gansburg
416.546.8770

LONDON
Rabbi Eliezer Gurkow
519.434.3962

MISSISSAUGA
Rabbi Yitzchok Slavin
905.820.4432

NIAGARA FALLS
Rabbi Zalman Zaltzman
905.356.7200

OTTAWA
Rabbi Menachem M. Blum
613.823.0866

RICHMOND HILL
Rabbi Mendel Bernstein
905.770.7700

Rabbi Yossi Hecht
905.773.6477

TORONTO AREA BJL
Rabbi Leib Chaiken
416.916.7202

GREATER TORONTO
REGIONAL OFFICE & THORNHILL
Rabbi Yossi Gansburg
905.731.7000

YORK MILLS
Rabbi Levi Gansburg
647.345.3800

WATERLOO
Rabbi Moshe Goldman
226.338.7770

WHITBY
Rabbi Tzali Borenstein
905.493.9007

QUEBEC
COTE ST. LUC
Rabbi Levi Raskin
514.485.7221

MONTREAL
Rabbi Ronnie Fine
Pesach Nussbaum
514.342.3.JLI

Rabbi Levi Y New
514.739.0770

TOWN OF MOUNT ROYAL
Rabbi Moshe Krasnanski
Rabbi Shneur Zalman Rader
514.739.0770

VILLE S. LAURENT
Rabbi Schneur Zalmen Silberstein
514.808.1418

WESTMOUNT
Rabbi Yossi Shanowitz
Mrs. Devorah Leah Shanowitz
514.937.4772

SASKATCHEWAN
REGINA
Rabbi Avrohom Simmonds
306.585.1359

SASKATOON
Rabbi Raphael Kats
306.384.4370

CAYMAN ISLAND
GRAND CAYMAN
Rabbi Berel Pewzner
717.798.1040

COLOMBIA
BOGOTA
Rabbi Yehoshua B. Rosenfeld
Rabbi Chanoch Piekarski
571.635.8251

DENMARK
COPENHAGEN
Rabbi Yitzchok Loewenthal
45.3316.1850

ESTONIA
TALLINN
Rabbi Shmuel Kot
372.662.30.50

GEORGIA
TBILISI
Rabbi Meir Kozlovsky
995.593.23.91.15

GERMANY
BERLIN
Rabbi Yehuda Tiechtel
49.30.2128.0830

COLOGNE
Rabbi Mendel Schtroks
49.22.1240.3902

DUSSELDORF
Rabbi Chaim Barkahn
49.21.1420.9693

HAMBURG
Rabbi Shlomo Bistriztsky
49.40.4142.4190

HANNOVER
Rabbi Binyamin Wolff
49.511.811.2822

GREECE
ATHENS
Rabbi Mendel Hendel
30.210.520.2880

GUATEMALA
GUATEMALA CITY
Rabbi Shalom Pelman
502.2485.0770

ISRAEL
ASHKELON
Rabbi Shneor Lieberman
054.977.0512

BALFURYA
Rabbi Noam Bar-Tov
054.580.4770

CAESAREA
Rabbi Chaim Meir Lieberman
054.621.2586

EVEN YEHUDA
Rabbi Menachem Noyman
054.777.0707

GANEI TIKVA
Rabbi Gershon Shnur
054.524.2358

GIV'ATAYIM
Rabbi Pinchus Bitton
052.643.8770

HAIFA
Rabbi Yehuda Dunin
054.426.3763

KARMIEL
Rabbi Mendy Elishevitz
054.521.3073

KFAR SABBA
Rabbi Yossi Baitch
054.445.5020

KIRYAT BIALIK
Rabbi Pinny Marton
050.661.1768

KIRYAT MOTZKIN
Rabbi Shimon Eizenbach
050.902.0770

KOCHAV YAIR
Rabbi Dovi Greenberg
054.332.6244

MACCABIM RE'UT
Rabbi Yosef Yitzchak Noiman
054.977.0549

MODIIN
Rabbi Boruch Slonim
054.300.1770

NES ZIYONA
Rabbi Menachem Feldman
054.497.7092

NETANYA
Rabbi Schneur Brod
054.579.7572

RAMAT GAN-KRINITZI
Rabbi Yisroel Gurevitz
052.743.2814

RAMAT GAN-MAROM NAVE
Rabbi Binyamin Meir Kali
050.476.0770

RAMAT YISHAI
Rabbi Shneor Zalman Wolosow
052.324.5475

RISHON LEZION
Rabbi Uri Keshet
050.722.4593

ROSH PINA
Rabbi Sholom Ber Hertzel
052.458.7600

YEHUD
Rabbi Shmuel Wolf
053.536.1479

ITALY
FIRENZE
Rabbi Levi Wolvovsky
39.389.595.2034

Share the **Rohr JLI** experience with friends and relatives worldwide

KAZAKHSTAN
ALMATY
Rabbi Shevach Zlatopolsky
7.7272.77.59.77

LATVIA
RIGA
Rabbi Shneur Zalman Kot
371.6733.1520

NETHERLANDS
DEN HAAG
Rabbi Shmuel Katzman
31.70.347.0222

NOORD-HOLLAND
AMSTERDAM
Rabbi Yanki Jacobs
31.6.4498.8627

PANAMA
PANAMA CITY
Rabbi Ari Laine
Rabbi Gabriel Benayon
507.223.3383

RUSSIA
ASTRAKHAN
Rabbi Yisroel Melamed
7.851.239.28.24

BRYANSK
Rabbi Menachem Mendel Zaklas
7.483.264.55.15

CHELYABINSK
Rabbi Meir Kirsh
7.351.263.24.68

MOSCOW-MARINA ROSHA
Rabbi Mordechai Weisberg
7.495.645.50.00

NIZHNY NOVGOROD
Rabbi Shimon Bergman
7.920.253.47.70

OMSK
Rabbi Osher Krichevsky
7.381.231.33.07

PERM
Rabbi Zalman Deutch
7.342.212.47.32

SAMARA
Rabbi Shlomo Deutch
7.846.333.40.64

SARATOV
Rabbi Yaakov Kubitshek
7.8452.21.58.00

S. PETERSBURG
Rabbi Zvi Pinsky
7.812.713.62.09

ROSTOV
Rabbi Chaim Danzinger
7.8632.99.02.68

TOGLIATTI
Rabbi Meier Fischer
7.848.273.02.84

UFA
Rabbi Dan Krichevsky
7.347.244.55.33

VORONEZH
Rabbi Levi Stiefel
7.473.252.96.99

SINGAPORE
SINGAPORE
Rabbi Mordechai Abergel
656.337.2189

Rabbi Netanel Rivni
CLASSES IN HEBREW
656.336.2127

SOUTH AFRICA
JOHANNESBURG
Rabbi Dovid Hazdan
Rabbi Shmuel Simpson
27.11.728.8152

Rabbi Dovid Masinter
Rabbi Ari Kievman
27.11.440.6600

SWEDEN
STOCKHOLM
Rabbi Chaim Greisman
468.679.7067

SWITZERLAND
LUGANO
Rabbi Yaakov Tzvi Kantor
41.91.921.3720

LUZERN
Rabbi Chaim Drukman
41.41.361.1770

UKRAINE
DNEPROPETROVSK
Rabbi Dan Makagon
380.504.51.13.18

NIKOLAYEV
Rabbi Sholom Gotlieb
380.512.37.37.71

ZHITOMIR
Rabbi Shlomo Wilhelm
380.504.63.01.32

ODESSA
Rabbi Avraham Wolf
Rabbi Yaakov Neiman
38.048.728.0770 ext. 280

UNITED KINGDOM
CARDIFF
Rabbi Michoel Rose
44.292.221.0733

EDGEWARE
Rabbi Leivi Sudak
Rabbi Yaron Jacobs
44.208.905.4141

ILFORD
Rabbi Rafi Goodwin
44.208.554.1624

LEEDS
Rabbi Eli Pink
44.113.266.3311

LONDON
Rabbi Nissan D. Dubov
44.20.8944.1581

Rabbi Mendy Korer
44.794.632.5444

Rabbi Baruch Levin
44.208.451.0091

Rabbi Yisroel Lew
44.20.7060.9770

Rabbi Gershon Overlander
Rabbi Dovid Katz
44.208.202.1600

Rabbi Yossi Simon
44.20.8458.0416

MANCHESTER
Rabbi Akiva Cohen
Rabbi Levi Cohen
44.161.740.4243

Rabbi Shmuli Jaffe
44.161.766.1812

VENEZUELA
CARACAS
Rabbi Yehoshua Rosenblum
58.212.264.7011

NOTES

NOTES

NOTES

NOTES

NOTES

NOTES

THE JEWISH LEARNING MULTIPLEX
Brought to you by the Rohr Jewish Learning Institute

In fulfillment of the mandate of the Lubavitcher Rebbe, of blessed memory,
whose leadership guides every step of our work,
the mission of the Rohr Jewish Learning Institute is to transform
Jewish life and the greater community through the study of Torah,
connecting each Jew to our shared heritage of Jewish learning.

While our flagship program remains the cornerstone of our organization,
JLI is proud to feature additional divisions catering to specific populations,
in order to meet a wide array of educational needs.

THE ROHR JEWISH LEARNING INSTITUTE,
a subsidiary of *Merkos L'Inyonei Chinuch,*
is the adult education arm of the Chabad-Lubavitch Movement.

TORAH STUDIES

Torah Studies provides a rich and nuanced encounter with the weekly Torah reading.

MYSHIUR
TALMUD LEARNING INITIATIVE

MyShiur courses are designed to assist students in developing the skills needed to study Talmud independently.

SINAI SCHOLARS Society
IN PARTNERSHIP WITH CHABAD ON CAMPUS

This rigorous fellowship program invites select college students to explore the fundamentals of Judaism.

JLI TEENS
YOUNG SMART JEWISH

IN PARTNERSHIP WITH CTEEN: CHABAD TEEN NETWORK

Jewish teens forge their identity as they engage in Torah study, social interaction, and serious fun.

ROSHCHODESH society

The Rosh Chodesh Society gathers Jewish women together once a month for intensive textual study.

TORAHCafé

TorahCafe.com provides an exclusive selection of top-rated Jewish educational videos.

BRILLIANT LEARNING, NATURALLY.

National JEWISH RETREAT

This yearly event rejuvenates mind, body, and spirit with a powerful synthesis of Jewish learning and community.

the LAND & the SPIRIT
ISRAEL EXPERIENCE

Participants delve into our nation's rich past while exploring the Holy Land's relevance and meaning today.

PEDAGOGY · CURRICULUM · MARKETING

JLI ACADEMY

Select affiliates are invited to partner with peers and noted professionals, as leaders of innovation and excellence.

מכון שמואל

THE SAMI ROHR RESEARCH INSTITUTE

Machon Shmuel is an institute providing Torah research in the service of educators worldwide.